Facilitating

with

Heart

Coaching for Personal Transformation and Social Change

Brie -
I cherish your openness & willingness to do
deep healing work. It's such a gift for me to
witness your sweet self love. I'm deeply inspired
Love, Martha

Martha Lasley

Acknowledgements

I am so grateful to the hundreds of facilitators, coaches and social change activists who have shared their hearts and transformational processes with me. When I first met my editor and writing coach, Nancy Coco, I was quite sure I'd never write another book, but she continues to inspire me to the point where I can't stop writing. My inspirational partners at Leadership that Works and Coaching for Transformation – Virginia Kellogg, Richard Michaels and Mary Kuentz – give me the loving spaciousness and sense of being held that is so vital to my well being. For more than a decade, Charlotte Morse has supported my creative process by making everything easy to read and turning concepts into drawings. And how about that book cover – her first draft was also the final! Lynda Smith Cowan gave me early encouragement and helped me design and conduct the interviews with many facilitators, coaches and social activists. I have many teachers, but I especially want to thank Marshall Rosenberg, Miki Kashtan, Sushma Sharma and John Heron. I appreciate all my co-facilitators over the years and all the participants who have contributed so much to my learning. I cherish my husband, Dave, who has helped me co-create a fabulous life filled with challenges, hope, and unconditional love.

Table of Contents

Chapter 1
Welcome to Facilitating with Heart

How wonderful it is that nobody need wait a single moment before starting to improve the world. — Anne Frank

The world needs competent, caring facilitators to bring people together and address the challenges of our times. It takes gutsy, dedicated people to deal with such haunting nightmares as child soldiers trying to reunite with their families, villages who want to stop female infanticide, urban gangs who are fed up, towns recovering from environmental disasters, and victims of sex trafficking reclaiming their freedom. It's a wonder we get any sleep at all. The need for facilitators is both widespread and close to home: a parent wants to reconnect with an estranged child, an entrepreneur wants to turn the workplace into a more humane environment, a teacher wants to help students become leaders, sisters want to resolve an old conflict, and social activists want to work more collaboratively to realize their dreams. Where others throw up their hands in despair, facilitators trust the process, help people open their hearts to each other, and transform nightmares into dreams.

I became a facilitator because I love to create nurturing environments for transforming distress into compassion. Inspired by people who make change look easy, I learned to facilitate by diving into the deep end of the pool. Sometimes facilitation *is* easy. Other times I'm clueless. So I read,, go to training, get tips from seasoned professionals, and continue to pick up new skills and insights every time I step into the fire.

The magical transformational moments sustain me, but I learn even *more* when things fall apart. In the spirit of learning what works and what doesn't, I interviewed facilitators, coaches, and social change activists, gathering stories about breakdowns and breakthroughs. In addition to their stories, I'm including plenty of my own – some euphoric, some horrific, but all learning opportunities. The beauty of facilitating transformation is that even when we hit a bump in the road, the process is life affirming and the opportunities for growth keep expanding.

This book is for you if you want to find new ways to enliven transformational processes that:

- Open groups and organizations to their passion, loving energy, and possibilities.
- Expand the opportunities for awakening growth and healing.
- Help people crack their hearts open and connect more deeply with each other.
- Enhance social change initiatives with compassionate sustainable practices.
- Support human evolution by living on the creative edge.

Facilitation supports human evolution because it calls out the best in people. Imagine a world where we believe in our collective wisdom to solve our own problems and know how to tap each other's deepest longing. Imagine interacting with teenagers, CEOs, prisoners, partners, or gang members from that perspective. We can apply facilitation skills to every part of our lives, at home, at work, or when we're alone. These life skills raise our emotional and spiritual intelligence and help us empower others to create more fulfilling lives and a better world.

As a trainer of visionary leaders and transformational coaches, I've led many workshops where people are hungry for growth and want a holistic approach to changing themselves and their organizations. Likewise, when I mediate disputes, I've noticed that people want far more than a desirable outcome. For example, after they agree on the tough decisions of how they'll share custody of the children, the parents want to trust they can talk to each other without someone storming out. After all, they're going to co-parent for years to come. Whether the couple feels heartbroken or relieved to be splitting up, more than anything, *they want to be understood*. Despite this basic human desire, and even with all the processes and tools available to support growth and recovery, there's only one thing that consistently liberates people – opening our hearts.

The Facilitating with Heart Process

When we listen to people's hearts, we connect with the part of them that's moving. By listening to the life energy, we hear what's stirring, what's awakening, what they're longing for. Putting our attention on the life force of the group we invite them into an intimate, safe space. By feeling the depth of their unique experience, and conveying our understanding of their experience, participants feel moved and empowered to open their own hearts. As we listen for individual and collective longing, we capture the essence of what is emerging in the group.

Typically a facilitator is not a content expert and doesn't give advice or participate in the decisions, but instead actively engages in the group's process. But to access the heart of people, and a group, we need to be more than a process expert – *we need to bring our own hearts into the process*.

Sometimes people come into the room completely closed to each other, but as they open up and others listen, really listen, they feel understood and their hearts melt. When the heart strings are pulled, people come closer together and they're more willing to engage in the process of collaboration and finding solutions collectively. If the facilitator sits there unmoved, participants tend to do the same. But as we step into each person's experience fully, and really feel their heartache, yearning or their joy… if we open ourselves to each and every person, they're moved to dive in with us.

I'm calling for a deeper level of interaction that is intimate, profound and moving. What makes this approach unique is that facilitators:

- Bring heart and soul into the facilitation process
- Create a culture of shared power and inclusion

2

- Transform judgment into compassion
- Support development of facilitation skills
- Share our own vulnerable work of personal transformation

As facilitators, we are compassionate catalysts, continuously creating openings for the light to shine in. I'm motivated to co-create a learning community of people who are actively committed to contributing to human evolution. Specifically I'm writing for both new and seasoned facilitators who aspire to integrate the physical, energetic, emotional, and spiritual dimensions of transformation.

I love working with transformation geeks: people who support deep change: enhancing growth at personal, group, organizational, and societal levels. Transformation geeks are everywhere – we practice the art informally with family, neighbors, friends, and colleagues. More formally, we develop human potential through a wide variety of professions – as facilitators, activists, coaches, consultants, mediators, counselors, and trainers. But we also work in non-profits, education, therapy, social work, politics, business, philanthropy, medicine, psychology, law, and many other professions.

My vision is to see people from every nook and cranny of the world skilled in facilitating heart connection. It won't be long before facilitation skills spread like mushrooms after a soaking rainstorm and a critical mass of people can support transformational processes. We'll be able to go to any of our neighbors, co-workers, or on-line communities where we'll find people who empathically witness our personal growth, help us transform relationships, mediate conflicts, develop organizations, or support social change initiatives. I'm writing to help people deepen these basic but extraordinary life skills of *Facilitating with Heart*. This crazy beautiful world is changing at the speed of light, which means my dream of a skilled facilitator in every family and every work group could be realized soon, so I'm writing as if it's already so. For some of us, we already have access to skilled facilitators and now we have the opportunity to reach out to the rest of the world and impact human evolution.

Create a culture of inclusion and shared power

Vibrant groups have one thing in common – participants are fully heard. The simple practice of listening deeply helps build a sense of inclusion, which improves the way people work together, plan, solve problems, make decisions, and collaborate. As facilitators, we enhance the sense of inclusion by providing a safe space for dialogue and ensuring that radically different view points are welcome. Originally, Robert's Rules of Order was devised as a structure to help everyone be heard, but there's a lot more we can do to create a culture of shared power and inclusion. Our role is to give each person the support to recognize their innate power, take ownership of what happens in the group, and take responsibility for the outcome. Instead of overpowering participants, we embrace our own power and the power of each individual, inviting people to challenge us and further our own development. Our empowering presence awakens people to their own latent or emerging power. The facilitator creates the space for empowerment, but is not the one *in power*, or the one with all the wisdom, or the one responsible for the results. Instead of having all the answers, we trust the wisdom of the group which unleashes people's innate power.

When I walk into a group, I can intuitively sense who has the power just by the way they carry themselves. This is particularly obvious in prisons where the powerlessness is bone crushing, and in corporations where the competition for power is both flagrant and covert. Many people who are vying for power have no intention of sharing their power with others until they realize that shared power means more power for everyone, including themselves. I define power as the ability to fulfill needs. If I use my power to meet only *my* needs, I don't have nearly as much power as when I mobilize resources to meet the needs of all people, all life.

Transform judgment into compassion to support transformation

Sometimes we lose sight of our shared power and find ourselves making moralistic judgments or comparisons. Instead of taking a pathological view and assuming we're going fix people who are broken, we take the view that people are already whole and moving toward a fuller expression of their wholeness. Instead of labeling groups as dysfunctional, or individuals as disruptive, we consciously open ourselves to seeing their full humanity and understanding their behavior as their best attempt at getting what they need. By seeing their positive intent and holding each person with care, a gentle compassion permeates the group. The openness and acceptance frees people to contribute their ideas and talents. When each person has an open invitation to show up fully, natural creativity is unleashed.

How in the world do we offer compassion to the snipers, bulldozers, jokesters and resistors? It's easy to facilitate people who are hungry for transformation, learning and mutual support, but what about the people who have no desire to change anything? The process is not about changing them, but changing ourselves; transforming our judgments into a warm pool of understanding and opening our hearts to everyone's full humanity. And I do mean everyone!

If we find ourselves judging anyone, and then beating ourselves up for being judgmental, that's a perfect opportunity to get curious about our own positive intent. Underneath the self-judgment, we'll find an unmet need. When we appreciate how that need drives our behavior, we open ourselves to deeper self-acceptance. From that place, we can more readily accept another's gifts, values, and desires. In the same way that we honor each part of ourselves, we can honor every aspect of the group, even when people cast disparaging looks or shout at each other. The challenge is to see each person and each expression as a gift. When people are fully heard and understood, they open to the transformational process and venture into a deeper space. A sense of movement replaces the static energy of judgment and diagnosis.

When a facilitator diagnoses or labels a participant, such as "passive-aggressive", the participant doesn't know what to do with the discomfort, except to move as quickly as possible somewhere else. Even minor judgments such as "She's reserved," leave people feeling pressure or isolation. The alternative – empathic uncovering of needs – changes the energy flow to joint exploration, discovery, and support. Instead of distancing someone by labeling them passive-aggressive, or reserved, we can connect with their desire for both safety and harmony.

4

The exploration of needs is an empowering process. We all know about needs, but digging beneath the surface and developing a deep understanding of the needs *right now*, give people such clarity about what's driving them *in this moment*. This process shatters the self-judgment and replaces the negative self-talk with an affectionate self-awareness. When people are deeply understood and received, that's when transformation is most likely to take place. As we move toward understanding of ourselves and others at the core, we build relationships and can simultaneously create shared visions, strategic plans, and compelling goals. Offering unconditional love or simply holding each person with positive regard helps the group generate creative ideas, resolve tough conflicts and achieve their objectives. Compassionate exploration of what is emerging creates a more open, loving environment where empowerment and healing can go deeper, feel more complete, and have a longer-lasting impact.

Support development of facilitation skills

The exciting role of a developmental facilitator is to help the group define and achieve their objectives, and *simultaneously* help participants learn to facilitate their own process. In traditional facilitation, we have our hands full just helping groups solve tough problems. So why would we take on the bigger task of developing the group's facilitation skills at the same time? The short-term fix leaves the group dependent on the facilitator. In contrast, a developmental facilitation process helps groups function more effectively now *and* in the future. They learn how to connect, communicate without blame, and streamline the decision-making process. Group members enhance their own facilitation skills as they go, which reduces dependence on the facilitator. Serving as a guide and catalyst, the facilitator helps people focus their energy while creating opportunities for profound learning, creativity, productivity, and ownership.

When we have two facilitators serving the group, we model shared leadership and develop open-hearted relationships that invite participants to step onto the playing field with us and share in the role of supporting the group's process. While one facilitator holds the direction of the group, the other can offer mentoring to participants as they work on their facilitation skills. As participants step up to the plate to facilitate, that doesn't mean we abandon our role; we simultaneously offer encouragement and mentoring for those who choose to get in the game.

To raise the bar even further, facilitators demonstrate openness to learning, not just from our fellow facilitators, but from the group. Early in creating the alliance with the group, we ask for permission to take risks, try new innovative ways of facilitating, actively solicit input and feedback, and co-create new opportunities for growth. Instead of putting pressure on ourselves to have it all together, we openly share our growing edges, publicly set intentions for what we hope to learn, and create opportunities for others to do the same. Instead of going behind the curtain with our co-facilitator to resolve issues and coming out with a smile, we openly discuss issues and concerns so that people can witness the power of live conflict, including the chaos and not knowing what will happen. We all learn more from what is happening now than from sharing case studies or anecdotes about conflicts already resolved.

When the culture supports the development of facilitation skills, we build capacity from within. No more unproductive meetings that cost thousands of dollars an hour. Instead, people take ownership of the meetings, recognizing that all of the people in the meeting are responsible for the outcomes. As more and more people develop facilitation skills, the confusing discussions, adversarial attitudes, power struggles, and mediocre decisions are replaced by open, productive dialogues. Wholehearted participation in planning, problem-solving, and decision-making at all levels results in saved resources. Around the world, in every sector, management and leadership styles are changing, and simple facilitation skills that help people connect at the heart level make a big difference.

Share our own vulnerable personal transformation

> Is devotion to others a cover for the hungers and the needs of the self, of which one is ashamed? I was always ashamed to take. So I gave. It was not a virtue. It was a disguise. —Anais Nin

As facilitators, we offer a wonderful vehicle for transformation for our clients. Many of us are drawn to the helping professions because we want to help or to make a difference. The danger is that we become "compulsive helpers" as a distraction from doing our own personal growth work or getting the help we need for ourselves. In any helping profession, it's easy to dismiss our own needs and avoid doing our own inner work. We put our attention on others because they suffer so much. Many in the helping professions become spectators, but as we witness the deep work of others, it opens us to identify our own suffering, connect with the desire to liberate our souls, and bring the rejected parts into the light.

When we focus on the growth and development of *other people*, the irony is that the beautiful messiness and energy shifts happen internally anyway. If we bring our hearts and soul into the process, once we get into the fray, we have nowhere to hide. Evan Harris from Sydney, Australia describes the inevitability of personal transformation as a facilitator:

> At some point we have to jump off the high diving board. In that messy situation, a grace enters. I belong to, rather than separate myself from, the group. The messiness comes from the process of breaking up barriers between myself and others. The walls crack and things get shaken up. The conflict jolts a few stones out of the wall and allows the grace to emerge.[1]

The stone wall that separates us from others crumbles when we choose to belong to the group. As we continuously do our own internal work, we deepen our self-love which opens our hearts to others. In turn, when we receive each member of the group with unconditional love, their own walls

---

[1] Evan Harris personal interview 2/20/2008.

come down. Undefended hearts radically shift the energy, the power dynamics, and the capacity of the group.

That's just a taste of what we'll explore as we venture into the challenges of facilitating. We're about to take a look at the model and values that give life to this process. Before we go on to the next section, put the book down, take three deep breaths while you connect with your deepest desires for a better world.

The COEUR Model

It takes a lot of heart and fierceness to facilitate groups that seek social change. At the root of the French word *coeur* (heart) is the word courage. It takes courage to sit in the fire with people as they uncover their passion and rage, and rise out of the ashes to co-create a better future. We start by creating a safe place for people to come together to connect across differences and make choices that benefit all of us. I trust that people want to open their hearts to each other, even when they claim they don't. This is not business as usual, because we engage people at a deep level, using more than just their brains. We breathe magic into the process just by focusing on the wisdom of our hearts. Our role as facilitators is to step into the fire by creating opportunities to:

Connect – create awareness of our shared humanity
Objective – clarify the shared purpose or aim
Empathize – discover the feelings and needs of each contributor
Unify – open to the collective desire for transformation
Respond – take actions that meet the needs of the group

Connect: How do we create awareness of each and every person's full humanity? Our role as facilitators is to open the group to their innate wisdom, so that we can appreciate the essence of each soul and open to the magic of the group process. We start with self-connection which makes it much easier to connect to the aliveness of each individual in the group. Becoming grounded and attentive to what's alive in *every* moment helps us facilitate deeper connections. From that place we generate curiosity, trust and openness. Even when a group member is deeply conflicted, wants to leave the group, or is filled with anger, we can hold the tension as an expression of passion and a desire to connect. Some of the things we do as facilitators are:
- Use breath work to notice that we all share the same air and the same universal desires
- Create safe space to practice radical self-honesty in every moment
- Do the inner work and the outer work simultaneously
- Tear our hearts open to the people we find most challenging
- Transform judgment into compassion

7

Objective: How do clarify the shared purpose and open the group to their shared vision? In this stage, we break things wide open by helping people express their passion, determine their desired direction and clarify what they really want to get out of their time together. They open to the great mystery, fresh possibilities and new pathways. We want to know what makes their hearts soar, so we explore both the short and long-term goals of the group. Collectively the group defines specific outcomes they wish to achieve. Even when a group has a clear purpose before the gathering, we invite them to talk about their hopes and dreams so that the group attunes to each other *now* and co-creates a shared sense of direction. We invite people to step into their full power – not power over others – but shared power where everyone can flourish. We all have our natural styles, but we encourage everyone to expand their range and step out of their comfort zone. In this stage we:

- Clarify the group's direction and then stretch into the unknown
- Set the intention of how we'll use our time and then let go
- Fill ourselves with curiosity, welcoming yearning and longing
- Encourage expression of passion and open the group to fresh discoveries
- Invite people to take risks and avoid editing themselves or censoring others

Empathize: How do we support empathic communication? To deepen awareness, we reflect each speaker's feelings and needs with compassion. Radically different from reflecting the content, we acknowledge each person's underlying motivation. Empathic reflection starts with a focus on the heart, or the positive intent behind every action and every expression. The beauty of this part of the process is that we transform judgment into awareness of the positive intent. In this way, we create an environment of acceptance, where every part of each person is welcome. Rather than focusing on what the group does not want, we attune to their hopes, dreams and deepest longing. As we identify the needs of the group, we check for shared understanding, which primes the group for action and movement toward collectively honoring and meeting the needs of the group. No matter how repulsed we are by the way they express themselves, we recognize that everything they do or say is an attempt to honor a value. So we identify their motivation and connect with the stirring in their souls. In this phase of the moon, we:

- Listen from the gut and take in people's essence
- Practice self-empathy by giving voice to what's happening right now in the present
- Nurture the scary, freaked out parts, giving them room to breath and come alive
- Hold space for a shift to intimacy as people discover that all parts of themselves are welcome
- Allow everyone to be fully heard, to deepen the understanding of each other's desires

Unify: How do we open to the collective desire for transformation? By creating safe space for people to explore the shadow, they show up, express themselves fully, and connect with their desire to contribute to a better world. We welcome divergent viewpoints and explore how they can co-exist. Often this stage seems mired in frustration, darkness and chaos, but in the shadows of despair, people connect deeply to their own humanity, and recognize their desire to change their inner and outer world. Here we look under the surface, notice what people are busy avoiding, and get people to talk about what really matters. When people start to feel utterly hopeless, or become mired in doubt, if we stay with the process, new possibilities emerge. Even if someone hijacks the group, calls people vile names, or threatens to walk out, underneath the antics, we hold a core belief that every person wants to contribute to the good of the whole. As people are deeply seen, heard and valued, their facades melt and they offer their gifts. Each individual comes to trust that they matter and that they belong. Inclusion does not mean compromise. We continuously sense and intuit what the group needs, and put our attention on what wants to be born. Everyone is activated and tuned into what is emerging because we invite them to put their attention on the heartbeat of the group. In the facilitator role, we:

- Create space for silence to support people in finding their voice
- Stay with the sexy turned on places *and* the dark scary places
- Point to what's wanting to be born or what's emerging now in the spaciousness
- Simultaneously honor the impatience to move forward and the desire to slow down
- Notice how spirit moves through the group – everyone contributes to the magic

Respond: What actions can we take that meet universal needs and move the group forward? It's as simple and as complex as getting people to ask for what they want. We encourage people to offer a proposal, but instead of being attached or rigid, they have an alternative strategy in their back pocket. In this way, they take a stand without getting locked into a position. With our attention on the needs of all, we tweak the proposals to honor the values of the group. Incorporating every wish can be a daunting task, but as long as everyone knows that their needs matter, they'll open their hearts to what is emerging. Ultimately, the group collectively creates an action plan that identifies who will do what by when. Everyone knows their part in implementing the solution. Not everyone gets their first preference, but the alternative is even sweeter because everyone's ideas, suggestions, and contributions are considered in the outcome. Some are excited; others are more cautious, but the entire group can live with and support the decision to move forward. We ask if anyone has a serious objection, or we can raise the bar by asking if anyone can't live with the plan. The willingness to dialogue and co-create solutions transfers into responsibility during the implementation phase. Everyone shares responsibility and knows their part in enacting the decision. Some are excited; others are more cautious, but every individual owns the outcome and supports the decision to move forward. In this phase we turn compassion into action and support the group to:

- Ask for what they *really* want, without holding back
- Generate inclusive alternatives that synthesize the needs of all the stakeholders
- Weave together requests so that the plan honors everyone's contribution
- Identify sustainable agreements and get clarity about who will do what by when
- Create empowering structures to confirm progress on the plan

Using this model awakens the heart and soul of the group and simultaneously moves people toward personal transformation and social change. Every step of the way we embody both compassion and fierceness. That's how we get people to step into the fire and stay there until the flame of group wisdom burns brightly. Supporting human evolution is challenging, sometimes heart-wrenching work, so it helps to have solid values we can rely on as a foundation.

Core Values of Facilitating with Heart

When it comes to creating a better world, embodying the values of *Facilitating with Heart* is far more important than learning about models, tools, or tricks of the trade. The values which guide this work are:

- Connection: Supporting compassion and understanding
- Choice: Recognizing individual freedom to choose level of commitment in every moment
- Compassion: Translating judgment into understanding, consideration, interdependence
- Transformation: Adapting to change and taking advantage of growth opportunities
- Transparency: Sharing information, observations, and interests openly and caringly
- Learning: Taking risks to cultivate awareness and develop new skills
- Vision: Unleashing passion to create a more desirable future

All of these values sound agreeable enough, but really living these values in the heat of the moment is both a challenge and a beautiful practice. Heart connection – that moment when people shift as they empathically experience each other – is the common denominator that facilitates true transformation. We don't have to agree or be in synch with others, but if we take off the armor and open our hearts, our understanding of each other deepens and creativity is unleashed.

Sometimes the opportunity for heart connection sails right by me, but I can still enjoy capturing the missed opportunities in hindsight. Come with me as I share a story about unexpected learning and transformation through heart connection.

When I volunteered to spend three days in a maximum security prison as part of the Alternatives to Violence Project, I expected to be searched by the guards before entering, but didn't know how much soul searching I'd be doing myself. I started out listening a lot, but revealed very little about myself. Sure, deep empathic listening is vital, but somehow I'd forgotten that mutual disclosure is a key ingredient in creating heart connection. Worse, I had very little understanding of the inner world of a prisoner. I was completely oblivious to the powerlessness it would evoke, when we offered them the opportunity to do a role play:

Imagine your girlfriend comes to visit you, and she flirts with another prisoner. How do you handle it nonviolently?

Every one of them looked at the floor and would not speak. Reluctantly a few people mumbled, "No way."

"Don't expect me to do that."

"Walk away. Only thing you can do."

"I wouldn't have nothin' to do with that ho."

In smaller breakout groups the men spoke more freely. Jules, the guy with low-slung pants and a steely gaze, said, "It depends how many people saw it. If a lot of people saw it…" He shook his head. "Well I wouldn't do nothin' right then. But when I get out, I would find her mother. I would shake da bed with her mother and if her grandmother isn't too old, I'd get her too."

I was rattled. So I asked a stalling, clarifying question, "You're talking about when your girlfriend winks at another guy, something like that?"

"Yeah. You don't know what it's like in here! Your girlfriend flirts with another guy, and you let that happen… that could get you killed. Know what I'm saying? If your girlfriend don't respect you, you got nothing. It's all about staying alive in here."

I started to get an inkling of what Jules was talking about. I couldn't quite imagine the extent of the powerlessness or how he coped with it. So I connected with his desire for respect, but I still didn't get it about going after the mother and grandmother. So I asked him, "is that about wanting to get your power back?"

He gave me the unmistakable look reserved for fools. "No. I got all the power I need. It's about making sure she know her whole family is hos. I want her to think about what I would have to *do* to make that happen. Know what I'm saying?"

Actually I didn't. What could that possibly do for him? To me this sounded like a need for shared understanding of suffering, and underneath that a need for dignity, but from my perspective, a crazy way to try to get it. Clueless, I could only guess his motives, "You want her to know how her flirting brings about suffering and loss of dignity?" He took that in, but I could see my words were a bit off the mark, until I used *his* words. "Oh, you want her to really understand what it's like for you in here."

"Yeah. Yeah. That's it."

He talked to me a few more times over the three days, each time deepening my understanding of what motivated him. I didn't dare tell him that I thought flirting was fun. Playful. Harmless. But finally I did anyway – something about his openness inspired me to reveal myself. I went on to say, "The second someone walks in the room, I know if I'm attracted. I could try to pretend otherwise, but what's the point? One way or another if I'm attracted to someone, any idiot can tell. For me, it's about being real." I could see from the glimmer in his eyes he could connect however slightly with my desire to be real. That's when the heart connection became *mutual*.

Everything shifted when I shared with the group something from my inner world:

"You all might think I'm here because I'm a do-gooder who wants to come in here and fix you. But I'm really here to work on my own tendency toward violence. When someone I love was tortured (tears), she went from a vibrant young girl full of life, to someone who couldn't get out of bed in the morning, and all I could do was fantasize about using a baseball bat on the animal who had hurt her. That's when I realized I wasn't very different from him. Or from any of you. I'm here because I want to understand and overcome my own violence."

They were struck silent when I told them I'm still heartbroken that I hadn't protected her, and cheered when I told them she has recovered – more than getting out of bed, she is getting married soon. They gave me their trust when I gave them mine. Our mutual trust opened up a healing process – giving voice to the desire to relieve the suffering their crimes had caused, and to let the victim's families know about their remorse.

On the third day, Jules opened up and talked about himself as a leader of men. I had a slight suspicion that he was talking about leading a gang, but I listened openly to his desire to lead young men out of poverty, out of low self-esteem, out of a dull despair, and into a life filled with possibilities. As I encouraged him to expand his vision, his dream of helping young men and protecting them from violence touched us all.

During our closing circle, the men shared from their hearts. One guy said, "Martha is like a mother to me, and I haven't felt anything like that in a long time." I was shocked to see several people tearing up, which I thought would be interpreted as cowardly, but they were deeply moved and respectful of each other's openness. Another sang a heart-wrenching song. Gospel. His vibrant energy turned the place into a church. But the ultimate compliment came from an intense guy who got right in my face to say, "Real knows real."

This experience gave me a glimpse of the possibilities that emerge from being open-hearted, real, and willing to work on myself. I was transformed by their willingness to be real with me and

Jules was transformed by my belief in his dream. My vulnerability helps me support the growth of individuals and groups, which in turn opens the door to development of organizations and society. Even the corrections officer was moved. As he escorted us to lunch on day one I asked what it was like for him to observe from the back of the room. He responded with a dismissive wave of his hand, "I've seen it all before. You can't change these guys. I don't even listen." I connected with his hopelessness about having an impact on inmates. Over the three days he became more and more attentive, and on the last day he gave us suggestions about coming more often – which programs would be well-received, who to talk to, and what to say. In some small way he'd accepted us, empathized with our desire to create growth opportunities, and wanted to support the work. There's a special tenderness I feel for all the participants who bring tough but *real* challenges that push me out of my comfort zone, inspiring me to experiment in new realms of chaos and creativity. Before we get into extreme situations, let's challenge some old viewpoints about facilitating.

Debunking Myths about Facilitating

Facilitating is the art of helping people realize their full potential. Instead of telling people what to do, we help them deepen their awareness and create their own solutions. Rather than giving advice, we empower people to expand and realize their dreams. We do this by believing in people and activating their talents, rather than trying to fix them or tell them what to do. Most advice is ignored anyway, not just because it's bad advice, but because it doesn't honor the inherent wisdom of the people we advise.

We facilitators come from diverse backgrounds and use radically different methodologies, but draw amazingly similar conclusions about what works and what doesn't. The field of facilitation has grown quickly, giving rise to some common misperceptions. Some myths about facilitation are widely held but don't hold up under scrutiny:

- *Better decisions are based on facts rather than feelings*—if you avoid talking about feelings, the *real* meeting happens out in the hallway afterward. Feelings are the portal to what really matters to the group, even when expressed by only one person.
- *Consensus is too time-consuming*—for important decisions, where you need commitment from the whole group to move forward, getting buy-in from the whole group saves time in the long run because implementing the decision takes far less time.
- *When things get too intense, take a break*—when people express intense emotions, they're giving you a gift, letting you know that they're touching on something very important. Taking a break diffuses the tension, but you miss the opportunity to discover what's really going on.
- *The facilitator should stay calm and neutral, even if personally attacked*—if a participant yells in your face and you pretend to be calm and neutral, you'll be perceived as inauthentic or closed off from your emotions. Instead, match their intensity, not by judging them or negating what was said, but by empathizing fully with their passion and sharing your own response.

- *Difficult people can sabotage the meeting and they need to be stopped*—seeing some people as "difficult" creates a sense of separation when they merely want to be heard.
- *Facilitators don't get emotionally involved*— if you shut down your emotions, the rest of the group will also retreat, and you'll miss rich opportunities for connection and transformation.
- *Facilitators shouldn't take sides* – Instead of taking sides with *one* person, you can be on the side of *each* person, by fully understanding their experience, their feelings and their passion.
- *Don't intervene when your co-facilitator is working with the group because you'll make her look incompetent*— co-facilitation can be a beautiful dance that starts with two people in synch with each other, moving as one body, speaking with one voice.
- *Facilitators can't resolve international conflicts when they struggle to create peace in their own families.* Facilitation is a continuous learning process that includes working on internal conflicts and family conflicts, which supports you in facilitating groups, organizations and social change. If you transparently share your personal struggles, you'll give others the courage to do the same, so that everyone learns from each other.

Now that we've explored some of the ways we break from traditional facilitation, let's look at some of the practices that inform and influence the best practices in the field.

Favorite Practices

I've learned about facilitating transformation from multiple modalities and cherish three of my favorite practices: Nonviolent Communication, Coaching, and Organization Development. In the spirit of gratitude and authenticity I want to share what I love about each practice, along with what drives me crazy.

Nonviolent Communication, developed by Marshall Rosenberg[2], has been the most liberating practice of my life and here's a short list of the things I most value:
- Empathic heart connection deepens intimacy
- Attentiveness to feelings and needs creates new awareness
- Loving consciousness builds awareness that everyone's needs matter
- Spaciousness for judgment opens the door to transformation and compassion
- Being seen, heard, and understood creates opportunities for transformation
- Making requests without attachment to strategies opens new possibilities
- Commitment to spiritual development and social change becomes a way of life

This heart-opening practice also brings some challenges. It took me years to become fluent in the language of compassion, because I had to change the way I was hard wired. Every minute was

---

[2] Rosenberg, M. (2003). *Nonviolent Communication: A language of life.* Puddle Dancer Press.

well spent, but I'd like to find new ways for people to learn NVC consciousness more quickly so that heart connection spreads more rapidly. Even worse than the time it takes to learn, when newcomers overuse the jargon it sound like someone singing out of tune or one of those robo-call messaging systems. I want more originality and spontaneity so that compassionate consciousness has broader appeal across demographics. Another area that troubles me is the practice of offering empathy relies so heavily on the facilitator. Instead of doing the work *for* people, we can hold space for the speaker to self-empathize, by asking them what they feel and need, rather than making our own guesses.

Although NVC is a tool for resolving conflict, when we start the process by looking at what isn't going well, we continue to look for additional problems to solve. However if we point our toes in the direction of creating what we want, I'm more hopeful about creating both personal and social change. Many NVC trainers are moving away from the energy of "unmet" needs and focusing on the energetic quality of the pure need, so I'm hopeful about this development. Lastly, as a community of practitioners, our emphasis on empathizing with others overshadows honest expression of our own needs; I want communion with people who value authentic expression and practice it as rigorously as we practice compassion for others.

Coaching has radically changed my perspective. As the author of my own life, I make choices from the heart and I focus on what I want to create. Thomas Leonard is often considered the father of personal coaching. He wrote six books on coaching and founded Coach University and Coachville.[3] The beauty of coaching permeates my life and other's lives in many ways:

- Asking empowering questions calls forth both wisdom and action
- Taking responsibility for creating our future awakens new opportunities
- Trusting in resourcefulness and willful choice creates a balanced, fulfilling life
- Sharing power fosters creativity and intentional relationships
- Articulating intentions and desires transforms them into action
- Identifying values of balance and wholeness helps people create lives they love
- Using simple coaching models leads to fast learning and wide dissemination

As much as I cherish the practice of coaching, I have a few challenges. As coaches, we often lead clients into action. I'd like to see coaches offer more spaciousness for clients to develop a deep awareness of emotions and needs and allow action to naturally emerge from that tender place of conscious choice and desire to shift. The other issue I'm concerned about is that as a profession, the emphasis on making money both helps us and hurts us. To prosper as a coach often means catering to the elite, which means people at the lower end of the socio-economic spectrum, those who need it most, don't have access. On the other hand, a thriving coaching practice gives us the freedom to do pro bono work and spread coaching more rapidly.

---

[3] Thomas Leonard authored six books on coaching and founded coachville.com.

Organization Development continues to deepen my belief in humanity as I facilitate systemic change. I cherish my work in organizations where we develop the capacity to improve interpersonal and group processes, enhance decision-making, develop shared leadership, transform conflict, and facilitate action learning. Applied Behavioral Science has evolved since Kurt Lewin co-founded the National Training Lab Institute[4], when the focus was on sensitivity training, but still supports me in being more present and available to myself and others. Appreciative Inquiry[5], a strengths-based approach to systemic change, is an exciting process that gets people fully engaged in improving organizational performance and building capacity. I'm especially grateful for the practices of:

- Engaging in discovery, dream, design, and delivery to awaken passion for social change
- Building awareness of authority, power, and group dynamics to create sustainable relationships
- Recognizing that each group member is *responsible* for what happens which fosters ownership
- Immersion in chaos and trust in the process which allows for openness to a new kind of order
- Receiving continuous feedback on impact which invites behavioral change
- Community building leverages support systems that contribute to human evolution

I'm especially appreciative of all my friends at the Indian Society for Applied Behavioral Science (ISABS) for helping me to trust working in the here and now. My greatest concern with organization development is the emphasis on diagnosis and labels which evoke judgments that disconnect us from our innate compassionate nature. The learning structure often creates "power-over" dynamics between consultants and clients, which is valuable for understanding the power dynamics, but I'm seeking more creativity in creating the dynamics that empower everyone.

Integration

Separately each of these practices are inspirational, but taken together, the synergy leads to deeper transformation. This book builds on the inspirational practices from the three traditions of Nonviolent Communication, coaching and organization development. Many of the teachings are imbedded in my heart and interwoven throughout the book. The awe, the wonder, and the challenges of each practice point me toward my desire to integrate multiple modalities so that we can develop new practices and co-create opportunities for radical change.

Interview Process

I'm grateful that many facilitators, coaches, and social change activists readily agreed to talk about their work. Working with Lynda Smith Cowan, we interviewed 50 people we admired. To start, we created a list of interview questions designed to gather stories about transformational

---

[4] National Training Labs. http://www.ntl.org
[5] Appreciative Inquiry Commons. http://appreciativeinquiry.case.edu/

facilitation experiences, but the process itself transformed quickly – we changed the interview questions, tossed them out, and went with the flow. As people described a transformational experience, I heard them saying things like, "I'm just realizing this now... or I'd never thought about it like this before."

The interviews themselves became transformational when I acted less like a journalist, and more like a peer. The dialogues became richer as we explored what's so intriguing about our work, and what's next for them in terms of their own growth. When I asked people what they loved about their own facilitation style, that really opened the kimono. I had a frustrating experience during one interview because I was attached to getting a story out of her. She kept talking in generalities, even when I asked for specific examples. When I finally let go of my strategy, and opened my heart to hearing whatever she wanted to say, however she wanted to say it, she popped. She described how she consciously "puts her arms around the room," holding the group and every person. I got into the flow by saying, "I'm going to do that right now with you – I'm putting my arms around you." She really opened up and told a moving story about how she transformed her terror – I never would have guessed that she ever felt sheer terror when facilitating groups.

Instead of treating the interviewees like experts, instead of separating myself from them, I became involved in the process and started sharing my reactions and how I'm challenged and inspired. Likewise, as I embodied the very facilitation skills as they described them, our conversations deepened and shifts happened.

Overview

Now that we've taken a look at what makes facilitating with heart special, shared the core values, shattered a few myths, told a personal story, and looked at an overview of some of the practices that influence the work, we're going to step into the field of facilitating deep change. I've set the book up the same way I'd set up a workshop, sequencing each step to build on the last. So in chapter 2 we'll look at setting the tone, inviting people into the sacred space of transformation. In chapter 3 we'll review many facilitation skills so that we can scope out the big picture and gain some early confidence. In chapter 4 we go right into the essence of the work, intimately connecting with the body, feelings and needs. Chapter 5 is all about movement, progress, and action, dealing with resistance and creating support. In Chapter 6 we hone the art of making requests and experiment with several decision-making models. Then we go deeper into heart connection, exploring coaching techniques and healing in chapter 7. In chapter 8 we'll compare several facilitation models, from traditional to evolutionary. Chapters 9-12 are all about the inner work of the facilitator including presence, authenticity, feedback and personal transformation. In chapter 13 we look at how we design the facilitation process. In the next three chapters 14-16, we'll get into organization development, social change and the business of transformation. The last section is full of resources to support our work as facilitators.

At the end of each chapter you'll have an opportunity to absorb the content by doing some field work. I invite you to journal or sit with the reflection questions, explore the discussion topics with your peers and experiment with the activities to enhance your awareness, personalize your learning and translate knowledge into action.

Exercises

Reflections:
1. What "mistakes" have you made as a facilitator?
2. How can you celebrate what you learned?

Small Group Discussions:
1. What strongly-held beliefs do you hold about facilitating groups?
2. What are your core values that serve you as a facilitator?

Activities:
1. List some of your favorite practices and brainstorm ways you can integrate them in your practice as a facilitator.
2. Create your own personalized facilitation model.

Chapter 2
Creating Sacred Space for Transformation

The difference between "changing" something and "transforming" it is that changing implies replacing, or in some way negating what is there now. Transformation, on the other hand, implies reaching deep within what is there now to find the seeds for a new shape, a new reality. It is more like the true meaning of education: from its Latin root e-ducare, to draw out, as in drawing water out of a well. You can think of the kind of transformation described here as drawing new water out of your old well — by going deeper than you ever dipped before. The way to get your bucket deeper into your well is by taking on powerful questions, instead of jumping at attractive-looking answers.

— John Scherer

So many times I've seen facilitators panic because the coffee pot isn't working, people arrive late, or the chairs are intolerable. They blame themselves or others, lose sight of the whole, and struggle to regain their footing. How do we kick things off so that we ease people into the work of transformation? The work we do together is sacred, so the way we come together is vital to the well-being of the group. The way we start profoundly impacts the expectations of the group, so let's explore how we open the group with care and grace. In this chapter we'll look at how to create sacred space for transformation, by consciously creating community, setting the tone, fostering inclusion and co-creating guidelines. We'll also explore ways to honor our time together and design inspirational openings and closings.

To give you a sense why the topic of creating sacred space is so important to me, I want to share a personal story. I designed a coaching course for a medical diagnostics company and delivered it in ten cities before one group fell apart. I've had a few "Let's kill the facilitator" experiences, but this one stands out because it could have been avoided so easily. The one thing that contributed to my sense of failure more than anything else is that I did not earn their trust at the beginning of the workshop. Here's how I remember it:

> Before I was introduced, the human resource director set a basket in the center of the room and told everyone to put their cell phones in it. Most people complied but a few stayed seated. Undeterred, she picked up the basket and walked around the room disarming everyone of their phones. One of the doctors

refused, "We can't give up our cell phones. Some people's lives depend on us." The HR director explained why it was important – last month more people were talking on their phone than participating in the workshop and she found it distracting. He didn't budge.

At the time, I had only basic skills as a trainer and I didn't have a clue how to deal with the impasse. I pretended it was their conflict and had nothing to do with me. Of course it had everything to do with me. How could I possibly manage a group that insisted on talking on their cell phones during the program or where a desire to save lives was not clearly valued? How could I help them navigate their dispute? I was lost. From there, the workshop never came together. This experience taught me a most important lesson: step over nothing. Avoiding the issue cost me their respect, trust and willingness to participate. If I couldn't deal with the cell phone issue, how could I possibly help them with their really tough challenges?

I'll spare you the details of the disaster that followed except to say that the CEO didn't participate in some of the coaching activities and we ended early, which was a relief to all, especially me. On the feedback forms, one of the participants gave us the lowest possible ratings and some cutting comments. Needless to say, that ended my coaching workshop tour in their facilities.

In hindsight, there are several things I could have done differently. I could have been completely transparent and said, "I have no idea what to do." Or I could have given them my solution, "Give your cell phone to someone who will come get you in an emergency." Or I might have empathized and asked for their solutions, "I hear that Toni wants to create an environment where people can put their attention on the coaching workshop and Buck wants to stay in contact with people whose lives are at stake. Can we strategize about some ways that both Toni and Buck can get what they want?" Which of these three options would you like to hear if you were about to give your next eight hours to a workshop leader you don't know? Any genuine solution is better than stepping over it, but my preference is to empathize and ask for *their* solutions. So now you know why I'm so passionate about creating sacred space – so that I can help people avoid such catastrophes, including myself.

Imagine yourself facilitating this group and that you trust your ability to connect with each person's needs simultaneously. You can easily acknowledge that their phones were not just phones, but tools for saving lives, that represent their commitment to their patients. Keeping their phones actually gives them a sense of security and ensures their ability to be present. What would you do differently? How do you honor all of the stakeholders in the situation? The HR director? The doctors? Their patients? Did you remember yourself, the facilitator? What about the patient's loved ones? Lawyers? Okay, I won't get too carried away, but let's begin the journey of uncovering needs as often as we can. Let's look at things through the lens of what really matters to each individual and to the whole group.

One of the things that I find important to manage early in a workshop is the way we build trust, by pushing the envelope, a little bit at a time, checking to make sure that people are with us. Sharing our vulnerability can build trust or erode it completely depending on how we handle it. To be transparent, I've been a little worried about sharing stories that reveal my fear, ignorance, and facilitation failures. I want to share real moments about my growth as a facilitator, but at the same time, I'm worried that you, the reader, will lose trust in me. I hope you'll connect with my vulnerability and maybe even see it as a source of wisdom and strength. As I write and imagine your varied reactions, I have no way of knowing if you're with me or if you stopped on page nine. I've read nine is the average number of pages that people read in books they purchase. The *average*! So if you're still with me, you might have grown up in Lake Wobegon – Garrison Keillor's hometown in Minnesota where all the children are above average. I share my angst about losing you, because this is exactly what I do in a workshop if the connection is tenuous. In this case, just naming my desire to stay connected to you, gives me a sense of relief and helps me get clarity about the direction I want to take. In addition to stepping over nothing, and sharing our vulnerability, we'll look at other aspects of creating a trusting environment for transformation, starting with community building.

Creating Community

In a world where families are scattered across the globe and neighbors barely know each other, people long for a sense of community, a place where they belong. To consciously create community in groups, let's think about how to design a space where people feel safe emotionally, psychologically, and spiritually. The space we create for doing transformative work is often referred to as the container, which becomes a leaky bucket if we ignore the process of creating community. We aren't guaranteeing a permanent relationship, but when we value each person and feel genuine concern for each individual, we give people the opportunity to connect right now. Surprisingly, the impermanence can give us more freedom to feel our present connection more fully – no strings attached. But how do we build a strong sense of community when the group only comes together for a week or infrequently? By making ourselves fully available right now, we give people the opportunity to be fully present with each other, a sustainable practice that people can use in every aspect of their lives.

Consider something simple like introductions, a key component of the community building process. The way we introduce ourselves sets the tone and conveys how we offer ourselves to the group. Short introductions with no interaction between participants can result in an inauthentic pseudo-community where people are polite, overly nice, and impersonal. Because they don't feel safe, participants interrupt the process to suggest little tasks, such as whether to adjust the heat or change the time for lunch. The trust level is much higher if the group starts with a brief check-in. When every voice is heard within the first five minutes, the safety level is ratcheted up another notch.

Longer, interactive introductions increase the trust dramatically, particularly when people talk about something meaningful. Talking in pairs before talking in the large group helps people find their voice and get comfortable. Giving people a chance to empty themselves of what they're leaving behind reduces stress, promotes listening, increases risk taking, and deepens community. Instead of "pretending we're all the same," people begin to talk about and accept differences, starting with differences in feelings, perpectives and backgrounds and easing into differences in religion, ethnicity, and socio-economic. The first time someone opens up and shares vulnerably, some members of the group may stiffen. To soften their anxiety, they distance themselves by quickly moving on to something lighter or taking up a task, but the retreat is only temporary as other people access their own courage to share themselves deeply. Slowly, the sense of community creeps into the group and all at once, we can see people physically relax into a sense of being held. Collectively, shoulders drop and the breathing deepens.

Setting the Tone

> For facilitation to be truly transformative it must come from a holistic approach — appealing to the mind, the body, and the heart. —Lee Mun Wah

In the first few minutes of any gathering, people intuitively absorb hundreds of pieces of information and quickly form opinions and expectations. The way we set the tone impacts the ambience and the receptivity of the community. The tone tells people who we are and what we care about. Right away they know if they feel at home or if they're in the wrong place altogether. We can kick things off to help the group deepen their trust, open to curiosity, and expand their sense of acceptance.

How do we create trust? As facilitators, we don't have to be the experts, the problem-solvers, or the only ones responsible for the results. We don't have to offer a life-changing piece of wisdom or make people change; all we need to do is create an opening for the group's exploration and discovery. Offering a welcoming presence invites people to explore whatever is meaningful. Holding our own agenda lightly helps us attune to their agenda. We simply provide space for reflection, empowerment, and authentic exchange. I will repeat that in case you didn't experience a sigh of relief. As facilitators we create an *opening* for the group's exploration and discovery and we don't have to be the experts, the problem-solvers, or the only ones responsible for the results.

We can create a container where people access inner wisdom, expand their resourcefulness, and take action. The tangible ways to create trust include regularity, reliability, clear boundaries, and follow up on requests. To support trust building in more subtle ways, we offer loving presence and empathic connection, whether people are experiencing joy, pain, or fear. Ultimately we want to create the space for people to feel safe, and at the same time, access their fierce courage.

As facilitators, we tap our own courage when we express ourselves vulnerably and authentically. We increase the sense of safety because we convey our trust in the group. For instance we can share a dilemma we're facing, processing the quandary out loud. "I'm torn about whether to sit or stand because I want to be on the same level energetically with all of you, but I think I'll stand for a while because my back is hurting and I might get some relief if I move around." We choose carefully what to share because building trust is a gradual process. If we're *too* vulnerable from the start, we rock their boat, and people will physically and emotionally retreat. For example, if a facilitator shares that he's feeling annoyed by something a participant has done, that might be a great tone setter in a workshop on authenticity, but in most settings, revealing too much at once is frightening and participants either retreat into silence or get up and leave.

When we invite people into a deep state of curiosity and wonder, we set the tone for a learning environment. Not by talking intellectually about how curiosity is the core of any learning experience, but by living in a state of curiosity. When we choose to see the world with the fresh eyes of a child, we adopt a curious mindset. No matter how negative or perplexing the topic, we can choose to stay open and curious. Instead of thinking that we know exactly what to do, we can acknowledge whatever is present or alive without being in a hurry to get somewhere else. By keeping company with our emotions, our life force will emerge. Without applying pressure, we maintain the state of mind of simply opening to what is emerging. It takes trust and discipline to believe that openness and curiosity really serves the group. When we free ourselves from the belief of having to know it all, we give ourselves and the group a gift.

To be curious is to be in a state of openness. If we embody the enthusiasm of a child exploring a creek, we affirm the process of discovery. The opposite of curiosity is judgment. There is no such thing as judgmental curiosity. However, we can get curious about our judgments by going upstream to the source. By listening curiously to our yearning underneath the judgment, we open.

We experience wonder when we connect to what is blooming – the creative force that embraces both apprehension and fascination. When we create space for awe, curiosity, and intrigue, we're often astonished and invigorated. If we apply that same sense of wonder to discomfort, if we get really curious when we're jittery, suspicious, or scared, we soften. When we offer curiosity in response to other's anger, fear, or apprehension, the authentic understanding of what they need opens us to the miraculous. A sense of wonder goes beyond genuine curiosity because we hold people with reverence. For a joyous perspective on wonder, go to the web site of Jon and Maureen Jenkins: the Collective Wisdom Initiative.[6]

Nobody personifies wonder like Duke Fischer. A mediator and trainer from Learning Laboratories in upstate New York, he seems to live in a perpetual state of deep curiosity, simultaneously exploring skepticism and new possibilities. He uses wonder not just as a way to contemplate or explore, but also as a process for bringing the desired future into reality. It's not a naïve starry-eyed process – he shakes things up by sharing his inner protagonist out loud, harnessing doubt by intentionally willing the desired future into the present moment. The discipline of noticing

---

[6] Jenkins, J. J. & M. (2006). *Sense of Wonder: Maintaining the Capacity to Be Surprised*, Excerpted from *Nine Disciplines of a Facilitator: Leading Groups by Transforming Yourself*. Jossey Bass.

and savoring moments of awe means he allows them to unfold without forcing, categorizing, or labeling the experience. Instead he listens to the unknown. Here's how Duke described his facilitation style when I interviewed him:

> I was working with a family where the teen wanted to dress cool, and the parent wanted the teen to dress safe. I helped them restack their perspectives by saying, "Tell me about safe. Tell me about cool." Once they heard what it was like for each other, then they could deal with clothing that was cool enough for the kid and safe enough for the parent.
>
> But first I helped them challenge their assumptions by being gentle and surprised. They hinted at something and I elevated it by saying, "Tell me more about that." I'm chronically confused. But I get to be with people in awkward, real spaces. If they say they need revenge, I stay with them, without pushing them or leading them. They're in the bubble, the fervor, the boil, and I just hold their reality. [7]

Building on trust, curiosity and wonder, Duke offers full acceptance to everyone in the group. To accept is to *hold what is happening with care*. However, "just accept it" is usually poor advice because it doesn't give us the space to accept the part of us that doesn't want to accept it. When we find ourselves bracing against whatever is happening, we can take a step toward acceptance by honoring the part of us that wants things to be different. To illustrate I offer this vignette:

> Lola feels disturbed that two people are having a side conversation while she is talking. In fact it's driving her nuts. She is getting more and more focused on the side conversation and less focused on the rest of the group and what they want to accomplish. She asks the group, "What the hell is wrong with me? Why can't I just accept that two of you are talking? I'm going into a full boil and also judging myself that my reaction is out of proportion, because it's such a small thing."
>
> As the facilitator I ask, "So just for a moment—what would it be like to accept the part of you that is boiling, and see it as a message that you want to be heard and understood?" I see Lola smile and breathe deeply. I may be on to something, so I continue, "Would you also like to accept the part of you that values acceptance?"

Acceptance is a practice of nonjudgment that allows us to be in the now. The art of acceptance is *not* about settling for less than what we want. Instead, we pay attention to everything that is, *including* what we want and don't want.

Dian Killian, co-author of *Connecting across Differences: A Guide to Compassionate Nonviolent Communication*, described her journey toward full acceptance in an interview:

---

[7] Duke Fisher personal interview 3/27/08 http://www.learninglaboratories.org/

My orientation for much of my life as a social change activist and union organizer was to go out and fix things. Transformation is about change. So if I want change, I take action: I go *do* something. Ironically, acceptance is a key element in transformation. It's counterintuitive. When there are aspects I want to change in my life, rather than going about changing them immediately, I start by just noticing them. It's a fabulous first step. I just notice my behavior, and implicit in that is acceptance. No judgment. I simply recognize it, and that's where change begins to happen—in awareness, in seeing.

Despite all my training in analysis and empathy, what actually contributes to transformation is presence. Yes, action will come from that, but we don't start with that; we start with acceptance. Other than food and water, what could be more primal than wanting the reassurance and affirmation that we exist and we matter? Having someone witness where I am in this moment is such a core human experience.[8]

Even more valuable than acceptance from others is self-acceptance. How we express our self-acceptance conveys our trust in ourselves, in others and in the universe. Likewise, our curiosity about what is happening now conveys our sense of wonder and openness. As facilitators, when we embody self-trust, it impacts the trust in the group. Our way of being permeates the group.

Fostering Inclusion

"Often we treat certain aspects of ourselves as junk, having no value. We try to throw parts of ourselves in the garbage. But a human being is an ecosystem, and everything in that system is of value to the whole." — Stephen Schwartz

A group is an ecosystem and each person contributes to the whole. Coming into a new group, many people start out wondering if they belong. As facilitators, we can invite people to expand their sense of belonging by practicing inclusion. We don't have to push people out of their comfortable nest before they're ready to fly, but some people appreciate a little encouragement. Talking in self-selected pairs or small groups can warm people up, or a group mingle can help people ease into contributing in the larger group. Even with these exercises, some people may wait for an invitation to join the group or test the waters before jumping in. Others like to show up fully from the get-go. In reality, we all get to choose our own sense of belonging. No one else can decide that for us. We each decide if we belong.

---

[8] Dian Killian personal interview with Lynda Cowan Smith 3/13/08 http://bnvc.org

We can invite people to speak by name. We can also honor their choice to remain silent as long as it is their informed choice. Using a talking stick is a Native American ritual that ensures that people are heard fully, because the group has an agreement that no one interrupts the person with the talking stick. It takes some people longer than others to gather their thoughts or they may be afraid to speak in a large group. To create balance, we can ask the people who have spoken to journal for the next five minutes, and those who have been quiet to get ready to speak. Ironically, when I've shared an observation, without judgment, that 20% of the people are doing 80% of the talking, the talkers talk even more. Sometimes we can support a sense of inclusion by being invitational or even directive, but ultimately we want to build awareness so that all members in the group create space for each other. A few lines that help reluctant participants join in:

- Let's hear from some of the people who haven't spoken yet.
- It's unrealistic to expect everyone to participate equally, but let's have a moment of silence and then open the floor to people who have not spoken.
- We've heard Ian and LaToya express their concerns. Does anyone else want to share?
- To take the pulse of the group, let's have a quick go-round where each of you says one word about how you're feeling right now.
- Shomi, I see you sitting on your hands and I wonder if you are holding something back. Is there something you'd like to say?
- Kendra, I've missed your voice in this discussion. Will you share your perspective?
- To get more voices to weigh in, let's take five minutes in pairs to explore the topic.

You could also offer an observation, such as, "The four white males have spoken more often than the six people of color. How can we create more balance?" Unless the group has already done a lot of work on power dynamics, I only recommend this approach if you have plenty of time to process the group's reaction.

In addition to encouraging those who have not spoken, we can further build inclusion by encouraging everyone to listen deeply to the people who express dissidence, feeling misunderstood, or seem stuck repeating a similar theme. Loud, angry, persistent voices are a sure sign that people want to be heard. We don't always recognize this because they may take more airtime than others, so we can make the false assumption that they have already been heard. But there's a big difference in speaking out and trusting that you've been understood. Reflecting what the talker has said builds the connection and gives them some relief that they have been understood and can stop talking.

Some facilitator behaviors do *not* foster trust or inclusion. Subtle, unconscious behaviors can close down the group and we won't know what hit us. For instance, if we make eye contact with a few people or we encourage some participants, they may perceive that we favor some participants over others. Or, when we evaluate some participants' contributions by saying "Great idea!" or "We seem to be getting off track," they perceive that we're judging them or taking sides. Likewise, when we ask leading questions, we steer or direct individuals toward decisions that they aren't fully committed to, often based on our own priorities. If we operate on unchecked assumptions, we start to treat opinions or perspectives as facts. Instead of offering our opinions, we can redirect content issues to members of the group.

One of my most memorable facilitation moments was in a workshop for a political party. I'd attended their opening session where person after person got up and spoke with deep passion, but I never got the sense that any of them felt understood or got what they wanted. The next day when I was facilitating a break out session, a woman joined the group 30 minutes late as we were talking about needs and declared, "I'll tell you what the party needs: for all the white men to shut the fuck up." Do you think she wanted to be heard? When anyone is crying out to be heard, we can simply empathize, "So are you really enraged because you want to honor the voices of women and minorities?" However, if many people are clamoring to be heard all at once, one of the easiest ways to foster inclusion and ensure that everyone is heard is to get people into pairs to give everyone more time to understand themselves and vocalize. We increase the likelihood of people being understood if their partner can reflect the essence of their comments and empathize. Another way to foster inclusion is to let people know that you've heard them and value their contribution. A few phrases that can generate a sense of inclusion:

- Several objections have been voiced. It sounds like the group really values autonomy and independence, and at the same time wants to make progress as a group.
- I've noticed many of you want to be heard and understood. Before speaking, would you be willing to say one sentence about what the previous speaker just said?
- As each of you shares your perspective, let the previous speakers know that you heard them. Start by saying, "What's ringing in my ears is…" and then share your own perspective.

We can honor diverse communication styles by expanding acceptability of the ways people express themselves. As facilitators we can support people who exaggerate, drone on and on, go off on tangents, or interrupt, not by making them wrong, but by capturing the essence of what they're trying to communicate. For instance we get more inclusion if we:

- Distill the message of someone who repeats himself
- Stop the interrupter by asking that we complete the current discussion
- Interrupt someone who keeps talking when the group has stopped listening
- Acknowledge the needs of someone who sees things differently
- Honor the discomfort when someone complains that the conversation is too touchy feely.

Val Liveoak is the coordinator of Peacebuilding en las Américas of FriendsPeaceTeams.org. She has facilitated Alternatives to Violence Project (AVP) workshops in prisons, youth groups, and community groups in Canada, Mexico, El Salvador, Guatemala, Kenya, Columbia, Cuba, Mexico, Burundi, Rwanda and USA. She shared with me:

> I'm timid of confronting conflict even after all these years of work. But I've
> learned to build community, even with groups who are desperate, unknown, or

hostile to each other. We have to overcome the barriers, whether it's the disparity between individuals or between ethnic groups, like the Hutsis and Tutsis in Burundi and Rwanda, or the mistrust of young people by older people in El Salvador because of gang violence.

There's nothing terrifically unique about the Alternatives to Violence Project, but I love the total immersion in affirmation. It's like a second language that I never learned as a child. Without being touchy feely, the Alternatives to Violence Project promotes continual reinforcement and noncompetitive teamwork. Our focus is on creating experiential learning for participants and we also develop facilitators. After each day, we do post-sessions called clinics to evaluate and talk about what we're going to do next. There we ask, just as we ask participants after each activity, what happened? How did we feel? What did we learn? How does this help us deal with conflict? We explore how we can transform ourselves, situations, and others.

In an advanced workshop in Africa with two facilitators from Burundi and one from Colombia, everything was going through translation. One of my colleagues, a University professor, gave a long sermon filled with, "You ought to do this..." which is not our preferred experiential method of learning. I was getting nervous because people were drifting off—as team leader I had an obligation to re-direct the process. When I just couldn't tolerate it anymore, I said, "Can we see what other people have to say?"

Later when we had our team meeting, she called me on it, "You interrupted me. I had a good reason for doing what I did." I responded, "You're right. I did interrupt you." I apologized, explained myself, and we forgave each other. Her gracious acceptance contributed to transforming power. She could have seen me as the "white person who thinks she knows everything," but she was open to letting something change in her. I was open to a need to look for a better way to work together. I experienced significant transformation and spent the night ruminating and journaling. The next day I woke up and felt around in my psyche, in my soul, like a tongue continuously probing a sore tooth, and found the burden of resentment gone, lifted from me. I had a sense of liberation from envy and jealousy. I've made many missteps along the way, but I let go of my own hurts and learned the skills to let people see that I am caring. Now I have a commitment to being open to conflict.

This was a unique experience, a religious experience. It wasn't unique for me to offend someone, but it was unique for us to air our differences, accept each other, and work together better than before. What helped was the affirmation from my Columbian colleague who said, "I've worked with Val many times. She speaks strongly, which we can find distressing in Latin American culture. But she thinks about what's best for participants and looks for a beneficial way of working." Her care gave me a sense of acceptance, if not unconditional love.

I'm beginning to look at retirement, passing the torch, so I'm developing a greater interest in mentoring, which brings up new energy. The most rewarding thing is to step back from the joy of doing it myself and invite or elicit the skills that I think are important. I am an amateur—I do it because I love it and it's a source of vitality. Every time I facilitate, I grow. The Alternatives to Violence Project is like a greenhouse where everything for my growth is dependable, constant, and sustained.[9]

We grow and increase our vitality when we look for ways to include all parts of others and ourselves. A sense of inclusion gives us the freedom to show up fully. When we continuously probe the sore tooth, as Val describes, we notice what we're pushing away, bracing against or excluding. When we make room for the parts of ourselves that irritate or stimulate others, our caring exploration opens our hearts and brings us closer to the acceptance of our full humanity.

Co-creating Guidelines

One of the ways we establish sacred space for empowered groups is by co-creating agreements. We can ask, "What will help you work well with others and get the most out of our time together?" For instance, at Coaching that Works, a school for training coaches, the year-long program starts with an invitation to step into agreements. A few things that come out of the discussion that help the group consciously co-create a learning community include:

Shared Leadership

When leadership is shared, each of us contributes as a leader. By being attentive to ourselves and others, each member can take the lead in creating a dynamic learning community.

Heart-Centered Communication

Going to the heart of the matter helps us take the direct route to transformation. If we trust the process and engage fully, we experience empathic connection. So we listen carefully—from the heart, where we can touch what's going on with people at their core.

Compassion

Instead of judging ourselves or others and then judging our judgments, we simply notice that judgments are a portal to awareness. When judgments arise, and we connect with our underlying feelings and desires, we create an open mind and heart. When we transform judgment into awareness of our longing, we open to our shared humanity.

---

[9] Val Liveoak personal interview. 4/25/08.

Authenticity and Vulnerability

When we share our growing edges, and open ourselves to transformation, we model behaviors that help others take risks. Sometimes we avoid vulnerability because we are afraid we won't be accepted. Yet our authenticity helps create deep community that leads to collective transformation.

Lightness

Even though we take our work seriously, we can create plenty of space for lightness, joy, humor, and playfulness. We always have the opportunity to see each other's light and spirit.

However, if we truly embody acceptance, most groups don't need a lot of guidelines. As facilitators we sometimes get attached to our favorite structures – some of us can't move forward without agreement on confidentiality or a commitment to staying for the full time allotted. When the group co-creates the guidelines, they end up with a process that they've all bought into which gives them a sense that they can work together well. It's not the actual guidelines that are most valuable; it's the process. For instance, I have a preference when people raise concerns, that they share their personal experience. The guideline I offer: When you raise a concern, identify specific behaviors and describe the impact on *you,* not what you think is happening to someone else.

Aside from logistical guidelines like turning off cell phones and coming back from breaks on time, some of the guidelines we might co-create include:

1. Listen and reflect interests and needs before choosing strategies or solutions.
2. Test inferences and assumptions for understanding.
3. Share relevant information in terms of observations and specific examples, rather than interpretations, judgments, or evaluations.
4. Discuss the "undiscussables" by transparently sharing observations, feelings, and needs.
5. Make specific doable requests that take the interests of all parties into account, instead of expecting others to understand implied requests.
6. Jointly design action steps by combining advocacy and inquiry, rather than promoting one position.
7. Choose a decision-making process that generates the level of commitment needed to implement the solution.

One of the challenges with participant-created guidelines is that people sometimes ask for ground rules that are vague and unenforceable, such as "speak respectfully to each other," or "be nonjudgmental." Instead of going along with these "feel good" ground rules, we can help the group articulate specifically what they want. That way we don't get caught in a conundrum of evaluating what is "respectful" or "judgmental", and what isn't or set up the expectation that we're going to enforce ground rules that are likely to alienate people. The power of these discussions is not in creating a power structure for enforcing the rules, but in cultivating the trust that we can work together and revise the guidelines as needed.

Holding Time

Sometimes we create community, set the tone, foster inclusion, and establish guidelines, but people get frustrated seeing the time frittered away on trivia without getting to the real purpose of the gathering. Small talk can be an unconscious way to avoid the tough issues, but often it's a strategy for building trust. One way to deepen trust is to honor our agreements about how we spend our time, without using time as a noose.

As facilitators, how do we honor a wide range of relationships with time? Do we start and end exactly on time? Or do we have a little leeway? Can we trust that time is our friend and that people will come together when they are ready? How do we honor each other's perceptions of time and simultaneously honor the sacred flow?

People from different cultures have diverse expectations about how we honor agreements about time. In Western cultures, people tend to think of time as a commodity and there is never enough, or time is wasted. In indigenous cultures, time is more circular, without differentiation between the past, present, and future. How we convey our relationship with time reveals our relationship with abundance, scarcity, and respect for others.

If we hold time too loosely, people come to sessions late, leave early, and the group energy becomes depleted. When people don't come back on time, people begin to wonder if the work matters. If people come back late and we call attention to it the very first time, we reinforce our shared agreements. If we skip over this, the group tends to come back later and later. The art of holding time includes sharing observations without judgment. We can ask if the group is avoiding something, if they need a lighter work load, or more free time.

As long as we don't make it a habit, asking the group to extend a session to address challenges is far better than ending without closure or wondering if the meeting will ever end. Without holding the group hostage, we can co-create a system for holding time. When we share the role of time keeper, we create an empowered group that makes agreements and holds each other accountable.

If one facilitator does all the rounding up each time a session starts, we don't share the onus of responsibility. So whenever I work with a new co-facilitator, I like to co-create agreements about time. Some of the things we can explore are how we:

- Estimate how long something takes
- Track and hold time
- Keep the group focused
- Share air time
- Work with fast- and slow-paced people simultaneously
- Honor differences about what "on-time" means in multicultural groups

We can give the group a good reason to come back on time by sharing what's next. We can also help them envision starting on time by saying, "Before we go for lunch, visualize yourself getting up from the table at 12:50, using the bathroom, and getting back in this room ready to start by 12:59." Even better, we can ask a couple of participants to take on the task of creatively getting people back on time. Similarly, participants can help us by monitoring other aspects of our agreements, such as ensuring we end on time, honoring how long we'll do a specific activity, or tracking an agreement to cover something later.

A common ground rule used by facilitators is for participants to share the airtime. Jane Connor, coauthor of *Connecting across Differences*, stands that rule on its head with a story she shared for this book:

> I had a transformational experience in an open session with the Miki Kashtan [the facilitator] where people could ask whatever questions they wanted. I asked the first question, and then had another burning question, but I saw there were a large number of people there, so I said, "I guess I shouldn't ask it because the rest of you may have something to ask." That led to 15 minutes of processing my judgments—dealing with how much space I am entitled to and my fear that people might not like me. All Miki did was take a little piece of what I'd said and took the time to unpack it.
>
> At first I thought, "Why is she doing this? This isn't that important. So much time on something so inconsequential." She was modeling what she was preaching, and the rest of the group was engaged. She conveyed passion and spoke with clarity that what she was doing was important. Her energy drew us all in. As a result, I was able to let go of an old message I received as a little girl about not being too piggy. The work that I did there led to changes I was able to implement immediately.
>
> I learned to trust myself and to go ahead and use the time that they were offering me. Before I would have said, "I need to stop because I used my share of the time." I learned to trust my assessment of the aliveness of the group and release my old rule that we need to divide things equally, which is not necessarily helpful. We can take care of ourselves and each other by being sensitive to whether or not needs are getting met. Who has what proportion of the time is not relevant if we're all engaged and learning.[10]

When the group's attention is on one person, on a content level, that person may be getting value that is unique to her experience, but as witnesses, the other participants can have deep, enriching, transformative experiences of their own. We feel a sense of oneness with our shared humanity and can touch the sacred beauty of our collective experience. Sharing time is a cultural

---

[10] Jane Connor personal interview 3/23/08.

norm that we rarely adhere to anyway – some people are more comfortable speaking while others are more comfortable listening. Ultimately we can support participants in making a choice about whether to speak or listen that serves both the individual and the group. Simply drawing attention to the choice, asking people to check in with their desire to speak, and making space for people to take some of the group's time can support awareness.

Spaciousness

Sometimes agreements about time evoke a sensation of tightness in me. I feel a sense of scarcity when I'd much rather facilitate from a place of generosity and spaciousness. I want to convey that I value everyone's time and yet we have plenty of time. Spaciousness is not emptiness, but depth of presence. In our modern world it's rare to meet people who embody true spaciousness in their lives. To keep up with others, we get on the fast track, even if we don't know where the track is headed. If we don't pause to reflect, we squeeze in all kinds of activities that don't nurture us. We can cram every minute full of activity, but to what end? For instance, spending time on the internet can be a huge sink hole where we wile away the time, but we also have access to wonderful insights like these on Meridith's blog (reprinted with permission):

> There are many kinds of spaciousness – there is spaciousness of physical form, of time, of presence, and I have discovered, of love...
>
> Spaciousness is always a beginning, a possibility, a potential, and a capacity for new awareness. If I can bear the truth of how things are and actively seek the truth, not just what is comfortable, I eventually find myself in the midst of a peaceful Presence...
>
> It is a blessing that love is relentless. Love waits for us to make space for it in our lives. When I step out, risk myself in love, let this love exude from my wholeness, I find an ever-deepening capacity within me for this spaciousness of love. [11]

Just reading Meridith's description of spaciousness, my lungs expand, and my self-imposed confinement withers. What a contrast to modern life! Spaciousness is a choice. We can live a harried life succumbing to restriction, or we can choose to continuously open. One way to expand into spaciousness is to practice compassion – we can even have compassion for the parts of ourselves that feel cramped or overwhelmed.

In our frenzied world, creating spaciousness gives people room to breathe, reflect, and deepen their awareness. With the intention of meeting people where they are, we can start by matching the group's pace even if they sound like a pinball machine, trusting that they'll hear their own frantic clip and slow things down themselves. Or we can gently guide them into slowing down by asking them to notice their heartbeat, take a few deep breaths, or hold silence for a few moments. Intuiting when people need more spaciousness is pretty simple since most people benefit from slowing down,

---

[11] Meridith's blog. Retreived from http://gracefulpresence.blogspot.com/2005/09/musings-on-spaciousness.html

especially when they're in a hurry. Jane Connor who lives at Pendle Hill, a Quaker spiritual community, says they *double* the amount of silent time upfront when they have a business meeting with a full agenda, *especially* if they have important decisions to make. She told me about a time when she awakened to the power of spaciousness:

> Transformation can be so simple. Two weeks ago Kanya Likanasudh was describing work she'd done with a couple where she slowed down the process and gave them space to sit with the beauty of each other's needs. She was giggling, totally thrilled with how it had gone. I felt touched by the emotional affect of her delight, almost envious because I want that delight in my work with clients. Her description gave me pause, and I took it in deeply. So simple. I wanted to stretch myself into the miracle of experiencing the beautiful needs. It wasn't a new idea – cognitively I knew all about needs, but I hadn't heard it in that form.

> I found her description of the process very powerful, which alerted me to try something different. The following week doing empathy work with students, I slowed it way down just by talking slower and waiting longer. It was Empathy 101, but something about the spaciousness was transformational for me. Now I use more spaciousness in my interactions every day. I was so surprised that such a simple idea of spaciousness could have such a profound effect. [12]

Noticing the group's rhythms and cadence creates room for spaciousness and new awareness. As facilitators, we need to be willing to play as little or as great a role as needed. We can spot new facilitators a mile away because they offer guidance even when the group doesn't need it. Knowing when to hold the space can be even more important than knowing when to intervene. If we set the container and get out of the way, participants will create, implement, and own their solutions.

Openings and Closings

Opening and closing rituals enhance the sense of spaciousness. In addition to setting the tone and bringing the group to closure, the beginnings and endings serve as solid bookends by supporting the work of the group. A few ways to create sacred openings are by choosing welcoming music, warm lighting, and comfortable seating. Are we already set up and eager to greet people as they enter? Have we gotten rid of any clutter and made arrangements for refreshments? Have we created a ceremonial entry or can people come and go whenever they choose? The boring go-round of your name and where you're from can be replaced by a centering meditation or an energizing activity that helps people become present. In the early stages of the group, participants often experience three types of anxiety:

---

[12] Jane Connor personal interview 3/23/08.

Acceptance anxiety – the need for love, acceptance, belonging, community

Orientation anxiety – the need to understand, for clarity, meaning

Performance anxiety – the need for competence, mastery, personal power, learning, growth

The group wants reassurance early in the program that the facilitator can simultaneously provide direction *and* freedom to choose. Some members have strong values of structure, order, and predictability, while others value autonomy, personal power, and freedom. Identifying and balancing a wide range of needs gives participants reassurance and helps them open up to the experience of the group. Ironically, voicing my own anxieties can empower the group because they accept their own anxieties and know they are not alone. Some of my favorite ways to mitigate anxiety are to get people talking in small groups early on, to share some meaningful connection, or do a "brain dump" to reveal all that they already know about the topic and relieve the stress of "knowing " or "not knowing."

The first words spoken leave a lasting impression. That doesn't mean we have to pre-plan a speech, because spontaneity can be very, very, inviting, but if we start out by saying, "I can't find my glasses," we've already lost some credibility. Although we may have missed a huge opportunity, we can always recover.

I never start a group by listing my credentials – that may be a tactic for people who don't trust who they are right now in the moment. I like to start with an opening question to establish the direction of the group. The beauty of starting questions is that they provide a starting place, stimulate excitement about where we're going, empower individuals to act, and engage them in the solutions. We can use them not only at the start of the session but for each item on the agenda. Figure 2.1 offers three types of opening questions – casual, de-energizing and energizing:

Figure 2.1

Opening Questions		
Casual	**De-energizing**	**Energizing**
Shall we get started?	What's the root cause of the problem?	Imagine…
Is everyone here?	What's important about this dilemma?	What if…
Shall we check in?	What's wrong with our current process?	Envision…
You have the agenda?	What data is needed to address this difficult situation?	Picture yourself…
Who'd like to begin?	What information do we have about this crisis?	Suppose…
How are you all?	How are we going to get out of trouble?	The ideal future…

I see the casual approach used by facilitators who like to ease into relationships, the de-energizing approach used when people are in trouble, and the energizing approach used by visionaries who want to create a better future. To ask energizing opening questions every time, we use the participant's language rather than facilitator jargon. We address participants directly instead of just talking about the issue, problem, or opportunity, and involve them as people, putting "you" into the question. Giving participants the opportunity to visualize themselves in action, as opposed to just *thinking* about the issue, helps them imagine *doing* something to get the results they want. Rather than just picturing resolution, we help participants explore what's different about *them* in the future.

To engage people on a visceral level, we can ask direct questions that enable them to create visual images of their own answers, instead of giving them canned solutions. For instance, when I worked with a group of social activists, I started the session with, "Imagine a world where you have unlimited resources to realize your dream and that you have hundreds of volunteers who want to support your vision." That set the tone for them to continuously explore the kind of world they want to co-create.

Like openings, closings take very little time but can be the most relevant part of the session. Closings may involve summarizing, reviewing outcomes, articulating next steps, or evaluating the process. A closing ritual helps people shift from the process to connecting with their internal transformation and commitments. Wrapping up a group gathering often takes the form of sharing new awareness or new intentions. In Figure 2.2 are some conventional closings that I've seen used many times in many contexts.

Figure 2.2

Closings Rituals	
Awareness	**Intentions**
What's the pearl of wisdom?	Who will do what by when?
What are you taking away?	How will you apply what you learned?
Let's harvest the learning.	What will you do differently?
What are you celebrating or mourning?	What will you commit to?
Take a minute to journal and share one insight.	Write yourself a letter stating your intentions.
Share one thing from your heart.	What is your first step?
Appreciate yourself or others.	Let's summarize the outcomes.
Mingle and give symbolic gifts to others.	Step over the line into commitment...
What gift do you give yourself?	Create support structures with a partner.
What do you need to say or do to be complete?	What is your action plan?
What did you learn that you can use?	Raise your glass to...

Tried-and-true closing rituals offer reassurance and predictability. By giving people an opportunity to capture the essence of their experience, they can take away their learning in some tangible form. Most of the closings listed in the table were once innovative but have since become part of my stock repertoire. Innovative closings can be a little more daunting, but more exciting because we've never tried them before. We make them up in the moment, based on our assessment of what the group needs to feel complete. As a result, they may be less graceful, but more authentic and powerful.

Exercises

Reflections:

1. What's important to you in creating a learning community?
2. What is your relationship with time and how can you connect with people who have a very different relationship with time?

Small Group Discussions:
1. What are some ways to set the tone for creating sacred space?
2. What guidelines would you like to see in place when you're in a group?

Activities:
1. Flip chart behaviors that foster inclusion and hinder inclusion for several identity groups: parents, people of color, white men, English as a second language, Lesbian, Gay, Bisexual, Transgender.
2. Design an activity to create spaciousness right now.
3. Share examples of innovative openings and closings you've tried or seen; then create fresh closings and openings.

Chapter 3
Facilitation Skills

The greatest gift you can give another is the purity of your attention. — Richard Moss

We can draw on our rigorous education, professional background, and inner reserves, yet still wonder if we have the skills and resources to help people with their toughest challenges. Most of what we use comes from experience, discovering for ourselves what works and what does not. As facilitators, we have many options in any moment. So why do so many facilitators perform like one-trick ponies, using one skill over and over again, regardless of the situation? Sometimes it's all they know. One facilitator, who is passionate about action and results, continuously asks the same question, with slight variations, "What are you going to do?" Another facilitator, enamored by the power of compassion, repeatedly empathizes with individuals in the group, even when they're begging for another way of interacting. Despite having many tools in our facilitator's box, we tend to move into default behaviors when we're in uncertain or atypical situations, using tried and true methods that give us a sense of comfort and predictability. So part of the challenge is to hone a variety of tools so that we deepen our inner trust in multiple options.

As we support groups in dealing with complex, controversial issues, we need a wide range of facilitation skills so that we can approach every moment creatively. We start this chapter with a helicopter view of 35 facilitation skills and examples. This introduction gives us a rough map of the territory before we explore five core facilitation skills in more detail: listening, riding the waves of energy, intervening, keeping the focus, and synthesizing.

35 Facilitation Skills

Acknowledging – helping people see things they may take for granted or are unable to see about their values, contributions, or impact on the group.
Example: "This group cares deeply about team spirit and making a meaningful contribution."

Articulating - succinctly describing what is happening in the moment by sharing observations, naming group dynamics, or group process.
Example: "The group seems both afraid and excited about confronting the director. I sense fear, excitement, and a desire to be understood. How can you use the group energy to request what you want?"

Asking Empowering Questions - using open-ended questions to evoke clarity, insight, and action.
Examples: "What is important about this?" "What stands out about the group process?" "What is next?"

Brainstorming - generating ideas, expanding new possibilities, or developing strategies.
Example: "Let's come up with all the ways you can have fun while getting the results you want."

Challenging - requesting that the group stretch beyond their perception of their limitations.
Example: "The challenge is to utilize everyone's talents to get over this hurdle, without leaving some people out. I challenge you to find new ways to include everyone."

Championing - believing in and encouraging the resourcefulness of the group and highlighting their desire or ability.
Example: "This group has demonstrated a lot of creativity throughout the planning process. How can you use that creativity right now?"

Clarifying - succinctly articulating the essence of what has been communicated, and speaking to the deeper message or implication in the words.
Example: "I'm hearing that members of the group want autonomy and a sense of community, and you're looking for ways to have both?"

Creating Trust - developing safe space to embrace five elements of trust: reliability, acceptance, openness, straightforwardness, and caring.
Example: "What are some requests you have of the group that will allow you to work well together?

Choosing Curiosity - stepping into the space of childlike wonder and "not knowing" for the sake of opening up possibility for the group.
Example: "One person said she wants to slow down; another wants to pick up the pace. I'm curious what really matters to each of you?"

Discovering the Wisdom - trusting the group to explore and discover fresh insights, new understanding, and alternative perspectives.
Example: "It sounds like the group learned a lot from the experience. What insights are beginning to form in you?"

Embracing Polarities - valuing needs that appear to be in conflict without making one need more important than the other.
Examples: "So group members seem to need both freedom and security. How can you have both?" or, "Imagine the experience of freedom and then envision the experience of security and notice the internal differences."

Establishing Accountability - creating structures to verify the action plan is on track or to remind people to actively live their values, vision, or goals.
Example: "What will you do and when will you do it?" or " How will you stay on track with your plan?"

Expressing Vulnerability - honestly expressing your internal experience to deepen authenticity and build connection.
Example: "I'm feeling overwhelmed right now and I really want to hear each of you clearly. Can we slow this down so that I fully understand each of you?"

Holding the Focus – keeping the group's attention on the original agenda and what is important.
Example: "Let's come back to the group's original intention – how do you support each other as change agents?"

Holding Silence – knowing when to be quiet so the group can fully experience the power of the moment and discover their resourcefulness.
Example: A group member says, "We seem lost and confused. Maybe we should ask the facilitator for the answer." You hold silence while the group experiences confusion and discovers its own answers.

Identifying Group's Agenda – listening for what matters, both in the big picture and in the moment.
Example: "The purpose of our meeting is to establish a long-term strategic plan, and right now two people have expressed a desire to clarify the outcomes of today's meeting."

Interrupting – cutting through storytelling to capture the essence of what was communicated, support the group's agenda, help them stay on track, or develop connection.
Example: "Hold up a minute. Joe, you said something similar a moment ago. I'm imagining that's because you really want to be understood. Would you like someone to tell you their understanding of what you said?"

Intuiting – trusting your inner knowing and expressing your gut reactions.
Example: "I have a sense (hunch, intuition) that there is a black veil over this whole situation. What are you not saying?"

Listening Empathically – listening for what the group wants at the core and reflecting feelings, needs, values, and vision.
Example: "I'm hearing a wide range of feelings about José leaving the group. Some are hurt or disappointed, and others are relieved. Underneath these feelings I'm sensing a need for inclusion. How does that resonate with you?"

Metaphor Making – using images, stories, and pictures to deepen learning and reflect the essence of the situation.
Example: "You've hauled this baby around for nine months; put your heart and soul into it, and now that the baby is in the birth canal wanting to be born, but a few parts of this collective body have given out from exhaustion."

Moving into Action – requesting actions that are aligned with the expressed group values.
Example: "What can each of you do this week so that we can launch this initiative on time?"

Observing – articulating what we see or hear and allowing the group to make their own meaning and choices about it.
Example: "Five minutes ago the group was physically very close and everyone was leaning forward. One person left the room, several people leaned backward and a few people looked at the floor when Tamal suggested you give each other feedback. What are you moving away from?"

Offering an Inquiry – asking a reflective question that helps the group explore new learning and insights more deeply.
Example: "How do your relationships impact the quality of the work?"

Planning – eliciting the direction, goals, action plan, and method for monitoring progress.
Example: "What are the action steps needed to accomplish this goal?"

Reading the Energy - paying attention to the flow and what is emerging, trusting your intuition (including the wisdom of your body, senses, emotions) to connect with the underlying forces.
Example: "The group energy has shifted several times during this process, tentative at the start, animated as you engaged in the dialogue, and subdued as you start to look at the action plan. What is the elephant in the room?"

Reflecting – receiving and mirroring back what people have said to move the group toward deeper wisdom or energetic shift.
Example: Jin says she's tired of being so nice and wants people to listen to her. You take in her desire, then reflect, "Jin, you want to express yourself more freely and you want to be heard. Lily, will you let Jen know what stood out for you about what she said?"

Re-framing – sharing a new perspective that opens up broader possibilities.
Example: "You said you think Paolo and Mary are in a stalemate. Perhaps they care deeply about this environment and want to create a solution that works for everyone."

Requesting – asking for a specific action without being attached to the outcome.
Example: "To deepen the learning, I request that each of you find a peer coaching partner that you coach every week. How many of you say yes? No? Counter-offer?"

Self-Managing - setting aside own internal reactions when triggered and staying connected rather than expressing judgment, opinions, or advice.
Example: Two members in the group have become romantically involved and others observe that the quality of the work is slipping. As facilitator, you feel challenged because you've been putting your own romantic relationship ahead of your work, and decide to take time to process your internal reaction after the session. Then you step into curious, focused listening where every group member's needs matter.

Setting Goals - setting intentions for desired outcomes that are specific, measurable, attainable, relevant, time-bound, and communicated.
Example: "What will you create and how will that look when it is complete?"

Synthesizing – summarizing, weaving in contributions, and creating synergy.
Example: "I've heard three areas of concern: including the business dimension, prioritizing academic honesty, and setting a realistic time line."

Tracking - knowing where you are in the process, remembering what's been said, what's complete and what's still open in the group.
Example: "I'm tracking that we aren't finished talking about the goals for the day, Sonya wants some time to talk about transportation and Gillian wants to brainstorm new ways to build teamwork. Can we finish with the goals and then come back to transportation and teamwork?"

Visioning – exploring the big picture and creating a visual picture of a better future.
Example: "Take away all the limitations and imagine you are successful beyond your wildest dreams. What if this team were the best team of all time? What do you see?"

At any given time, we have a wide range of facilitation skills to choose from. We use our intuition and senses to determine ways to intervene that awaken the soul of the group. One of my favorite skill building practices is called "The Three-Headed Facilitator." Here's a simple way to learn and reinforce facilitation skills:

1. A small group forms a circle in the front of the room to work on building their relationships, while the rest of the group forms a horseshoe around them to practice a range of facilitation skills.
2. Each person in the horseshoe chooses three facilitation skills to work on – preferably ones that they rarely use.
3. After the small group has talked for about 3 minutes, the facilitator asks for three interventions, where the people in the horseshoe name the skill they are about to use first, and then state their intervention.
4. Ask the small circle in the front to express their emotional response physically by exaggerating their body language or facial expressions so that we can see the impact of each facilitation skill.
5. Then the small group responds to the three-headed facilitator in any way they are moved – they can respond to one, two, three, or none of the interventions.

We do this for about 30 minutes with the intention of practicing as many skills as possible. Occasionally the mentor facilitator offers support, say if a participant names one skill but actually uses another. Or the mentor might say, "The group is working, so now would be a good time to practice the skill of silence," or "The group could use some support in making requests that are connected to their needs." Not only do people get a visceral experience of a wide range of facilitation skills, but those working in the small circle are often amazed at the transformation of their relationships as they look at multiple pathways to consciously co-create their relationship.

Listening

The greatest gift you can give another is the purity of your attention. – Richard Moss

Of all the facilitation skills available to us, listening is fundamental to opening the possibility for transformation. Pure, focused listening invites people to look within. With so many places to put our attention, what do we listen for? We're so busy listening to other people that we forget to listen to ourselves. By listening deeply to ourselves, we have a greater capacity to listen to another, and both practices open us to listening for transformation. Each practice nurtures the other. We can practice the three levels of listening shown in Figure 3.1 separately and eventually we listen to all three levels at once.

Figure 3.1 Levels of Listening

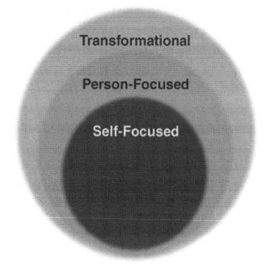

Self-focused Listening

Self-focused listening includes listening to your body, sensations, emotions, and needs. When we bring our awareness to self-focused listening, we shift from reacting and judgment into the wisdom of the entire body-mind system which makes intuition more accessible. When we cultivate inner awareness and follow our intuition, we are more in tune with what is happening in the moment. Modeling deep inner listening sets the tone for others to do the same. Self-awareness enhances our ability to listen deeply to another. If we are triggered or have judgments about what someone is saying, we can take a moment to self-empathize and translate our judgments into our inner feelings and needs.

Examples:
- Staying present with or exploring the meaning of the butterflies in your stomach.
- Listening to your intuition telling you to explore your feeling of alarm.
- Trusting your desire to share a metaphor.

Person-focused Listening

When we practice person-focused listening we narrow our focus so that all our attention is on the other person. Listening to the content and word choice helps us get clarity about what is most important to the speaker. But we can also hear what the person is not saying. We pay particular attention to body language, feelings and needs. We take in the nuances of their mannerisms, pace, volume and tone, witnessing their process of discovery. Conscious, clear, empathic listening fosters self-awareness. As we listen to the content of the story, we pay attention to underlying desires.

Examples:
- Hearing the change in emotions when the person shifts to new revelations.
- Listening for the needs and values at stake as the voice gets louder and more energized.
- Attuning to the underlying desire for relief when the person says he doesn't want to talk about sadness.

Transformational Listening

With *transformational* listening we hear all that's happening within ourselves, each individual, the group energy, the environment, and then sense the meaning and potential movement. Hearing the whole symphony, we have a heightened sense of the flow of the conversation. We can intuit and recognize the openings, new possibilities, emerging opportunities, and forces that generate change. Knowing when to hold silence is key, so that we can tune into the need for spaciousness, the desire to shift into deeper awareness or move to a new perspective.

Awareness is inherent in transformational listening, which creates an environment that fosters opportunities for profound transformation. We intuit fresh openings, arising feelings, shifting motivations, and emerging insights that help people become aware of what is waiting to be born. At the heart of transformational listening is listening for what's emerging right now.

Examples:
- Acknowledging the celebratory tone as people discover empowering perspectives.
- Getting in synch by hearing and supporting an "aha" moment.
- Holding space for new consciousness as people discover their gifts that enable them to make a meaningful contribution.

Here's a true story about a guy who listens deeply at all three levels and can easily shift his focus between the three levels, even in challenging situations.

> Darrel listened when Sylvia, an old girlfriend he hadn't seen in 19 years told him he had an 18-year old daughter. He was ecstatic! His first thought was, "Instant grandchild for Dad!" He felt distraught when he learned that Sylvia had never told a single friend or family member about the birth of their child, Darrel put his exuberance aside and shifted into listening deeply to Sylvia's experience (level one listening).

> As Sylvia talked about her grandfather's ties to the KKK, her family's probable response to a bi-racial child, and the secretive adoption process, Darrel listened in awe to the depth of her pain, and the intensity of her experience. He noticed Sylvia lowered her voice as she described why she didn't tell him about the pregnancy 19 years ago. "I wanted to protect both you and the baby from my family," she said in a pained but relieved voice. Tears flowing, Darrel reflected, "When you gifted our baby with adoption, you were doing it out of love and protection." Sylvia interrupted, "What did you say?" Hearing his words a second

time, Sylvia sobbed with relief. She had always thought of "giving the baby up for adoption," and was deeply relieved that he understood her positive intent (level two listening).

Darrel could read the energetic shift as she was understood for her intention to give her baby the gift of a better life. Her broken heart began to heal. Sylvia was flooded with emotions and was grateful that over the next few weeks Darrel was available to listen to her desire for healing, love, and acceptance. As he came to know how long she'd been suffering alone, he allowed her plenty of spaciousness for her story to unfold and for the healing to begin (level three listening).

His gift was his capacity to listen deeply to himself, as well as to Sylvia. The opportunity to be there for someone who needed him was a deeply satisfying experience. Their daughter's name and location remain a mystery to both parents, but a master of patience, Darrel is still hopeful about meeting his daughter and is filled with lots of new questions and thoughts about her existence. For right now, he is focused on his reconnection with Sylvia, their mutual caring and shared transformation.

Not everyone is the natural listener that Darrel is, but everyone has the ability to learn. We can hold our attention on one area, bounce quickly from one to the other, or listen simultaneously to all three levels, staying continuously aware of our inner experience, their inner experience, and the emerging opportunities for transformation. By integrating each level of listening in our consciousness, we have access to our deeper intuition. We create trust by being curious listeners, staying in the moment, and reflecting core values. Only then do we reduce resistance and cultivate openness, receptivity, and engagement. This higher level of engagement creates the space for intuition to evolve and opportunities for transformation to emerge.

Reflection

> When you listen to somebody else, whether you like it or not, what they say becomes a part of you... the common pool is created, where people begin suspending their own opinions and listening to other people's... At some point people begin recognising that the common pool is more important than their separate pools. — David Bohm

It's one thing to listen at all three levels; it's another to let people know we're listening. Reflective listening is an active way to express compassion and open people's hearts – ours and theirs. When we listen for what is most important, our reflections lead to deeper understanding of values, fears, and dreams that connect us to the heart of the experience. Listening for content so that we can analyze or critique might make us look brilliant but rarely helps us connect to the opportunities for transformation. The power of reflection is in giving people confidence that we understand their experience.

The old stand-by expressions such as, "I follow you," "I'm with you," or "I understand," don't contribute to connection as much as capturing the essence. Instead of saying we understand, we *show* that we understand deeply, without judgment. Even if our reflection isn't quite accurate, when people see that we *want* to understand, they experience an energetic shift and willingly explore more deeply. Instead of saying, "I'm hearing..." we take ourselves out of the equation by saying, "You're saying...?" The focus on "you" seems like a little thing, but can have a huge impact.

Beware of one of the most disempowering behaviors of facilitators – altering participants' words. Sometimes we change their words to offer reassurance, or tone it down because we can't handle the pain. Even if our intention is only to condense or clarify someone's words, we invalidate their experience unless we reflect the force of their rage, the depth of their longing or the fullness of their happiness. We can paraphrase by paying attention to the particular words, which seem to catch the essence of what the person is expressing, and checking for accuracy.

Instead of parroting the entire story, we focus on the micro-shifts while matching the tone and energy. Here are three examples of reflections that connect the listener with the speaker:

> Speaker: I am not developing the team the way I had hoped.
> Listener (mirroring): I can feel the disappointment about not developing the team the way you had hoped.
> Listener (articulating): Are you sensing some new desire emerging from your disappointment for developing a better team?
> Listener (reframing): It sounds like you can envision another kind of team?

Reflections generally build trust and help people get clarity, but can also be overdone. Excessive reflections can disrupt the flow and prevent the listener from absorbing, really letting their felt sense of the experience infuse them and authentically become part of them. Duke Fisher, a facilitator from Learning Laboratories, describes the importance of avoiding rote reflections:

> The one thing I can't stand is when facilitators sleepwalk their reflections. Once I was on the other end of mediation, and I was really upset about my nephew exposing my five-year-old to porn. The mediator said, "It seems like you really love your kids." Duh. That's what you heard? That's not listening. That's smoothing. I'm not playing softball here – I'm outraged. You might as well say, "I'm not listening," than tell me it seems like I love my kids.
>
> That's why I hate using a needs list – it's so shallow when there's so much more. A lot of phenomenal listeners struggle with technique and lose their authenticity. Teaching people to listen, we have to have the courage to be in the moment – not to hide from their pain or meanness. When I change their words to neutral

language, they get a message that I'm judging them. We need to have the courage to be with what they're actually facing. Be fearless. Stay with them. If they want revenge or they're feeling horny, stay with them by using their words. Otherwise if you sweeten it, before you know it, it's not real. People don't need us for the easy stuff. They want us because we help them be with the things that are dicey, embarrassing, or humiliating. [13]

One of the ways to avoid "sleepwalking our reflections" is to steep ourselves in the moving energy. We can understand people more deeply if we "try on" or embody their experience. If we're not sure what to reflect, we can guess, aiming more towards the desire for transformation, rather than the details.

Reading the Energy

To expand the power of listening we use more than just our ears. Our whole body becomes a receptor as we read and interpret the energy of the group. Riding the waves of energy is a life-long learning process. As we continuously scan the room for emotional reactions, we notice the many ways that people reveal that they are bursting at the seams, smoldering, opening up, losing patience, hiding, devastated or done.

Have you ever considered how many factors impact the group energy? The light, sound, the last group that was in the room, what people have eaten, seating arrangements, what's going on back at the office, how people slept the night before… the list is endless. We process what we see, hear, and feel, noticing the posture, tone of voice, facial expressions, changes in breathing, heart rate and tone of voice. As we receive all that information and more, and then notice how it lives in our bodies, we may begin to notice shifts in energy. Is the energy stagnating, spiraling downward, or getting ready for lift off? What we *do* with the energy is another story, but the first step is developing the capacity to read the group. If we're unsure or if we want to develop greater accuracy, we can check in with the group, asking them for *their* read on the energy. One of the first times I asked this question, a woman responded, "The room is getting much lighter." I didn't actually read the energy the same way, but as soon as she said it, it was so… I could actually feel the light coming into the room. Now perhaps she was ahead of me, or perhaps her reading impacted the group energy. Whenever we ask for a reading or give a reading, that in itself impacts the group's energy.

Occasionally group members have very different experiences – some are in awe of what is going on, some are bored, while others are terrified, but regardless, most people experience the energetic connection of the group. Because each individual's experience permeates everyone else in the group, even those who insist they are not impacted, the group can largely be in synch. Sure, one person may be riding the wave of angst and another finds the same wave thrilling, but the entire group is going for the ride. Collectively we share the energy of the group whether we're

---

[13] Duke Fisher personal interview 3/27/08 http://www.learninglaboratories.org/

experiencing frustration, hunger, or bliss. Our self-awareness and self-acceptance are immutable parts of the group energy.

A facilitator from Vermont, Marsha Smith shared a story about a time when facilitating didn't work the way she'd hoped. Every facilitator has a rough day now and again, which usually stems from misreading the energy, not naming it, or stepping over it. I'm moved by her example of what happens when you read the energy but don't act on it:

> Prior to the meeting I interviewed every participant—each an executive director of a component service agency, and they were unanimous about what they wanted: to be more connected with each other. I had been told that the individual directors had trouble getting along, but this seemed like a straightforward facilitation.
>
> What I didn't know was that a significant decision had been made between when I'd interviewed them and when we met. The decision effectively eviscerated the strategic plan and eliminated one of the executive director positions. He had moved his family to the U.S. in order to implement that very plan, and now the future he had imagined—on which he had literally banked—had disappeared. No one told me this.
>
> When we gathered, the energy level was zero. The man who had just lost his future—was sitting with legs outstretched, head back, arms crossed, eyes closed. Another woman sat with her head on her knees and her arms folded over her head. When I asked them what was going on, all they could say was, "We're tired." I've seen plenty of people roll their eyes and give each other knowing looks, but here the intensity was different. They didn't speak of their hostility, but I could feel it. My biggest mistake was that I didn't stop right there. I wish I had said, "I don't buy it. Being tired doesn't look like that." Instead I went forward. I pulled out every trick, but I could do nothing right. I had no foothold. At the end they clapped. The clapping haunted me.
>
> Later the guy who hired me told me the missing information about the changed decision. Only then could I see that I was a sacrificial lamb: I got what was intended for him. I was shocked and confused by the very present but unacknowledged rage in the room, cowed by the level of hostility. I felt like a canary in a mine shaft: I was the first victim of the buildup of some pretty powerful toxins.

I carry this story with me in my heart as a warning against blindness and avoiding what feels too dangerous to acknowledge, no matter how clear it actually is—I have more willingness to see what's there and name it.[14]

Why do we step over the undiscussables? We don't want to invade other's privacy. We're scared or don't trust ourselves. We think the group won't like us. What will happen to the beautiful plan we had for the day if we step into the whirlwind? What will happen if we don't? We want to give people choice and respect their readiness to explore the tough issues.

So how do we create safe space for exploring the intense emotions that lurk just below the surface? We read the bubbles as they break through the surface – sharing our observations about body language, sharing our own energy and mixed feelings as an opening for participants to share theirs. They're more likely to share in pairs than in a larger group, so asking them to tell a partner what they need can surface what's really going on.

The energy lies in the emotional life of the group. Because the mood can range from constricted to stimulating to frenetic, our awareness of the energy is vital to helping us choose from our repertoire of interventions. Awareness that everything is transitory helps us step back, and view the situation with fresh eyes. Figure 3.2 offers ten aspects of Group Dynamics that can contribute to our understanding of the group energy.

---

[14] Marsha Smith personal interview 6/24/08.

Figure 3.2

Aspects of Group Dynamics

Goals:	Non-existent	Co-created	Instant Agreement
Conflict:	Avoided	Explored	Destructive
Interventions:	Ignored	Considered	Unquestioned Acceptance
Tracking:	Disregarded	Attentive	Inflexible
Humor:	Absent	Enjoyed	Disruptive
Posture:	Closed	Opened	Sprawled
Focus:	Task	Balanced	Relational
Structure:	Aimless	Flexible	Controlled
Decisions:	Analytical	Blended	Emotional
Awareness:	Self-focused	Shared	Other-focused

This chart is adapted from the work of Brendan Reddy.[15]

Collectively these dynamics inform our choices about when and how to intervene. Notice that the center of the chart offers a balance, but that doesn't mean that the outliers are undesirable. Taking one example, when a decision needs to be made, thinking analytically moves the group forward. At other times, the decision can't be made until people have expressed their emotions. Any group needs a blend of both behaviors.

Connecting Energetically

There's a big difference between talking and connecting energetically. Meeting people right where they are changes the way we think and the way we connect. I've heard many people say that empathy is not about the words, but I do not completely trust this claim. I've seen hundreds of references to Mehrabian's experiments with communication (of feelings and attitudes) claiming that

---

[15] Reddy, W. B. (1994). *Intervention skills: Process consultation for small groups and teams.* Pfeiffer & Company. p. 90.

only 7% of the meaning of a message is derived from words, 38% from tone, and 55% from body language.[16] All three elements are important, but I find words particularly soothing and connecting, even when I don't understand the language.

When I introduced empathy practice to a group of social workers in the slums of Mumbai, half of whom were transgenders (people whose gender identity does not mesh with their assigned gender at birth), I experienced the power of empathy without words.

> Out of 20 people in the workshop, there were 16 different mother tongues, so I had a translator on each side whispering in my ear the whole time, which felt incredibly sweet. Whatever incentive I had to learn another language was completely destroyed. On the second day when the group was working in pairs, two people felt triggered about their beliefs regarding how transgenders should dress. Since neither of them spoke English, Shridhar Kshirsagar (my co-facilitator) worked with the woman in jeans and I got to work with the woman in a sari. She poured her heart out, her body glistening with tears and sweat. When she paused, I reflected back my own feelings and compassion for her, "I don't know what you're saying; I just know you're suffering and you want some relief and understanding." Back and forth we went, me aching to reach out to her, and her craving to be understood. After about 20 minutes, she sighed deeply and seemed to shift. She hugged me and when we debriefed in the large group we both shared (through translators) what a moving experience it was for each of us, even though we didn't understand a word. She wasn't trying to impose her will; she was deeply concerned for the other's safety, and believed wearing a sari would protect her from violence.

In India, *hijras* (transgenders) are paid to dance and sing at birth ceremonies and bless the bride and groom at weddings. But public violence against *hijras* is brutal and they face extreme discrimination. Taken from their birth families at a young age, they join a *hijra* family which usually consists of a guru and five or more *chelas* (students) who assume the surname of the guru. What little income they make goes to the guru, who manages the household. Because so little else is available to them, 95% of transgenders in Mumbai work in the sex industry and about half are HIV positive. If they undergo a sex change, which is rare, anesthesia is rarely an option, and then they spend ten days alone in a room without food. If they survive, they are considered one of the chosen and are revered by the transgender community. Larger than any language or culture is the universal need for understanding. Our heart connection means so much to me; she has changed me just by sharing her experience.

---

[16] Mehrabian, A. (2007). *Nonverbal Communication.* Aldine Transaction.

Intuition

The only real valuable thing is intuition. — Albert Einstein

Our intuition comes from a deep well of experience. It often has a mystical, illusive, sometimes magical feel to it, when actually, our intuition is always available in every moment. Sometimes intuition quitely tiptoes into our consciousness and sometimes it comes as a full body slam, jolting us at the core. We integrate information from multiple sources, assimilating our gut reactions, receiving a flood of warmth, hearing a song of hope, noticing patterns, listening to angelic voices or the vibrating of longing. The practice of developing our intuition means rejecting nothing, riding the waves of energy as they flow through us, accepting both the niggle of doubt and the urge to meet the challenges head on.

To expand our intuition, we find that beautiful place within us that trusts our divine experience, where there is no pressure to figure it out, be right, conform, or make others change. Intuition comes as a whisper or a melody that guides us from within, even when the suggestion seems incomplete. Instead of witholding our intuition, we can accept the invitation to explore, to follow the yearning and expand the way we experience the world. By allowing the grace to enter our hearts, we feel comfortable speaking before we have all the answers, before we've found resolution, before we have gift wrapped our words and tied a ribbon around the package. If we wait for inner harmony to express ourselves, we miss out on the now and others are deprived of our experience. The exploration itself becomes the gift as we move from darkness toward the light.

If our intuition is under-developed, an image comes to us and immediately we doubt its value— we seek confirmation or a stronger sense of knowing, so we filter or withold our thoughts and feelings, living in a state of fear or suppression. Our uncertainty grows when we second guess our inner experience which we know to be true. We have the opportunity to become a living testament to God by accepting and sharing the full experience of our heart. For example, I received the image of a badger calling out to be heard and a hummingbird longing to be seen. On the surface, the two animals seemed to be at odds, but I wanted them to coexist. Ignoring one or the other would leave me divided. To offer compassionate presence to all the energy as it flows through me creates the space for me to be with all that's on the inside and on the outside.

By honoring ourselves just as we are, without name calling or labeling, we learn what it means to love and accept fully. It becomes safe to use fear as a gateway to love. Anger becomes the stairway to the temple. As we accept both the inner terrorist and the divinity within, we embrace the whole gamut of the human experience and it becomes safe to be who we are. We can give shame, disgrace, and humiliation a place to rest and surrender to the fullness of our experience.

Using Silence with Intention

At all times preach the Gospel... and if you must, use words. — Saint Francis

How do we know when to hold silence? When people struggle to articulate their experience, the temptation as the facilitator is to jump in and save them from their distress. In silence they give birth to new ideas. Likewise, when we speak while someone is crying, we interrupt their cathartic process. We aren't doing them any favors by rescuing them. Offering silence gives them the space to wrestle long enough for the words and fresh insights to emerge. Saying just enough is an art form to be cultivated. Kaethe Weingarten, author of *Common Shock* says:

> Many people feel that asking questions from a position of curiosity is pointless since they are already good at understanding what people mean. They think that understanding another quickly makes a positive contribution. I think not. People often develop what they mean as they realize that their listener has no preconceptions or pre-understanding. It may seem contradictory to the task at hand, but in order to listen well to another, we have to be able to extend our *"not understanding"* as long as possible so that the people we are listening to can themselves develop an understanding of their meaning.

As I've become more and more comfortable facilitating, I use fewer and fewer words because I trust the process and the wisdom of the group. As a reminder, WAIT is an acronym for "Why Am I Talking?" Finding time for silence is a precious gift. We have all the time there is. We create spaciousness by slowing down, listening, pausing, so that something new emerges. When someone is silent in response to another's expression or question, we may have hit on something they want to consider. If we resist the impulse to jump in, they get to swim in the experience. We don't have to supply the answer or let them off the hook with a question or another response. If we have a strong intuition, we can check out what is happening by simply asking. Aliveness does not mean fast-paced. We can expand our range both by keeping the dialog moving and by holding space for silence.

In Robert Greenleaf's essay *The Servant as Leader*, he talks about saying *just enough*:

> As a leader, one must have facility in tempting the hearer into that leap of imagination that connects the verbal concept to the hearer's own experience. The limitation on language, to the communicator, is that the hearer must make that leap of imagination. One of the arts of communicating is to say just enough to facilitate that leap. Many attempts to communicate are nullified by saying too much.[17]

---

[17] Greenleaf, R. (1982). The Servant as Leader http://www.greenleaf.org

54

Greenleaf also says, "A commentator once observed: 'If you have something important to communicate, if you can possibly manage it—put your hand over your mouth and point.' Someday we will learn what a great handicap language is."[18]

However a lot of people feel uncomfortable with silence – what about them? They have good reasons for their discomfort – silence takes us to the chaotic but magical mystery of *not knowing*. Different from the old adage "ignorance is bliss," choosing to face our terrifying edges means we learn to trust that not knowing is filled with profound possibilities. These same options are available anytime our demons have us by the throat. In the same way that coming face to face with our nightmares is both terrifying and provocative, we can lean into the contraction of silence, knowing we're about to give birth to something new. When I coach one person in a group setting, sometimes I offer suggestions to the rest of the group about ways to deal with any discomfort with silence:

- Notice what your discomfort wants for you.
- If you can't bear the silence, journal about it.
- Listen for transformation.
- Envision silence as a separate entity: pay attention to the intention and energy of the silence.

Particularly if silence is accompanied by tears, someone in the group often intervenes with a wisecrack to relieve the discomfort or with words of support designed to wipe away the tears. Usually tears are a sign of self-connection, so if we can get the group to honor the silence, we collectively hold the space for transformation.

Laura Turner, a natural health practitioner and author, talks about the benefits of silence:

> Silence. Why does it work? From a physics or scientific standpoint, the electrons within the molecules of the body actually speed up when the body slows down. It seems difficult to understand at first, but the key is its reciprocal process. When the body slows down, the energy surrounding the body and passing through the body speeds up, literally directing the body: instructing it.
>
> Grace, balance, and growth are often natural extensions of this process. When you take some time to be still and offer your goal up to the universe, you can then become aware of the divine direction. To do this, first become aware of your surroundings. Then aim to find time each day to move toward your worthwhile goal. Keep it close to your heart. Know that there are many distractions in life, but if you take time to rest and stop for one moment, it could be the moment you will receive your greatest inspiration. [19]

---

[18] Greenleaf, R. (1982). The Servant as Leader http://www.greenleaf.org

[19] Turner, L. Personal alchemy: Three steps to positive transformation. Retrieved from http://www.enhancedhealing.com/articles/view.php?article=746 2010.

By slowing down, we generate spaciousness and stillness which gives everyone the room to breathe and birth new awareness or new ideas. If silence is golden, then knowing when *not* to intervene may be the most important skill in the tool box. Unnecessary interventions waste time and turn the attention to ourselves. Infrequent interventions give more weight to our words when we actually do intervene.

Interventions

As we look at ways to intervene in a group's process, we listen deeply so that we're fully connected to our intuition, the needs of the group, and the opportunities for transformation. We'll start by looking at how we balance two types of interventions: process and task. Process interventions focus on *how* the group works together, while task interventions focus on *what* the group is working toward. Many groups have a low tolerance for process work because they value accomplishment and tangible results. If we're disconnected from the important tasks, the group can descend into processing things to death. When the facilitator joins the group in the bottomless process pit, the despair is palpable because everyone has disconnected from the purpose of the group. The mission is lost. The flip side can also derail groups if we only work on the task and neglect relationships. If we value the end result and focus only on what the group accomplishes, without developing heart connection, the capacity of the group diminishes.

We need to balance both process and task, while we simultaneously hold space for the group to feel some discomfort when they perceive the focus is too much on one or the other. Working with the discomfort of the process can lead to breakthroughs. Before a process intervention, we can ask ourselves, "How will my comment about the process foster awareness and help people change?" Staying on task has its own rewards. When making a task intervention, we can ask ourselves, "Is this what the group really needs right now or am I trying to rescue them from wrestling with their discomfort?" If we have a preference for task or process, we can unconsciously push our own point of view on the group. Ideally we want to tap the resources of the group to help them support both process and task. The following chart shows some examples of task interventions and process interventions.

Task Interventions	Examples
Brainstorming	"Let's brainstorm some options..."
Building on	"What I like about what you're saying is...and I think we can..."
Integrating	"Raoul's idea about ... fits well with Jaimala's concept of ..."
Reflecting before disagreeing	"I hear your concern for... What we need now is..."
Initiating or proposing	"Based on what you've all said, I propose that we..."
Observing the process	"I notice that the group is discussing the pros and cons of Lupita's proposal before hearing all the options."
Orienting the group to task	"We still have two decisions to make. Are you all willing to stay until 5:00 to wrap this up?"
Recording content	"I want to make sure we have all the ideas down. Will you get Malika's point about the cost/benefit analysis up on the chart?"
Testing for consensus	"I sense that we're in agreement on... Does anyone object?

Process Interventions	Examples
Asking for reflection	"To ensure understanding, will you let Roberto know the key points you heard from him before you respond with your opinion?"
Gate-keeping	"Let's pause a moment. Lisa, are you reiterating what you've already said, or is there something new you want us to know?"
Harmonizing	"I see a lot of similarities between the two strategies. What's similar is . . . and what's different is..."
Holding multiple needs	"Some people want to slow things down for understanding; and some want progress. I propose a strategy to honor each person's interests..."
Including	"Jorge, what is your perspective?"
Inviting personal responsibility	"It sounds like you don't like the direction the group has taken. What would you like to do about it?"
Reinforcing	"Mikael, I appreciate your vulnerability, because now others feel more comfortable sharing their trepidation."
Requesting Connection	"I see you moving away from the group. Will you describe how Tony's words impacted you?

We need to balance our interventions between process and task based on the organizational, regional, or ethnic culture. Some cultures value relationships above all else, while others care only about completing tasks. And in most cultures people care about both process and task, so we need a range of responses that accommodate both sets of values. Instead of forcing people into changing their behavior, when we create opportunities for reflection and awareness, new behaviors are often the by-product.

Caution about interventions that can disempower the group:

- Taking Over: benevolently give advice instead of honoring the group's self-direction.
- Over-Teaching: fascinate and seduce the group by offering teachings and steering people away from self-directed awareness or action.
- Comparing: evaluate the group's effectiveness based on other groups by telling them they're better communicators, visionaries, or leaders.
- Avoiding: Skirt difficult issues and direct the group to talk about less controversial issues.
- Prescribing: Tell people what to do instead of empowering them to create their own solutions.
- Manipulating: Influence the group to do something that's in the facilitator's best interest instead of the group's interest.
- Eliciting: work to get the group to come to a conclusion already made by the facilitator.
- Hiding Covert Process: proceed without sharing what the facilitator is doing or why.
- Lagging: Offer an intervention based on something said long ago.
- Cutting Off: Stop the process as the work intensifies out of fear or protection.
- Thwarting Integration: allowing insufficient time for insights to emerge or awareness to be integrated.

Focusing the Group

When the group has wandered or is spinning its wheels, the gut feel is instinctual and often shared by most of the group at roughly the same time. Someone feels misunderstood and keeps repeating himself. Another calls for a decision, any decision, just to get the group moving again. Ironically, this is not the time to offer a perfectly logical solution because people are on divergent paths. Simply acknowledging the group's confusion and the struggle to integrate can visibly relieve the tension.

Too often we accelerate toward the solution before people have had a chance to express their divergent points of view. Some groups foreclose way too soon, but others take years to make simple decisions and people eventually give in to a less than optimal solution, give up, disengage or leave because they're overwhelmed, impatient, depleted or bored. Amidst all the chaos, how do we know whether the group is exploring a fork in the road, going down a dead end or avoiding the bumpy road ahead?

As soon as we recognize that we've taken a detour, which is usually accompanied by an energetic slump, how do we honor what's just been expressed and circle around to the original objective? Keeping the group focused reduces frustration and keeps the process on track. A few examples of statements to re-focus the group:

- Now we have several issues on the table. I'd like to complete the ones we've started and then come back to this if it's still important. Does that work for you Kally?
- Before we go there, can we check in with Lisa to see if she's finished with her request?
- Just as we start to see the light at the end of the tunnel, it's not uncommon to get derailed. We've piled additional requests on to the train. Can we come to agreement on the original intention, and then explore these additional options?

In developmental facilitation, we can support participants in developing their skills in re-focusing the group by asking:

- Can you tie that into the big picture of where we're headed?
- Who can point the group toward the end goal?
- To help the group stay focused, will each of you write down what you'd say next if you were facilitating?

Facilitators rarely give participants the chance to explore shared facilitation, thinking that they have to "own" the facilitation to be of value. When we give part of our role away, we take some of the pressure off ourselves and empower the group to facilitate themselves, which ultimately increases our value.

Tracking

The facilitation skill that I'd like more competence in is tracking, or paying attention to and holding all that has happened, all that is incomplete, and simultaneously keeping the group on track. It's not enough to remember names and who said what. Asking permission to put something in a "parking lot" is one of those tried and true methods that feels a bit generic but is effective for helping people to feel heard and trust that their issue will be covered eventually. It helps to remember the exact words of each speaker, but we can allow the felt experience of each speaker to imprint our heart. When we make a practice of connecting everything said to at least one thing that's already been said or seen, then we can easily draw the thread through every idea expressed. Another way to track what's going is to visualize a linking system – noticing which issues are connected to others.

When I've mentioned that I'm often in awe of the way some facilitators track so many details, they've given me a few tips that seem obvious, but can be really helpful:

- Write down names and capture the actual words.
- As soon as you start to feel overwhelmed, name all the things you're tracking, and ask if you've missed anything.

- Request that volunteers track some parts and remind you later.
- If someone brings in a new topic on top of an unresolved issue, ask if he would be willing to bring it up later.
- Request that the group finish up something that isn't complete before you go on to a new issue.

Are you tracking right now that we're nearing the end of a chapter on facilitation skills, exploring ways to keep the group focused and looking at ways to hone our tracking skills? Sometimes I get so caught up in the present moment, that I forget to hold the bigger picture and the direction we've set. The image of putting all the needs or issues on the table, nesting one concern within another, or drawing a mind map with dotted lines of how issues and desires are connected helps me to track the direction. In this moment I want to illustrate the power of tracking with an example:

> Yannai Kashtan comes from a family of facilitators. When he was five years old, in an open-space style retreat, in a confident voice that the whole room could hear, he offered a session on alternative rocket fuels that about 20 people attended. The moment that stands out in my memory was when two people started to talk at once. He said to one of them as he pointed to the other, "Can you remember what you want to say and say it after she is finished?" [20]

He simply slowed things down by alerting the group to who was going to speak next. When facilitators queue people up, by saying to the people with hands up, "Let's hear from Meg, then Gina then Henri," people visibly relax and can put their attention on the speaker. Another way to enhance inclusion and keep the energy circulating is to call on people from different sections of the room.

Taking the Lead

Some facilitators take the lead by brute force while others are reluctant to take the lead at all. Somewhere in between these two extremes we find ways to both use our expertise and empower the group. The challenge is to provide direction and empower people at the same time. I cringe when I see the way some facilitators take the lead or refuse to take the lead. I'm especially discouraged when I hear people attempt to steer the group through domination by saying:
- I'm in charge, so I'm going to stop the discussion now.
- Okay, we've wasted enough time on this. Now we're going to…
- You've taken us off topic.

On the other end of the spectrum, I feel even more unsettled when a facilitator has no opinion, offers no guidance, or displays no confidence by asking:
- Is it okay if we move onto something else?

---

[20] BayNVC Leadership program 2004.

- We're not getting anywhere, are we?
- What do you think we should do now?

Every group wants a sense of direction. The people who take the lead are sometimes held with reverence and sometimes with disdain, so I enter this exploration with full appreciation of the difficulties of leading a group. To move the group forward, we need to master the art of knowing *when* to take the lead and *how* to take the lead. To complicate matters, facilitators have no inherent authority to lead unless the group consents. If we lose the consent of the group, we need to know how to re-establish our role.

At times, everyone in the group wants to be led, but they also want their autonomy, so how do we create the delicate balance of leading people to their own autonomous decisions? Usually a collaborative approach empowers the group, while a dictatorial approach disempowers people. But not always. When a group is rudderless and people are fed up with the process, they just want a benevolent dictator to tell the group what to do. As much as we want to trust the group to discover their own direction, we also need to know when to step in and offer guidance. Although a facilitator is more of "a guide on the side than a sage on the stage," there are times when the group will breathe a collective sigh of relief if the facilitator offers clear direction. When we take the pulse of the group, we can provide direction that creates willing followers.

So how do we take charge without creating a power-over dynamic? If the facilitator doesn't believe in the proposed direction, neither will anyone else. But on the flip side, if we go too far by insisting that our proposal is the best choice, rebellion is right around the corner. When a facilitator timidly or reluctantly takes the lead, people don't follow, and they feel confused about the real role of the facilitator. Lack of leadership manifests as allowing the group to flounder for too long, continuously changing the agenda, or offering multiple options without moving forward. Some actions we can take to help bring people back into the fold:

- Synthesize where the group has been and offer a new direction forward that takes into account all the needs that have been expressed.
- Slow things down with a moment of silence.
- If people are highly charged, give them a chance to be heard in pairs, get clarity about their request, then come back to the large group.
- Offer a range of options for finishing up anything incomplete.
- Use a pre-arranged signal to request silence, such as ringing a chime or raising a hand.

There's an art form of getting the attention of the entire group. We start to talk, then stop until we have silence. Continuing to talk while some are still having side conversations gives people the sense that we don't care if people are listening, when in actuality, we don't know how to ask for the group's attention and get it. You can also give participants a signal that they have one minute to wrap up so that they're prepared to transition. Walking toward people who are still talking helps them shift their attention toward the whole.

Even after laying the ground work, most groups have a life of their own. I've seen a slew of ways to bring a group to silence, many of them straight from the grade school classroom:

- Raise your hand if you can hear my voice (repeat this until you have silence).
- Massage your lips.
- It's time for…

Whether you're working with children or adults, to ensure collaboration and reduce the sense of domination, avoid using practices that evoke shame or convey impatience.

- I'm waiting.
- It's my turn to talk.
- We're running out of time.

Since these words *can* be delivered with compassion, ultimately, our voice and body language are crucial instruments for taking charge of the room. Even if people aren't complete, if we have their trust and they know we're acting on behalf of the whole group, they'll stop talking just because our body language tells them that we have something valuable to offer. If we start talking and then notice we don't have the attention of the whole room, and we simply stop talking and wait, the group tends to shift their focus toward the facilitator.

Synthesizing

> We each carry some portion of Truth. To reconcile, we must listen for, discern, and acknowledge the partial Truth in everyone. — G. K. Hoffman

The art of synthesizing relies on the skills of deep listening, riding the waves of energy, knowing when to intervene and focusing the group. How do we pull it all together when one person in the group wants to go faster and one wants to go slower? One person wants to focus on building relationships and another wants to focus on getting the work done? One person wants to express their individuality, another wants group collaboration? As facilitators, how do we synthesize all the needs that are expressed in the group?

Imagine that the group is one person – one person with many voices. If we treat the group the same way we treat an individual, we'll notice that there are multiple needs at one time. It's not that one voice is right and another is wrong; they're all contributing value. When an individual is torn between one strategy and another, we help them uncover their needs by hearing each voice of their inner committee and help them build a sense that all their needs matter. It may seem impossible at first, but these needs can coexist symbiotically. When we name the needs that are on the table so that every voice feels understood, then the individual or the group is ready for movement. By synthesizing all that we've heard, we help the group create strategies to meet multiple needs at one time or choose to attend to one need first and then another.

In *Newsweek* magazine September 9, 1985, Issadore Barmash concludes, "After a lifetime of work, I've never seen a meeting end happily." One counter-example is that for over 300 years, the Quakers have held transformational business meetings that build true consensus. Called "meetings for worship for business," they rely on participants' sharing from religious assumptions: Every person has "God" within and he or she is "seeking God's truth."

The process works because everyone is secure in these assumptions. Consensus is sought, not so much as a polling of the collected wisdom of those present, but rather as a collective discernment of God's will. When I asked Campbell Plowden, a gifted facilitator in the Quaker tradition, about the art of synthesizing, he responded:

> The ability to synthesize is the goal of the clerk of a Quaker meeting. The role of the clerk is to present the question that the group is being asked to consider. Since Quakers believe that there is "that of God in every person," and that Quakers meet to discern the truth, all present are invited to share their views since the truth may be best expressed by any person. Once views are expressed, participants are encouraged (either directly or indirectly) to let go of their particular view and be open to hearing the truth embodied in the views of others.

> The clerk calls on people to contribute to the discussion if needed and at a certain point to state his view of the group's view. This may be a view expressed by one person, a combination of views, or some new expression that the clerk discerned emerging from the discussion. The expression of the "sense of the meeting" unifies the point or points that resonate with divergent views. Sometimes the clerk calls for further reflection before a single "sense of the meeting" can be adequately expressed. Once the clerk puts out his or her view, the group is again invited to comment on how well this expression hits or misses the mark. Sometimes a meeting works through this process to a point where participants can unify around a particular expression; sometimes it doesn't. It is common practice for serious matters to be "held over" for a future meeting to consider the issue again.

> Sometimes people equate the process of reaching consensus with the Quaker quest for a sense of the meeting. While the process is sometimes similar in format, the underlying principle, and thus the result, is often very different. Consensus is a secular process that often means reaching a compromise solution that seems like the best accommodation of everyone's views. Seeking the "sense of the meeting" is an acknowledgement that the group has tapped into the vein of truth coming from God that resonates with the people gathered for this purpose. Working with this process requires faith and patience because it is often slower, but once reached, it is easier to implement and has a greater chance of succeeding because people have full buy-in once they have agreed to a particular course of action. It took our meeting several years to come to terms with a more

progressive policy about gay unions under our care, but once it was reached, our community has become very strong in its embracing of all of our members.

So for me, the ability to synthesize doesn't begin with learning a set of skills; it begins with a philosophical and spiritual belief in the values and process. That said, the skills that seem important are being a good listener to people's words, a keen observer of people's tone and body language, and a willingness to hold one's own opinions at a distance so that they don't get in the way of an honest and objective reflection back to the group of the clerk's sense of the meeting. I am working to deepen my spiritual side that would open me up to accomplish these tasks, but this is a path that many people pursue in their own ways. The rest is just practice.[21]

Synthesizing combines many skills like listening deeply, tracking, sensing direction, and holding each person's needs and values. When do we summarize? When we sense that the group could use some support in seeing how each idea connects to the whole, some of the phrases that we can use to synthesize:

- Here's what I've heard so far…
- The common threads seem to be…
- Here's how I see the connection with all that's been said…
- My sense of the ideas expressed is…
- I'd like to summarize the collective wisdom of the group …

Ultimately we want the group to facilitate their own process, so after modeling, we can support group members in developing their own synthesis skills. I particularly like to ask the group to synthesize when I start to lose track of what's been said. As my memory becomes less reliable, I find myself taking in the essence of each expression, taking notes about content, or relying on the group to help me hold all that's been expressed. I might ask:

- Who would like to summarize the desires that have been expressed?
- Who can link all these ideas in one synopsis?
- What needs are on the table?
- What do all these suggestions have as a common thread?
- From all that's been said, can one of you provide a condensed version of what's important to the group?

I'm often pleasantly surprised that some of the quiet people who listen deeply have a great capacity for synthesizing – they just need to be invited to capture it all for the group.

In this chapter we've taken in the panoramic view of many facilitation skills. After scanning the horizon, we stopped at a few vista points to take in the beauty of listening, riding the waves of

---

[21] Campbell Plowden personal interview 2/28/08.

energy, interventions, focusing the group and synthesizing. We've set the tone, taken in the overview, and now we're ready to expand awareness by going within.

Exercises

Reflections:

1. Referring to the facilitation skills that start on page 39:
   - Which three facilitation skills have you already developed?
   - Which three facilitation skills would you like to deepen?
2. If you knew you could receive reliable information from your intuition right now, what is the question you'd most like to ask? Formulate a question daily for a week, honoring the answers that come from the wellspring within.
3. Practice the skill of synthesizing by capturing the essence of each section of this chapter. Write one or two sentences for each of the six sections.

Small Group Discussions:

1. Get into small groups of four. Practice reading the energy in your group. Articulate the energetic messages people are conveying right now.
2. Dialogue about the power and discomfort of silence. As you share your insights, practice expanding your comfort zone with silence.
3. Remember a time when you were involved in a group that lost its focus. Brainstorm ten things you could say to help the group return to the original purpose of the meeting.

Activities:

1. In small groups of four, each person chooses one task intervention and one process intervention from page 57 and then the group collectively brainstorms examples that you can use in the moment.
2. To expand your capacity to listen for transformation, listen to a partner for 30 minutes, reflecting the essence of their desire once a minute.

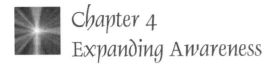

Chapter 4
Expanding Awareness

What we are is far superior to what we want to become. —Tara Singh

Exploring what motivates people is the life force of the Facilitating with Heart process. When we peel the onion and connect with the many layers of each individual's deepest needs, we enhance the heart connection, which serves as the opening to transformation. Since the body displays feelings, and feelings are stimulated by needs, the direct route to awareness is to observe the body, intuit the feelings, and uncover the needs. In this chapter we'll start with a look at the LEAD model, a way of embracing people and helping them expand their awareness. Then we'll delve into how awareness of the body leads us to awareness of emotions, which are intimately connected with our deepest needs.

With so much happening at both the individual and the group level, where do we put our attention? In any group we're fed so much information at once – how do we decide what really matters in the moment? In cultures where the intellect is sacrosanct, we often miss the subtle cues provided by the body. We don't even notice when people crumple or expand if all we care about is what they think. But the body reveals the complex changes of the internal experience. By expanding our awareness of the body, we come to recognize every change in the body represents an internal shift. Even slight changes in how we're feeling show up in our faces, our posture, our voice. The emotions are the gold mine within. When we go down that tunnel, we'll find that emotions lead us to the nuggets of what people need, what they want, or what they dream about. Since everything people do or say is an attempt to meet a need, expanding our awareness of what people need *now* is invaluable.

LEAD Model

The purpose of the LEAD model is to lead people inward to their innate wisdom. The process deepens awareness by fostering self-connection, insight, and learning. The four aspects—love, empathy, awareness, and desire—provide a simple, powerful process for connecting with the core of our being. We can use the LEAD model to help people get more clarity about their heart's calling. By heart's calling, I'm not talking about a quest that takes you across continents and changes the world; I'm talking about what your heart is calling for right now in this moment.

All four components help inform the changes people wish to see in themselves and in the world. Instead of pressuring groups into action, this spacious approach of witnessing the process leads people into new awareness and profound self-connection. The practice of loving people unconditionally right where they are and empathizing with their deepest longing provides the most fertile ground for transformation. Ironic, huh? Loving people *just the way they are* is the very opening they need to create a shift. Figure 4.1 shows the four aspects of the LEAD model that invite people to open.

Figure 4.1 Lead Model

Love	Connecting with life-giving forces Choosing unconditional positive regard Expanding trust, openness, vulnerability Enjoying radiance, magnificence, individuality Embracing open-heartedness and curiosity
Empathy	Listening with full compassion Reflecting range of feelings and emotions Honoring needs and values Engaging heart, soul, and spirit Embracing polarities and desire for wholeness
Awareness	Reading body language, voice, affect, and non-verbal Riding the waves of energy — being with the flow Resonating with aliveness, life force, and power Tapping intuition, inner sources of wisdom Staying with what is present, here and now
Desire	Exploring natural openings and what is emerging Paying attention to insights, movement, new direction Creating from expansion, resourcefulness and prosperity Actualizing growth, development, and evolution Making requests and decisions from the heart

Here's an example of an individual coaching session using the LEAD model:

Love

Nicole: I'm not sure what I want to work on right now. Everything is going really well...

Coach: Wow, let's savor where you are right now.

Nicole: The best part is my team – they are amazing. They would do anything for me!

Coach: You sound so pleased about the team you have pulled together and the support you get from them.

Nicole: Well, they're encouraging me to take the CIO position, but I like it right where I am.

Coach: Sounds like you have clarity about what you want.

Nicole: Yes, I'm so energized by my team because they care. Why would I give that up?

Coach: You have a commitment to caring – the deep honoring of yourself and the way you've created caring work relationships.

Nicole: Most of the time, that's true, but there's one thing that bothers me. My boss dumps on my team. You know what she said yesterday? When Brendan offered a suggestion during a brainstorming session, she said, "That would be suicidal. If you don't have any better ideas than that, keep your mouth shut."

Empathy

Coach: I hear your outrage! Sounds like you really value respect and caring...

Nicole: Yeah... I don't get any work done because I'm always trying to protect them from her. I don't know if it's intentional or if she doesn't even know that she's destroying the morale.

Coach: So you're baffled and have a need for an environment where people can thrive?

Nicole: No... Actually, right now I'm angry with myself that I didn't have the courage to stand up right then and say, "All ideas are valued here." But I have to be careful not to piss her off.

Coach: It's frustrating to want to support your team, *and* also want a good relationship with your boss, yes?

Nicole: Yeah, we're being bought out by another bank, in the middle of the biggest economic meltdown in history. Unemployment is 10% in this city. I'm a little scared to confront her because she could fire me.

Awareness

Coach: I'm hearing a shift in your awareness. You want to create a more supportive work environment *and* keep your job.

Nicole: Actually, that's not it. I've survived a merger before – I'm not going to lose my job. I'm just using that as an excuse. I don't know how to talk to her about the vicious things she says.

Coach: (silence)

Nicole: I mean how do I tell my boss she has absolutely no people skills?

Coach: Sounds like you really want to work on yourself – to find the courage and tact to support her professional development...

Nicole: My hands are shaking.

Coach: If your hands could speak, what would they say?

Nicole: I'm scared. It's hopeless. My only hope is that she'll get ousted in the merger. You know what else she said?...

Desire

Coach: Hold on. I get it that you're frustrated by many things she says, but if I heard you accurately, your fear is connected to your desire to change *your* side of the relationship – to confront her in a caring, supportive way.

Nicole: Mmm. You know, what I really want to be able to do is to treat her like anyone with a problem, even though she's my boss.

Coach: What part of yourself do you need to tap so that you can have this conversation with her?

Nicole: Oh! I just got something. You know how I started this conversation saying my team would do anything for me? The reason I value that so much is that I want to be that way. More giving. I want to throw myself into my relationship with her. Instead of writing her off, if I could treat her the way my team treats me and I think she'd respond.

Coach: I hear your passion.

Nicole: When I look at it this way, I'm pretty confident that I can change the relationship by changing my behavior.

Coach: So what does changing yourself look like?

Nicole: I think I'll start with a conversation with her tomorrow and I'm going to focus on my desire to *give* to her. Now I have a sense of peace and hopefulness about this.

In this example of the LEAD model of coaching, the coach starts out empathizing and then moves into supporting Nicole in doing her own work. The coach gently guides her using the four phases as a loose structure to support her inner resourcefulness. Continual reflection invariably helps the tension dissolve into inner knowing. The LEAD model isn't usually linear; it's more typically a spiral that takes people into the depths of their souls.

The process of using the LEAD model in a group is more complex because there are a lot more people to love simultaneously. If we practice using the process with one person, then we can more easily do it with a group.

Wisdom of the Body

The body is an opening, a way to union even though we may perceive it to be an enclosure, a little fortress with some awareness inside. The body is a passageway, an entry into a cathedral. It is the door to spaciousness. When we become aware of the body in this way, we begin to experience life differently and might even feel the presence of invisible forces, wisdom bearers that can give strength, compassion and understanding to us in our everyday affairs. — Stephen Schwartz[22]

We can use our body as a fortress or as a cathedral – protecting ourselves from the possibility of pain or danger, or opening ourselves to the beauty and wisdom in every cell. We're taught to trivialize our bodily sensations because we're afraid of suffering, eros, or narcissism. So many of us close ourselves to our deepest yearnings, our desire for love and freedom, our hunger for expressing from the deepest parts of ourselves.

Our desire for change often starts in our bodies. Bodily sensations act as a portal to emotions and awareness. To accept the sacred nature of our bodily experience, to attune to our body's vibrations gives us a felt sense of our internal wisdom that nourishes us. If we don't know how we're feeling, we can scan our bodies for sensations and experience the waves of energy, which invariably have a message that helps us discover our emotions. We may notice trembling, tensing, aching, or tingling in different parts of our bodies.

The world of thought and evaluation is a tiny fraction of the knowledge that is available to us. Paying attention to the body gives us a deeper sense of our innate wisdom. Without evaluating or manipulating our experience, or pressuring ourselves to change, we can come to new discoveries just by witnessing and opening to what is. If we attend to the subtlest cues and stay very quiet, we come into contact with our energy. Whether we're experiencing pure bliss, mild restlessness, or utter outrage, riding the waves of energy and honoring the emerging forces within is an act of self-respect. Working with the list of Bodily Sensations found in the resource section on page 381 is a starting place for deepening our awareness of the urges that permeate our body which opens the door to becoming more aware of our feelings.

You can tap the unique gifts and learning style of each person, recognizing that some have cultivated body awareness and others have a practice of armoring, ignoring, or conquering the body. In an effort to feel in control, some people hide their fear or strong feelings, ignoring their body, and spend most of their time using their heads to analyze or rationalize. To create structures that engage people in the process of their own lives, ask questions that bring attention to their bodies:

- What is your body trying to tell you?
- What part of your body holds your fear?

---

[22] Schwartz, S. (1993). *Angelic dialogues*. Riverrun Press.

72

- Where do you physically feel the joy coming from?
- How does your anger live in your body? What shape and color is it?
- What posture would help you shift from confusion to clarity?

Increased self-awareness of the body brings natural shifts in behavior and lifestyle as people consciously choose to live their lives fully connected to their desires. Instead of asking questions, we can further empower people by offering observations and creating space for them to make their own meaning:

- You leaned back and closed your eyes when you said the words, "I want a partner."
- When you described your plan, you sat up taller and moved your head forward.
- One side of your mouth smiled when you said you value risk-taking.
- You stuttered when you said "sincerity."
- Your right leg is in constant motion and you are speaking louder now.

Fluency in the subtleties of body language helps us connect more intimately and heightens our intuition, compassion, and insights. When we explore our own body, emotion, and needs as we interact with others, we can increase our awareness of how our energy shifts. Our body serves as a barometer of what is happening in ourselves and in others. Inner awareness allows us to become more present, which helps us create the space for people to explore their body's energy and the hidden parts of themselves. We can become aware of the shifts in another person by becoming deeply aware of the changes in our own body.

Authenticity stems from congruent emotions, language, body, thoughts, and actions. We're perceived as authentic when our inner world matches our outer expression. This inner and outer alignment helps us choose actions that bring momentum into our lives. Exploring new kinesthetic experiences helps us develop sensory awareness which contributes to greater choice. When the body is alert and free of muscular tension, the whole person is more open to listening, learning, and taking action. How do we free the body from old habits and unlock our intuition and creativity? Imagine what possibilities open up when we feel energized and connected to our intuition, creativity, and choice!

How do we support people in honoring the intuitive wisdom emanating from their bodies? We learn to read the nuances of body language which serve as a portal to understanding emotions and needs. The heart gives us access to far more intelligence than the brain alone,[23] and other body parts also contribute to our understanding. An internal, felt sense of love, care, compassion, and appreciation produce measurable, qualitative change in the heart's electrical field. In every moment, our subconscious speaks to us through our body, using a language that is as rich and informative as the language of our native tongue. Our body communicates continuously, informing our intuition, also known as sixth sense or somatic intelligence.

---

[23] Childre, D. L. & Martin, H. (2000). *The heartmath solution. The Institute of Heartmath's revolutionary program for engaging the power of the heart's intelligence*. HarperOne.

Dian Killian, the founder and Director of Brooklyn Nonviolent Communication, describes the value of physical empathy:

> Once I was really distraught about a past experience. The pain was very intense, and I started bumping my head with my hand, which was metaphorically like banging my head against the wall. This was an effort to release the pain, to express it, although this was instinctual and not a conscious choice.
>
> I experienced a profound level of cynicism, blame and judgment in my relationship with my father growing up. During the moment when this pain was coming up, a very powerful and transformative simple action was when Miki [the facilitator] reached over and took my hand in a gentle but assertive way so that I was no longer hitting myself. I was hitting my head out of frustration, not causing physical pain, but it was a powerful symbolic gesture. She wasn't willing to be witness to me being violent to myself, which was a healing moment for me.
>
> That's why deep empathy can be so powerful because the visceral re-lived experience now is different from the initial experience. It's so powerful to have a juxtaposed, radically different experience from the original experience. I felt a huge release of energy, which is a hallmark of shifting – there's a sense of joy and freedom.
>
> At the New York Intensive, someone volunteered in a large healing circle, and I said, "Okay... let's stay with your body. I'm not even curious what's going on in your mind right now. Let's just empathize with your body." She scanned her body and said, "I notice tension in my back. This is familiar to me. I often have problems with my back."
>
> I said, "Let's listen to what your back has to say. And we just gave empathy to her back, almost like talking to her back as if it were a person. "What's going on for you? What sensations do you notice? Is there anything your back wants to say at this moment?" After we did this for 10 to 15 minutes, she was amazed that the pain was completely gone. Before closing the session, I asked if her back had anything else to "say." At that point she checked in with herself and there was nothing else her back wanted to "express" at that moment. When her back had been "heard," the pain ended. Mind-body connection is key to transformation because our physical experience is connected to our emotional experience. When we're stressed, angry, or sad, our bodies clench up or close up; I'm sure we all have experienced this—tight jaws, pain in our necks or backs, headaches etc. Empathy, and especially empathy for the body, which releases emotions we're holding, can lead to physical release too.

Emotional freedom technique (EFT) involves tapping on acupuncture points in the body while connecting with thoughts that you have in the moment. People have had profound healing and shift around chronic physical conditions. In addition to tapping on acupuncture points, you say, "I absolutely and completely love and accept myself." No matter what is up for you, you can release it doing EFT, which I consider a physical form of self-empathy and a way of further integrating empathy in the body.[24]

When we respect the body's intelligence, we raise our consciousness and can make meaning from our immediate experience without the filters that accompany verbal expression. Language is more abstract—one step removed from our actual experience—because we edit, label, and summarize our somatic-emotional experience.

Instead of relying so heavily on conversation, we can facilitate growth by using the body as a rich resource to process emotions, instincts, and intuition. Listening to the full wisdom of the body reveals emotional patterns, energy shifts, and opportunities for transformation. Including the body helps people understand their needs at the cellular level and fully embody their conscious choices. Since learning happens in the body, a daily embodiment practice helps people shift an old habit to a new one.

Sources of Information about the Body:
Information about the body comes from multiple sources:
- Breath—the pace, rhythm, volume, and location
- Posture—position and balance
- Flexibility—spinal flexibility and movement
- Blood—pace, rhythm, volume, and pressure
- Eyes—movement patterns

The pace and rhythm of the industrialized world exacts a toll on our physical well-being and creativity. People may feel overwhelmed, physically or emotionally, by the speed of movement, thought, speech, and breathing. To enter a rejuvenating flow state, we need a balanced physical structure, heart connection, and a calm, compassionate awareness of ourselves and others.

Although the rational mind, emotions, body, and soul, function together as one integral unit, each component can contribute to awareness. When we live and breathe as one harmonious unit, we experience alignment. Living from the inside out fosters authenticity.

---

[24] Dian Killian personal interview with Lynda Cowan Smith 3/13/08. http://bnvc.org

Feelings and Emotions

There can be no transformation of darkness into light and of apathy into movement without emotion. — Carl Jung

Once we notice physical sensations, we understand how the body connects us to our emotions and feelings. At home and at work, we're taught to consider feelings a sign of weakness or neurosis. As a result, some people are proud to keep their emotions under control, and even claim, "I'm not feeling anything," but the only time we aren't feeling something is when we are dead. Even if all we can feel is numb, frozen, or still, we always feel something. Connecting to our feelings, just sitting with how we feel, without trying to change it, leads to a radically different awareness of our internal state. As we give ourselves the space to understand our feelings, they shift, which leads to deeper understanding and awareness.

When people are uncomfortable with their emotions, it helps to start getting acquainted with socially-acceptable feelings: happy, uncomfortable, irritated, disappointed, and concerned. Once safety has been established, we can add feeling words that are less acceptable: afraid, angry, anxious, distressed, hurt, uncertain, and insecure. Cultural taboos place many feelings off limits and consequently, many people have no idea what they are feeling. So it helps to have a list handy to reconnect with what is really going on inside. In Figure 4.2 shows some examples of feelings.

Figure 4.2

Feelings	
Affectionate	Angry
Excited	Disinterested
Hopeful	Tired
Joyful	Embarrassed
Peaceful	Sad
Refreshed	Yearning
Grateful	Tense
Confused	Vulnerable
Scared	Agitated

In the resource section on page 396 you'll find a list of feelings for easy reference. *Experiencing* our feelings is an expansive process while *thinking* about naming our feelings contracts our energy. Allowing ourselves the full spaciousness of our feelings expands and shifts our energy. However, if we start thinking about our feelings, we can simply notice our feelings about the thoughts, and return to the flow of expanding energy. Staying with whatever is alive, without forcing ourselves down a particular path, helps us experience our feelings, and our lives, more fully. Once we have familiarity with our feelings, the list can actually interfere with experiencing our feelings fully as we step out of our experience to label it.

I appreciate how Marice Elias, coauthor of *Emotionally Intelligent Parenting*, describes emotions:

> Emotions are human beings' warning systems for what is really going on around them. Emotions are our most reliable indicators of how things are going in our lives. They are also like an internal gyroscope; emotions help keep us on the right track by making sure that we are led by more than cognition.

When we label our emotions as good, bad, or terrible, we color our experience which changes it. Too often we put a positive valence on some feelings such as happiness or excitement, assign a negative valence to feelings like fear, sadness, or hurt, and avoid completely anything that implies shame, guilt, depression, or anger. If we remove the ball and chain and sit patiently with our internal reactions, we find at the core of every emotion a pure wave of energy that is free of moralistic judgment. When we see how our body holds our emotions, we develop self-compassion and find that no emotion is more positive than another. Opening to the delicate mystery of emotions generates a sweet acceptance both within and outside ourselves.

Even when we have a thorough understanding of the beauty of each emotion, we can find ourselves struggling with a particular emotion. For instance, a low threshold for anger or timidity could actually awaken us to the profound messages these emotions have for our souls. Instead of closing ourselves off from our anger or admonishing our timidity or hiding our true feelings behind a hand of cards, we can accept these emotions as gifts. When we embrace all our emotions, they no longer have a vice-like grip on us and we can experience life more fully and freely. The six core emotions that are evident across cultures are happiness, sadness, surprise, disgust, anger, and fear, according to researchers Ekman and Friesen.[25] When we allow ourselves full expression of our emotions, without trying to nail them down with particular words, we find our unique energetic expression that comes through in the way we hold ourselves, move, and speak.

We often use the terms emotions and feelings interchangeably, but I appreciate the special usage ascribed to the word "feeling" by John Heron, a prolific writer about human inquiry:

---

[25] Ekman, P. & Friesen, W. V. (1975). *Unmasking the face. A guide to recognizing emotions from facial clues.* Englewood Cliffs, New Jersey: Prentice-Hall.

By the term 'emotion' I mean the intense, localized affect that arises from the fulfillment or the frustration of individual needs and interests. This is the domain of joy, love, surprise, satisfaction, zest, fear, grief, anger, and so on. Thus defined, emotion is an index of motivational states.

By 'feeling' I refer, with special usage, to the capacity of the psyche to participate in wider unities of being, to become at one with the differential content of a whole field of experience, to indwell what is present through attunement and resonance, and to know its own distinctness while unified with the differentiated other. This is the domain of empathy, indwelling, participation, presence, resonance, and such like.[26]

So how do we build awareness of emotions and feelings? Many people are alienated or cut off from their emotional state and struggle to identify their internal reactions. If asked what they're feeling, they identify their thoughts. Starting a sentence with these words invariably means the speaker is sharing *thoughts,* not *feelings*:

- I feel that…
- I feel you…
- I feel as if…
- I feel like…
- I feel I…

Following the word "feel" immediately with an emotion (internal state) helps people connect. To relieve alienation, you can awaken capacity for experiencing feelings and support emotional awareness by asking:

- What's your internal reaction?
- How do you feel when you think she's betrayed you?
- What do your bodily sensations tell you?
- Do you feel sad, angry, or hurt?
- Which feelings on the list or cards resonate with you?

Ultimately we can support awareness if we have access to a full range of emotions ourselves. If we have a low threshold for a certain emotion, say rage, it may be because we have an innate value of tenderness and vulnerability that we'll do anything to protect, even if it means numbing parts of our own bodies. On the flip side, sometimes we become fixated with one emotion, where we are fascinated by or stuck in an emotional state. If we repeatedly tell stories that justify obsession with one emotion, such as, "I can't stop feeling this way…He always makes me feel…I've been depressed for days…" we need to do the internal work of deepening our awareness. Building our inner reserves helps us become more available to the groups we facilitate.

---

[26] Heron. J. (1992). *Feeling and personhood.* London, Sage Publications. p 16.

Occasionally people are unable or unwilling to experience the shift to a full range of emotions, but the question is why? Instead of enabling people to wallow day after day, year after year in the same pool of emotion, we can help them get relief from fixation by shining the light on that intense emotion, noticing micro-movement toward other emotions and uncovering what needs are met by fixing attention on one emotion.

Feelings Mixed with Judgments

Sometimes people confuse their feelings with their judgments. For example, if I say I *feel* abandoned, betrayed, or manipulated, that's actually what I *think* other people are doing to me. My actual internal feeling may be hurt, sad, or angry. We can separate our emotions from our judgments by asking, "How do I feel internally when I *think* someone has abandoned me?"

Self-judgments or self-evaluations such as: bad, crappy, great, good, excellent, inadequate, worthless, terrible, horrible, positive, and negative actually describe what we *think* about our experience, not what we *feel*. Translating our evaluations into feelings builds facilitator awareness. If we struggle to identify our emotions, we can shift our focus toward our bodily sensations. Say I have a judgment that I'm being manipulated and can't seem to touch on how I feel about that. I can ask, "Where does that live in my body?" or "Where do I feel this sense of manipulation?" or "When I think I'm being misunderstood, does my whole body experience it? Does it live primarily in my chest or belly?" These questions help us shift from thinking the judgment to the felt sense of our experience, which gives the feelings a place to call home. Rather than seeing a feeling as something dangerous happening outside of ourselves or that someone else is causing our emotions, we develop self-intimacy by honoring our internal emotions. We can differentiate between feelings and thoughts by extracting our judgments.

The beauty of feelings that are mixed with judgments is that they help us viscerally connect with deeper needs and desires. Too often people ignore how they feel or want to change how they feel *without recognizing the needs* connected to their feelings. As facilitators, we can help people explore what is under the surface and learn about the source of their emotions.

Because of our need for harmony, it's not uncommon to want to de-escalate emotions. When I attended a workshop with Roger Schwarz, author of *The Skilled Facilitator*, he explained that when people get emotional, most beginner facilitators would say, "Let's take a break." Skilled facilitators will know they've hit pay dirt because it means people are talking about what's *really* important.[27] Substantive movement comes from self-awareness and direct experience more than thinking your way out of feelings or challenges.

Connecting with Intense Emotions

I grew up in a household where only three feelings were acceptable: happy, thrilled, or excited, so I tend to freeze when I'm confronted with intense anger. When people express their emotions at high levels of intensity, they're letting us know they're touching on something vital to their well-

---

[27] Personal interview with Roger Schwarz 3/15/00.

79

being. Instead of reacting like deer in the headlights or with judgment, we can acknowledge intense emotions as an opportunity and train ourselves to listen for the unmet needs, even when we're triggered. Just as a lightning rod channels the currents of electricity so it is not destructive, our body has the capacity to digest emotions that create distress. The first key to working with the realm of emotions is to breathe and remind ourselves that we do not have to save the person, supply the answer, or change their experience. To help them step into *all* of it, we can ask them about what they notice, breathe deeply, and pay attention to the energy. Anger is just another word for frustrated love. With practice, we can see intense emotions as passion and notice that:

- Anger as an intimate experience
- Hopelessness as the desire to trust again
- Terror as an opportunity to reclaim what really matters
- Fear as a signpost of where to move next
- Rage as a mobilizer for social action

Although emotions are universal, how we express ourselves varies widely from culture to culture. Since emotions play a valuable part in the change process, I encourage people to fully express their emotions in whatever way is comfortable for them. When emotions are expressed with intensity, that's usually a sign of a deeply met or unmet need. When emotional expression is suppressed, that's another sign of an unmet need. Awareness of emotions is the precursor to change. Especially when people are triggered by anger, we need to create emotional and physical safety to create open, honest dialogue.

When we're working with people from emotionally-reserved cultures, where people rarely express emotions openly or understate their emotions, we can help them feel safe if we meet them where they are. For instance in many corporate cultures, the full extent of acceptable emotions is: annoyed, irritated, uncomfortable, disappointed, concerned, happy, or excited. Other emotions are considered "overly emotional." In an emotionally-reserved culture, if someone claims he's mildly irritated, but we interpret his body language as fuming or outraged, we have a choice about helping him express himself more fully, or meeting him right where he is, in the space of emotional safety. To help people ease into emotional awareness, we can offer metaphors such as, "The line has been drawn in the sand," or "you've hit a brick wall," or "you're pushing the rock up the mountain," before articulating the emotions – "maybe you're feeling tense, hopeless, or exhausted."

In contrast, people from emotionally-expressive cultures feel very comfortable with their feelings and overtly express their emotions. People from outside perceive them as dramatic when they describe how much they're suffering from the air conditioning, or how ecstatic they are that everyone is on time. They're more likely to express at top volume, greater range of pitch, faster speed, with more animated gestures, dramatic facial expressions, and use profanity because they're much more comfortable with emotions. If we understand their strong statements with less emotional language, they won't stand for it. They welcome an emotional outburst because it gives them the freedom to express fully and trust that the real issues will be explored. The same emotional outburst in emotionally-reserved cultures leaves people feeling threatened or frozen. They find ways to change the focus or create reasons for leaving the room. Usually we have both reserved and expressive people in the room. Instead of insisting on drawing out the emotions of reserved people or defusing the emotional content of expressive people, we can help everyone feel more comfortable with their unique personal expression – that's empathy! By being present to emotions, regardless of how they are expressed, we can foster connection, understanding, and change.

Needs Awareness

One does not come to a so-called state of wholeness by trying to bypass neediness. We must go through it, dignify it and find what we really need on this earth, what we are longing for. – Stephen Schwartz

A basic premise of *Facilitating with Heart* is that every feeling is connected to our desire to meet our basic human needs. Understanding our needs and other's needs takes us right to the core. Some of the most common human needs are for connection, autonomy, peace, meaning, play and contribution. Compassion comes from heart connection and awareness of feelings and needs. Whether we're practicing self-compassion or compassion for another, awareness of needs is a portal to the soul. Though expression varies, needs are universal, existing across cultures.

Although each of them defines and frames needs differently, the Chilean economist Manfred MaxNeef includes nine categories in his needs matrix[28]; Marshall Rosenberg offers seven basic categories of universal needs in his book *Nonviolent Communication*[29]; Tony Robbins works with six umbrella needs[30]; and Abraham Maslow's hierarchy of needs features five levels. John Abbe says that when we inquire deeply into our own and each others' needs, we find behind all of them a single source. He doesn't like to put a label on it because that can invite argument about what it *really* is, but others refer to the primary need as God, love, spirit, consciousness, Universe wholeness, or oneness.[31] Whether I work with individuals or groups, I encourage them to create their own needs list, using language that works for them. Some prefer to distill and drill down to their core needs, while others want a wide variety of needs to choose from.

Seeking the positive intent of every thought, every word, and every action leads to understanding and connection. Giving ourselves the gift of empathic self-connection in turn allows us to connect more deeply with others. But how do we practice self-connection and radical self-care? Empathic connection starts with awareness of our feelings and needs. The distinction between needs and strategies (which are ways to get our needs met) gives us the freedom to understand ourselves deeply without being attached to getting our needs met in a particular way or by a particular person. Refer to the resource section on page 403 for a list of needs.

---

[28] MaxNeef, M. Retrieved from http://www.rainforestinfo.org.au/background/maxneef.htm
[29] Rosenberg, M. Retrieved from http://cnvc.org/en/what-nvc/needs-list/needs-inventory
[30] Robbins, A. Retrieved from http://tonyrobbins.com
[31] John Abbe personal interview 4/29/08. http://ourpla.net/

Of all the places to put our attention, understanding the nuances of human needs awakens profound opportunity for deepening awareness. In every moment, if we hold our awareness on a person's needs (which can shift as often as every 20 seconds) we stay present to their unfolding. People often want a quick fix – for their relationships, finances, career, health, or any dilemma they face. But if we point them toward their underlying needs *before* they move into action, their action plan becomes more real and satisfying. Giving people a list of needs can help them deepen their consciousness, but eventually they too can name their needs in every moment without using a list.

The Empathy Labyrinth, developed by comedian and puppeteer, Marc Weiner[32], is a deceptively simple tool for slowing down and enhancing needs awareness. Using the four steps of Nonviolent Communication, the heart of this deeply transformational process involves trying on a wide variety of needs, identifying the top five, sitting with the energy of each need, and imagining how it would feel for each need to be deeply met. I personally find the Empathy Labyrinth a magical process for enhancing self-intimacy, using it to resolve inner and outer conflict. I've even used it to

The Empathy Labyrinth

explore a newly-hatched opportunity. I've seen many, many users experience a sense of wonder and awe, and they're often blown away whether they use the large, outdoor version or the table top version. A minister from Virginia described his experience with the Empathy Labyrinth as a direct line to God. This doesn't surprise me because I find that slowing down the process allows people to go deeper and deeper. For example, one user of the empathy labyrinth iniquired within, "Why do I need connection? Because I want to contribute." And "Why do I want to contribute? Because I want love."

When we stop and sit with each need and follow the energy, we come to our deepest needs, which are often about love or connecting with God. Everyone has a different way of expressing this, and usually words are inadequate. Steeping ourselves in what we're longing for has a profound impact. When people walk through the Empathy Labyrinth in pairs, they experience the connectivity of our shared human experience.

Another empowering process that uses movement to deepen awareness was created by Gina Lawrie and Bridget Belgrave from the UK. They developed the Dance Floors so that people can experience Nonviolent Communication in action.[33] Of the seven dances, three are for role-playing a dialogue with another and four are inner dance processes designed for personal transformation. Working with the Dance Floors with the support of a trainer or a partner helps us integrate multiple learning styles: auditory, kinesthetic, and visual.

---

[32] Marc Weiner personal interview 4/15/08. The empathy labyrinth. http://theempathylabyrinth.com
[33] Lawrie, G. & Belgrave, B. NVC Dance Floors. http://www.NVCDanceFloors.com

When it comes to building awareness, I consider the practice of identifying needs the single most valuable source for opening the space for transformation. To facilitate growth, we can cultivate needs awareness both in ourselves and others. Everything we do is our best effort to meet our needs, even "unacceptable" behaviors like interrupting, stealing someone's boyfriend, screaming at the television, or using taking up arms. We don't do these things because we're evil; we do them because we need to be heard, need comfort, need to belong to a group, or need to protect our way of life. Illegal, dysfunctional, anti-social or violent behaviors rarely get us what we *actually* want, but awareness of why we act the way we do can help us choose different behaviors altogether. Every one of us is driven by our personal needs. Fortunately for humankind, one of the primary needs of all people is to contribute to others.

Building on the person-centered approach of noted psychologist Carl Rogers, Marshall Rosenberg has enhanced the practice of empathy, going beyond presence by reflecting feelings and needs. Listening for what people care deeply about involves listening between the lines. When we attune to needs, it helps us connect with primary motivations, the first step in connecting with the heart. When we see and hear a person's deepest needs, and they sense our understanding, the doors open to new opportunities for personal transformation. We pay particular attention to anything we hear twice, which is usually a sign that people want to be heard.

As transformational facilitators, our role is to help people develop a close relationship with their inner worlds. If the person is in the habit of believing the inner critic, translating judgments into unmet needs or desires can lead to self-acceptance and growth. For example, if someone says, "I'm not smart enough or dedicated enough to realize my vision," we can ask, "So you are longing to trust your intelligence and to connect with your inner drive?" Another empowering question might be, "What need are you meeting by holding that belief?"

Differentiating Between Needs and Strategies

Sometimes we mistake needs for strategies, which are actually the ways we attempt to meet our needs. For instance, "I need to go to bed," is probably a strategy for rest, and "I need to go back to school," is probably about a need for learning, while "I need a raise," might be about needing respect, recognition, or sustainability. Suppose you are asked if you have a need to dominate…will your heart open? If you tense or feel apprehensive, that's a clue that you're looking at a strategy rather than a universal need. One way to determine whether a need is universal is to notice that our hearts open when we recognize that we all have the same human needs. Sometimes we're so attached to the strategy that we can't see any other way to get our needs met. But if we look a little deeper, we'll find the needs underneath the strategy, which cracks open the door to multiple ways to meet the needs.

When someone in the executive team says, "I need a new production manager," a novice facilitator might ask action questions, and soon the team has a plan to write the job description, talk to a headhunter, interview prospects, and hire a new production manager. By contrast, an experienced facilitator slows down to clarify the unmet needs before moving into action.

Suppose the conclusion that they need a new production manager stems from outrage that the shipment was rejected, and she needs trust. Peeling back the onion, she becomes aware of the need for reliability, clear communication, and stronger relationships with customers.

Once she is aware that her deepest need is stronger relationships, many strategies will emerge to meet that need. She may decide to develop her relationships with peers, take her team out to lunch, or expand her network by joining a nonprofit board of directors of a social justice organization. She may still decide to hire a new production manager, but the important thing is that she's doing so with an awareness that her primary need is to build stronger relationships.

Human needs are universal and are very different from strategies that include actions, people, and timeframes. Finding a production manager is a strategy to fulfill a need, so awareness of the core need helps us choose strategies that are more likely to sustain us. What follows are a few examples of strategies that can be translated into needs:

Examples of Strategies: Possible Needs
> I need to have sole custody of my daughter: safety, predictability, or to be loved.
> I need you to come home earlier: inner peace, loving connection, or trust.
> We need to go to the store: sustenance, companionship, or organization.
> You need to mow the lawn: beauty or support.
> We need to stop the war: safety or peace.
> We need to escalate the war on terrorism: safety or peace.

Notice that we can choose very different strategies for meeting similar needs—to stop a war or to escalate a war on terrorism are both strategies for safety and peace. Our success in getting our needs met and others' needs met is directly related to how clearly we recognize what they are. Differentiating between strategies and needs helps us open to multiple life-serving choices. Awareness of other's needs helps us to understand them at a deeper level and co-create strategies that meet the needs of more people.

Often this awareness begins with an exchange about needs that are *not* met because they come to our attention through our powerful feelings. Choosing effective strategies requires awareness of needs that are met by the status quo, so that we don't sacrifice needs that are currently being met in seeking to address those that are not. For instance, I travel a lot for work which means I get to do work I love—spreading empowering coaching and facilitation skills— but I also need connection time and to protect the environment by spending time with family and reducing my carbon footprint, so it's a tradeoff. A solution that meets both needs is to facilitate more groups by teleconference, which allows me to create the kinds of relationships I want in other countries as well as at home.

Pseudo Needs

Let's explore the range of feelings and needs connected to two very common strategies: money and control. When we think of **money** as a strategy, we can explore some of the possible feelings and needs. Maybe I feel worried and see money as a strategy for comfort or sustainabilty. Or maybe my relationship with money gives me great happieness because t allows me to meet my need for contribution and generosity. When I think of **control** as a strategy, some of the feelings and needs might be that I'm nervous because I need competence. Or I feel anxious because I need to belong. Thinking about control as a strategy I might feel excited because I need order and reliability.

Other words or phrases that are commonly thought of as needs but are actually strategies are listed below, followed by some of the needs the strategy may be attempting to meet:

Revenge: Shared understanding about suffering or healing from woundedness

Justice: Trust that my needs, our needs, or their needs matter

Fairness: Collaboration or a sense of caring about all needs

Compliance or Obedience: Order, predictability, or shared understanding

Control or Power Over: Predictability or sustainability, trust

Influence: To contribute or make a difference in our well being

To be Understood: Shared reality, connection, trust

Attention: To matter, connect, feel closeness

Status: To belong, to matter, or feel personal power

Whatever language people use, we have a choice of judging their words or empathizing with their inner experience.

Empathy

The word, "empathy" didn't come into common usage until the 1880s when the German psychologist Theodore Lipps coined the word, *einfühlung*, which means feeling into. True empathy is feeling with, or participating in communion with another. Empathy is comprised primarily of two components: heart connection and awareness of another's feelings and needs. Because most people don't get nearly enough empathy, this practice opens people to inner awareness like no other. The practice of reflecting feelings and needs involves guessing what a person feels and needs right now. Although there's nothing rote about empathy, the simple model, "Are you feeling x because you need y," can deepen awareness and connection.

A powerful way to build understanding is to reflect the emotions and needs of the group. For example, Kendra says, "I can't wait to get out of here!" A few examples of empathic reflection are:

- So you're feeling disappointed because you need teamwork?
- Are you excited because you want options?
- Maybe you're outraged because you crave respect?

By offering several rounds of empathy, people often shift to a new awareness of their needs. They may say, "No, that's not it at all. I just want to go for a drive on my Harley." So we try again, "Oh, so you want some freedom?" After several empathy guesses, eventually they'll say, "That's exactly it," or simply, "yes." People are so unaccustomed to paying attention to their needs that sometimes they are stunned and need a moment to take in the beauty of their need. Silent empathy can be even more meaningful than spoken empathy so we can listen for the silence before the shift. We might hear the transformation as an energetic thunk, an "aah" or a slowing down. By staying present with shifting emotions, we can hear the energetic changes that propel the person into awareness, and eventually into action.

Even if our guess is off the mark, our attempt to feel into another's experience is a force that builds heart connection. Sometimes we find it difficult to empathize when we need empathy ourselves. That's why a regular practice of self-empathy contributes to our ability to empathize with others.

By putting the oxygen mask on ourselves first, we can serve the larger world. Connecting with our inner experience is a prerequisite to connecting with another, connecting with groups, and connecting with spirit. The practice of self-empathy sounds a bit like taking a bubble bath, or it can seem more like an archaeological dig. Listening to our own heartbeat and tuning into our feelings and needs is a rigorous practice that continually deepens self-awareness. We can use it for mundane moments, understanding deep bliss or dealing with deeply distressing events. When we're triggered or steeped in judgment, our needs can remain elusive despite a serious search. Many practices build awareness, but the practice of self-empathy coupled with the awareness of emergence is the most direct route to opening our hearts. For a Practice in Awareness of Emergence, by Jim and Jori Manske, refer to the resource section on page 389.

Transforming Distress into Light

Another practice that deepens awareness harnesses the energy of distress in life-serving ways. In the spirit of gratitude and exploration, I've adapted this process by merging the work of many practitioners: Marshall Rosenberg, Susan Skye, Robert Gonzales, and Meganwind Eoyang.[34] I

1. Describe the stimulus of my distress.
   a. What triggers me?
   b. Describe the moment I first felt pain.
   c. What am I seeing, hearing, smelling, etc?
2. Express my reaction.
   a. What am I telling myself?
   b. What is my judgment of others or myself?
   c. Voice all the judgments until I have clarity about my core belief or deepest judgment.
3. Scan my body.
   a. Sense my body from the inside and experience the wisdom of the body.
   b. What physical sensations do I notice?
   c. Notice any desires in the body – for attention, expression, or movement.
4. Experience my feelings.
   a. What am I feeling?
   b. Give voice to my internal emotions.
   c. Honor my deepest feelings without pushing them away.

---

[34] I recommend workshops with any of these teachers. See http://cnvc.org; http://baynvc.org; or http://www.nvctraininginstitute.com

5. Experience my needs fully.
    a. What do I want?
    b. Underneath that, what am I longing for?
    c. Mine all the needs, digging deeper until I identify the bedrock need.
6. Mourn the unmet need.
    a. Feel the pain of the unmet need.
    b. What if this need were *never* met?
    c. Grieve the loss.
7. Sense the radiance of the need.
    a. Stay with the distress and add the image of a bright light, sustaining this attention until clarity emerges.
    b. Feel the alive energy associated with the exquisite need.
    c. Reaching for life, imagine the deep satisfaction of this need fully met.
8. Take action.
    a. What requests can I make of myself that will help me remember the radiant need?
    b. What requests can I make of myself to help me honor or meet these needs?
    c. What requests can I make of others that would be most likely to get my needs met?

I used this 8-step practice with a woman named Raquel because she was deeply frustrated with her relationship with one of her staff. She started out complaining about Tarik who stayed out all night drinking and didn't show up at work on the day of an event they'd been planning all year. With a little encouragement, Raquel shared her judgments. She thought he was unreliable, inconsiderate, uncaring, and disrespectful. Her body slumped and she felt drained and hurt. Going a little deeper, she noticed her deep disappointment was about her need for caring and her desire to establish mutually-supportive relationships. Her voice was wracked with grief as she thought about the possibility that she'd never have the kind of caring relationships she craved. As she stayed with her distress, and added the image of a bright light, she began to dream again, and could feel internal certainty that the respectful relationships she longed for were possible. She held that sense of peacefulness as she imagined the need fully met, when she requested a meeting with Tarik about redesigning their working relationship.[35]

The transformation of internal distress into light is the psychological alchemy of turning base metal into gold. Holding the light of awareness intently on an internal emotional state alters the frequency of the energy and completely transforms the initial emotion. As we mourn, we touch the sadness of the unmet need, but if we stay with it, we touch the energy of the beauty of the need as it lives in us. Connection to the heart activates healing and transformation. Grace Harlow Klien, a life-long facilitator, gives a haunting account of her own personal journal of the pain and beauty of being with such mourning. This inner practice can also be brought into dialogue so that we stop blaming others for our unmet needs. Instead of wallowing in scarcity or despair, we can connect with aliveness and our core authenticity. Even when our needs remain unmet, the practice of putting our attention on our needs is nurturing and energizing.

---

[35] Although this is a true story, I've changed the names by request.

Exercises

Reflections:

1. Scan your body and notice any sensations – what stands out?
2. What feelings are connected to your bodily sensations? Just stay with the feeling and notice what happens when you put your loving attention on your feelings.
3. What needs of yours are deeply satisfied right now?
4. What needs of yours would you like to meet more fully?
5. Without taking any action, just notice your needs throughout the day.

Discussion:

1. In a group, explore what you are feeling right now. Peeling the onion, how do you feel about that feeling?
2. Remember the last time you really wanted control or money. Discuss what's going on underneath by connecting with your feelings and needs. Brainstorm additional strategies for meeting your feelings and needs.

Activities:

1. Empathy Practice:
    *   Have a 20-minute conversation with a buddy who talks about something that's important to him. Every minute or so, reflect what he is feeling or needing. Are you feeling x because you need y?
    *   Afterward, remember three things you were thinking about during the session. Connect each of your thoughts to your own needs. What needs were important to you in that moment?
    *   Think about three things you would like to say to your buddy in the future. What needs would you meet if you said those things? What needs would be met if you don't say them?
2. Use the LEAD model in a coaching conversation and put your attention on what is emerging. Notice any shifts in you and in the person you're coaching.
3. Name ten things you'd like to accomplish during your life time. Identify all the needs you'll meet by each accomplishment. With each need, ask yourself: if that need is met, then what will I need? Notice any themes about your needs and share with a partner.
4. Distress often has a dark, shadowy, disturbing image associated with it. Ask a partner to put his full attention on his distress for a minute or more; then add the image of a bright light and sustain this attention until clarity emerges and the emotion is transformed.
5. Identify any internal distress, and walk through the 8-step Transforming Distress into Light process on page 86 first using it alone and then with a partner. Discuss what you learned.

Chapter 5
Finding Direction and Taking Action

Give to us clear vision that we may know where to stand and what to stand for - because unless we stand for something, we shall fall for anything. - Peter Marshall

One of the most unbearable things to witness is a group that goes around and around, eventually sinking into an abyss where all the energy is drained. The light fades from their eyes as people talk on and on, saying similar things over and over, repeating themselves, reiterating, and then restating, while the facilitator is little more than a spectator. People are thinking, "Can somebody save us from this meaningless drivel?" or wondering, "How can I get out of here without anyone noticing?"

As facilitators, ultimately we want to trust the group to find their own compass, but we also need to know when to step in and help the group move into action. Facilitation is more than a chance for expanding awareness; the purpose is to help the group gain sufficient clarity to explore options, choose their direction, and implement changes that revitalize people. Sometimes the process of using the LEAD model to deepen inner awareness feels complete, but true learning is more than new awareness; real change happens when we translate new awareness into action.

While the LEAD model heightens awareness, the GROW model lends itself to finding direction and taking action. When goals are built on awareness of values, the path forward is more compelling and as a result people implement their plans wholeheartedly. Many groups are task oriented and value efficiency. In order to feel engaged they need solid evidence that the group is making progress. To make good use of the group's time, we first need clarity about what people really want before they spring into action. Accomplishing things that don't really matter serves no one. In this chapter we'll look at ways the facilitator can move the process forward, starting with the structure of the GROW model, and then expanding possibilities, prioritizing action steps, offering challenges, developing leadership and creating support systems for continuous movement and growth.

GROW Model

To facilitate learning, ability to change, or achieve desired results, I use the GROW model as a structure to help both individuals and groups design their future. This focused approach works particularly well in business settings or with groups that are task oriented. According to John Whitmore, GROW stands for:

- GOAL setting for the session, as well as short and long term.

- REALITY checking to explore the current situation.
- OPTIONS and alternative strategies or course of action.
- WHAT is to be done, WHEN, by WHOM, and the WILL to do it.[36]

Figure 5.1 GROW Model Questions

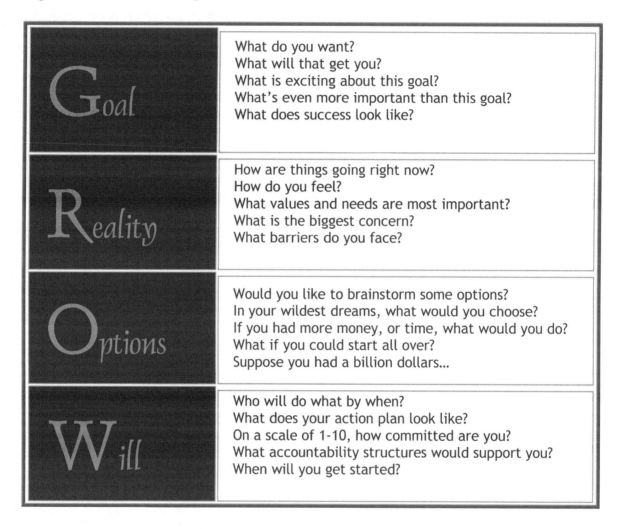

Goal	What do you want? What will that get you? What is exciting about this goal? What's even more important than this goal? What does success look like?
Reality	How are things going right now? How do you feel? What values and needs are most important? What is the biggest concern? What barriers do you face?
Options	Would you like to brainstorm some options? In your wildest dreams, what would you choose? If you had more money, or time, what would you do? What if you could start all over? Suppose you had a billion dollars...
Will	Who will do what by when? What does your action plan look like? On a scale of 1-10, how committed are you? What accountability structures would support you? When will you get started?

Figure 5.1 offers a few examples of the questions asked at each stage. The GROW model is a structure that helps people identify what matters and move forward into action. It may sound counter-intuitive to start with the goal instead of the reality, but opening with what people want provides direction and clarity. Even when people come into the session with a lot of clarity about their goal, when we explore the broader goal, or deepen the awareness of related goals, the group gets more clarity. For example, I used the GROW model with a board of directors who told me the

---

[36] Whitmore, J. (2009). *Coaching for performance.* Nicholas Brealey

executive team was dysfunctional and couldn't resolve their conflicts. As we looked at their goals for the organization, it became clear that they needed leadership development at all levels: the board, executive team, and managers. Their initial goal was to resolve a conflict, but as they went a little deeper, they found they needed a system-wide approach to improve leadership skills.

The purpose of the reality stage is to empathically uncover the emotions and motivation connected to the desired change. With that awareness, the process helps people self-connect, go deeper, and understand the nuances of their motivation. Traditionally the reality stage is used to help people identify weaknesses, barriers, resistance, and budget constraints, but the flip side is even more important. Identifying the group's strengths, including their relevant experience, access to resources, and past successes all support movement toward the desired future. To uncover the *real* situation, we identify the hard facts and also recognize that emotions and values take us directly to the heart of the matter.

In the options stage of the model, we support people to brainstorm strategies to meet their needs. This is the rowdy, outrageous, fun phase where anything goes. Letting the imagination run wild awakens creativity and gives people a range of options to choose from. We get out the magic wand and give people full permission to dream. Sometimes the accountants in the group roll their eyes if I say, "Imagine you have an unlimited budget," but invariably this exploration helps people identify new possibilities, and then they can find much less expensive ways to get what they really want. Flinging the doors wide open taps the group's resourcefulness. Likewise, we can also ask, "So how would you do this if you had no budget and very little time?" to help the group find less costly alternatives.

After generating a wide range of options, we move into the Will phase and help the group create compelling action plans. This is where the rubber meets the road. We find out what people will actually do and when they're going to do it. In this phase, we ask for commitments and build in accountability structures by asking three simple questions: What will you do? When will you do it? How will we track our progress?

If we spend a lot of time in the Goal stage and even more time in the Reality stage, the options stage goes relatively quickly because people are connected to their values and bursting with ideas. Likewise, the Will stage tends to be short because people are fully engaged and have the vision and drive to take ownership of the action plan. The more time spent at the Goal and Reality stage, the easier it is to find the Options and Will. If we see hesitation in the Will stage, where people are reluctant to commit to action steps, that's usually because we haven't spent enough time in the goal or reality stage to identify the vision or what people really care about. If the action plan doesn't materialize, or if the commitment level is below a 7 on a scale of 1 – 10, we can revisit the goal to make it more compelling or replace it with another goal that people can readily commit to implementing. So the GROW model is not always linear – sometimes we circle back to clarify the goals or expand the reality.

To follow is an example of the GROW model in action. I've streamlined the example to highlight the facilitator's role, whereas in actuality, the team members said a lot more and the facilitator intervened much less often.

Goal

Jamel: Okay, we know what we want to work on today – better collaboration between departments.

Facilitator: What's important about collaboration?

Arianne: We have a great team, but there's some sort of underlying competitive spirit with other teams that keeps us from really coming together on projects.

Facilitator: What would "coming together" look like?

Sunita: Breaking down the walls between departments. Appreciating what each group contributes.

Hayden: That really strikes a chord with me. Each department is so territorial, we end up working against each other. Imagine the possibilities if we worked together!

Facilitator: Ah, let's do just that... what *are* the possibilities if you all worked together?

Jamel: We'd support each other instead of trying to outdo each other. We could get through this looming re-org with a lot fewer scars.

Hayden: Coming to work would be a whole lot more fun. All the friction and the fear of change would vanish.

Arianne: If we build bridges between our departments, we could create some synergy.

Facilitator: If you were to integrate support, fun and synergy, what would you envision?

Jamel: We'd challenge each other and learn from our mistakes. We'd work as a team – no superstars. We'd have team spirit across departments.

Sunita: You know what the problem is? The closer we get to the go-live date, the more frazzled they get. We thrive on pressure. But the other groups can't take the heat.

Hayden: Exactly. The only way to build team spirit is to get some traction. Stop wasting time on building relationships. Execute.

Arianne: That's not the problem. Want to know the real issue? With the re-org, some jobs are going to get cut. They're scared.

Hayden: Yeah. That's why they're pointing fingers and blaming each other. Competing for recognition.

Jamel: It's different for our department. Our jobs are safe.
We don't have a clue what it's like for them. But we can't stop the changes. We need to move forward.

Facilitator: Move forward to what? What do you want to get out of *this* session today?

Jamel: A plan for partnering across departments, even though we know we're going to lose some people.

Arianne: We don't want to be callous about losing people. As we go through this transition, I'd like to see how we extend the supportive environment outward to other departments.

Reality

Facilitator: What makes you proud to be part of this team?

Sunita: We're smart.

Arrianne: We like each other. Some of us even hang out together after work.

Hayden: We get things done. Fast.

Jamel: That's what makes us close. But maybe this great "family" thing we have going in our department has actually kept us from connecting with people outside our department.

Facilitator: What's missing?

Sunita: Real connection with other departments, accepting differences of opinions, pooling our resources for the good of the whole.

Jamel: If we truly want to collaborate with the other departments, we need to build relationships, and spread the team spirit into the rest of the organization.

Options

Facilitator: I'm hearing a strong desire for partnering with other departments, and building an organization-wide esprit de corps encourages respect and collaboration. What are some ways to move in that direction?

Hayden: Cross-functional training. Shadowing.

Sunita: Yeah, they need to understand more about the architecture of this project so they aren't asking us to do the impossible.

Arrianne: More importantly, we need to understand *their* parameters.

Sunita: We need to take the time to get to know each other. I want to celebrate our shared milestones – quick, easy fun ways to remind us we are all on the same team, working toward the same goals. Celebrating our success together.

Facilitator: Going beyond what's possible, what would take you beyond your wildest dreams?

Hayden: Jamel: Work isn't in my wildest dreams... How about a summit in the Carribean?

Jamel: I'm not sure exactly how this would work, but I'm thinking about a department-to-department mentoring program. Something that would really expand the expertise and tear down the walls we've build around ourselves.

Arianne: We could trade departments for a day. Create some healthy chaos.

Will

Sunita: Let's look at what we're actually going to *do*.

Jamel: I'll invite people from other departments to sit in on our next meeting – to begin working together and sharing ideas.

Arianne: I would really like to take the lead on setting up a inter-departmental meeting to get rid of the silos collectively.

Hayden: Where the purpose would be to create more unity. I can create the agenda.

Facilitator: So who will do what by when?

Jamel: I'll put together notes from today's meeting and arrange the time and space for our next meeting by Friday.

Arianne: I'll check on the availability of the conference room for our fun gathering. I'd like to get this on the calendar going forward - the 2nd or 3rd Friday of each month. I'll email you the date and time by Thursday. Would each of you email me your ideas for our first gathering, and let me know how you'd like to help? Could you do that by Tuesday next week?

Hayden: Anyone willing to facilitate our next meeting, using the GROW model?

Sunita: I will. I and am excited about the opportunities we can create together – not just us, but the whole organization.

Evaluating the Process

Facilitator: This sounds like a good stopping place. I appreciate your desire to collaborate and your commitment to moving forward with a plan. Let's generate some feedback on the process, specifically how the GROW model is working for you.

Sunita: The model gives our conversation structure and keeps us focused.

Arianne: My favorite part is the Options phase. I felt most engaged when we were brainstorming ideas. I think we could spend more time exploring all the possibilities.

Hayden: I'm concerned our goals aren't measurable. We need to be more rigorous about the actual goals and determine how we will know if we've reached them. We could identify smaller objectives on our way to the one big goal.

Jamel: For me, I like the way the GROW model allows each of us the opportunity to co-facilitate. It's easier to step into the facilitator role knowing we have shared guidelines.

Facilitator: Sunita, you're facilitating the next meeting, so will you track these two suggestions: make sure the goals are measurable and spend more time on options?

Sunita: I'll remember that and I expect everyone to track these suggestions with me!

One of the things I especially appreciate about the GROW model is its simplicity. Anyone can use it without a lot of training or practice. Hanging the model on the wall during a meeting gives people a sense of the flow and the entire group becomes facilitative very quickly. The GROW model has a reputation for being fast but not very deep, which is exactly what some groups want. However we can change the depth by lingering in the stages, especially the reality stage whereby we deepen awareness and enrich potential options before moving into action.

Possibilities

When I ask people about their goals, they often start by telling me what they don't want: I'm tired of the cut-throat atmosphere at work; we're running out of money; I'm not in love anymore. Or they talk about other people: my boss doesn't appreciate me; my son doesn't want to go to college;

the project manager doesn't do his share of the work. Out of habit, people spend most of their time thinking about what they don't want. Where we put our attention grows, so if we can get people to focus on what they *do* want instead of what they *don't* want, we're half-way around the field. In many cultures we're taught that wanting anything at all is selfish. This mindset can be a difficult hurdle, especially for people taught that their role is to serve others. Learning to think in terms of what we want is the first step in going after it. Once we have clarity about what we want to manifest, we can implant the intention and spend some time imagining the visual picture of the desired outcome.

When we are in the sacred relationship of assisting human beings in becoming more aware, the opportunities for transformation flourish. By drawing into consciousness deeply-held dreams and longing, we magnify the potential of the group. The very act of opening minds and hearts to possibilities frees the imagination and initiates movement. When we recognize the power of intentions, we awaken creativity. Offering plenty of spaciousness brings people to a stillness of mind that becomes a hotbed for imagination, ideas, and inner knowing.

We can help people access their inner wisdom and get the creative juices flowing by encouraging them to consider all the possibilities without censoring themselves. To access their wildest dreams, they can imagine they have a magic wand, a billion dollars, a thousand volunteers, or unlimited wisdom. Ironically, my favorite way to generate new possibilities is to repeatedly finish the sentence, "It would be impossible to…" Exploring impossibilities reveals what is most important.

Sometimes groups are completely overwhelmed with too many possibilities. In every moment they have a choice. One way to move forward is for the group to imagine they're at the banquet table of life. From all the options, they only choose the most soul nurturing food. Instead of trying to jam another thing into an already-packed schedule, we start fresh, with a spirit of abundance and full choice. When the group explores what is most important right now, and simultaneously moves toward a future of greater possibilities, they can make satisfying choices.

Choosing and Prioritizing

> There is one elementary truth, the ignorance of which kills countless ideas and splendid plans; that the moment one definitely commits oneself, then providence moves too. All sorts of things occur to help one that would never otherwise have occurred. A whole stream of events issues from the decision raising in one's favor all manner of unforeseen events, meetings and material assistance which no one could have dreamed would have come their way. —W. H. Murray

As much as we enjoy imagining and envisioning an ideal future, making it all real is even more exciting. Some people enjoy the freedom of choice so much that they swim in the endless sea of possibilities without ever moving forward. For people who love options, autonomy, and a wide range of choices, making a commitment or choosing a focus can feel restrictive, like strangling a part of themselves. Acknowledging their commitment to freedom helps ease them into the realm of awareness that they do commit and they do make choices, even if their choice is to wallow. From there they can open themselves to explore other possible commitments.

Other groups rush into commitment without fully exploring whether the path has heart. So we can help them create a balance between exploring unlimited choices and forward movement. As long as the action plan is based on values and taps the life force within, we can support movement toward fulfillment. If we sense any hesitation about the action plan, we can ask them to stand on a continuum, "How confident are you about the plan on a scale of 1-10?" Anything less than a 7 indicates they haven't chosen a compelling action plan or that serious barriers are in the way. Asking how they can get to a ten can reveal any barriers or point them in a new direction.

Challenges

If you aren't living on the edge, you're taking up too much space. – Alan Zimmerman

One way to challenge people is to make outrageous requests that take them to new levels of awareness or action. We all have moments when we fall asleep at the wheel of life. A bucket of water thrown in the face can be boldly refreshing, as long as we have trust and we've given each other permission to call each other forth. The purpose of challenging people is to wake them up to a more exciting future, challenge them to play a bigger game, or let them know we believe in them.

A challenge is not about what *we* want the group to do, but about encouraging or holding the group members to what *they* want. A few examples of supportive challenges follow. I challenge you to:

- Create a plan to increase cultural competencies within the next week.
- Only say yes to things that move you toward the goal for the next week.
- Build on the previous speaker's ideas when you express your own.
- Break down the walls by meeting with people from other departments daily.
- Expand your decision-making capacity by choosing three decision-making processes, and apply each of them separately to this problem.

Without being attached to our challenges, we give people the option to say yes, no, or make a counter offer. If they don't hesitate to say yes, we probably haven't given them a big enough challenge. Ideally they tweak it and make it their own, moving from the outrageous to a difficult but possible action.

Leadership Development

Although many people hold a common belief that leaders are born, not made, anyone can develop leadership skills. As facilitators, we see every person in the organization as a leader, and part of our role is to develop leadership capacity in any group. We support leaders in connecting with their power—the ability to see what needs to happen, tap resources, and make things happen. As facilitators, we intentionally help people see their strengths and open new opportunities for growth.

Regardless of the hierarchal structure, we support leadership development at all levels so that people can collectively create a better future. We facilitate groups of people to support each other in developing their leadership competencies so that they can play at the top of their game. In the resource section on page 398, you'll find a list of Leadership Competencies that you can adapt for giving feedback on individual leadership.

Behavioral Change

Behavioral change is one of the most challenging and results-oriented niches for coaches and facilitators. We cannot infuse willpower, but we can help people:

- Understand their motives and best interests
- Take responsibility for changing their behavior
- Explore their resistance to change
- Recognize their power to change
- Support them in taking action to change

Marshall Goldsmith has been a pioneer in 360° feedback (from your boss, peers and direct reports) and was named by Forbes as one of five most-respected executive coaches. As a behavioral change coach he uses *feedforward* to help leaders not only change their behavior, but also change *perception* of their behavior. First the leader determines the behaviors that will make the biggest difference in leadership effectiveness and then engages key stakeholders to support behavioral change. The next step is to collect feedback on observable behaviors as a benchmark and create an action plan for changing behavior. Then additional *feedforward* (suggestions on how to improve their leadership in the future) are collected each month as the basis for revising their leadership development plans. These monthly five-minute conversations with seven key stakeholders provide inspiration, evoke creativity, uncover additional areas for improvement, and ensure follow-up.[37]

Resistance to Change

Why do we resist change even when change is for the better? Why is our comfort zone so appealing even when we're miserable? We may feel overwhelmed, fear the unknown, or lack clarity about the benefits of the change. For change to fly, we need to be able to envision a significant improvement in our lives before we're willing to take the risk. Resistance is a force that is trying to

---

[37] Goldsmith, M. Feedforward. Retrieved from http://www.marshallgoldsmith.com/approach/index.asp

tell us something important. My business partner, Virginia Kellogg, has helped me understand the beauty of resistance to change. She says:

> If we feel ourselves "grinding away" trying to push people through their resistance, we can simply stop and *go into the experience of the resistance*. Getting really curious about the resistance rather than trying to get people out of the resistance comes from tuning our listening to that energetic stance of arms out in front, holding something at bay. There is no need to *do* anything about it, no need to direct them out of it, and no need to rescue them from their resistance.

Resistance shows up as "bracing against" something, but if we push back against the resistance, we miss what they are "embracing." People always have the choice to explore their emotional resistance, and when we point people toward choice, they have a sense of control, ownership, and partnership. We can invite people to exaggerate their bracing by choosing a posture or a movement that embodies what they are bracing against. As they hold it, they become fully present and experience resistance in their bodies. We can also ask what they are protecting or embracing. By going into the resistance from either door, they build awareness and often a shift will happen when they get clear about their underlying needs, and new choices.

A spiritual thinker who suggests that the body doesn't need to be transcended or the personality fixed, Stephen Schwartz describes how people open through their feelings:

> In the dialogues, I would just follow someone until the very net of their own conflict caught them. There wasn't any place to take it on a conceptual level, and something would split open. Then, and only then, could I feel that person, could they feel me, could the people in the room suddenly be aware of the real human connection. From this phenomenon I realized that communication can't take place through beliefs — no matter how great the beliefs, no matter how powerful or sublime or spiritual. If you take the lid off the belief, you can see that it was an idea protecting you from something you didn't want to feel, something very raw and vulnerable. [38]

Some people don't shift even after we've tried everything. Occasionally I've seen people get really, really stuck. I've been stuck a few times myself— more than a few times. Empathy is the most powerful experience I know for helping people move, but there are times when they still spiral deeper into the abyss. If clients talk about the same issue week after week, without any sense of progress, I recommend therapy. Usually my referrals are based on the therapist rather than the type of therapy, but some of the types I find especially useful are: Eye Movement Desensitization & Reprocessing (EMDR), feminist therapy to recover self-esteem, family system therapy, group therapy, and relationship therapy.

---

[38] Safransky, S. The prayer of the body: An interview with Stephen R. Schwartz. *The Sun Magazine*. October 1992. Retrieved from http://www.thesunmagazine.org/archives/1233?page=1

Dissatisfied with the effectiveness of therapy in some cases, Frank Farrelly[39] developed provocative therapy, a process that promotes transformation in people who struggle with chronic, recalcitrant behaviors. He plays the devil's advocate, court jester, or mischief-maker by siding with the client's self-judgment, finding laughter in the absurdity, and puncturing old belief systems. Clowning with clients, without losing the sense of the sacred, he offers laughter as clients explore the edges of their limitations. The Latin word "provocare" literally means to "call forth," but he puts safety first. Some of his interventions fly in the face of conventional therapy. He sometimes:

- Stops paying attention or misconstrues their comments
- Jokes or offers outrageous suggestions
- Insists they continue with the behavior even when they want to stop
- Makes the client ludicrously responsible for absolutely everything that has happened
- Laughs at the absurdity of their beliefs

Some of the outrageous language might include:
- What's wrong with that?
- If that happens you'll probably die.
- You must have gotten really bad parenting.
- Either it's your karma or you're in a bad soap opera.
- This has been going on for a decade? Three more decades should be about enough.

Whether they're shocked, shaken, confused, or angry, people often have breakthroughs simply because the facilitator jolts them into discovering their own insights. Behaviors that seem so impossible to change suddenly become so repulsive that people can't change their behavior fast enough. I wouldn't have believed it if I hadn't experienced a breakthrough myself with provocative therapy. Laughing at people is so antithetical to a spiritual, empathic approach – it sounds ridiculous, even cruel. I couldn't imagine actually saying such things. But when I actually tried it with a group, there was something about the laughter that loosened me up so that I could receive their empathic caring in new ways. The jolting insight for me was that inconsequential as it seemed, I wanted to be fully heard about something that happened thirty years ago. Back at home, when Dave and I got into a gridlock where he was trying to get me to tell him how I was feeling and I was revealing nothing, I remembered this insight. So I started talking about the 30-year old incident and Dave said, "You do realize you've told me this before?" I yelled back, "Yes! And I didn't feel heard then, and I don't feel heard now!" Then he silently empathized, with his hand on my back as I cried and talked until I'd said everything. When I got it all out and really felt heard, I remembered the provocative therapy session and I started laughing... David started singing full throttle, "I haven't got time for the pain... I haven't got room for the pain..." which I found very amusing, very cathartic.

I tell this story because I'm a big believer in shaking things up and trying something new if the same old approach isn't working. I also believe like Jerold Bozarth, probably the most prolific

[39] Ferelly, F. Provocative therapy. Retrieved from http://www.provocativetherapy.com/

author on unconditional positive regard, that persons experience empathy in idiosyncratic and emergent modes. Sometimes paradoxes, jokes, random comments, and even sarcasm can stem from or be perceived as empathy[40]. Without these alternative forms of empathy, whereby people maintain their suffering state, a sense of safety can be lost even when safety is prioritized by a facilitator.

Support Systems

Another thing that can break down resistance and get people moving again is creating an ideal support system. Some people have all the support they need, but most of us benefit from a pit crew that gives us regular tune-ups, by reminding us of our direction, keeping us on track, and ensuring that we perform optimally. Why settle for anything less than giving and receiving in ways that are deeply satisfying? We can start by assessing our current level of support, then imagine our ideal support team, and bridge the gap by creating a support network. To flesh out your understanding of how to identify, evaluate, and build support in your life, engage yourself with the following creative process.

On a large piece of paper, use the balance wheel below, or create your own wheel based on your values or most prominent needs. Start by evaluating your level of satisfaction in each area on a scale of 1-10, with 10 being very satisfying. Write the names of people who support you in each wedge of the wheel. Imagine your ideal support team, and add names of people whom you'd enjoy having on your support system. Write the names of people you'd like to ask for support in each area of your life. When thinking about the support you want to *receive*, also think about the types of support that you want to *give,* since support is a two-way street.

Figure 5.2 Support System

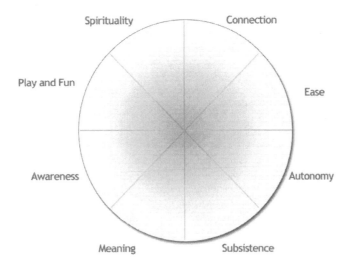

---

[40] Bozarth, J. (1998). *Person-centered therapy: A revolutionary paradigm.* PCCS Books. (Ross-on-Wye, UK)

What if your support team is nonexistent? Make it up! Add people like Gandhi, your grandchild who isn't born yet, Joan of Arc, your first teacher, even Bart Simpson, whomever you imagine could support you. Include the butterfly in the window, the old oak tree in the park, the wind rustling the tall grass, the North Star or anything that could offer you support. After imagining the perfect support team, then go out and create a real support team. In some cultures the value of independence and individuality is so strong that people can't begin to imagine what full support would look like, so this is an opportunity to recruit an all-star team! Everyone needs support – and there are many ways to expand our support system. Next we'll look at how we use decision-making processes to support diverse groups.

Exercises

Reflections:
1. Use the GROW model to self-coach on a goal of your choice.
2. Design your ideal support system using the Balance Wheel on page 380.

Small Group Discussions:
1. In small groups brainstorm some outrageous possibilities of actions the group could take.
2. In small groups, discuss, "What will you commit to doing? Short term? Long term? What does your heart say about this plan?"

Activities:
1. Use the GROW model to support someone to reach a personal goal.
2. Now use the GROW model to run a meeting, and ask the group to assess the value of using the model.
3. Focusing on your own hopes and dreams, make five outrageous requests of yourself. Share these with a partner. Now focus on your partner's hopes and dreams and make five outrageous requests of her.

Chapter 6
Making Shared Decisions

Each indecision brings its own delays and days are lost lamenting over lost days... What you can do or think you can do, begin it. For boldness has magic, power, and genius in it.

—Johann Wolfgang von Goethe

In some cultures, shared decision-making is seen as a sign of weak leadership, and in others the ability to facilitate shared decisions is the sign of true leadership. Nothing crushes a group more quickly than giving them the autonomy to make decisions and then taking it away. If we don't clarify who has the power to make decisions, be prepared to see the air sucked out of the group when all the dialogue, deliberation, and brilliant solutions are usurped by the person in authority. It's easy to talk a good game about collaborative decision making; it's another to fully embrace it, so transparency is vital.

Nothing builds team spirit more than the ability to efficiently make decisions that everyone can support. If I'm working with scientists, I'm unlikely to ask them to make decisions based on their emotions. If I'm working with Quakers, I wouldn't use a model that relies on taking a straw vote. With youth, I wouldn't ask them to sit still for very long. With an academic department, the faculty might agree on a recommendation where an administrator will ultimately make the decision. The importance of the decision, size of the group, level of awareness, and time constraints all impact which facilitation model or decision-making process we use.

Helping people gain clarity about what they *really* want and making clear, doable requests engages their hearts in the decision making process. So we'll kick this chapter off with an exploration of requests, a vital component of the decision making process, and then we'll take a look at several decision making models and processes.

Making Requests

If I only have time to share one skill with a group, I usually choose to support them in making requests because I value the improved understanding, clarity, and potential for transforming the culture. Too often, requests are implicit rather than explicit. Every time anyone speaks, it's for a reason. We may not be aware of it, but each time we talk, we almost always want something back even if it is only acknowledgement that others have heard us. Here's an example. Jack says, "It's cold." We don't know if he is requesting that we build a fire, give him a jacket, fix him a drink, go skiing, buy tickets to the Caribbean, or something else. We can only guess what he wants – not a very effective way to communicate.

Requests are a gift—an opportunity to contribute to the requestor. Sometimes we struggle to understand what someone is actually requesting, so we can support them in articulating their request. We may have to explain that "It's cold," is not a request and one can't expect others to figure it out. Without this, Jack might later retort, "I said I was cold and you did nothing!" The frustration that results from implied requests and resulting misunderstandings confound people, but we can support them in articulating their request. The first step is identifying the need they are trying to meet. The second step is identifying the request that is most likely to meet that need.

When people soft-pedal their requests, or expect others to read their minds, we can make it a lot easier by helping people turn their implicit requests into explicit requests. Often getting to the root of their desire is as simple as asking, "What is your request?" Other times the request is more elusive, but we can elicit the implied request by empathizing with their feelings and needs and asking:

- What do you need right now?
- Can you be more specific about what you want?
- Do you have a request?

Or we can guess their request. "Are you asking for …" or "Does that mean you want …?" Many of us find it difficult to make requests. We pride ourselves on being fiercely independent; we're afraid to hear someone say no, or we're afraid they'll say yes out of obligation. Many people hear the word "no" as "You don't like me," or "I don't matter to you." Exploring and dismantling all the limiting beliefs we hold about requests helps us ask for and get what we want.

When we make a request, we start with connection, using words, tone, and energy that invite dialogue, as opposed to demanding action or insisting on ultimatums that elicit one-word answers, submission, or rebellion. A request starts with "will you?" or "would you be willing to…" not "Don't you think it would be a good idea to…" or "Do you think you could maybe…." Requests include a specific action and a defined time frame. Our requests are more easily visualized and executed if we ask for what we *want* rather than what we *don't want.* "I don't want you to talk to me that way," is neither clear nor doable because I haven't asked for what I *do* want.

Most requests fall into two categories: action requests or connection requests. Action requests make it clear what we want people to *do* and give them an opportunity to do something about our request right now, often by making an agreement. Specific, clear, present, doable requests are more likely to lead to agreement compared to vague, implied requests. A few examples of action requests:

- Would you be willing to take the bus?
- Will you agree to pick up the materials by Friday?
- Can you sign the contract now?

In a hurry to get things done, we often go straight to action requests which can be disastrous if we don't first establish connection. Connection requests give us the opportunity to increase understanding *before* we move into action. One connection request is to ask the listener what she heard so that I have clarity about how she's interpreting what I said. Another connection request is about her reaction to what I said, "Will you tell me your reaction to what I just said?" In the first instance I want both of us to understand what's going on internally for me, and in the second, I want both of us to understand what's going on internally for her. For instance, connection requests might sound like:

- Can you tell me what you heard me say?
- How do you feel about what I just said?
- Would you like to know what I heard you say?
- Would you like to know how I feel about what you said?

Requests that are specific, clearly worded, and doable make it much easier for people to respond to what we want. If we let them know why the request is important to us, we increase the chances of satisfaction dramatically. If they understand our needs but don't like that particular request, it helps to have alternative requests waiting in the wings so that we can negotiate a mutually-satisfying outcome.

Once we hear why they don't want to honor the original request, we can also *ask* for a counter-offer, "I hear you saying 'no' to my original request, so I'm wondering if you have another way that we can both get what we want?" When we ask for a response in the present and we're open to hearing their answer, even if they say 'no', we're more likely to create shared understanding. We can expect responses to sound similar to three options:

- Yes, I will…
- No, I won't…
- Counter-offer: I won't do that, but I will…

If we put our request out there, we can just let it float around in the ether or stick with it long enough to get an answer. It's better to have a 'no' than to be unclear about whether we've really co-created an agreement. We often make the mistake of *thinking* we have a joint understanding when people don't respond, but if we keep asking until we have a clear agreement, both the communication and the results are much more satisfying.

Ideally we want true agreement, so if someone says yes out of habit, pressure, or a desire to conform, it's worth asking if their yes is truly a yes. If we notice a little hesitation, we can ask the respondent to really check in emotionally to examine any doubt or discomfort. Often people will respond with, "Well actually…" and then voice their objection or offer a revised plan that suits them better. Without this clarity, a "yes" response can be meaningless in terms of its reliability moving forward. We can revise the agreement so that we have 100% "yes" and confidence that we can fully honor the agreement.

When we break agreements, we impact other's lives and the ripple effect can come back to haunt us. But if we hold everyone's needs compassionately, the *way* we break agreements can actually *build* trust. Instead of damaging relationships, if we empathize with the other person's needs, then describe our own needs, and co-create new agreements that meet both sets of needs, we can avoid a lot of suffering.

When we respond to requests, instead of offering a one-word "yes," we get shared clarity if we articulate what we're actually agreeing to. To prevent confusion and disappointment, we don't say, "I'll do whatever you want," because who knows how that will be interpreted. Instead we state exactly *what* we're saying yes to. An example that could reduce frustration for both parties: "I *will* design the social entrepreneur workshop, but I'm *not* going to do it this afternoon."

The word "no" can be difficult for requestors to hear. Unconsciously we may connect a current "no" with the first time we heard the word "no." Underneath every "no," we're actually saying "yes" to something else. So if we can let the requestor know what we're saying "yes" to, we improve the chances of being heard accurately. Here's an example of saying no by explaining what I *will* do, "You matter to me. On Monday I'm meeting with the Skoll Foundation so if you need the design completed before Tuesday, let's find some other way to get it done." See how much easier that is to hear than, "No. Can't do it."

Here's an example: I wasn't paying attention when I booked a flight and didn't realize it conflicted with a coaching teleclass series. Argh! When I found out the change fee would be $750 to reschedule my flight, I called the class organizer to see if we could skip a week. I think it helped her to know that I cared about her reputation, her need for reliability and reduced stress, and that I was *willing* but not eager to pay the fee. From there we devised a new strategy that worked for both of us.

One way to show our compassion when we want to break an agreement is to address it as soon as we know we aren't going to keep the agreement. Notice I didn't say "can't keep the agreement" or "have to do something else," because we always have a choice. Waiting until the last minute or until after the time frame has passed damages trust, which can take a long time to rebuild. I'm writing this as I'm sitting at the airport, unsure if my flight will be delayed a day, in which case I'll need to cancel several agreements. With some of those agreements, I'm confident that people will easily accept rescheduling, but there's one I'm fretting about – a class with 23 people. Do I tell the organizer now that there *might* be a problem and risk stimulating unnecessary anxiety? Or do wait until I'm sure the flight will be delayed? We've all been in situations where we're on the fence about when is the prime time to break an agreement, and I assert that sooner is usually better than later. But even when we "forget" to alter an agreement, we can still express regret and care for the others' needs, which can go a long way toward regenerating trust.

Traditional Decision-Making

The voting process, where majority rules, may be the fastest way to make group decisions, but the least effective in getting buy-in, so implementing the decision can take much longer. Some groups never vote, including Quakers who prefer to seek unity, while other groups wouldn't take any action whatsoever without a vote. We can choose from many decision-making processes such as the popular force field analysis, decision matrix, or cost/impact analysis.

Decision Matrix: We chart a decision matrix so that we can evaluate the alternatives in a relatively important decision. We start by brainstorming the criteria that we'll use to evaluate the alternatives. If the group wishes, they weight each criteria based on its importance. The next steps are to mine the alternatives, dialogue, and then evaluate each alternative based on the selected criteria. We can weight each and rate each criteria individually and then as a group. Decision Matrixes help loosen individuals' attachment to a particular solution by bringing breadth to the process.

Force Field Analysis: We start by identifying the current and the ideal future state. Then we analyze the situation in terms of "driving forces" and "restraining forces." The driving forces are the forces that are propelling some type of change from the status quo. Restraining forces are the forces that are hindering a change from the status quo. Once we've identified the forces, we generate strategies to maximize the driving forces and minimize the restraining forces. Usually we get a larger payoff from the latter. Then we choose the best strategies to implement to produce the desired outcome. Force field analysis helps when a change is likely to occur but motivations and consequences are not clear.

Cost / Impact Analysis: After brainstorming alternatives, we look at each one separately and rate the degree of positive impact or expected return that the alternative will have on the goal or issue or problem on a scale of 1-5. Then we look at each alternative in terms of the cost to implement on a scale of 1-5. In addition to monetary impact, other costs to evaluate include: impact on morale, retention, the environment or the larger community. Because we look at the impact on human life, this approach often evokes great controversy. The cost to implement the alternative is only a part of the cost; we also look at the cost to relationships, impact on reputation, good will, and fit with the long-term strategy. Then we create a matrix, listing each alternative on the left side, with the criteria across the top, and then plot the scores in each area.

Each of these processes can shed some light on a new path forward but don't always help people stay connected to their emotions and creative flow. Nor do they ensure that everyone has a voice. For that we need more evolved decision-making processes such as Sociocracy, group Decision Making, Transformative Circles, and Autonomous Collaborative Group Decision-Making. When do we use each process? We can consider the prevalent needs of the group, time constraints, comfort level, and familiarity with each process.

Sociocracy

A form of governance that gives everyone a voice and equal power in the decision making process is sociocracy. Developed by Gerard Edenburg,[41] the simple process is based on consent and can be used by any kind of organization. The four main principles of Sociocracy are:

1. Decision Making by Consent. Decisions are made only when no one has a significant argument against the decision (no paramount objection). Before that point is reached, each reasoned argument is included in the discussion. All decisions are made by consent unless the group agrees to use another method.

2. Circle Organization. The organization's structure is made up of semiautonomous circles. Each circle has its own goals and the responsibility to execute, measure, and control its own processes. Each circle exists within the context of a higher-level circle. No circle is fully autonomous; the needs of its higher-level circles and lower-level circles must be taken into account.

At the highest level, there is a "Top Circle," which is similar to a traditional board of directors, except each member represents a different part of the organization's environment: legal/governmental, financial (including investors), cultural, technical field, workers, and management.

3. Double-Linking. Circles are connected through a double link: One person is elected by the lower-level circle and one (who has overall accountability for the lower-level circle's results) is chosen by the higher-level circle. Each belongs to and takes part in the decision-making of both circles.

4. Elections by Consent. Individuals are elected to roles only after open discussion results in a clear choice, with no reasoned objections. First, each person writes his or her name on a ballot as well as the name of a nominee. The meeting leader reads each nomination, asking members to explain why they chose their candidate. After discussion, people can (and often do) change their nominations. Finally, the chairperson formally proposes the person with the strongest arguments, and everyone then has a chance to present objections. This may continue for a few rounds, and when there are no more objections to a candidate, the selection process is complete. If no one is suitable, the circle has to find someone to fill the vacancy.

Decision-making meetings, as practiced in Sociocracy, are an efficient means of communication that build on trust. Despite the sound of it, consent is usually more efficient than autocratic decision making. Decisions stick and are not sabotaged due to discontent. Likewise, the highly-disciplined process helps the group stay focused and move swiftly through examination of an issue and actual

---

[41] Sociocracy. 2010. Retrieved from http://en.wikipedia.org/wiki/Sociocracy

decision- making. For example, one company reported a reduction of 50% in the number of meetings after it introduced Sociocracy.[42]

In addition to the four principles, people using Sociocracy follow agreements that:

- No secrets may be kept.
- Everything is open to discussion.
- Everyone has a right to be part of a decision that affects them.
- Every decision may be reexamined at any time.

To learn more about facilitating decision-making sociocratically, check out the Twin Oaks web page on Sociocratic Facilitation.[43] I often share Brian Robertson's work on Holacracy, a variation of Sociocracy that embodies the Integral work of Ken Wilber. Interested readers may consult Brian's succinct article that makes the process easy to understand.[44]

Group Decision-Making

High functioning groups take everyone's needs into account while making a decision as quickly as possible. This group decision-making model provides a structure for choosing a course of action and is especially useful if a difficult decision needs to be made quickly.

1. **Explore the desired future:** What do we really want? In an ideal world, what will be different? What is our goal?
2. **Identify decisions to be made:** What do we need to decide to get to our desired future? What do we want to determine?
3. **Analyze the issue:** What needs are important to the group? What data and resources do we already have, and what additional information do we need? What barriers keep us from creating our ideal future? Where else can we find resources?
4. **Establish criteria:** What criteria will help us determine whether everyone is satisfied with the solution/decision? We may choose to rank or weight the criteria according to importance.
5. **Generate options:** What are some possible solutions that would meet most of our established criteria? What options have we overlooked? What could we do in the absence of constraints?
6. **Evaluate options:** What is the best alternative according to our criteria? Which option is the most likely to help us create our desired future? Which option will solve the problem for the long-term?

---

[42] Endenburg, G. (1998). *Sociocracy as social design*. Eburon.
[43] http://www.twinoaks.org/clubs/sociocracy/facil.html
[44] http://www.holacracy.org/downloads/HolacracyIntro2007-06.pdf

7. **Implement the solution:** What resources do we need to implement the decision? Who will do what by when?
8. **Monitor and evaluate the outcomes:** How well did our chosen solution actually meet our selected criteria? How close are we to our ideal future? What do we need to do to course correct?

When I used this process with a board that had spent a year wrestling with whether to replace their CEO, they were able to make a difficult decision in two hours. One of the things that made it hard is that the CEO was a close personal friend of several members on the board. Not only did they make the decision, but they decided how to do it compassionately. They also established an action plan with next steps that gave them the confidence to execute the decision quickly.

Building Consensus

As an alternative to majority rule, consensus decision making creates inclusion, participation and cooperation by involving as many stakeholders as possible, actively soliciting input from those impacted by the decision, and striving to reach the best decision for all members. The approach is both egalitarian and solution-oriented. Each member has equal input and has the option to offer suggestions, amend or block proposals. The power to block a proposal can result in "tyranny of the minority" which is similar to "tyranny of the majority" when majority rule exploits diverse smaller interests. The consensus process has an advantage over majority rule because it invites collaboration rather than competition. However, because of the emphasis on compromise, many view consensus as a lose-lose proposition, whereas majority rules at least creates a win/lose dichotomy. However, the intention of building consensus is to create win-win solutions.

The primary role of a facilitator is to help the group make agreements they can live with, if not enthusiastically implement. The actual process of building consensus is more important than the outcome. One way to visually check the pulse of the group regarding a decision is to ask them to stand along a continuum line from one to five, indicating their position regarding the emerging decision:

1. I enthusiastically support the decision; I believe it represents the shared wisdom of the group.
2. I find the decision perfectly acceptable, but I don't feel especially enthusiastic about it.
3. I have some reservations about the decision, but I'm willing to support the decision.
4. I do not completely agree with the decision and need to express my objections. However, I can go along with it.
5. I am opposed to the decision, and I think we need to do more work before we can achieve consensus.

When everyone reaches levels 1 – 4, you have consensus and you're done. If people are at level 5, ask them, "What would move you closer to a one?" Invite them to share in pairs before asking the 5's to share in the larger group. After revising the decision based on the suggestions that emerge, and you think everyone stands somewhere between 1 - 4, avoid asking, "Is everyone satisfied?" or "Has everyone been heard?" unless of course you want to open the dialogue back up. To raise the threshold, ask, "Does anyone have a paramount objection?" or "Is there anyone who can't live with the decision?"

One of the things I enjoy about this process is that people are out of their chairs and physically moving, which invites movement intellectually and impacts the decision making process. As they stand along the continuum, we can notice subtle movements in their body language as people share their reservations and hopes. As they reveal their thinking to the group, if we watch their body language, we have more information about where people are leaning. This information helps raise the capacity to empathize and consider all viewpoints.

Large Group Decision-Making

One of the trickiest parts of facilitation is working with large groups in ways that each individual trusts that they matter, and that everyone else in the group also matters. The author of *Intervention Skills*, Brendan Reddy says, "As group size exceeds about 12 members, attaining consensus decreases dramatically."[45] The larger the group, the greater the fragmentation, loss of identity by members, and "social loafing."[46] Reddy asserts that large groups are difficult to manage because even competent group members let someone else do the work, so he suggests using break-out groups, which rings true for me. However, Miki Kashtan, a master at using Nonviolent Communication to make group decisions, has given me hope that large groups can make decisions quickly and compassionately if well facilitated. She has taught me about holding compassion for all, and many times I've watched her work with individuals, while taking a strong stand for holding the needs of *all* the people, even those not in the room. That doesn't mean that every person's needs will be met, but when I see her expressing her care for everyone impacted by the decision, I see the group open to making decisions based on everyone's needs.

Several elements contribute to facilitating large group decision-making. First we need to determine the value the group places on the importance of the decision. Second we take the pulse of the group and read the spaciousness of the group to explore options. By hearing objections to the proposal with openness and curiosity, everyone feels heard, and even if the decision is not their favor, they have the satisfaction of knowing they've contributed. After we synthesize all the needs that have been expressed, we can then alter the proposal to match the concerns that have surfaced.

---

[45] Reddy, W. B. (1994). *Intervention skills. process consultation for small groups and teams.* Pfeiffer & Company. p. 32.
[46] Latane, B., Williams, K., & Harkins, S. (1979). Many hands make light the work: The causes and consequences of social loafing. *Journal of Personality and Social Psychology.* p. 37.

For instance, if the group is trying to decide whether to move the chairs from rows into a circle, this is a low-intensity decision. But if the group is trying to decide whether or not to use a new process that could prevent bankruptcy and job loss, the members of the group may express much higher levels of anxiety.[47]

Choosing the Threshold

One way to encourage people to come forward with their needs, and at the same time use our power to move the group forward is to evaluate the importance of the decision and set the threshold (level of satisfaction with the decision) accordingly. "Is anyone disappointed?" is an example of a low threshold. "Is there anyone who can't live with the decision?" sets a much higher threshold. If we want full participation and agreement, so that everyone can easily contribute to the decision, we set a low threshold. However, we raise the bar when the decision is of low importance so that we can reach closure and devote our resources to more important issues. Miki Kashtan from BayNVC (Bay Area Nonviolent Communication) has experimented widely with setting thresholds to help large groups make decisions based on everyone's needs. This section is based on my evolving understanding of how Miki uses thresholds.

To make group decisions we can determine how high to set the threshold based on reading the energy of the group and internal sensing. We have more flexibility if we change that threshold based on the situation. A few examples of a range of thresholds:

- Is anyone unwilling to take the next five minutes to explore this issue?
- Any objection to trying this solution for six months and then revisiting the issue?
- If you have an ounce of willingness, will you…?
- Would anyone suffer greatly if we move forward with this decision?
- Knowing that many people have a preference for x, please raise your hand only if you absolutely cannot bear to move in that direction.

If we raise the threshold high enough, we can get the group to go in a certain direction, but that can appear manipulative. Why not just say what we want and take the lead to save the group from a lot of turmoil? One way to make a choice *for* the group when they are not aligned is to say, "I'm really committed to honoring everyone's needs, and since it looks like we're not going to come to an agreement within the next 10 minutes, we'll keep things the way they are, and I'll make myself available during the break if anyone would like to explore a better solution." If someone still expresses dissatisfaction, after hearing them and tweaking the proposal, you can raise the threshold further by saying, "Is there anyone who can't live with the decision to leave things as they are for the next three hours, and we'll meet over lunch to co-create a better solution for the afternoon?" As part of our request, we can also point to the exasperation in the group, or the need for movement, or share the observation that people have left, which points to group awareness and raises the bar further still.

---

[47] Personal interview with Miki Kashtan 6/9/08.

When the stakes are higher, we may still start with a low-threshold request and move to a higher threshold. Because we're fairly confident the group will agree, it might sound like, "New research shows that we can improve our process and save 50% on production costs. Is anyone unwilling to explore this possibility?" An example of a higher threshold: "Because we're facing bankruptcy, we will implement the new process immediately; unless any of you objects strongly enough that you would consider quitting."

We can continuously revise the proposal as more needs surface so that the decision is more satisfying to the group. The primary skill here is to stay open to the objections and underlying needs. Instead of harboring judgment about the person who isn't going along with the majority, we can respond with curiosity, trust that their contribution is a gift, and incorporate multiple needs into a revised proposal. Synthesizing the vast array of needs is the art of assimilating all that underlies the yearning and offering a new proposal that more people find satisfying.

Transformative Circles

Most group process work is done sitting in chairs, but often there's a better way to foster transformation – get people up and moving. If their bodies are moving, this generates movement in other areas – emotions, relationships, and actions. A structured way to process group experience is to create a large circle on the floor, divided into 8 pie-shaped sections using masking tape. Then the group participates in five rounds: judgments, attention, reactions, needs, actions. Place a card in each section of the circle as shown in the resource section on page 418. As a group, the participants start in phase one by exploring their judgment silently. Guided by a few questions for them to reflect on, they move to different areas of the circle. Keep the circle and change the cards for each phase. In the next four circles (attention, reaction, needs, actions) as you ask the questions and they settle into a section of the wheel, ask a member of each area to share out loud. The diversity of experience helps people understand each other's reactions and brings them together, as they "try on" each other's experience.

While there are an infinite number of cards to use, and ways to process what comes up, I offer here a generic place to start, but encourage you to tailor the process. I use Transformative Circles to help groups understand their diverse emotional reactions. For instance, when people receive their 360° feedback from their manager, peers, and direct reports, their reactions range from ecstasy to humiliation. Some are baffled. Some get exactly what they expected. I've seen stoic leaders in conservative organizations become so overwhelmed that they can't hold back the tears, "I never knew people thought so highly of me." Others are seething, plotting their revenge. Before they get private coaching, I like to process the group experience collectively because it sensitizes them to the wide range of experiences, helps build awareness of the impact on the whole team, and opens the door to supporting each other's growth and development.

Other ways you can use the Group Process Circles:
- Mergers and acquisitions in organizations
- Families going through divorce

- Teams exploring new opportunities
- Addressing change initiatives
- People working with trauma or tragedy

Participatory Decision-Making

Participatory decision-making can be a rigorous, liberating, and spiritual practice. At the heart of the participatory decision-making process is full empowerment for everybody. As a group searches for a solution that meets the most needs, one way to facilitate the process that honors both individual autonomy and group collaboration is for all participants to determine their preferences privately, silently, and then share them aloud in turn. Although we keep it light, easy, and playful, we don't avoid the first crucial step of determining personal preference. In this way, we continuously discover where each person stands. This process keeps our relationships clean, creative and respectful, by avoiding collusion, control, or going along with the majority. Autonomous decision-making ensures that cooperation is authentic and not imagined. Each person can check in with the deep inner motivation in the belly, to get a sense of where they truly stand, as a basis for creative agreement. Then people think about the whole, valuing diversity as they begin to explore proposals that will honor everyone. In this way, immanent, embodied spirit is a spacious co-creative partner to the contract. Honoring each other as autonomous beings grounds us in sacred energy. As we disclose our preferences and bring them into the light, we proceed to a negotiated, shared decision.

John Heron describes participatory decision-making in his book Participatory Spirituality:

> Participatory decision-making integrates autonomy, co-operation and hierarchy. In this inquiry, each person moves between and integrates these three positions, and moves between three phases. There is an autonomous phase: each person states clearly their individual, idiosyncratic preference, in relation to the matter being discussed. Next a hierarchical phase: people start to think integrally on behalf of the whole group, and one or more participants state integral proposals that seek to honour diversity-in-unity, and that resonate strongly with the group. Then there is a co-operative phase of negotiating an agreed decision, after debating, selecting and refining the most resonant integral proposal.[48]

As people share their preferences, everyone listens open-heartedly for the best interest of the group, allowing themselves to be influenced by each other. Working together to solve difficult problems, people often go through a difficult period where resolution seems impossible. Some people in the group experience profound discomfort unless they recognize the difficulty as a blessing. The same way that judgment masks important needs, the chaos of the decision making process is a gift. Given the space to touch the collective despair and hopelessness, someone in the group invariably offers an idea that elicits hope. The idea itself may sound ridiculous, amusing, or

---

[48] Heron, J. (2006). *Participatory spirituality: A farewell to authoritarian religion*. Lulu Press. p. 44.

114

half-baked, but the glimmer of hope sparks an energy shift, and new possibilities come forward. Facilitators who don't have deep comfort with the depth of despair and hopelessness, or want to rush through the process, don't get to experience this magic.

Many facilitators rob the group of their transformative experience because we don't have the courage to stay with the intensity or the heart to explore the depth of the challenge. Likewise, if we don't recognize the "aha" moment, and we allow the group to pounce on and demolish the idea before it fully emerges, the fresh insights don't surface. When facilitators regularly encounter the mysterious shifts that take place, we come to expect transformation, which impacts the outcome. But if we try to force the transformation or the miracle, it won't happen. No one can be forced into transformation – it arrives spontaneously in unlikely moments. We can co-create solutions by setting intentions, while holding them loosely, and maintaining a sense of how wonder might manifest itself.

We hold the intention of embracing chaos, allowing the old order to collapse so that a new kind of order can emerge. Often silence ensues. And then the space opens up and a new proposal emerges. Instead of tidying it up prematurely, we hang in there with the confusion to see where it goes. If people complain or blame others for their own discomfort, we can interrupt, asking them to sit with their values to support self-connection. Ordinarily, cynicism, skepticism, judgments, and labeling prevent people from living in a state of wonder. But if we get curious about those judgments and beliefs, if we encourage everyone to explore with the same sense of wonder, we have fresh opportunities for embracing the whole, including the shadow.

When it looks like we're close to unity, we can take a straw poll, using thumbs up, thumbs down, or in-between. Ask to hear from the folks with thumbs down first, to hear their creative input for tweaking the solution. As they speak, celebrate diversity by honoring idiosyncratic creativity and heterogeneous perspectives. We can ask, "What would it take to move you to thumbs up?" and adjust the solution accordingly.

This practice of participatory decision-making requires a deep level of trust in ourselves as facilitators, in the decision making process, and in the wisdom of the group. Surprisingly, "letting go" is an advanced facilitation skill that comes only with experience.

Exercises

Reflections:
1. What decision-making process would you suggest to:
   - A board that wants to develop a succession plan when the leader retires
   - A non-profit that wants to develop a lay-off plan because they lost 50% of their funding
   - Three school districts that are merging to save costs
   - A family foundation that suffers from infighting
   - The founder and the executive director who have both said, "Either she goes or I go."

Small Group Discussions:

1. Translate these implied requests into doable requests starting with two examples:
    - My flight is late. <u>Do you want me to cancel the meeting?</u>
    - It's too noisy. <u>Would you like to leave now?</u>
    - My computer crashed. _____
    - She said she'd deliver it today. _____
    - The stock market dropped 500 points. _____
2. In small groups, create a list of requests with a wide range of thresholds.
3. Practice generating statements to move from lower-to higher-threshold decision-making to match the scenario.

Activities:

1. Make three requests a day for a week and notice your internal state throughout the process. Ask for feedback on how your requests were received.
2. Check with yourself to see if you're forcing yourself to keep an agreement that you no longer wish to keep. Break or alter the agreement to your mutual satisfaction.
3. Using the guide in the resource section on page 418, try the Transformative Circle process with your family or friends to explore something controversial that just happened or something that you're considering in the future.
4. Use the Participatory Decision-Making process with your partner or family to make an easy decision.

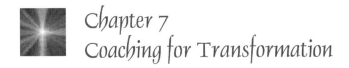

Chapter 7
Coaching for Transformation

There is a vitality, a life-force, an energy, a quickening that is translated through you into action and because there is only one of you in all of time, this expression is unique. And if you block it, it will never exist through any other medium and be lost.
— Martha Graham

To practice advanced facilitation skills, we need to be willing to go with people to the depths of despair and the heights of glory to awaken the hidden parts of the soul. In this chapter we'll look at ways to deepen the work of facilitation by coaching individuals in the group. We'll enhance the art of empowerment by helping people embrace inner polarities, interrupt internalized powerlessness, and create the space to grieve and heal. We'll also look at the power of values, purpose and vision work and open up the spiritual dimension.

Generally facilitators work with groups while coaches work with individuals, but the skill sets used in both professions are remarkably similar. Much of the focus of facilitation is to resolve conflict while the focus of coaching is on creating an ideal future. However coaches support individuals with their internal conflict and facilitators work with groups on designing their future. Ultimately, both coaches and facilitators create space for expanding awareness and moving forward.

Developing one-on-one coaching skills is a progressive way to ease into developing facilitation skills. I found working with groups challenging until I discovered that I could work with a group the same way I work with an individual. The many voices, emotions, and needs of an individual are almost identical to the many voices, emotions, and needs of a group. Rather than seeing group members as adversaries with diverse needs, the simple practice of treating the group as one entity (the same way I'd treat one person) gave me more confidence to facilitate groups. Somehow I can wrap my arms around the challenges by seeing both an individual and a group as a complex system that is moving toward more congruency. When each voice within the system is heard and understood, tension is relieved and people are transformed. Even when some people don't speak, their presence can still be honored. I don't give equal attention to *every* voice or *every* thought in an individual or in a group, but if I honor each voice, everyone softens.

Coaching

Principles of Coaching

At Coaching that Works, a school that develops holistic coaches, we rely on our affirmative beliefs about people. We can create powerful relationships based on these six principles of coaching:

1. Wholeness: People are whole and simultaneously moving toward a fuller expression of their wholeness.
2. Resourcefulness: Awakening inherent resourcefulness and wisdom activates creativity.
3. Natural Openings: Transformative action arises from recognizing and choosing natural openings.
4. Possibility: Much more is possible than any of us can imagine at any moment.
5. Polarities: Fully embracing both sides of any polarity leads to internal alignment.
6. Freedom: People are inherently free and always have the power to choose.[49]

When we fully integrate these beliefs, we empower people to realize their deepest longings. As simple as it sounds, we all meet people who want us to join them in believing they are broken, unimaginative, stuck, or without choice. They say things like, "No one can help me; I've never been good with money; I have no friends; I'll never find a job I like." Some people choose chronic suffering because they feel more alive when complaining about their dead lives, "I have to be a workaholic or I'll drown in debt; I can't get out of this draining marriage; I hate living in this deteriorating city." Empathy provides some relief, and we can take that a step further by believing in their ability to create the life of their dreams. Coaches can shake people out of their entrenched belief systems.

Occasionally I haven't believed in people fully and only realized it in hindsight. When I can see this and admit it, the relationship blossoms. For instance, I worked with a client whose boss recommended coaching to improve her leadership skills, I got the impression she had no desire to lead. I saw her as a number cruncher, not a people person. Most of our sessions focused on minutiae even though she wanted relief from perfectionism. I jumped to the false conclusion that she couldn't be both a visionary and a detail person. As embarrassed as I am about not supporting her more fully early in the relationship, I appreciate the way I witnessed her chew her way out of the cocoon rather than pushing her into leadership. Within a few months she became a partner, bought out the others, expanded the business, and *still* I didn't see her full potential. When I shifted my limiting perspective and started believing in her, she took the reins and opened up to her wildest dreams. She is much more powerful in the driver's seat using me as her copilot and map reader. My presence and attention to her process provided the opportunity for introspection, creativity, and growth. Whenever judgments or labels seep into the coaching relationship, I work on my own limiting

---

[49] Developed by Richard Michaels and Virginia Kellogg 2006 http://CoachingthatWorks.com

beliefs and remind myself of these core coaching principles so that I can see each client's full magnificence.

Empowerment

I've taught coaching skills to graduate students at several universities, most of whom have had many years experience as managers. Invariably they come into the course with a major misconception: they think they're strong managers because they give good advice—they can identify and solve people's problems. It's quite a shock to their system to learn that they've succeeded *despite* these behaviors, not *because* of them. Often they're quite skeptical about the power of asking questions and claim, "But that's why I'm the leader – because I have the experience and the answers." Naturally they don't change their minds by only reading a book, but by experiencing the power of coaching firsthand. After their first session or two where they abstain from giving advice, they're astounded by the process of using empowering questions and empathic statements to help people identify the change they want to make, brainstorm possibilities, and find their own solutions. They're often surprised when the person being coached raves about how much the coach helped them, but they're really blown away by the process when they experience being coached.

The two primary directions of empowering questions are to invoke either insight or movement. Questions that invoke insight explore the inner life by building awareness of emotions and values, while questions that invite movement propel people toward creativity and action. In addition to clarifying feelings and values, the call for introspection helps people address inner polarities, explore new territory in depth, or create a new viewpoint. We support people in connecting at the heart level to get at the root of an old belief or pattern or bring light to an inner conflict. Understanding inner motivation can be a blissful experience, so much so that people don't have any desire to take action. Once people repeatedly have self-connection to their deepest longing, they want movement. When we recognize the inner shift toward movement, we shape our questions to support them in creating needs- based action plans and empowering accountability structures. Both types of questions work better open than closed.

Open-ended questions don't have yes or no answers. They start with "What" or "How," not "Do you…" or "Are you…" Closed-ended questions, those that result in a yes or no answer, limit exploration, possibility, and dialogue. In contrast, open-ended questions invite engagement, body-mind connection, and specificity. Empowering questions are often simple, intuitive, or spontaneous. Using their language, we can ask people the questions that they haven't already asked themselves, such as:

- What happens when you reflect deeply?
- How can you bring light to your inner conflict?
- How can you use your fear as a resource?
- Specifically, what do you want to do?
- What advice does your highest self have for you?

In the resource section on page 391, you'll find a list of empowering questions. I encourage you to read through it only to get a sense of variety or to generate your own questions. But don't keep it in front of you while coaching or facilitating, even if you're on the phone, because you'll be much more present and creative without a list.

Disempowering Questions

Now that we've explored empowering questions, don't get the false impression that any question will do because many questions leave people feeling flat and lifeless. What makes a question disempowering? Disempowerment comes more from the tone, expectations, and judgments we hold, but the way we word our questions also has a strong impact. Besides closed-ended questions, a few examples of questions that disempower people and flatten the process include:

Information questions
What did you study in college?
Who else was in the meeting?

Usually you don't need such information. Even if you don't have the entire context, you can still facilitate effectively.

Why questions
Why did you do that?
Why are you going to get help?

"Why" questions can generate resistance to change. They ask for the story, the logic, the thinking behind the choices, and they often imply judgment or criticism. "Why" questions frequently solicit defensiveness or rationalization. Some "why" questions have the simple intention of uncovering values or needs which many people find supportive.

Leading questions
Have you tried…?
Wouldn't it be better if you…?

All of these questions can sound like thinly-disguised advice, which is not as empowering as helping people discover their own solutions. Likewise, don't bother asking questions if you already know the answer.

Shrinking questions
Aren't you taking on a little too much?
Do you really think you're ready?

Out of a desire to protect people from possible failure, we sometimes encourage people to shrink. As we become more masterful facilitators, we help people expand their vision but still address potential barriers creatively; e.g., "How can you get past the barriers?"

As people evolve and build their self-connection, instead of "doing the work *for* people," we can contribute more by helping them move toward "doing their *own* work." Another way to empower people is by shifting the coaching skill to the client.

Figure 7.1 Shifting from Support to Empowerment

Supportive Coach does more of the work	Empowering Client does more of the work
I sense that you feel discouraged because you need progress. Does that resonate with you?	What do you feel and need right now?
Do you want to focus on x or y...	Where would you like to focus?
What will you do? When will you do it? How will I know?	How would you like to take responsibility?
Would you like to explore your disappointment or your hunger?	I don't know where to go with this – what does your gut say?
Here's a challenge for you...	What's the challenge you'd like to give yourself?
My intuition tells me ...	What does your intuition tell you?
I appreciate you because you contribute to my...	What do you appreciate about yourself?

In Figure 7.1 the columns represent supportive and empowering options. Although the right side of the chart offers more empowering interventions, the left side can be very fruitful. The more the coach models each skill, the easier it is for people to do it themselves. Early in the work with new clients, we spend more time in the left column, but as people evolve and take responsibility for their inner and outer work, we acknowledge their increased capacity by shifting to the right.

So one of the questions that arises is, "What data do we use to intuit when to shift from support to empowerment?" This isn't just a rhetorical question – but the answers are a bit elusive. The danger is that, in our desire to contribute, we stay in the supportive zone far longer than is productive. The other possibility is that we move too quickly to empowerment before the client has the self-connection, comfort, or skill level. Ultimately we want people to make their own meaning when we offer observations. Instead of asking suggestive questions, or questions we *think* we know the answer to, sharing observations can help people explore their inner world and determine where to point their toes.

When people are in a curious state rather than a judgmental state, or if they are highly aware of their needs, or at least have access to them, that's a great time to ask them to identify their feelings, needs, and requests *for themselves*. My experience is that people need a lot of help with self-empathy because they habitually think about strategy before getting clear about what they really need. When people are disconnected or unaware of their needs, we can help them reconnect *before* asking them to explore their creativity. Applying that to myself, if I'm coaching someone who says she wants to make a living playing poker and I'm triggered because a dear friend is addicted to gambling, I have several choices. If I'm not self-connected and can't stop thinking, "You idiot. How will you ever be able to support your family?" that's a signal that I need to get empathy from someone else. But if I am more aware, I can self-empathize right then and there – I'm alarmed because I want to contribute to my client's well being and support her in creating a meaningful life. From this nonjudgmental, self-connected place, I can get curious about her values, what needs she's hoping to meet by becoming a professional poker player, and support her in developing her own self-awareness.

Values, Purpose and Vision

Values

Each of us cares deeply about our personal values. Our values are our deeply-held desires that guide us in creating a fulfilling life. When we honor our values, our hearts sing. However, it breaks my heart to see people confuse values with ethics or morals because when we get into right/wrong, good/bad thinking, we lose our ability to connect with our common humanity, desire to contribute, and intention of making the world a better place.

Finding compelling language that describes the key driving forces in our lives gives us clarity about our deepest longing, what we stand for. Most of us have four or five core values that we've held since childhood. To clarify our values, we can explore peak experiences when life was exceptionally sweet, when we recognized our highest selves, or when we were at the top of our game. values don't change much over time, but our awareness of our values often shifts. My fellow explorer, Glenda Mattison from Toronto, believes that values are "chronically unmet needs." When we first discussed this, I argued that values can also be deeply *met* needs. For instance, one of my top values is learning – I almost take it for granted because it's such a deeply-ingrained value. Not only do I teach graduate courses for the sake of my own learning, but I spend about 25% of my time (5 days a month) going to workshops or some other venue to learn something new. So I experience that my needs for learning are deeply met almost all the time.

A year after we had this discussion, I had a stunning learning experience in India with people who matched my hunger and joy for new discoveries in the area of awareness and group dynamics. What shocked me was that having my need for learning met so deeply, along with the mutuality, made me realign my thinking with Glenda's assertion that values are chronically unmet needs. Until then, I'd always thought of my need for learning as fulfilled. But when I got a taste of what learning *could* be, it became clear to me that my need for learning was previously only partially met.

I continuously deepen my awareness of values—mine and others—to the point where I can tell you what value is most important to me in any moment.

Values Clarification:

1. List your top values, expanding your list until all your top values are included. Then group like words together until you have a list of your top five clusters of values. As you say the words aloud, imagine the satisfaction of honoring each of these values fully, and select the words that resonate deep in your soul.

2. Ask two people who know you what your top values are. Just listen to their responses since their words could open a window to your soul.

3. Use compelling language to describe each of your values – imagery, a metaphor or an experience when you were fully honoring that value.

4. Use your values list to make a key decision – something you've been procrastinating about and are ready to move on. If you decide one way or another, which values will be honored and which will be fulfilled?

5. For a week, track the way you're spending your time and notice which values you're honoring and which are taking a back seat. Notice anytime you feel a deep sense of satisfaction or dissatisfaction and record which values are impacted.

6. Score each of your top five values based on how much you are honoring your values right now on a scale of 1 – 10. What short-term or long-term action will raise your score on each value?

7. What's the *one* value you'd most like to pass on to your children or the next generation of children as the key to a fulfilling life?

Purpose

> We don't know yet where we are called to go. We leave anyway because some inner voice tells us that if we do not, there will be hell to pay. Then we wander for a while in the strange place called "don't know." Don't know where I am going. Don't know what is coming next. Don't know who I am anymore. This is courage, not confusion; it is wisdom, not folly. It creates the space for something new to be born. – Joan Borysenko

Who am I? What am I meant to do? Why am I here? How do I create the space for something new to be born? Finding our calling or unique personal purpose is the ultimate quest. Fortunately, we don't have to go very far since the answers are already inside. Seeking the Holy Grail is not about arrival but rather about continuously stalking our destiny. How do we support each other in finding our deepest calling? One way to identify our unique purpose on earth is to journal, repeatedly answering the question, "What is my soul purpose?" Repeatedly asking the question and taking time to listen for the answers helps us explore our soul's code. Free-form writing eventually reveals the answer, sometimes in under half an hour, or after many months. Questions that help us discover the essence of our purpose include:

- When have I felt in alignment with my life?
- When have I experienced flow, passion or fulfillment in my life?
- What are my gifts that I most enjoy offering?
- What am I drawn to consistently?

When we discover the words that resonate deep in our soul, we feel a sense of bliss, often accompanied by tears. Another way to get to the same place is to go on a long walk in a quiet place, allowing ourselves to be drawn toward anything that attracts us whether it's flowers, trees, animals, or clouds. With a partner we can explore imagery and metaphors until we've captured our pure tone that vibrates our inner tuning fork. When we identify our purpose and live our lives on purpose, life is sweet. We feel fulfilled and joyful about making a difference. We're in a state of flow and things come easily.

Vision

> Dreams contain nearly limitless power to lift us up in a world that seems determined to hold us down. Dreams have the power to pull us forward in the face of adversity. Dreams have the power to sharpen our focus and fill our lives with energy and passion. Dreams have the power to renew our strength and shield us from criticism and negative thinking. Dreams remind us that the biggest accomplishments always start with the biggest dreams.
>
> —Burke Hedges

To facilitate shared vision, we can use the *Courageous Visions*[50] process to expand personal and organizational visions. We start with describing what you want your life to be like ten years from now, and then describe a vision that is both exciting and challenging. If the thought of telling a friend about your vision makes you feel a little uneasy, you probably have a balance of excitement and challenge.

---

[50] Lasley, M. (2004). *Courageous visions: How to unleash passionate energy in your life and your organization.* Discover Press.

Your vision should be more of a story than a statement, so include a description of what motivates and propels you. Think about all you want to accomplish in your life in order to feel complete. Address issues that are relevant for you, such as:

- Life Contribution
- Career
- Recreation
- Relationships
- Spirituality
- Finances

Instead of limiting our vision to our current circumstances, we can dream wholeheartedly! Storytelling is a moving way to get people in touch with their visions. You can walk people through seven simple steps of the process found in the resource section on page 417, so they become more engaged with their visions.

Once we've done some inner work, understand our values and needs, have clarity about our purpose and vision, we're often compelled to support others on the journey of self-awareness and transformation. Every journey inward, every shift, and every movement toward bliss strengthens our ability to be present for others.

When people have clarity about their values, purpose, and vision, the transition into action usually flows easily and naturally. When people set goals and create action plans that come from soul-connection, it's easy to facilitate movement and progress. Occasionally they get blocked and that's when coaching becomes even more valuable. Whether they're torn between two alternatives, telling themselves they're powerless, or need to heal an old wound, a coach can create space for their longing and tap the innate power to transform themselves.

Embracing Inner Polarities

> *The outward freedom that we shall attain will only be in exact proportion to the inward freedom to which we may have grown at a given moment. And if this is a correct view of freedom, our chief energy must be concentrated on achieving reform from within.*
> — Mahatma Gandhi

We each have a community of support—our inner healer, teacher, lover, warrior, gardener—all the archetypes are available to support us at any time. Sometimes they seem at odds with each other, but the integration of our many selves contributes to our ultimate well being.

My business partner at Coaching that Works and founding member of the Kripalu Center for Yoga and Health, Richard Michaels, talks about how he coached a woman to step into her power simply by being present and embracing polarities:

My facilitation style draws me into the moment. I'm more fully alive when I'm in the flow where my intuition and my heart are working. What really excites me is the inclusion of all parts of a person and the powerful change that comes from that simple practice. When I'm working with someone and creating space for the parts that they might have judgment about or have feelings of shame about, when they get to be held without all that judgment, a part of the person shows up more fully.

At a workshop on Kick Starting your Goals through Coaching, one woman volunteered to be coached on exploring the emotions and energy of viewpoints. At the get-go I could see her power and the emotion in her eyes. The first viewpoint she stood in was tremendous grief, which brought me totally into the moment, brought the room into a space of feeling. Her son had died six years ago. Her words cut through the silence. Disarming. Disrobing. I felt almost naked. I was no longer the teacher – I had to drop trying to be a certain way. My heart and intuition took me fully into the stillness.

She was a talented psychotherapist, but her son's death had slammed her so deeply that she couldn't practice. Paralyzed, she had closed everything down. She expressed great grief and loss, and said she could not move on. Invited into another viewpoint, she described a volcano with a bunch of little clouds, each with a word or a message for her. She had a lot of power within wanting to erupt or explode. She recognized the impact she wanted to bring into the world, but her body collapsed and she said, "But I just can't come into my power because I really can't break through that grief and sadness. It's still with me." There was a part of me that wanted to stay with that, heal that, but I knew that wasn't the place to go. She was grieving the loss of her son and also grieving the loss of her power.

I said, "That grief is real. It's a part of you and by stepping into this other part, we're not pretending the grief is gone or doesn't exist. We're acknowledging the grief is one part of you and it's not the only part of you. Knowing that, I invite you for a few moments to step fully into this volcano." A new expression came across her face. She just ripped. She said, "I am letting it go. I am a powerful woman. And here's what I have to give to the world..." She was totally in her power. In that moment she was acting out of making space, not pushing the grief out, but letting it be fully expressed. Her grief claimed that it was here to stay, wasn't going to move, and it was in charge. By making space for her grief, and giving her the opportunity to fully be in the volcano, her power came out, and she was able to talk about how she would feed this new part of her that was emerging.

The experience brought me into a deep stillness and appreciation in myself. I was recovering from a bad fall, so she brought me to a place of empathy and connection. She inspired me to feel that deeper faith of owning my power and accepting all parts of myself with greater relaxation. We're in this together. And out of that, what a blessing! Her strength, my strength came out of being with what is. The whole group was very present and open as a result of this woman going to a very deep place which gave everyone permission to be authentic. What just came to me now in thinking about her volcano was that I see new fresh growth of spring flowers blooming by the mountain lake as I step into the natural life process of being reborn.[51]

Richard describes a common inner struggle. We feel torn when two hungry inner voices are vying for our attention. The voices sound like polar opposites because each wants something different. The power of embracing both polarities is that we allow these inner voices the space to co-exist in harmony. Instead of settling for an either / or mentality, we create space for both to be fully understood and appreciated.

Sometimes needs appear to be in conflict when in actuality they are symbiotic. If we nurture them, they feed on each other. Only the strategies for getting our needs met are in conflict. Once we have clarity about the value of each need, we can find strategies that meet both sets of needs. Here's a practice that builds on the work of Marshall Rosenberg, author of *Nonviolent Communication*[52], for "embracing polarities" which can be used by yourself, with another, or in a group. Start by taking a look at the needs of the chooser and the needs of the educator. The chooser is the part of you that chooses to *do whatever you've done*, and the educator is the part of you that wants to educate you about what you *should have done differently*. Imagine that both the chooser and the educator love you, even though you may be irritated by some of their actions, tone, or advice.

Embracing Polarities Activity
1. Situation: What happened? What was said or done?
2. Judgmental Chooser: What judgments do you have that defend the choices you made?
3. Judgmental Educator: What judgments do you have about what you should have done differently?
4. Empathic Chooser: What needs and values were you *trying* to meet by your actions?
5. Empathic Educator: What needs or values of yours did your actions *not* meet? Connect with these exquisite needs.
6. Inner Mediator: (Slow this down.) Hold the needs of the chooser in your left hand and cherish the needs of the chooser. Hold the needs of the educator in your right hand and cherish the needs of the educator. Bring both hands into the namaste position and hold both sets of needs close to your heart. Imagine both sets of needs being deeply met. How can you

[51] Richard Michaels personal interview 3/20/08. http://CoachingthatWorks.com
[52] Rosenberg, M. (2003). *Nonviolent Communication: A language of life*. Puddle Dancer Press.

restore wholeness in yourself or others who were affected by your action? Allow plenty of silence until clarity emerges.

Consider this example: Raul wanted money to buy a birthday gift for his daughter. He gambled on line and lost $5,000. Afterward, he wanted to overcome his addiction to gambling. His *chooser* gambled on line and lost; his *educator* told him to overcome his addiction. Without judgment, starting with the chooser, identify what needs Raul was trying to meet by gambling on line:

- Independence and choice?
- Fun and excitement?
- Hope that he could relieve some financial burden?
- Contribute to another's well being?

Then take a look at what needs Raoul's educator is trying to fulfill. Identify what needs Raul's educator was trying to meet by telling himself to stop gambling:

- Protection from disaster?
- Valuing stability?
- To act from intelligence and choice?
- Contribute to another's well being?

Often the chooser and educator want the same thing – in this case, to contribute to another's well being – but they each have different ways of getting it.

The purpose of this embodiment activity is to foster self-acceptance and self-intimacy, and transform judgment of past actions into compassion.

Through embracing polarities, sometimes what appears to be self-sabotage or ignoring current needs and values, at the same time satisfies *other needs and values*. Taking time to honor old behaviors and the sweet needs the person was trying to fulfill removes some of the self-judgment and releases the tension. Consequently people can look for new ways to fulfill both sets of needs. This process can work for the facilitator too.

Transferring this practice to myself, I can self-empathize with my chooser *and* my educator, embracing the needs of both inner voices. For instance, in this moment, one voice in me is saying, "Let's move onto a new topic," but another voice is saying, "Give them an example of how you honor the chooser and educator yourself!" The chooser has already moved onto the next section, and is thinking about how to interrupt internalized powerlessness, but my inner educator is saying, "Come back!" If I look at the needs of the chooser first, I realize my needs are for movement, for the discovery that comes from delving into a new topic, and to give value to you, the reader. My inner educator wants to offer an example because I value clarity and depth. Or perhaps it's a desire to contribute to you so that I can trust that you can actually envision and therefore use this chooser/educator model. Then there's a part of the educator who just needs a moment of self-connection, which leads to more intimate connection with you, my reader. Interestingly, both voices want the same thing – connection with myself and to trust that I'm connecting meaningfully with you. By honoring both inner voices, I can move forward in ways that honor both sets of needs.

Transforming Internalized Powerlessness

> To stay with that shakiness—to stay with a broken heart, with a rumbling stomach, with the feeling of hopelessness and wanting to get revenge—that is the path of true awakening. Sticking with that uncertainty, getting the knack of relaxation in the midst of chaos, learning not to panic—this is the spiritual path. Getting the knack of catching ourselves, of gently and compassionately catching ourselves, is the path of the warrior.

— Pema Chodran

We become powerless when we believe what's said about us without finding out what's true on the inside. We collude with oppressors by believing we aren't enough – not smart enough, wealthy enough, or beautiful enough to be loved. If we hate our lives or ourselves, we exacerbate the pain and suffering within. Self-acceptance often goes against our moral beliefs or cultural conditioning, so it takes real courage to interrupt patterns of powerlessness.

Since traumatized people can be both oppressors and oppressed, understanding internalized powerlessness helps us heal trauma at both the personal level and in catalyzing social change. The free book, *Power-Under – Trauma and Nonviolent Social Change* is available on line.[53] The author, Steven Wineman, offers important new insights that can help us to break cycles of violence. Analyzing connections between oppression, trauma, and internalized powerlessness, his book shows how trauma is a link in complex chains of domination.

Here's an example of shifting powerlessness in my life:

On the first day of a week-long workshop, a beautiful woman came up to me, looked deeply into my soul with the eyes of a seer, and told me a mysterious, vibrant story. The short version of her story: "I told a German man, 'I know who you are. You are the man who gave those women such hope when you promised you would marry them. They loved you. Believed in you. You lured them onto the ship, took them across the water, and sold them as slaves.' He was surprised that I knew who he was."

Mesmerized by her tale, I intuited that she had a deeper message for me personally, so I asked her, "Why are you sharing your story with me?" She answered, "You could be his sister." I wanted more, but she responded, "That is

---

[53] Wineman, S. (2003). *Power-Under: Trauma and nonviolent social change.* Retrieved from http://www.gis.net/~swineman/Power_Under.pdf

all I'm going to say." Abruptly, she turned and left. I couldn't seem to get my jaw to close.

Why me? But right away I knew. She chose to tell me this story because I'd been so inactive, ignoring so many opportunities. When I read my ancestor's will, where he had left livestock, land, slaves, and his "mulatto woman Aggie" to his son John, I wondered if Aggie was his daughter, sister, niece, or cousin, but did nothing to understand what her life might have been like, or confront myself or my family about our murky heritage.

A day later I went for a long walk with the mysterious seer and told her that some of my ancestors were slave owners, including an American ambassador to Italy in the 1700s, a prolific writer and avid proponent of the white man's right to lynch. She seemed to know all about it and understood my distress, despite her own. She talked about her mixed-race heritage and about her work with a group of elders from the Cherokee nation who build connections between tribes. I expected her to brace against me, but instead I could feel her take me into her heart. She explained, "The reason I told you that story is because I sense you have a gift. You could be a leader in facilitating the healing of old wounds." Me? Heal wounds? I don't think so. My tribe doesn't believe in illness, let alone notice woundedness. "No coughing allowed," my mother would say at the first hint of a cold. Only one emotion was acceptable: full-tilt happiness. Despite my skepticism, the seer had touched some latent desire. I knew I was being called, but would I answer the call? And how in hell does anyone answer a call that large?

For a long time I felt powerless – I didn't even know where to begin. Reading about oppression and understanding it were a far cry from doing something about it. Starting with faltering baby steps, I've worked on transforming white privilege, dismantling "isms," and building bridges across cultures. I've been teaching a graduate course on Leveraging Workplace Diversity and working in under-served communities who don't have easy access to resources. I've only opened the door a crack, but I'm on the path toward taking action, rather than keeping my powerlessness to myself.

Grieving

As facilitators, we're on an upbeat path to help people create their ideal future. If we continually reframe everything into what we want, we can step over the grief work that gives us relief from pain and suffering. It takes a lot of courage to stay present to broken-heartedness and accept deep sadness. A fear of going into the pain is that we may never come out. Sometimes people recycle old pain, by revisiting it over and over, again and again, because it's safe and familiar. They trust themselves most when they suffer. The way they treat themselves when they suffer is exactly what they need to keep them feeling real and alive. Just recognizing this cycle helps people develop the freedom to choose *how* we want to stay connected to our realness and aliveness. Two practitioners who help people open their hearts to mourning are Jeyanthy Siva and Dian Killian.

As a child in Sri Lanka, Jeyanthy Siva often play-acted adults. She paints a vivid picture of two professional mourners who traveled to the house after her grandfather's funeral, and she and her cousin mimicked their behavior by crouching, facing each other, holding each other's shoulders, rocking back and forth, and wailing. In this way they helped the family mourn and let out their grief. She explains that the word "mourning" in Tamil is translated as "celebrating sadness."[54]

Grief work is no picnic, but it offers such sweet relief. One way to ease into grief work is the practice of micro-mourning as described by Dian Killian, co-author of *Connecting across Differences.*

> Mourning is a key element in transformation. Especially if we're stuck. Micro-mourning, as I call it, is just noticing where you are – confused and overwhelmed, without trying to shift it or trying to make it different than what it is. I can just say, "Wow, I'm just really overwhelmed at this point, and I don't know what to do…" That can also lead to a release of the energy because any kind of demand energy creates tension. When our bodies are tense, it's harder to make decisions, and we don't notice all the choices that are available. At a very pragmatic level, staying with the mourning of not knowing what to do creates an opening energetically. It gives you some space. A great number us of go pretty quickly from, "I don't know what to do" to "I have to do *something*" and then, from this place of urgency or desperation, we choose a strategy that's not an effective contribution to ourselves or others. I'd rather sit with I *don't* know, which can release the contraction and tension."[55]

Healing

If the world is to be healed through human efforts, I am convinced it will be by ordinary people whose love for this life is even greater than their fear. – Joanna Macy

In many cultures we give away our power by relying heavily on professionals, but there are many ways we can heal ourselves. Our original woundedness – the first time we find out that we're not okay – haunts us until we reclaim the vitality connected to our original experience. Loneliness can exacerbate the pain of the wound and perpetuate disconnection and powerlessness. The first cut

[54] Jeyanthy Siva personal interview 3/7/08. http://www.europeanpwn.net/index.php?article_id=218
[55] Dian Killian personal interview with Lynda Cowan Smyth 3/13/08. http://bnvc.org

goes deep, and we often protect ourselves from further pain by shutting down. Fortunately, we can respond to this underlying fear and vulnerability by embracing our earliest unmet needs. This path of transformation can be thorny but liberating. We can expect to turn our lives inside out as we alter our belief systems, uncover the deepest motivation of our behavior, create reverence for our essence, and honor new choices. Once we open to this spiritual investigation, there's no turning back as we expand our loving relationships with self, others, and higher power.

Healing comes when we turn toward our pain rather than away from it. We breathe into our woundedness and stay with the raw pain with the same attentiveness we'd give to a great work of art or someone on their death bed. If we blame someone for the pain or we want revenge, we just notice the bodily sensations without pushing them away. When we attend to the injury, releasing all the pressure to change it or fix it, love unfolds from that place of hurt. Instead of telling ourselves to get over it, we get into it, by completely accepting all the feelings connected to the wound. Underneath the hurt is a prayer or a longing that connects us to wonder and awe. That opens us to sacred possibilities, which feed us and reveal new direction. Woundedness becomes a sacred passage toward self-intimacy. The open, vulnerable body is the entry way to the temple

Extraordinary healing opportunities live in each of us. Even after much inner work, most of us continue to find new pockets of pain that we can release. The flip side of woundedness is that it can also be the source of our power. While recovering from woundedness, we're in touch with our innate ability to heal, which puts us in the extraordinary position of being able to support other's healing while we manifest our own. In the same way that teachers teach what they want to learn, we heal ourselves when we open ourselves to supporting other's healing. Healing is a part of radical self-care which is inextricably linked to healing and caring for others. Mutual healing has far more possibilities than healing alone.

Healing Trauma in Groups

> One brief way of describing the change which has taken place in me is to say that in my early professional years I was asking the question: How can I treat, or cure, or change this person? Now I would phrase the question in this way: How can I provide a relationship which this person may use for his own personal growth? — Carl Rogers

Working to heal trauma in a group can be far more intense than one-on-one healing work because people have high needs for safety and security to release long-term suffering. It takes a lot of peripheral awareness to hold a group while doing deep healing work with an individual. Publicly releasing the emotions of trauma can elicit shame. If we invite people to expose their pain and suffering, we need to be very careful to create real safety before doing deep healing work. We can start by offering a road map. If we explain the process and why we're doing what we're doing, we give people a sense of predictability and increase the level of safety. By letting the group know what to expect in terms of possible moments of stuckness, chaos, deep pain, or the wide range of ways that people release suffering, we provide a sense of reassurance.

We add to the sense of inclusion if we give group members something to do, whether we ask them to hold loving consciousness, point their awareness toward body language, take notes on phrases that stand out, breathe deeply if they experience tension, or self-empathize if they notice judgment. When we give people options about where to direct their awareness, they can self-connect. Otherwise they may downplay their discomfort or direct their frustration toward the facilitator or other group members, which gives us more to hold.

While holding the container for healing, we can also hold the space for learning opportunities. Multiple teaching points arise in the set-up and the debriefing, but it's a little more difficult to awaken people to learning opportunities during the healing process. One way to do this is to invite our co-facilitator to make brief process comments aloud or on the flip chart, such as:

- Notice that the facilitator gives plenty of time for self-reflection.
- Watch the way she mirrors body language.
- What changed in her voice?
- Come closer if you can't hear.
- If you're finding this stressful, self-empathize by connecting with your feelings and needs.

Comments about the process help observers feel more included, and help the person doing the deep healing work to trust that they are making a contribution to the group. Before beginning, we can ask everyone to hold the space for transformation and ask for specific support from group members – someone to hold time, another to deal with any intrusions, and another to support anyone who may become too distressed to stay in the room.

Sticking to time constraints can be difficult since we never know how long healing might take. So in the set-up, we can give the group an opportunity to make conscious choices about how the group honors time, instead of individuals autonomously making choices about their other time commitments. If we're working within an agreed time frame, we can get permission from the group to add more time, reconvene later, or continue with part of the group.

Much of the time, we're juggling multiple balls in the air which can include ascertaining the will of the group, asking and testing for agreement, creating a sense of belonging for all, and holding shared leadership. At the same time we're spinning plates, creating openings for teaching points, harvesting learning opportunities, all while honoring time agreements.

Whatever happens, we need to save time at the end for the group to process their experience since everyone in the group is affected emotionally by trauma work. If you don't process trauma work, observers take the trauma out of the room with them which reverberates throughout many people's lives. If we sense a strong reaction, we can put people into pairs to share their experience before debriefing in the group.[56]

---

[56] This section on Healing Trauma in Groups evolved from a discussion with Philomena Moriarty and Sam Trumbore on 8/26/08.

Spiritual Dimension

> *Spirituality is that sphere of experience that lies beyond the commonplace world of our surface lives and that opens our awareness to the ultimate and core realities of existence. There are two realms of spirituality. They are distinct yet complimentary. Together they form a whole. Either alone is incomplete.*
>
> *One realm (spirit)...turns upward toward the light, ...helps us to disidentify from the commotion of the strategic mind so we can reclaim the inner quiet, peace, and wholeness of our true nature. It is about cultivating the blissful experience of being fully present in the moment and one with all creation.*
>
> *The other realm (soul) leads not upward toward God but downward toward the dark center of our individual selves and into the fruitful experience of nature...it shows us where and how to make our stand. On this half of the spiritual journey, we do not rise toward heaven but fall toward the center of our longing.*[57] —Bill Plotkin

The soul is the unique consciousness or core essence of an individual, while spirit is the light that permeates all things, the universal love that connects one soul to another. To experience the fullness of life, both our soul and spirit need to flourish. Spiritual renewal comes from recovering our longing for meaning, bringing our unique gifts fully into the world, and expressing our full selves. When we engage with people's yearning for change, we uncover their deep desire for belonging, love, and a sense of oneness.

Soul embraces the essence of our particular individuality, the essence unique to each of us. People often refer to soul as the "real me," because it taps what is most wild and natural in each of us. Spirit is the life force or animating energy that underlies and is the cause of all creation. When people experience the interconnectedness of life, they experience themselves and interact with the world in ways that are more connected. This spirit, God, or life force is referenced in many traditions.

I consider it vital to stay alert to how Spirit moves through the group. Others may call it something else, but the practice of seeing each individual as a manifestation of God keeps me in a state of awe and wonder. My faith in the possibilities, trust in people, and confidence in the outcome stem from my openness to all that is mystical, magical, and evolutionary. An exquisite example is Kanya Likanasudh's description of a workshop in Thailand:

> I facilitated a workshop for the Foundations of Friends of Women for 24 counselors who work with abused women. They came from all over Thailand. When I found out the workshop coincided with a national religious holiday, I felt

---

[57] Plotkin, B. (2003). *Soulcraft: Crossing into the mysteries of nature and psyche.* New World Library.

so much freakin' pressure. Moreover, these people were "ordered" by their bosses to come, which goes against my value for choice. I was sweating because this was my very first NVC workshop.

On Saturday we were supposed to be in session until 9:00 pm. In the afternoon, a woman asked my "permission" to end the session at 5pm so people could go to the temple to circumambulate, part of the ritual of this Buddhist holiday. In Thai culture, it took a lot for this woman to make this request in front of the whole group because she was breaking from the pack. I didn't want to make a unilateral decision, which is the habit in this hierarchical culture—I wanted the group to make the decision. So I asked her to she asked the group. People were shy, but people who spoke all agreed with her. They wanted to go to the temple. Then a man spoke between his teeth and said, "This is a Buddhist holiday and there are Christians and Muslims in this room." I knew right away that this sentence was loaded. So I asked if someone could guess his feelings and needs.

Their guesses were thoughts and strategies, not feelings and needs. Then the director of this foundation started to say that religion is such a sensitive issue and it's really hard to talk about this because we each have different point of view. As gently as I could, I interrupted her and asked for her to hold her thoughts for a moment while we were guessing the man's feelings and needs. I was scared because I broke off from the hierarchical norms. She was higher in position than I was and older, so I was not supposed to interrupt her. Finally, someone put together a feeling and a need and the man smiled and his face became relaxed. He said he felt so good to be understood. I sensed the energy in the room was so alive! People were experiencing the power of NVC.

The man wanted choice—for people who don't want to go the temple to not have to go, and also for us to still get through all of the material we were learning. The woman who brought this issue up said she wanted the same thing. I asked everyone to hold silence and take a few breaths as this was a crucial moment in any conflict when the two people could see each other's needs and humanity, regardless of strategy.

After that exchange, it took us less than 5 minutes to come up with a solution: we would not take a long break in the afternoon and have dinner 1/2 hour later. People felt good that they'd come up with a solution that worked for everybody and I was feeling smug and thinking, "Yeah, it worked!"

Then another participant, let's call her Lek said, "But I was hoping to go to work during break." I thought, "Oh my god, here we go again." I sensed agitation in the room and in myself.

The boss who earlier lectured about the delicate nature of discussing religion, said that this was such a small issue and the woman manager had enough power to order someone else to take her place.

However, Lek, who was older than the big boss and thus had higher ranking in age, stood firm and said she wanted to check with the people at her office. During the mini-break, she spoke to people at work and excitedly reported back to the group, "I made an observation, feeling, need, and request to the people at work and, with some juggling on their part, they are WILLING to take our places. I want to try out what we are learning. I want to make a request rather than an order. It feels so good to know my subordinates were there because they are willing to rather than because I ordered them to."

Throughout this dialog, my translator mimicked my movements. I got up, she got up. I sat down, she sat down. I had a sense that we had become one. Sometimes my sentences would come out in Thai, sometimes in English, sometimes in "Thenglish". The translator did not miss a beat and explained, "I needed to take on your energy in order to translate it." I learned to trust the process. I don't need to have the answers. To be in the moment and experience the synergy helped the group build the quality of connection that allowed us to come up with the solution we came up with. Instead of describing the process, we all had experiential learning. The air was thick, and the connection between people was palpable. Partly I think it was the warmth that I have for the people there, but I also felt the presence of what Christians might call Holy Spirit, or Samboghakaya in Tibetan Buddhism, a sense of something higher.[58]

Is it any wonder that Kanya's connection to herself, her translator, and the participants paves the way to connecting with something higher? Nothing happens without connection. Action complements the deep work in the realm of soul and spirit. The soul and spirit find fulfillment in taking action. There is a world of difference between action for its own sake and action where there is alignment of body, mind, emotion, soul, and spirit.

Working with the Natural World

Listening to the natural world deepens the quality of our connections. My business partner, Virginia Kellogg, helps people connect with nature as a portal to the soul. One of her clients told me, "I live in the city. I am not 'nature girl'. So I was amazed that Virginia got me to do things in nature that I never thought I'd enjoy. I am glowing." Virginia describes the value of getting people out of their habitual environment and into a natural environment:

---

[58] Kanya Likanasudh personal interview 4/29/08.

Nature gives us an easy and powerful way to work in the realm of soul. The wildness of nature matches the inner nature of the soul. Even a small amount of time in a wild place will begin to awaken the soul.

I send clients on nature walks or for quiet time in the wild. First we create a context for this experience by crafting a question to sit with. Sometimes they have a conversation with something in nature (or the earth itself). We structure the time for talking and then listening. They notice that nature is a mirror and step into silence and openness in order to see themselves.

This work in nature is about opening to the possibility that the entire universe is a resource for growth. The earth is waiting to be in relationship with us all, and stepping into that relationship can bring profound insight and knowledge. The beauty of vision questing is that people move into a ritual space that removes distractions and invites them into deep conversation with the Sacred Other and their soul. Solitude, poetry, storytelling, dance, drumming, chanting, artwork and dreamwork also call out the deepest soul stirrings, help people make sense of themselves in a less heady way, and touch deeper into who they are.

Exercises

Reflections:
1. What empowering questions from page 391 stand out for you that you would like to ask yourself?
2. What unfinished grief would you like to explore in yourself? Make a list of anything you still have grief about and mourn fully. Celebrate your sadness.
3. How do you create space for mourning and self-connection without encouraging wallowing in despair?

Small Group Discussions:
1. Complete the "Tell Your Vision" worksheet in the resource section on page 417, and tell a friend about your vision.
2. Choose an incident that doesn't sit well with you. List the needs of your inner chooser. List the needs of your inner educator. Empathize with both sets of needs and look for new strategies that could meet *both* sets of needs.
3. In small groups discuss the first time you learned that you were not okay? How is your deepest wound also your greatest gift?

Activities:

1. Review the Supportive/ Empowerment table on page 121. With your coaching partner, start your coaching session with ten minutes of support (left column) and the last ten minutes of empowerment (right column). Share feedback with each other about the impact of supportive vs. empowering coaching.

2. Choose one:
   - Journal until you've identified your unique purpose.
   - Walk until you've identified your soul purpose.
   - Weave together metaphors until you've identified your soul purpose.

3. Complete the "Liberate your Dream" worksheet in the resource section on page 401, and celebrate your dream.

Chapter 8
Facilitation Models

You must learn to be still in the midst of activity and to be vibrantly alive in repose. — Indira Gandhi

Although we may find several facilitation models we love, we end up tweaking them based on our experience, or we create a model of our own. I like to work with multiple models so that I can choose the one that is most likely to meet the needs of the group. Some facilitation processes that I find meaningful are Nonviolent Communication, Appreciative Inquiry, Dynamic Facilitation, FIRED UP, and Empathic Mediation.

Nonviolent Communication

The purpose of Nonviolent Communication is to facilitate heart connection and compassion. The process offers three ways to build connection: through honest self-expression – sharing in ways that inspire compassion; empathy – listening with compassion, and self-empathy – practicing self-compassion.

Empathy involves understanding the essence of another's experience, connecting with the heart and reflecting the speaker's feelings and needs. This practice fosters understanding, whether we're empathizing with another or with ourselves, and can be done silently or aloud. Empathy often relieves distress, which helps the person become more available to hearing another. The four steps of Marshall Rosenberg's model are 1) observations, 2) feelings, 3) needs and 4) requests. As simple as it sounds, many people have found it takes years to master because by connecting with the heart of each step, we're actually changing decades of habitual, judgmental ways of responding. If you'd like to hear the four steps in action, check out an entertaining demonstration delivered by Sam Trumbore and Philomena Moriarty during a Sunday service at http://www.trumbore-media.org/podcast/Making-Peace-with-Each-Other.mp3[59] or go to http://NVCTraining.com for additional recordings. Practice groups, empathy partners, and journaling are all ways to support the change to more heart-centered communication. Former baseball player Tony Scruggs describes his journey toward heart connection:

> In the major leagues I played baseball with people making millions of dollars.
> They had everything and did not appear to be happy. By age 24 I had reached all

---

[59] Sam Trumbore and Philomena Moriarty's NVC demonstration at UU Church 10/10/08

of my goals, and I thought, now what? I walked into a bookstore and for the first time in my academic career, I did not have anyone telling me what I had to read. As I started reading Tony Robbins, Wayne Dyer, Deepak Chopra, and Eckhart Tolle, I began integrating the concepts of transformation, oneness, abundance, detachment, present moment awareness, and synchronicity. A floodgate of tools transformed my life. I lived in the raw possibilities beyond right and wrongdoing. It's been a decade-long journey of integration, since that original stroll into that bookstore, as the tools are now a part of my consciousness and my life. For the past few years, I've been boiling with excitement, ready to explode. Overflowing with childlike enthusiasm, I've been wanting to help people shift their emotional state and support their awakening.

At the same time I've experienced an inner restlessness, so when I met Marshall Rosenberg, I thought, "Wow dude, you are so totally speaking to me." After ten minutes with him, my intent towards other people went from, "Here's what I believe you should do to make your life better," to, *"I'm open to wherever you are, right now."* He gave me a bridge from my island of tools to go anywhere I wanted to go. I'm still excited about contributing to other people's well-being, but instead of holding them with the subtle demand of "knowing what will help them," my way of being with them is as an offering. Instead of preaching to the choir, Nonviolent Communication has given me a way to be with people that's new, that's more in alignment with the way I want to be. In spite of the richness of all the other teachings, the missing piece, for me, was the communion, the real heart connection, which happened by accident before, but now I call on it consciously. Before, heart connection would happen, and it felt really wonderful, but I had no real idea how we got there. Now I live there, and I have more of a sense of empowerment and choice. I hit the ground running because my island now has a drawbridge that enables me to connect with anybody at any moment.[60]

The rest of this section on Nonviolent Communication is an excerpt of an article I wrote for Group Facilitation Magazine, *Difficult Conversations: Authentic Communication Leads to Greater Understanding and Teamwork,* where I'm introducing NVC to facilitators who work in a business setting.

Difficult conversations can lead to crisis or harmony. The Chinese word for crisis combines two symbols: danger and opportunity. When it comes to challenging conversations, we usually only remember the first meaning, danger. Real conversations can become highly emotional, trigger old battle wounds, and motivate us to confront, freeze, bolt, or attempt to smooth things over. Or we can choose lively, caring discussions to explore the tension and discover new options. The piano maker Theodore Steinway said, "In one of our concert grand pianos, 243 taut strings exert a pull of 40,000

---

[60] Tony Scruggs personal interview with Lynda Cowan Smith 4/8/08.

pounds on an iron frame. It is proof that out of great tension may come great harmony." Authentic communication can turn tension into creativity and harmony.

Imagine yourself at a tense planning meeting where the financial director reports, "We need to lay off 20% of the workforce." The marketing director responds, "That's the stupidest thing I've ever heard. We need to lay *you* off so we can hire new people who are serious about growing the business." Are you ready to add fuel to the fire, would you prefer to crawl under your chair, or do you have the skills to facilitate an authentic, productive conversation?

How do we develop facilitation skills so that we can embrace challenging conversations rather than avoid them? First, we need an effective process that leads to understanding and productivity. While smoothing things over may look quick and easy, in the long run, radical honesty and directness help teams perform at their highest potential. Roger Schwarz, author of the *Skilled Facilitator*, says that most meeting facilitators call for a break when the emotional energy escalates, but skilled facilitators know they've hit "pay dirt." Intense emotions mean that people are talking about what matters most. Emotions serve as a barometer indicating the level of importance.

Support and understanding are two of the most important universal needs, but we often sweep them under the rug, telling ourselves that we don't have time for that nonsense, especially in a fast-paced workplace. But the sense that "I matter, you matter, we matter," gives rise to high-functioning work groups that improve relationships, build team spirit, and contribute to the growth of the organization. Steve Bates, a writer for HR magazine, says, "...study after study indicates that employee emotions are fundamentally related to—and actually drive—bottom-line success in a company." Emotions are directly connected to whether our needs are met or unmet.

Figure 8.1

Components of Nonviolent Communication	
Observations	Observations differ from judgments. Observations are what we see and hear in a videotape vs. what we think, judge, or evaluate.
Feelings	Feelings are not the same as what we are thinking. Feelings are our emotions or gut reactions vs. interpretations of what someone is doing to us.
Needs	Needs are universal desires that are separate from strategies, positions, or ways to get our needs met. Our needs are our internal longing, not what others should do.
Requests	Requests are strategies for getting needs met - very different from demands. Requests involve asking for what we want vs. insisting on what we want.

Everything we do or say is an attempt to meet our needs. Sometimes our positions for getting our needs met seem to be in conflict, such as "We need to hire more people" and "We need to fire more people." However, when we deepen our understanding of each other's needs, we open to new visions that can satisfy all parties. The key is to understand the needs fully first, and then come up with strategies that will meet everyone's needs.

In this model, instead of speaking in ways that alienate others, we connect by sharing our observations and reactions and by becoming aware of each other's needs. Rather than becoming attached to particular positions, we explore the underlying needs we hope to satisfy. From this shared awareness, we can request strategies that work for everyone.

What do these steps look like in practice? Let's apply them to the situation above, the planning meeting where layoffs are being considered. The financial director, Susan, has suggested laying off 20% of the staff; the marketing director, Jack, responds by questioning her ability and judgment. Noting that Jack seems the most agitated, you decide to address him first.

> You: Jack, when you heard Susan say that we should lay off 20% of the staff, (observation), I'm guessing you were feeling pretty alarmed (feeling), because you're concerned about the company's effectiveness and growth (need). Is that accurate? (request)
>
> Jack: Yes, she's clueless! Doesn't she know we're launching two new products this quarter? If we have any chance of success, it's crucial that we have adequate staff on board, especially in marketing!
>
> You: So hearing this plan (observation), you're really concerned (feeling) about the life of the company? (need)
>
> Jack: Yes, I care about the company—I've been here ten years. But I also care about my job and I can't do it without adequate staff. The last guy in her position made the same mistake and I ended up paying the price. Sales plummeted! We're still recovering, three years later.
>
> You: So you're worried about the company (feeling) but also want some understanding about what's involved in adequately marketing products? (need) You want the staffing and resources to do your job well, and feel confident about success. Is that right?
>
> Jack: Yes, that's it.

Having heard Jack's concerns, you now turn to Susan to see that she's understood what Jack has said. At first, she may need some help; it's not unusual, especially when tempers are high, for one person to hear a message very differently from what the other expressed. If you're not confident that Susan has heard Jack, you can check back with him and/or share with Susan what you have heard Jack say:

> You: Before we go on and I hear your concerns, Susan, I want to make sure that we have clarity about what Jack has said. Could you tell me what you heard him say?
>
> Susan: He said that I remind him of my predecessor and that I'm making the same mistakes he did. He thinks I'm screwing up.
>
> You: Thanks Susan. I'm glad I checked. What I heard Jack say is that he wants sufficient staff to successfully launch the new products this fall. He wants to build an effective department and is worried that he won't have the resources to do so. Can you tell me what you just heard me say?
>
> Susan: He wants to make sure his department can adequately market these new products.
>
> You: Right. That's what I understood. Jack, is that what you wanted to express?
>
> Jack: Yes. It's crucial that these new products do well.

Once you're confident that Susan has understood Jack, you can turn to her concerns. Wanting to include Jack, you can check with him first to see if he's ready to hear what Susan has to say:

> You: It's important to me that everyone is understood (need), so I'm wondering now Jack if you're ready to hear where Susan is coming from? (request)
>
> Jack: A little anxious, but ready...

After several rounds of listening to each other in this way, both see that they share similar objectives. They both care for the life of the company, fear for its future, and want to see the company succeed. Having heard each other, they come up with a mutually agreeable solution. Susan agrees to postpone any layoffs in the marketing department for six months, until after they launch the new product line. Jack also agrees to new sales targets and acknowledges that if they don't reach their goals, some layoffs may be necessary. Jack ends the meeting more motivated than ever to market the new line. Susan has a greater understanding and appreciation of the challenges that Jack faces in his department and agrees to involve his input in the future.

It may take several rounds of guessing feelings and needs before both parties feel understood. Once the needs are on the table, you can encourage all those involved to make requests that honor each other's needs. Because they feel understood, each person involved is much more likely to listen to the other's ideas and create strategies that work for everyone.

The outline above can be visually summarized in this model shown in Figure 8.2.

Figure 8.2 NVC Distinctions

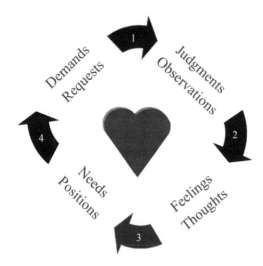

The inner options in green (observations, feeling, needs, and requests) represent ways of connecting with energizing, productive forces. The outer options in red (judgment, thought, positions, demands) represent alienating forces or habitual ways of communicating. The four steps and choices are:

1. Stimulus: We can either pass moral judgment or notice our observations.
2. Reaction: We can attune to what we're thinking or what we're feeling.
3. Awareness: We can decide on a position or explore what we need.
4. Action: We can choose between making a demand or make a request.

Let's explore the distinctions between observations and judgments. The statement, "Derek is a poor manager," at first might sound like an observation. As far as you're concerned, it's a fact: Derek is simply not doing a good job—anyone who worked with him would agree. But this statement in fact offers no clear observations; all we are given is an evaluative word, "poor." A clean observation might sound something like, "Derek tore up the report, pounded his fist on the table, and did not say goodbye when he left." Or perhaps your evaluation comes from more subtle observations, such as "Derek raised his eyebrows when one of his employees made a suggestion." We don't know what the raised eyebrows mean unless we check. When we state what really happened instead of telling people what we imagine is going on, we reduce the likelihood of defensiveness and open the door to authentic conversations.

As facilitators we help individuals translate evaluations, labels, and assumptions into pure observations. So if someone claims another is wrong, domineering, sexist, liberal, brilliant, or evil, we help them unpack their judgments and support them in identifying what is actually happening. We do this by asking for data and hard facts. We can test observations by asking what a video camera would capture. Honing in on what people *actually do and say* helps people release their stories they have about each other.

In many organizational cultures authenticity suffers because people think they have to check their feelings at the door, but in actuality, everyone is always feeling something. When people equate emotions with being needy or weak, they often avoid expressing themselves fully. In cultures where feelings are off limits, I sometimes show a tape of Martin Luther King trembling during his "I Have a Dream" speech so that we can see how full emotional expression helps us connect with the speaker. Feelings reveal our needs, wants and desires, which lead to understanding, collaboration, and team work.

If we are not accustomed to identifying and articulating our feelings, we can confuse feeling with thinking. How often have you heard "I feel manipulated" or "I feel like leaving," or "I feel that this conversation is going nowhere?" These are all examples of using the word "feeling" to describe what we are thinking. Manipulated is not a feeling; it's what I *think* someone is doing to me. Whenever I say, "I feel that... I feel you... I feel like... I feel as if...," you know you're about to hear what I'm thinking, not what I am feeling. To connect with what I'm feeling instead of what I'm thinking I can ask myself, "How do I feel when I *think* that someone is manipulating me?"

The list above includes words about what we "think" another person is doing to us. We can translate any of these interpretations of others' actions into feelings and needs. For instance, when I say, "I feel manipulated," it may be that I'm feeling disappointed and needing independence and choice. When we face a crisis, we often rush headlong into the solution, without discovering what really happened, without connecting with our feelings and needs or to the feelings and needs of others.

Taking the time to discover what we really need results in long-term solutions that work for more people. The Chilean economist Manfred Max-Neef suggests that there are only nine basic needs: subsistence, protection/security, affection, understanding, participation, leisure, creation, identity/meaning and freedom. The needs are "the same in all cultures and all historical periods."[61] The language that we use to describe these needs changes. The needs are the same, but we may choose different words to describe them to different people. The language that resonates in business cultures is different from the language I use when talking to fellow facilitators. Instead of talking about observations, feelings, needs and requests, I ask about highlights, reactions, challenges and requests in a business setting. Even though I'm more comfortable using words that are familiar to *me*, using *their* language builds trust and empathic connection. There are many words that describe variations of our basic needs, such as values, wants, desires, cravings, or longings. We can help people get clarity by separating our needs from the thousands of strategies we might choose from to get our needs met. One of the ways that people entangle themselves in challenging conversations is when they insist on a position or premature strategy without understanding the needs. Although every action is an attempt to meet a need, team members often take very different positions for

---

[61] Max-Neef, M. & Ekins, P. (1992). *Real-life economics: Understanding wealth creation.* London: Routledge.

meeting those needs. They can lose sight of those core needs if they get caught up arguing the merits of this position versus that position. Both Susan and Jack had different positions (hiring and firing) for meeting similar needs. When people insist on a specific solution before they have explored all the needs from all departments, plans are usually poorly conceived, poorly received, and poorly executed.

When we discover and understand all the needs first, the resulting solutions are much more effective and satisfying to all involved. We get buy-in and cooperation that result in long-term productivity. "I need more money in the budget, and I need you to work longer hours," are not needs; they're tactics for getting needs met. To guess the actual needs we might ask, "Do you need more options and more support?"

We also have a choice when it comes to making demands or requests. We can announce "It's my way or the highway," but that only invites submission or rebellion, not teamwork. Alternatively, we can ask for what we want with a willingness to revise our positions. Requests invite options, and better strategies evolve when people recognize they have a full range of choices.

Although Rosenberg's model is simple, it only works if we follow one of Stephen Covey's principles, "Seek first to understand, then to be understood." Imagine accepting frustration, complaints, and rebellion as gifts. Instead of hearing an outburst as a judgment, you can listen curiously for the unmet needs simmering just below the emotions. Instead of seeing co-workers as whiners, you can see them as hungry to get their needs met. When your boss is furious, ask yourself, "What unmet need is the driving force?" When you connect with what others want, you can help them move away from blame and toward productive strategies. When *you're* scared, what do you really want? Probably you need reassurance and effectiveness, among other needs.

Feelings and needs awareness is a fundamental skill for today's leaders who are shifting from paternalism to partnership. Such partnership means mutual respect and that employees are included and engaged at full capacity. Many leaders are unsure how to engage employees fully, but powerful questions can get you started: How do you feel? What do you need? What energizes you? Several research firms have found that roughly half of the workers in America show up and do what's expected of them but don't go the extra mile. "Employees want to commit to companies, because doing so satisfies a powerful and basic human need to connect with and contribute to something significant," says Carol Kinsey Goman of Kinsey Consulting Services. When we connect with what energizes employees, we can quickly get to the heart of the matter; doing so helps workers engage fully and improve their performance. By listening for feelings and unmet needs, we can collaborate to find strategies that work for all of us. When we listen to each other with respect and curiosity, we appreciate each other's contributions and build on opportunities for expanding the vision. When we engage in passionate wholehearted conversations, we pave the way for win-win solutions, shared vision, and higher productivity. This is not possible in a culture that expects people to leave their honest feelings and their humanity at home.

Appreciative Inquiry

Throughout the organization development field, there's an emphasis on changing how people work together—how they communicate, resolve conflict, solve problems, and learn. But there is very little emphasis on changing how people think, except in the area of Appreciative Inquiry (AI), which focuses on the life force of an organization and helps people put their attention on what they want to create. Developed by David Cooperrider and Suresh Srivastava at Case Western Reserve University, AI is a social change process that has had a far-reaching impact in both nonprofits and corporations. The practice of inquiring into organizations changes them. The seeds of change—that is, the things people think and talk about, the things people discover and learn, and the things that inform dialogue and inspire images of the future—are implicit in the very first questions we ask.[62] Appreciative Inquiry brings together large groups of people to mobilize collective imagination and collaboration. This energizing process has been deeply influential both inside and outside the Organization Development world. The process leads to new innovations and projects that elevate organizational performance and bring communities together.

Appreciative Inquiry is a process for connecting with the life force of individuals and groups that allows new possibilities to emerge. We ask empowering questions that awaken the full potential of the organization. Instead of focusing on what's wrong, we can choose to focus on what's already working well or on what is possible. That does not mean we step over problems. Instead we use the issues that arise to co-create new opportunities for learning and new ways of interacting. AI offers an upbeat alternative to consultants who look for problems to solve. The process is based on:

- attention to what is most energizing or fosters aliveness
- strengths-based approach that leverages what's already working
- storytelling process that fosters connection
- process that empowers people to have a profound impact without a lot of training

Four Phases of Appreciative Inquiry

1. Discovery – Appreciating

In the discovery phase, we clarify values and use storytelling to capture the best of *what is*. We discover what gives life and energy to the organization. We start by asking people to interview each other in pairs, gather stories that capture memorable experiences, and discover organizational strengths and assets. Sharing and collecting these stories helps build organizational capacity by valuing and expanding on the best of what already exists. As we collect these stories, we can ask ourselves the following questions:

- *When it comes to your organization, what do you take pride in?*
- *What energizes people?*
- *What are the best stories about the organization?*

---

[62] Cooperrider, D & Whitney, D. (2008). *Appreciative inquiry handbook.* Berret-Kohler. p.103.

2. Dream – Envisioning

In the dream phase, we get out our magic wands and imagine *what might be*. Together we think big and share our hopes for our work and our relationships. We look at individual and organizational calling to explore our greater purpose and deepest wishes. In this phase, we act out our dreams to dramatize the possibilities and stretch the imagination.

Questions for this phase:

- *What is the world calling your organization to do?*
- *If you had no constraints, what new possibilities would you explore?*
- *If you surrounded yourselves with life-giving forces, what would that look like?*

3. Design – Co-constructing

In the design phase large numbers of people come together to co-create the future organization. In small groups we explore the lofty images of the dream stage and determine what's possible. We align values, structures, systems, and mission with the ideal by talking about *what should be*. In this phase, the team crafts provocative propositions which stretch the organization. We design by exploring possible actions and making choices that will create a more desirable future.

Questions for this phase:

- *What choices can turn our dreams into reality?*
- *How does each piece look in an optimal system?*
- *To create a more desirable future, what actions do you choose?*

4. Delivery – Sustaining

In the delivery phase we develop action plans to realize the provocative propositions. In an open forum, we ask employees to determine their contribution and how they wish to serve. We establish personal and organizational commitments to fulfill these contributions and determine *what will be*. Small groups collaborate on the new initiatives that grow out of this process. Because people are deeply involved in the first three phases, commitment and alignment come easily in the fourth phase.

Questions for the delivery phase:

- *What action plan do you need to put into place to create a wonderful future?*
- *How can you bring about lasting cultural change?*
- *What do you need to do to sustain your preferred future?*

Sara Orem, author of the book *Appreciative Coaching*, told me about her early days of using Appreciative Inquiry.

> I worked in a bank that had just gone through downsizing, and the workforce was pretty wrung out. As the change agent, I was responsible for marshalling the troops, but gathering got harder and harder. Changes were imposed – people had no choice. They were tired.

When I first started using Appreciative Inquiry, new energy came into the room – the talk, interaction, enthusiasm, and willingness to engage shifted. I could viscerally feel it in my body – my anxiety lowered and my feet were tingling in anticipation. Asking participants what they were proud of created an entirely different electricity in the room. They were willing, even anxious, to talk about how to use things they were good at to create something new and different.

I thought, "If this works in a room of 1500 people, it's got to work one-to-one. Since I wrote my book *Appreciative Coaching,* new research shows that it's easier for us to change the synapses in our brains when we look at what we've already done well. It's much more difficult to change by looking at what we don't do well.

We don't ask people to talk about their successes nearly enough. Exploring peak experiences, they say, "Nobody has ever asked me about this before. I haven't thought about his in 20 years. I feel calmer than I've felt in 3 months," just as a result of thinking about something they were really proud of doing.

I started to use it in all kinds of places to see if worked all over. When I started using AI on myself, I felt a sense of gratitude for the method. In a community of practice, while subcontracting with a small consulting firm, 12 of us would meet once a month about our learning. We asked people to engage around the four AI questions:

What gives life to you now?

What are your peak experiences?

What do you value about yourself?

What do you want to be different?

While I enjoy the butterfly nature of exploring, it's also frustrating. AI isn't appropriate all the time. It's not the only thing that works. If the organization is so full of conflict that they can't even talk to each other, forget it.

When an HR director calls me in because the COO has to learn to be a better speaker, I know that's not the place where I will start. I start with exploring times when that person has been in a public place and knew something that works. That's what I want to build on.

My short attention span was a problem for so much of my adult life. People would say, "Decide what you want to be when you grow up and be it." I don't think I'm a creator. I'm an integrator. I used to put myself down. I thought creators were brilliant. They have courage that is rare. I look for ideas that excite me. My

thinking shifted when I started valuing my vast range of experience and noticing my ability to integrate.[63]

Awakening groups and organizations to their energizing forces gives everyone a lift and supports the change process. Occasionally I work with groups who just can't go there. Their pain is palpable and they need some space to grieve before they can move toward celebration. Blending Appreciative Inquiry with the practice of empathy gives us the best of both worlds.

By expanding what people do best, new conversations and deeper connections emerge. Transforming the beliefs that people hold about themselves changes how they act. We can change an organization's belief systems by crafting and seeding catalytic questions that generate unconditional positive regard and elicit generative thinking that results in long-lasting change efforts.

Dynamic Facilitation

Jim Rough developed a transformational approach to wrestle with complex issues which he calls Dynamic Facilitation (DF). A major advantage of this approach is working with participants "as they are." They don't have to learn a special language or abide by elaborate ground rules. As DF facilitators, we create the container for transformation by taking an active role without being directive. We do this by encouraging people to speak their truth openly while still providing safety for everyone.

By ensuring that participants feel completely understood, facilitators enable them to focus their attention on listening to others. Unlike many styles of facilitation, in this approach we start by asking for solutions. People come into the meeting with solutions in response to the challenges and pain. So we help participants purge what they already know and listen deeply to their solutions, which creates space for fresh ideas. If people complain or have a problem with other's solutions, we encourage them to offer their own solutions.

As we record what each person says, without pointing out the shortcomings of the ideas, each person becomes a valued contributor. When we listen deeply to people, their posture and body language changes as soon as they feel fully understood. They visibly relax and their voices soften. If we are aware of the signals, we can sense when to stop drawing someone out because they've searched in their heart, have found what they want to say, and feel satisfied that others understand because they can see it up on the chart.

If we allow conversations to emerge, groups naturally move through three stages on their own without the facilitator cajoling or pushing them through steps of a process. The three stages of Dynamic Facilitation are:

1. Purging: sharing what we already know
2. Transition: feeling discomfort at not knowing what to do with all that's been said
3. Excitement: sensing creative possibilities emerging

---

[63] Sara Orem personal interview 2/28/08.

In the *first* stage of purging what participants already know, we draw them out, help them feel heard, and record their contributions. We create a mind map, capturing the essence of what everyone says, using *their* language on one of four flip charts:

1. problem statements or inquiries
2. solutions or ideas
3. concerns or difficulties
4. data or perspectives

Charting each person's contribution helps people feel understood. By purging preconceived solutions we give people a chance to let go. We welcome complaints because every concern has a potential solution behind it.

In the *second* stage, the group faces the challenge of how to make sense of the walls full of chart paper. The discomfort of this stage is palpable but doesn't last long. A few minutes can feel like hours. Instead of rescuing them from their discomfort, we hold the creative tension. Silence can be our most empowering option. Simply waiting and trusting the *not knowing,* inevitably leads to creative inspiration. People start to pop with new ideas, saying things like, "Whoa! I just had a crazy idea… We could…" Even if the idea isn't the perfect solution, the shift in energy sparks additional solutions.

In the *third* stage, we keep recording individual contributions, but new creative ideas are flowing, and the group senses that something new is emerging. We welcome every idea, recognizing that they could be part of the puzzle.

Dynamic facilitation assures choice creating because we:

- invite people to speak authentically from the heart
- protect creativity by turning judgment into concerns or solutions
- follow the energy while inviting caring, curiosity, and creativity
- celebrate self-organizing shifts and breakthroughs
- capture new insights and solutions

We welcome everything that's said, recognizing how much people care and that their distress could be a gift in disguise. Yet we actively intervene at the micro level to support each participant's contribution. In their *Dynamic Facilitation Manual and Reader,* Rosa Zubizaretta and Jim Rough give an example, "If someone interrupts during a sensitive moment, the facilitator might say, 'Excuse me, I really want to listen to what you are saying, but first I want to make sure that I have really heard what this other person has to say.' As soon as the facilitator has finished with the first person, he or she will turn back to the person who was interrupting to listen and draw out that person's contributions in full. Or, depending on the circumstances, the facilitator might redirect their attention to someone who is in obvious distress, and then come back to the person who was originally speaking. Regardless of who goes first, the larger point is that each person will be heard, and it is the facilitator's job to hear each person fully."[64]

We also protect people from judgment by asking them to state the problem or concern. Sometimes we place ourselves physically between two participants in order to interrupt a volley, debate, or judgment. We might say, "I really want to hear what each of you is saying so I can record your ideas, but I can only listen to one person at a time." Instead of judging people as "interrupters" or "overly emotional," we simply notice that they are overflowing and they too want to be heard. When we see the genius behind the whine or complaint, we shift to new ground. We advocate for each voice to be heard and actively protect participants from anger by inviting them to direct intense emotions toward us and welcoming their contributions with unconditional receptivity. As a result people feel safe. Jim Rough values authentic dialogue and describes a time when he worked with a group that was concerned about terrorism:

> As the conversation began, one woman criticized every idea offered. Seeking her solution, I asked, "What would you do?" She started to give me an answer that sounded a lot like what others were saying – bolster security, strengthen the borders. Talking from her head, these were logical answers. When I said, "your answers sound similar to the others," she sighed and settled into herself saying, "I'm just afraid... I don't know what to do." There was a period of silence. Everybody was there with her. No one was jumping in to speak. The rhythm of back and forth was gone. Finally somebody said, "When I feel like a terrorist, I just want to be listened to." Then the group found a whole new energy of possible solutions. Questions flew. How could we create a listener for the terrorists? How could *We the People* become the listener? Now we were accepting the transformational possibilities in the situation, in the terrorist, and in ourselves.

> Following the thread of her frustration opened everyone to realize the genuine fear. In the new spirit of openness, she recognized her own terrorist tendencies when she undermined the ideas of others. My job is to help the group go to this place of new openings. It's not brainstorming. It's more heart-stirring. We call this process "choice-creating."

> Most people think of creativity in a cognitive way. "Choice-creating" is creativity in a heart-felt way. It is transformational. From the experience of choice-creating each of us changes. If I'm in my head, I keep my distance from the problem. But the heartfelt creativity of choice-creating changes me, so that I leave different than when I came.

---

[64] Zubizaretta, R. & Rough, J. (2002). *Dynamic facilitation manual and reader.* http://www.diapraxis.com/dfmanual.html

Our culture is fundamentally structured to facilitate a level of conversation that involves discussion, debate, judgment, and battling for supremacy. I'm interested in shifting our quality of conversation and our thinking to "choice-creating," where everyone seeks what's best for all. To facilitate this high quality of thinking, I have to do my inner work. I need to know about this transformational potential in myself and others. I need to trust that from this high-quality of thinking doors will open. "Impossible" problems can be solved.[65]

The beauty of Dynamic Facilitation is that when participants are fully heard, a collective "aha" or sigh of relief comes when the group resonates with an insight that strikes a chord. This collective breakthrough experience leads to actions that the group is excited about implementing. When decisions emerge in this way, high energy and commitment come from the group's shared discoveries.

The Dynamic Facilitator's invitation is simple: "Trust me. Trust yourselves. Trust the process."[66] Just creating the conditions for reflection leads to self-organization. By trusting the process, we allow breakthroughs to happen. Simply by staying present to what is emerging and simultaneously letting go of any attachment we have to breakthroughs, transformation happens in its own way in its own time.

Another kindred spirit, Alan Seid, has developed a facilitation process that blends best practices from three worlds: Dynamic Facilitation, Nonviolent Communication, and Coaching:

I worked on a 20-year comprehensive plan for land use policy, where urban sprawl was the issue and the economy, jobs, and the environment were at stake. Loggers, business people, and hippies were all in one room without a facilitator. For 18 months, we worked on the plan. The animosity was thick, but we identified common ground and did some effective bridge-building.

From that experience I developed a new way of facilitating and shortly afterwards I worked with a co-housing group that really wanted to do things on their own and had resisted using facilitation for years. The results were mind-blowing. I labeled four flip charts, 1) Issues, Problems Data, Observations 2) Feelings, Needs, Values 3) Solutions, Broad Strategies and 4) Action Steps. The directionality goes from left to right, moving from the past to the present to the future. Everything that was said went up on the charts as I reflected back what they were saying. We started with problems and moved toward understanding each other and creating solutions and action steps.

The group had been stuck for years, but I empathized, kept my eye on people, and went with the energy of the group, asking "What do you have to say? Let's

---

[65] Jim Rough personal interview 3/18/08.
[66] Adapted from the Dynamic Facilitation Workshop with Jim and Jean Rough 2/5/08 and Zubizaretta, R. & Rough, J. (2002). *Dynamic facilitation manual and reader.* http://DynamicFacilitation.com

get it up on the sheet." They combined items on the third sheet and prioritized using a dot vote system. But when we got to the fourth sheet, I asked them to pull out their calendars. They froze. They were not expecting that because they were so entrenched in feeling good and not taking action. I could see people with lumps in their throats, so I connected with them right there. But they'd just had an authentic conversation, so they were able to move into action in a compassionate way. [67]

I find it heartening that so many facilitators come to similar conclusions via different pathways. I especially enjoy the creative experimentation and willingness to share evolving models that support personal, group, and social change. I have no doubt that the models we use are powerful structures that give us a sense of order; but it's the experience of being fully heard that opens people's hearts which is where new strategies emerge.

Here and Now - Experiencing the Moment

"All we have is right now." — Marca Cassity

I find the value of focusing on the here-and-now electrifying. Without it, no real connection takes place. Instead of languishing in the past or dreaming about the future, the now is an opportunity to get real about our current experience. Talking about someone else or somewhere else is an insult to the people who are present, to the rich exploration that is available to us right now. By focusing on the here-and-now, our authenticity comes into sharper focus and the opportunity for intimacy increases exponentially. Fear of intimacy is the primary reason that people take flight into there-and-then.

For instance, I was in the middle of debriefing a session with a co-facilitator when she started talking about her past experience with another co-facilitator who took more than ten opportunities to offer teaching points to the group. Knowing that people often take flight to there-and-then to ease into talking about what's going on in the here-and-now, I started to look at how her example might be similar to *our* dynamic in the now. Instantly I could feel some discomfort about the teaching tone I was using with her and got in touch with my desire to explore from a place of honoring each other's wisdom. When I shared this with her, she asserted that wasn't why she brought it up, but she could see what I was talking about and why I might have that discomfort. I pay attention to the discussion about the past and the future because it's always tied to the now. Similarly, talking about *others* is connected to *our* relationship, which can be very revealing. When people start talking about people they're angry with, attracted to, or hurt by, my ears perk up, because their memories are triggered by things that are happening right now.

---

[67] Alan Seid personal interview 10/07/08.

Facilitating the Process

Process is distinct from the here-and-now. Every process comment refers to the past. Process comments refer to what has *just* happened or can refer to repetitive behavior or patterns. No group focuses strictly on the here-and-now, but the purpose of using the past is to generate understanding and change behavior in the present. *What* we're trying to accomplish is qualitatively different from *how* we try to accomplish it. Our process says more about what we value than the end results. Awareness of our process – how we interact in our relationships – impacts our transactions.

Irvin Yalom says that process illumination is the power source of the group:

> The focus on process—on the here-and-now—is not just one of many possible procedural orientations; on the contrary, it is indispensable and a common denominator of all effective interactional groups. One so often hears words to this effect: "No matter what else may be said about experiential groups (therapy groups, encounter groups, and so on), one cannot deny that they are potent – that they offer a compelling experience for participants." *Why* are these groups potent? *Precisely because they encourage process exploration. The process focus is the power cell of the group...*where else is it permissible, in fact encouraged, to comment, in depth, on *here-and-now behavior, on the nature of the immediately current relationship between people?*[68]

In a learning laboratory, where the only guidelines are to focus on the here and now, I've seen connection to myself and others improve dramatically. The purpose of focusing on the here-and-now is not to form long-lasting relationships with group members, nor is it a dress rehearsal for real life. Although we experiment with new behaviors for the sake of learning, the process is real.

Here's how Jane Connor describes the impact of focusing on the present with an old friend:

> I started paying attention to the here-and-now in conversations, and people started revealing themselves, which I found very connecting. When I told a friend I was confused by his laughter, he revealed that he was doing some deep healing work that was painful, but he was grateful to be alive. This simple exchange gave me a better understanding of him, and we connected with each other more genuinely. It gave me a sense of empowerment to notice that I become more alive and present when he was alive and present. [69]

Occasionally I have intentional here-and-now conversations with Jane. Instead of talking about what we've been *doing*, or our relationships with *others*, our focus on *us* in the present invariably helps us explore what's real in *our* relationship, which brings us closer and deepens our awareness of each other. A writer for the New York Times, Sandra Blakeslee, gives us another reason to stay in the here-and-now:

---

[68] Yalom, I. D. & Leszcz, M. (2005). *The theory and practice of group psychotherapy*. Basic Books. p 150.
[69] Personal interview with Jane Connor 3/23/08.

At best the future is imaginary and the past is distorted. Every time we access our memory, we automatically alter it based on the current context, and our revised memory is then returned to long-term storage in place of the original memory.[70]

Our connection to the present moment is an invitation to accentuate what is real.

ORID

Since 1976, ICA Canada (Canadian Institute of Cultural Affairs) has been doing community development using the ORID Process to structure dialogue and access group wisdom. They use a collaborative approach to whole-systems change. Grounded in the depth of human spirit, the ORID process invites all perspectives as a way to co-create solutions that work for everyone. The four steps of the process are objective, reflective, interpretive, and decisional. Each phase of the process has a different purpose:

Objective (observations) – Getting the Facts, Information, Sensory Impressions
- What happened?
- What did you see/hear?
- What words or phrases caught your attention?
- What events do you remember?
- What else happened that contributed to the discomfort?

Reflective (reactions) – Personal impact, Associations, Emotions, Images
- What was your first response?
- How did you feel?
- What excited you; what frustrated you?
- What is your reaction to what has happened?
- What has been the hardest for you?

Interpretive (importance) – Meaning, Values, Significance, Purpose, Implications
- What are the main issues?
- What's really behind all this?
- What are the implications?
- What are the needs or values you are holding here?
- What are the insights?

Decisional (direction) – Resolution, Action, Next Steps
- What change is needed?
- What do you want?

---

[70] Blakeslee, S. Brain-Updating machinery may explain false memories. *New York Times*, September 19, 2000.

- What shall we do to heal?
- What are you committed to?
- What are the next steps?

ICA Canada's joint initiative with the Maasai leaders of Il Ngwesi, Kenya, has produced some remarkable results over the last year. Highlights include:

- 1,800 people have been tested for HIV.
- 200 peer educators are now offering HIV/AIDS awareness sessions in their villages.
- 6 local HIV/AIDS Voluntary Counseling and Testing (VCT) counselors have been trained.
- 88 community care coalition members have been trained to provide support to those testing positive for HIV/AIDS.
- Family Health International has provided funding for local staff salaries and an office for the continuation of the project.[71]

Facilitators who use the ORID MODEL usually create their questions in advance, which provides a lot of structure, but dampens spontaneity in my experience. Still I value the process and appreciate Brian Stanfield's lists of questions in *The Art of Focused Conversation*. He shares sample questions for focused conversations in seven categories: evaluating and reviewing, preparation and planning, coaching and mentoring, interpreting information, decision-making, managing and supervising, personal and celebrative.[72]

FIRED UP

Similar to the ORID process, I developed the FIRED UP process as a structured discussion that accesses group intelligence, awakens creativity, and uncovers group passion. The primary difference is that we intentionally hold space for creativity and passion to emerge:

Facts
Importance
Reactions
Exploration
Direction
Unleashing Passion

Facts – Objective observations, Information
- What actually happened?
- What did you see or hear?
- What words or phrases caught your attention?

---

[71] Institute of Cultural Affairs Canada http://www.icacan.ca/index.html
[72] Stanfield, R. B. (2000). *The art of focused conversation*. The Canadian Institute for Cultural Affairs.

- What events do you remember?
- What's going on right now?

Importance –Values, Needs, Underlying Meaning
- What do you need?
- What are the implications?
- What are the values you are holding here?
- What are the insights?
- What is at stake here?

Reactions – Feelings, Emotions
- What was your first response?
- How did you feel now?
- What moves you?
- What internal images come to mind?
- What's your gut reaction?

Exploration – Creative ideas, Strategies, Alternatives
- What are our options?
- Five years from now, if things were perfect, what do you envision?
- If you had a magic wand, what would you do?
- What ideas excite you?
- What are some other alternatives?

Direction – Action Plans, Decisions, Next Steps
- What change is needed?
- What's the consensus of the group?
- What actions will you take?
- What decisions are you committed to?
- What are the first steps?

UP – Unleashing Passion

Each of the five phases of the FIRED UP model is connected to the body. If we check in with what's going on in our bodies, we access multiple intelligence areas that can provide important information about the decision we want to make. We scan the body starting at the top and moving downward, looking for sensations and messages. If the group is stuck, when they check in with their pelvises, they often come back with words like, "frozen, numb, or locked up." Drawing attention to that body part, they can start to notice micro-movements that get the energy flowing again and awaken ideas about taking action, which unleashes passion. I also use this process with individuals, and after the decision-maker has checked in with each body part, I often ask for an inner dialogue, which sounds something like, "Does your heart have something to say to your head?" Body awareness helps people come alive when they give voice to the muted, disowned, or hidden parts of themselves.

FIRED UP

Phase	Body	Question
Facts	Head	What is happening?
Inquire	Heart	What's important?
React	Gut	How do you feel about it?
Explore	Pelvis	What are the possibilities?
Decide	Legs	What are the action steps?

UP – Unleashing Passion[73]

Here's an example of tapping the wisdom of the body using the FIRED UP model with Angelica who says she is conflicted inside and finds it difficult to support the organization's plan for eliminating human sex trafficking.

> Angelica: I know I've talked on and on and I'm blocking the progress of the group, but this plan will take forever to implement and meanwhile so many people are suffering. I can't bear that. I can't seem to move forward because I don't believe this is the best plan. I'm really stuck.

> Facilitator: I hear how conflicted you are and that you want some movement. Are you willing to try a process that uses the wisdom of your body to help you get clarity?

> Angelica: I'll try anything, because I feel awful about this.

> Facilitator: Okay, so let's start by checking in with your head. What does your head say about this dilemma?

> Angelica: I need peace of mind.

> Facilitator: Now connect with your heart. What does your heart have to say that's important?

> Angelica: I'm heartbroken that so many women and girls are suffering. I'm suffering. But I'm also a vehicle for safety.

> Facilitator: Now check in with your gut. Give voice to any feelings in your gut.

> Angelica: I feel some softness in my belly. My belly wants more levity and lightness.

---

[73] Lasley, M.. (2004).*Courageous visions: How to unleash passionate energy in your life and your organization.* Discover Press.

Facilitator: What about your pelvis? Tune into the creativity that's available to you there.

Angelica: Totally frozen. I need to defuse the tension. Just saying that I'm melting a little... I'm getting a desire to move.

Facilitator: Go ahead and move...

Angelica: Standing up helps. I can see that I'm moving toward my own healing, not from a place of desperation, but from trusting myself and the group.

Facilitator: Now give voice to your legs. What do your legs want for you?

Angelica: To give myself plenty of space to do my own healing work, without rushing it. I don't have to pressure myself or the group to fix everything quickly.

Facilitator: Is there one part of your body that has something to say to the other part of your body?

Angelica: Ya, my heart wants my legs to know, "I'm okay if you take baby steps." Whoa. I have a rush of relief that goes through my whole body.

Facilitator: Just stay with that for a minute.

Angelica: ... So much shifted in me. I'm not holding any tension, only peace and I'm soaring with hope.

Facilitator: Since you can come back to this place anytime, how would you like to remind yourself that this inner state is always available to you?

Angelica: I want to leave for a few minutes to write about this experience and integrate what I've learned.

Facilitator: Anything you want from the group before you go?

Angelica: I can see that many of you are moved by the change in me, but I don't want to hear from any of you right now... I'm grateful that you gave me the space to look at what was blocking me.

The entire group can explore the wisdom of the body simultaneously. Each person in the group holds the issues differently, but they can still visit each area of their bodies, give voice to the wisdom dwelling there, ear each other's desires and unleash their collective passion.

Empathic Mediation

Traditionally, mediators support disputants in reaching an agreement, where the parties themselves determine the conditions rather than accept a solution proposed by the mediator. The impartial mediator doesn't have a vested interest in the outcome, but I've seen way too many green mediators push for resolution without understanding that the real purpose of mediation is to dialogue to rebuild connection. Many disputants come into the process *thinking* they know exactly what they want in the signed agreement, and then become aware that what's even more important is to be heard and understood by the other party. Resolving conflict is rarely about the solution and never about finding out who is right and who is wrong. A tremendous amount of energy can go into taking sides and evaluating positions. In contrast, dialogue helps people understand and appreciate different perspectives and develop compassion for why people act the way they do.

As mediators, we develop presence in the midst of conflict by listening empathically to each party, translating judgments into needs, and supporting collaborative resolutions. In my experience, the most transformative mediation practice is the translation of judgment, blame, criticism, and demands (which tend to stimulate defensiveness or counterattack), into the underlying human needs, such as care, respect, freedom, safety, or trust. To illustrate, "he's so selfish" could be translated into a need for consideration; or "she's so greedy" could be about a need for trust or caring. By translating judgment into needs, we support disputants in more clearly communicating their desires, which opens them to hearing each other more compassionately and generates new possibilities for collaborative solutions.

As divorce mediators, Duke and Sharon Fisher help families face real crisis: couples come in with a sense of dread, wondering, "Where are my kids going to live?" and, "How am I going to face financial ruin?" Duke describes the process:

> We help people avoid the horrific experience of adversarial divorce. Conflict resolution is really hard work. Emotionally draining. Hurtful. We think, "Man, that sucks," or "Wow, that was painful." It's hard to like people when they're in crisis or in a lot of pain. But it's a double-edged sword because we're doing something important, worthwhile. We get to be in the room with powerful emotions and get to see couples create plans for their separate lives. The process pushes my edges—participants feel frustrated with the process and with us, but if we can help them avoid family court, keep them out of the system, the end result is worth it.
>
> After the divorcing couple works out an agreement, their attorneys, who often don't understand how divorce mediation works, may tell them, "You have a right to this. You have a right to that. This mediator doesn't know what he's doing." So we work with all of that.
>
> I'm drawn to the work – there's such a huge need for competent conflict resolution. Not just theory and practice, but actual mediation. The stuff that's available is so bad – it's all based on ideas but not on reality. The material on bullying on the web is garbage – adults who don't have a clue, telling kids what to do, "If you're bullied, tell your mom." Kids aren't going to do that! Or the advice on abstinence, "Leave food on your face to make yourself less attractive." These

adults don't understand kids at all! Instead I work with people who are very real. I get follow-up calls from educators and kids who say, "My life is different because I have new skills."

In abuse and neglect cases, I represent the child or the victim. But I also include abusive stepparents, judgmental social workers, and frightened school officials, so that we create a plan that everyone supports. I meet with the directors to talk about a collaborative approach because we have to meet the needs of everyone at the table. Everybody has to be on board. In the volatile stuff I get invited to do, I need to stay unstacked - I don't prioritize one person's needs over another. It's an ethical commitment to facilitating without leading—I will not give an opinion, nudge, hint, or suggest. I just stay present in the moment. I stay on their agenda, help people speak their truth. When push comes to shove, I stay out of the fray. I do not get involved in telling participants what to do.

The work is based on a Trifecta of values that come together during mediation: connection, authenticity, and influence. These core skills enable people to build a bridge.

In our role as mediators, one way we help people build bridges is by helping them differentiate between interests and positions. When disputants focus on positions and strategies they've already decided on, before they've clarified their interests or needs, they often skip over the underlying concerns. In contrast, when we uncover the needs of all the parties and get them all on the table, we find that the needs are not in conflict. Only the positions, solutions, and strategies are incompatible. By uncovering all the interests of each party, they have more compassion for each other, and we are then able to help them co-create solutions that are more likely to meet the needs of both parties.

For instance, I worked with parents who could not come to a custody agreement because they both adamantly wanted their children on Christmas day. They were in deadlock until they heard why that strategy was important to each other. The mother wanted *stability* for the children and believed that the tradition of waking up in the house they'd grown up in was a way to reduce the upheaval of their parents' splitting up. The father wanted to *deepen the family bonds* and believed that taking the children to visit his elderly parents would help them to know that they were loved. Both parents softened when they felt understood by the other. Knowing that each of them wanted the children to be treated with care and tenderness, they came up with a plan so both could get what they wanted, which included each parent spending time with the children on Christmas.

Four Contexts for Mediation

There are four ways you can enter the mediation process, starting with the most common:

1. You mediate your internal process – empathizing with the chooser and educator[74]
2. You enter mediation as one of the parties involved in a dispute

---

[74] The process of empathizing with the chooser and the educator is described on page 24.

3. You enter mediation informally, without being asked
4. You're asked to mediate two parties in conflict

Although sometimes mediation is court ordered, it usually begins because two parties have hit an impasse and recognize that they need some help to communicate. In a formal context, when both parties have agreed to mediation, we set the tone of the mediation with a simple introduction to the process, letting them know our role and that we want to support both parties. Sometimes the opening is as simple as, "We are here to help you understand each other." I often ask for a moment of silence in the beginning for both parties to set their intentions or to imagine how they would like to feel when the mediation is over or what they envision would happen in the next couple of hours for them *both* to feel deeply satisfied.

If they're agitated, it's unlikely that they'll be able to hear my assurances of confidentiality or how I'm going to operate, so I like to let people start with a very short introduction and then clarify my role or the process later, as needed. If one disputant talks more than another, that's when I'll let them know that they are *both* going to get a chance to be heard. If they rush into strategies, that's when I explain that I'm interested in helping them uncover each other's needs *before* we explore strategies. Later in the process, if they seek guidance from me about forming an action plan or an agreement, I share that I'm not going to tell them what to *do*. Although I could explain all the nuances of the mediation process and ground rules up front, I'm more inclined to bring things up as they arise, because it empowers both parties to create their own flow and to trust that they can enter a dialogue in the future without formal parameters.

A common ground rule in mediation is "No interrupting," but many people have no desire to adhere to this ground rule. In some cultures, interruptions are a sign of comfort and familiarity – anything else is perceived as overly-polite, inauthentic, or strained. Forcing a Eurocentric norm on the group imposes a sense of right and wrong that can feel foreign and unnatural. Instead of judging someone for interrupting, serving as a traffic cop, or doing what is "right," we can model the desired behaviors ourselves by giving people the space to be heard. Ironically, one of the ways to set the tone is to interrupt the process ourselves to slow things down or ensure people understand each other e.g. "I'm concerned about fully understanding each of you, so I'm wondering if you can hold that thought until Sheri has fully expressed what she wants to say. Would that work for you?"

Because they have been unable to work out the difficulties on their own, many disputants start the process by talking to the mediators about the other party, instead of to the other party. A common intervention is, "Would you like to say that to *her*?" Or we can give people the freedom to choose, because eventually they'll start talking to each other as trust is built. When I interpret that one or more parties are withholding, caucusing is a way to hold private conversations to give each person a chance to be understood. In general we use caucusing as a last resort. Instead we advocate for transparency and empathize with needs for emotional safety and self-expression. To follow are the five steps of mediation developed by Marshall Rosenberg, Ike Lasater, and John Kinyon.

Five Steps of Empathic Mediation

1. Ask person A, "What needs of yours are not met by this situation?" Identify A's needs.

2. Say to person B, "I hear that person A has a need for X." Ask B to reflect A's needs.

3. Ask person B, "What needs of yours are not met by this situation?" Identify B's needs.

4. Say to person A, "I hear that person B has a need for Y." Ask A to reflect B's needs.

    Keep repeating steps 1-4 until all needs are identified and reflected back to the satisfaction of the other person. Pay attention to the quality of the connection, and once both people have received enough empathy and have demonstrated that they've heard each other, move on to

5. Strategies: Co-create solutions by exploring strategies that honor all needs. Collaborate on making agreements.[75]

Although we make the language our own, if we hold the intention of moving through each step, both parties are more likely to feel understood. To illustrate the five steps, here's an excerpt from an actual empathic mediation with a couple working on a parenting plan. The names have been changed to protect their privacy.

> Sasha: Of course I want you to see Malika regularly. She's your daughter. I just want you to come when you say you're going to come.
>
> Justin: Sometimes I have to work overtime..."
>
> Mediator: Hold on. I want to hear about that, but first I want to make sure I've heard Sasha's needs. So can you hold that for a minute?
>
> Justin: Uh, sure.
>
> Sasha: I'll tell you what I need. If you say you're coming at 5, I don't want you showing up at 7.
>
> Mediator: Sasha, is it that you need consideration and want some reliability so that you know what to expect?
>
> Sasha: Exactly. I can't wait around forever. I have a *life*!

---

[75] Adapted from the work of Marshall Rosenberg, Ike Lasater and John Kinyon.

Mediator: Justin, can you let Sasha know you heard her need for consideration and reliability because she has a life?

Justin: I get that, but she doesn't understand that I have no control...

Mediator: I want to hear about that in a minute, but first can you let her know that you heard what she said about needing consideration and reliability.

Justin. I guess so. She needs me to be more considerate and reliable so she can live her life the way she wants.

Mediator: Sasha, Did he get that right?

Sasha: Yeah, but I also want him to know that I know the real reason he's late, it's because of that whore who...

Mediator: Before we talk about that, I want to make sure Justin gets a chance to be understood about overtime. Can we come back to this part in a minute?

Sasha: Okay.

Justin: You're the one who has a different boyfriend every night and I don't think our daughter should have to put up with that. She's only ten and...

If the two parties are talking to each other, some facilitators trust the process and don't intervene. But when the parties are making accusations, and I don't put a stop to it, new wounds are created and we'll never get around to addressing the original pain. By translating everything into interests or needs, I'm helping them both slow down and see each other's positive intent.

Mediator: Wait. Let's slow down and really look at your needs Justin. Is it that you're worried and want to be sure your daughter is growing up in a healthy environment?

Justin: It's more than that. Her mother wears those slutty clothes and dresses my daughter the same. It's not right.

Mediator: So you care about Malika's clothing; are you really worried and you just want to keep her safe and protect her from harm?

Justin: ... Yes. I don't want her to get hurt.

Mediator: Sasha, will you tell Justin that you heard his needs - he cares about her safety and wants to protect her from getting hurt?

Sasha: If he really cared about protecting her, he...

Mediator: Before you tell him that, can you just let him know you heard his needs?

Sasha: He *says* he needs to keep her from getting hurt.

Justin: Fuck you! The way you say that - it's like you don't believe I care about her.

Mediator: (takes a deep breath to slow things down and then speaks with intensity) Are you completely enraged, because you want to be known for your fierce love for you daughter?

Justin: I love her more than anything!

Sasha: Actually I know that. I guess what I'm really upset about is that I want you to respect me.

Justin: (softly) Really? I thought you hated me...

Sasha: Well I'm not saying I want to get back together again, but I'd just like to know that you still care about me.

Justin: (choking) This is really hard for me to say now that I'm married to someone else, but I'll always care about you.

Now that they have opened their hearts to each other, this isn't the time for me to say, "Okay, how about that parenting plan?" They need some time to grieve their losses and enjoy the reconnection, before they sign up for some happy action plan. But I want to acknowledge their movement.

Mediator: Let's just take a moment to appreciate your desire to raise your daughter together and find a way to care for each other at the same time.

Sasha: Well, I probably should just enjoy the moment, but there's something that is really bothering me... That woman, oh God, I can't even say her name, if she ever hits Malika, you'll never see my daughter again.

Justin: She would never...

Mediator: Justin, based on what Sasha just said, can you reflect her feelings and needs?

Justin: I'd say she feels vindictive and needs to make you think my wife is evil.

Mediator: I'm hearing something else... Sasha, are you terrified and would you like to know that Malika will find happiness, even when you're not there?

Sasha: It's so hard to be away from her. She's so young... and this divorce has been so hard for her... I just want her to be happy.

Mediator: And you just want some reassurance that she will recover from the pain of the divorce? And that she'll be happy? That she has a wonderful future ahead?

Sasha: mmm...

Mediator: Justin, even if you don't agree with what she's said, can you tell Sasha the needs you hear?

Justin: She just wants to make sure Malika is happy.

Sasha: Yes! I feel so bad about what's happened to her and I just want her to get her childhood back.

Justin: So she can be a care-free little girl who isn't carrying the weight of the world on her shoulders? That's what I want too.

At this point both Justin and Sasha are feeling warm toward each other and connected about their desires for their daughter. Connection is the real purpose of the mediation, so I could have stopped here, but I sensed that there was more.

Mediator: There were a couple of times I interrupted you both, and I want to see if there are any other needs that either of you want to express.

Sasha: Actually, I'm ready to look at how we work out our schedules now. Are you?

Justin: There's one other thing... That guy you were seeing who just got out of prison?

Sasha: I'm not seeing him any more.

Justin: I know, but I don't want my daughter around people like that.

Mediator: It sounds to me like this is the same need - you both care deeply about Malika's safety. Do you have any requests you want to make of each other?

Sasha: Don't try to tell me who I can and can't see.

Mediator: So you want the freedom to see who you want, but what is your request of Justin?

Sasha: I'm not sure.

Justin: Well I know what I want – don't bring ex-cons into the house.

Mediator: That's what you don't want. Can you make that into a doable request?

Justin: Will you think about who you bring into the house.

Mediator: How will you know she's thought about it? What do you actually want her to do?

Justin: hmm...

Sasha: Get your approval before I date anyone?

Justin: ... no... I guess I just want you to know that I get really worried when I see the parade of guys at your place

Sasha: Shut up! A parade of guys? Are you fuckinuts? Do you know how pitiful you...

Here I made a judgment call – they're both triggered, but I move toward the tension by empathizing with the person in the most pain.

Mediator: I'm a little torn about which of you to focus on right now because you're both upset, so I'm wondering Justin if you can wait to be heard, and tell Sasha what you think her needs are.

Justin: uh... no idea. Revenge?

Here I'm saying to myself, "Martha are you crazy? He's not going to be able to hear her needs when she's this angry. Just tell him what you think they are, and then ask him to reflect."

Mediator: Revenge isn't actually a need. Would you like to ask her if she's furious because she wants respect?

Justin: Is that what you want – respect?

Sasha: I'll tell you what I want. Quit stalking me. Quit fantasizing about the men in my life. I'm tired of you saying I'm a bad mother.

Mediator: You'd like recognition that you're a really, really caring mother. I haven't heard Justin say that you are a bad mother. What I heard him say is that he wants to know if you want respect.

Sasha: Oh, I didn't hear that. Yeah, I want some respect for being a good mother. You have no idea! I'd do anything for her!

Justin: I know you would. (pause)

Now they are on common ground and have made a tentative connection. I'm tracking that I've interrupted them several times but can't quite remember the issues. So I give them the freedom to explore further.

Mediator: Are there additional needs that you want to get on the table before we look at the parenting plan?

(silence)

Mediator: Justin, do you still want to talk about overtime and your schedule?

Justin: Nah. Not really. It doesn't look there's going to be any overtime for a while. I can get there on time. And if I'm going to be late, I'll call.

Sasha: Good. I'd like to have her on Wednesday nights. So we can go to dance class. Is that okay with you?

Justin: Sure. I'm not working weekends anymore, so I'd like to have her every other weekend.

Sasha: Okay. And I don't want you sending her home with dirty laundry. She can keep some of her clothes at your house and you can wash them.

Justin: Our washer was broken—that won't happen again. Quit worrying about that. I want my name on the emergency card at school. I didn't like finding out that she was sick at school a day later.

Sasha: So go down to the school yourself and tell them. You don't need me to do that.

Justin: I can't think of anything else.

Sasha: I can. Could you buy her some clothes once in a while?

They made a few more requests of each other and when the mediator asks if they want to put any agreements in writing, they both say no, usually a good sign that they have more trust in each other than in a piece of paper. Does this mediation sound like it's way too directive? Filled with interventions? That I'm putting words in their mouths? It does to me. In the next section on transformative mediation, we'll explore another mediation style that I also enjoy because there's an inherent trust in people to resolve their own conflicts without as many interventions from the mediator. But first let's explore a few key mediation skills. And by the way, what I just said is a facilitation skill that I love using – telling people what's to come so that they have something fun to anticipate as we prepare for it with some skill building.

Mediation Skills

Mediation skills are similar to facilitation skills, but call for even more diligence simply because the parties are often enraged, with each other, if not the mediator.

Empathy: When a disputant expresses pain in a judgmental way, we empathize with their needs. Then the other disputant will be more likely to be able to hear the other party. "It sounds like you've really been struggling financially and would like to be able to buy winter coats for the children."

Reflection: To ensure understanding, we can make a request of a disputant to reflect the needs of the other party. "Marc, I think Kay would like some understanding for how much she has been suffering since the accident. Would you let Kay know that you heard that she's been in a lot of pain? Even if you see if differently, can you just let her know you heard what she said?"

Tracking: We keep track of all the needs that are on the table and track where we are in the process. "I'm tracking that I interrupted you earlier and you wanted to talk about payment for the damages. Then we'll come back to Luanne because you want to have better relationships with your neighbors."

Interruption: We interrupt to rebuild the connection. If someone talks longer than we can listen attentively, we stop them, reflecting the key points. "Just a sec... I want to make sure I'm getting the most important pieces here..."

Self-Connection: Even if we don't voice it, our judgments about disputants come out in our body language. Fortunately, our judgment can lead us to awareness of our need. The goal is to name our judgment in silence and translate it into feelings and needs. This quick check-in can allow us to return to full presence. "Whoa – he might move to China or Serbia... I'm feeling a bit hopeless, wanting to support them in creating a parenting plan that they can both live with."

Self-Expression: We share transparently with both parties what is going on internally. "I care about each of you, so I feel really sad when I see that you're about to walk out, because I want to support you in co-creating the relationship you want. I can feel how much you're both suffering – it touches me – so before you go, I ask you to say the *one* thing you really want the other person to know."

Request: At any time mediators have four ways to create connection: self-empathy, self-expression, empathizing with others, or helping others express themselves. To support their choices we can make requests that help them connect. "You've said a lot. Would you like to stop for a moment to see if Steph has understood what you've said so far?"

Of all these skills, self-expression can be the most difficult to express and the most transformative. Jim and Jori Manske had been mediating for years when they first started using NVC as part of their mediation process. They describe the experience of revealing themselves transparently to the disputants:

The nascent paradigm shift that emerged in spite of our conscious incompetence with the NVC process included two deep and lasting insights that have revolutionized our mediation practice. First, during the mediation process, we broke the taboo of revealing our own uncomfortable feelings and needs to the disputants. Secondly, rather than acknowledging feelings and thoughts, which had been our previous style, we crafted our reflections of what we heard the disputants share by focusing on their feelings and needs. The outcome of this shift included (1) a shared sense of vulnerability; and (2) a quality of connection based on a shared focus on each person's well-being. This outcome seemed to both astonish and please all of us.[76]

Years later, the disputants wrote a book about their divorce experience which included a statement that Jim and Jori "were extremely skilled at getting to the crux of the matter." The practice of sharing their own feelings and needs with disputants is highly unusual in most mediation practices. I consider transparency an advanced mediation skill for people who are highly self-aware and have confidence that they can own and describe their experience without moralistic judgment or blame.

Another mediator, Meganwind Eoyang from California, had worked with a couple for several weeks that weren't making much progress. She tried to stop them in the middle of blaming and criticizing each other, but they continued. She interrupted them again, but again they didn't stop. Out of exasperation, Meganwind said, "I would like to end the session now and ask you to leave." The couple was shocked. The mediator explained, "I don't want to schedule another session with you because I don't see that I have anything to offer you if you're unwilling to work with me." They responded, "No, no. We've worked with two others and we're getting a lot out of this. Please continue to work with us." They were able to proceed from there.

So empathic mediation is not just a Pollyanna approach; it's a rigorous process of listening deeply and getting clarity about what people really want. Now we'll look at another mediation model, transformative mediation.

Transformative Mediation

Transformative Mediation is based on the work of Robert A. Baruch Bush and Joseph P. Folger, who support the balance of two fundamental aspects of human nature: personal autonomy and connecting with others. In addition to being motivated by their individual gain, people want to recognize and relate to each other. The work of transformative mediators is to support empowerment and recognition shifts by encouraging dialogue and shared decision-making. Despite the way conflict destabilizes human interaction, people can restore their self-confidence and responsiveness to others through dialogue. The empowerment shift and the recognition shift generate satisfying interactions which are even more important to disputants than a favorable resolution. As transformative mediators, we measure success not by whether parties reach agreement, but by shifts toward responsive interaction. Once people change the way they interact with each other, they often find ways to resolve their differences. The more important goal is that people gain new insights and deeper interpersonal understanding.

---

[76] Manske, J. & Manske, J. NVC mediation: Creating dynamic connection. Retreived from http://www.nonviolentcommunication.com/press/article_PDF/JJMankse/NVC_Mediation_JJManske.pdf

I've been experimenting by blending empathic mediation with transformative mediation for years. The empathic approach to mediation aims for heart connection, relies on multiple interventions to protect the parties from stimulating additional pain, and supports them in understanding each other's needs before creating solutions. The philosophy of transformative mediation is to trust the people and the process. By giving a lot of leeway to participants we trust that the parties can connect without a lot of interventions or over-dependence on the mediator. Both processes help people to strengthen their communication skills.

Wanting to integrate the best of both worlds, I mediated a dialogue between two people who hadn't seen each other in years: the son was terrified and his father was bewildered. I started out intervening often. When I interrupted the father to change his language from talking *about* his son to talking *to* his son, I knew I'd gone too far. Even though he was receptive and turned to talk to his son instead of me, my body and language suggested that I didn't have faith in them or the process. He would have eventually talked to his son on his own, without any high-handed directives from me. I backpedaled and said, "This is *your* conversation. If I'm getting in the way, just tell me to stop talking." I held silence for about ten minutes, even when the conversation turned to other people in their lives. The son intervened himself, asking to shift the focus back to *their* relationship. I could have done that for them, but it was so much more satisfying to see them find their own way of rebuilding their connection.

Beginning mediators commonly overuse interventions – it's a way to get a lot of practice with a variety of skills and a strategy for dealing with our own fear of failure. On the path to mastery we don't need to litter it with extraneous interventions that create dependence on the mediator.

Creative Approaches to Facilitation

Most of the approaches facilitators use have a track record. So it's refreshing to see people create new ways of facilitating transformation. When we venture into uncharted territory, we assume nothing. Nothing is sacred. Rules change. Perspectives are challenged. Anything is possible. When we use a fraction of our creativity, they use only a fraction of theirs. Observing other facilitators at work, creating new processes on the fly, inviting participants to create their own process, all contribute to our learning and potential for creativity. For example, Karl Rohnke, the author of Silver Bullets created the helium pole activity with Outward Bound groups using aluminum tent poles. Two lines of people face each other with their forefingers pointed toward each other holding a tent pole on top. The challenge is to lower the helium pole to the ground without losing contact. Invariably the helium stick rises even though everyone in the group is trying to lower it to the ground, evoking a lot of fault finding and laughter. Eventually the group works together to lower the pole to the ground. Karl Rohnke has several creative alternatives to this activity, including using large hula hoops. In a workshop with business managers, he showed them how to make their own "helium poles" out of rolled up newspapers. Another creative facilitator, Harrison Owen, noticed that many people claimed they learned more at conference *between* sessions, so he created open space technology, a way for large groups of people to self-organize and talk about what is most important to them.

In addition to his work as a mediator, Duke Fisher also works with at-risk youth, using a radical, creative approach to facilitation that helps kids explore contemporary, real issues in their lives.

I work with a college where a large number of freshmen are on academic probation. They're not hedonistic, stupid, or lazy. They're from difficult backgrounds - they all have their stories. If we judge them, it's very difficult to have influence, so we created a mentoring program that taps their strengths. Instead of using successful kids to mentor unsuccessful kids, we train mentors and tutors who have been on academic probation themselves to connect with their strengths, reach out to others, and design plans based on needs. By double-dipping into the at-risk population, we create internal capacity for academic success which boosts them up.

To dramatize issues that matter to kids, we also use guerilla theatre, where the audience doesn't know they're interacting with improv actors. The students come together and share their personal stories and how they connect to the issues. Then they choose an issue to dramatize, whether it's dating violence, drug and alcohol use, or whatever matters to them. The group at the college chose to dramatize a story about student pregnancy by creating a 5-member panel that presented the issue in front of 100 high school faculty. One of the students played the part of a student teacher who co-chaired the student government. She described a 7th grade girl who got a lot of attention because she was pregnant. The other girls were cooing, offering her a lot of positive reinforcement in ways that the student teacher deemed unhealthy. She worried that pregnancy would become contagious and expressed a lot of fear for the students. The pregnant girl was a leader in student government, and she was asked to step down while pregnant. The rest of the panel shared their opinion on pregnancy in junior high school, and the audience of faculty members responded. Some emphatically supported the student teacher's choices; others were outraged.

Then I told the teachers they had been watching a dramatization of a story that belonged to one of the panel members. The woman playing the student teacher revealed, "My name is Sharon and I'm dramatizing the role of my teacher. I was actually a 7th grade student who became pregnant." Debriefing the experience, teachers who had said, "You did the right thing. I support you in removing her from student government," felt guilty and exposed because they hadn't handled her gently enough. Both students and teachers raved about the experience, saying, "Wow! This gave me some insights into myself." It's a layered experience. Scary.

Improvocation is a short cut to getting real. Some folks feel you're exploiting their emotions when they unwittingly become part of a dramatization, but they all agree that the veneer comes off. When we encourage people to be authentic, by design that's risky. The dramatization brings out undercurrents—secondary reactions, and those involved finally say what they've been withholding. It's not the story they practiced in the car, but the *real* story. These rare moments of authenticity are special. We spend most of our life under control, editing our words, or playing a role. Ironically, our role-playing brings out real stuff that feels edgy. I help people find the courage to show themselves when they're not at their best. Bitchy. Cranky. Volatile. As the facilitator, I always feel a lot of anxiety. Giving myself permission to be real means I'm scared a lot of the time.

When I work with kids, I get permission from the school system to use language that's real. In the handouts, I write "fuck", not "f@%#*." Otherwise, they sense the lack of authenticity, and they think, "This guy doesn't really know what it's like." I do a lot of storytelling, not about some woman in Ohio, but about what happened to me this morning. That level of authenticity builds trust. [77]

Creativity blossoms when we're not attached to results. We need to have the courage to trust our instincts, but where does that courage come from? The opened heart. When we trust our own heart, and all the other hearts in the room, we are more willing to try out new ideas, blend two existing processes together, and make things up in the heat of the moment. Now that we've experienced several different facilitation models, we'll look at how facilitators develop presence.

Exercises

Reflections:
1. Spend an hour or a day focusing on the here-and-now and notice how your relationships change. Notice how this simple practice deepens your awareness, facilitates real connection, and opens your heart to intimacy.
2. Repeatedly ask yourself, "What quality of life do I want to have in this moment?"

Small Group Discussions:
1. Choose an internal conflict and use the 5 Empathic Mediation Steps to fully-hear both sides of yourself. Then try the same thing with a friend. Discuss your learning.
2. Compare the value of transformative mediation to empathic mediation.

---

[77] Duke Fisher personal interview 3/27/08.

Activities:

1. In triads, mediate a dialogue between two people role-playing a conflict. Ask them to choose a scenario that has meaning for one of them. Get feedback from each party.

2. In small groups work on the same issue using a different facilitation model each time:
   - Nonviolent Communication
   - Dynamic Facilitation
   - ORID or FIRED UP

Chapter 9
Facilitator Presence

We've come to believe that the core capacity needed for accessing the field of the future is presence. We first thought of presence as being fully conscious and aware in the present moment. Then we began to appreciate presence as deep listening, of being open beyond one's preconceptions and historical ways of making sense. We came to see the importance of letting go of old identities and the need to control and, as Salk said, making choices to serve the evolution of life. Ultimately, we came to see all these aspects of presence as leading to a state of "letting come," of consciously participating in a larger field for change. When this happens, the field shifts, and the forces shaping a situation can shift from re-creating the past to manifesting or realizing an emerging future. — Peter Senge

Many people are asleep about their presence, completely unaware of the tacit cultural agreement to stay dormant. It's not the mastery of presence that is difficult, but rather giving up the conventional comatose habit. In this chapter, we'll awaken to the power of presence. We'll look at how we impact the group through charisma, our bodies, and subtle energy. We'll also ascertain how to balance autonomy, collaboration and leadership. And we'll end with the tango as we learn the dance steps of co-facilitation.

As facilitators, we wear many hats – leader, teacher, coach, student, and friend are only a few. The most valuable tool we have is ourselves. Our presence, posture, voice, and energy impact the group in every moment. As we model creativity and transparently share our facilitation choices, we help the group members develop facilitation skills in the process.

We all know presence when we see it. We don't even have to see it; we can feel it. When someone with a compelling presence walks into a room, heads turn. He or she embodies awareness and compassion, and something else – mutual empowerment.

Ironically I became aware of new ways to access presence because I came unraveled when I lost track of the time at a weekend workshop. Afterwards a participant came up to me and said, "You should read John Heron's book, *The Complete Facilitators Handbook*." Even though I've facilitated hundreds of groups, I was embarrassed, telling myself that I'd failed her. I brushed off her suggestion, thinking, "Yeah, yeah, yeah, I've read enough books on facilitation to endow a library, but when I'm faced with challenging situations, I choke." When she sent me an excerpt, I ordered the book immediately. My jaw kept hitting the floor. Even though it was a heady, intellectual read, I couldn't stop salivating, so I wrote to John and asked if I could study with him. He shot back, "I am in my 80th year and I don't do that anymore. But if you come to New Zealand, I'll work with you for up to 90 minutes a day five days in a row."

While I considered this option, I asked if instead he'd be willing to work with me over the phone. Our first session had a dramatic impact on me. In less than an hour he helped me deepen my awareness about my presence, voice, language, and intention using a practice he called charismatic time.

That night as I lay sleeping, I dreamt that I went nose to nose with Jack Nicholson to teach him about presence. Although Jack couldn't hold my gaze, I woke up exhilarated that I'd boldly chosen to teach presence to Jack, the master of presence. Here's a description of one of the exercises John led me through called Experiential Presence:

> Stand up and arrange your experiential body so that you can be present throughout it all at once. Find your way into the exhilarating feeling of simultaneous extension in all directions. Your posture will assume a stance like those found in the *mudras* (sacred postures) of Tantric practice, or in the martial arts such as Tai Chi and Aikido: knees somewhat bent, legs well grounded, arms out from the side, elbows bent; spine, neck and head aligned with a subtle feeling of levity, the back elongated and widened. Now move slowly, maintaining this same experiential presence throughout your moving form, coordinating the integrated, extended awareness from the *hara*, the center of gravity — and levity — within the lower abdomen. Form into pairs and share your findings with each other. End with experience-sharing in the whole group.[78]

You'll find a full description of charismatic time and additional presence exercises in Heron's book, The Complete Facilitators Handbook. I'm especially intrigued by the idea that when we embody our soul's longing, others are drawn to us. As presence emerges, we exude authenticity from every cell of our body, and every movement is infused with meaning. The practice of reclaiming my posture, giving full attention to my spine, noticing gestures and how my body moves in relation to space helps me open to the presence of others. When I slow down my speech, pause, and fill the silence with awareness (not anxiety), I notice that people are fed by this. When I am present to my own soul, other people feel it, which becomes the basis of empowering relationships.

When we release our embarrassment of being seen, we become fully present and aware. Everyone starts to notice us, including ourselves. We begin to notice how our personal presence changes when we stand in the middle of the group, to one side, outside the circle, or close to one person. As we move around in a group and notice our impact, we get in touch with the implicit mana or magical power of everyone in the room. When the group is in a U shape, like a uterus, and we step into the womb of the group, we're aware of the energy and what the group is giving birth to. We all share the same experiential space, so our experiential space subtly interpenetrates everyone else's which creates a state of interpersonal empathy.

---

[78] Heron, J. (1999). *The Complete Facilitators Handbook*. Kogan Page. p 242.

To be present is to dwell in the mutuality of the group, a form of everyday applied mysticism. Theater training and facilitator training are similar because the way we portray ourselves indicates our personal power. Along with awareness, presence is a vital component of personal power and can be identified by posture, demeanor, carriage, facial expression, gaze, gesture, voice, and phrasing. Our personal presence or stage presence comes from our physical bearing, awareness of every part of our body, and our physical movement within the space. Skilled athletes, whether they are divers, ballet dancers, or aikido martial artists know where their body is in relation to everything around them. Attuned to our personal longing and meaning, we're perched for both personal transformation and leading social change.

> Personal presence is the ability to be fully available, open to all our senses, and responsive to our environment by authentically expressing who we truly are. By being completely in the moment, experiencing the now spontaneously, without attachment, we connect deeply with others. Through complete self-acceptance and acceptance of others, we deepen our consciousness. Trusting our intuition, opening to not knowing, experiencing our full range of emotions, all contribute to our ability to empathically connect with everyone's needs, including our own.

When we support full presence, we experience the moment. Rather than recommend a course of action, we can help people come into their own power where their natural awareness emerges.

Charisma

First say to yourself what you would be, then do what you have to do. — Epictetus

Charisma is a source of personal power, intimately connected to presence. I'm not talking about power or charisma used to dominate, control, or oppress others, but the opposite. Empowering ourselves is the basis for empowering others. Personal power is accessible to everyone and can be cultivated by developing presence. Unique personal style is not acquired or created. As a person becomes more and more authentic, their distinct style is revealed. The unique way we relate to others reflects what we deeply value.

When Charlie Seashore, founding father of National Training Labs, introduced me to Sushma Sharma, his respect for her was palpable. He raved about her facilitation skills, acknowledged her leadership as president of the Indian Society for Applied Behavioral Science, admired her understanding of group dynamics, and described her thriving practice as an organizational development consultant. After several minutes of praise, I started to feel embarrassed, wondering if he'd ever stop. But Sushma just nodded her head and calmly received all the praise. I thought she might say, "That's enough," but instead she let him continue to search for the elusive quality that he couldn't quite articulate. Finally he stopped speaking. Sushma smiled and said, "And there's one more thing – I am very sensual." It wasn't what she said, but the way she said it – her voice and body exuded sensuality. Connecting with her unique personal style helped make me aware of my own desire for more boldness, more self-love, and more full expression in my own life.

I usually think of motivational speakers or politicians as the people who really need charisma to succeed; whereas, facilitators are much more laid back and relaxed, going with the flow. But charismatic facilitators have a deep impact on groups because the ease of connection is palpable. Our presence – that aware, lived, embodiment of our personal power – invites trust and vulnerability. Although the reaction of others tells us a lot about our own charisma, our reaction to ourselves is even more revealing.

Early in life I learned about charisma from my sister, Janet. She lights up any room. She has her picture on the front page of something on a regular basis, enthralls Oprah's audience, and receives awards left and right. Even when she's on chemo, which is a lot of the time now, she still manages to entertain everyone and keep us all crying and laughing. I've always felt comfortable in her shadow. Her perspective of me is a little different from my self perception – that I uplift people by bringing calm energy into the room and I've got my own brand of charisma. We all do. Charisma is not just for the rich and famous – we can all access and develop our unique charismatic presence.

John Heron has taught hundreds of facilitators about presence and defines charisma as "the ability to be empowered by one's own inner resources, the wellspring within, and the ability thereby to elicit empowerment in others."[79] He goes on to say, "Personal power is rather like the original light of the soul taking charge of its earthly location and its human relationships. Our whole culture runs a strong tacit taboo which conditions people to bury such a propensity and keep it repressed, and to feel diffident and embarrassed when invited to manifest it. This awkwardness, hidden behind conventional social behaviour, is very strong. So the move from being silently present to actively manifesting personal power is a challenge."[80]

Charisma can either empower or disempower others. When we balance our personal charisma with invoking charisma in others, people become inspired. If the purpose of the group is to develop certain competencies, and we give away our skills and empower people to develop their own charisma, then our charisma is put to good use. In contrast, if presence is used to teach, but participants become dependent on the facilitator's energy, they don't become charismatic themselves.

If we become the center point, the star, radiating our light outward, by answering every question or evaluating each suggestion, we disempower the group. Instead of promoting the model that "the guru is enlightened" we can give people the support to catapult themselves into freedom. As charismatic initiators, we fire people up to take charge of their own destinies. Our empowering presence in turn awakens people to their emerging power. If starry-eyed students remain astonished, they give away their power. If we overdo it, they feel disempowered, yet if we hide our own charisma, others may completely miss the opportunity to step into their own power.

---

[79] Heron, J. (1999). *The Complete Facilitators Handbook*. Kogan Page. p. 216.
[80] Heron, J. (1999). *The Complete Facilitators Handbook*. Kogan Page. p. 224.

A facilitator who over-awes the group creates ardent followers. Likewise, over-teaching can be a seductive process. When we enthrall the whole room or we go on for too long, we don't develop the peer relationships that invite people to challenge us and further our own development. However, there is an alternative: embracing our personal power while we simultaneously embrace the power of others.

Ultimately we move toward using our charisma for the greatest good. To deepen our awareness of how our charisma impacts others, we connect with our intention – what impact do we *want* to have when we speak or take action? By continuously scanning other's body language for reactions, we deepen our understanding of our *actual* impact. Then we look for ways to bridge the gap between our intentional and actual impact, making conscious shifts in our language and our thoughts.

Embracing the Body

Personal power, presence, and charisma are intimately connected to the body. When we are in contact with our personal bodily rhythms, we develop a more alive way of being. We move toward harmony with ourselves and with the rhythms of the universe when we experience life through our body. By feeling the person inside, we generate a presence that allows genuine connection with our inner core, with others, and with the rest of the world. Living in the body awakens us to our feelings and sensations. When we cultivate love of the body, tenderness emerges and we experience a richer, more harmonious life.

Instead of excessive reliance on conceptualizing and abstract thought, experiencing our life through the body puts us in touch with purpose and meaning. We can also rely on the intelligence of the body to guide us through crisis. Our body's innate capacity for sensing and empathy brings new awareness and choice into our daily lives and helps us heal both physically and emotionally. The body offers such a rich cache of information, that the question, "Where do you feel that in your body?" starts to sound repetitive. Mary Kuentz, a faculty member at Coaching that Works, eventually tells her coaching students to *stop* asking that question so that they can expand their repertoire of coaching skills.

When we embody our inner experience, our entire body is in a state of awareness and attention. From a genuine embodied presence, we give birth to words, thoughts and actions that inspire and empower. By connecting to the wellspring within, alert presence is concurrent throughout the whole body. Liberated, flowing gestures come from the center. Our free flow of subtle energy permeates other people.

The way our bodies move in relation to the space elicits the attention of others. Poised expectantly for interpersonal empathy, the whole body is aroused. Our bodies reflect our personal archetypal nature. When our body, gestures, posture, facial expression, and words are congruent and connected with our inner wellspring, we are inwardly empowered, outwardly exhilarated. When we stand tall and expansive with our heart area open, the body becomes a source of communication. Eye contact with one person at a time and peripheral contact with the group creates a sense of shared power. When we face another squarely, with deep relaxed breathing, our connection deepens and we create spaciousness and comfort. As we embrace our bodies, we practice the art of harmonizing ourselves with the universe.

Posture

Walking around with a book on our head may lead to perfect posture, but that only covers up our inner experience. Our posture sends a strong message about our inner world. Our stature is reduced when we disown our heart area, disregard our thighs, or hold our neck taut. We negate our personal power physically when our body is dozing or looks like this:

- Chest concaved
- Head jutted forward
- Fingers pointed
- Spine slouched
- Legs or arms crossed
- Eyes slitted
- Throat constricted
- Jaw tensed
- Pelvis pulled back
- Diaphragm contracted
- Arms held limp and lifeless

For instance, constricting the diaphragm is a common way to suppress longing. Sometimes this suppression shows up as tightness in the diaphragm or shallow breathing. The constriction can be released with movement, breath work, empathy, or touch. Just putting our attention on this area helps us return to the wisdom of the body and connect more with who we really are. Amplifying the constriction or exaggerating the movement can release whatever we're holding in that part of the body.

Fortunately we can reclaim our personal power just by changing our posture. Consciously releasing tension and aligning our posture allows an emotional release. We can physically rearrange the body to discover the power of presence so that we become supportive, alert, expectant, and open-hearted. Notice what happens internally and externally when we attend to spatial awareness and:

- Move the heart area forward and offer it to others
- Extend the spine
- Move thighs apart, uncross the legs, and ground the feet
- Connect with sparkle
- Change proximity to others

Self-alignment comes from internal and external congruence. When we use the body consciously, our gestures, facial expression, gaze, proximity to others, movement, touch, breath, and voice match our internal experience, and we communicate full authenticity. Slowing down our breath and breathing into the wisdom of the body opens us to Spirit, guidance, flow, and connection.

Subtle Energy

Whether you call it chi, life force, Holy Spirit, prana, Shakti, manna, or radiant subtle energy, the concept that energy can be harnessed for profound transformation and healing is nearly universal. Chinese acupuncture, Sufi dancing, healing by prayer, telepathy, mystical transmission, or heart-based intuition are all practices that heighten consciousness. In many spiritual traditions, the energetic frequencies are influenced by prayer, meditation, worship, devotion, love, and service. Although we can't see, hear, taste, or touch subtle energy, it permeates everything, and we sense the vibrations in our body and our emotions.

Nick Totton shares the basics of subtle energy work online, including a few exercises for building awareness of subtle energy. He says, "Working with these exercises will lead you into more and more subtle discriminations of energy and of what needs to happen. Dialogue opens up many more possibilities—what are they experiencing? What do they feel is trying to happen? The goal is to move flexibly between energy work and all the other kinds of work, e.g. verbal, bodily, etc. Color and imagery seem to be for many people especially important dimensions of subtle energy."[81]

Like water, energy is not positive or negative – it's part of the river of life. Wherever we put our attention, the energy flows. Instead of ignoring, suppressing or trying to still the energy, we can move with it. Without trying to control it, we can simply perceive the energy without expectation. We can gather and release energy simply by paying attention to it.

Balancing Autonomy, Collaboration and Leadership

How do we know when to lead and when to get out of the way? What level of intervention will serve the group? When we're insecure in our facilitation skills, we tend to control the group with the tentacles of an octopus, trying to impose direction, intervening way too often and our efforts to suppress only invite rebellion. As we tighten our grip, we lose more and more control, which sucks suck the life force out of the group. In contrast, if we use our leadership to foster autonomy and collaboration, we create an environment where power is welcome, shared, and honored.

Irvin Yalom, author of *The Theory and Practice of Group Psychotherapy* says:

> These group techniques or gimmicks are servants, not masters. To use them injudiciously, to fill voids, to jazz up the group, to acquiesce to the members' demands that the leader lead, is seductive but not constructive for the group.... Too *little* leader activity results in a floundering group. Too *much* activation by a leader results in a dependent group that persists in looking to the leader to supply too much. ... using gimmicks to make interactions, emotional expression, and self-disclosure too easy - misses the whole point. Resistance, fear, guardedness, distrust — in short, everything that impedes

---

[81] Totton, N. Retrieved from http://www.orgone.org/articles/ax6antot.htm

the development of satisfying interpersonal relations — must be permitted expression. The goal is to create not a slick-functioning, streamlined social organization, but one that functions well enough and engenders sufficient trust for the unfolding of each member's social microcosm. Working through the resistances to change is the key to the production of change.[82]

Internal resistance is a fascinating resource that we have access to only if we give it the space it is calling for. As facilitators, when we encourage the expression of resistance and really welcome the sun *and* the rain, people grow into their full power and show up more authentically. Virginia Kellogg, a coach and quilter, started using creative quilting as a healing process when her brother died. She describes how quilting helps people embrace and move through their resistance:

> My nourishment comes from understanding my soul path, which includes surprises, intimacy, working on the land, quilting, and coaching. I completely believe that people can create whatever they want. Even when I work with women on expressing themselves through quilting, I hold the space for them to explore, pushing them and letting them go.
>
> I worked with a long-time quilter who was terrified to get out of measuring everything precisely. Her goal was to discover a piece of herself that she hadn't found. I had no idea what it looked like. She had dreams about it, came in with images, but was stopped by thinking that it had to look a certain way.
>
> A big piece of facilitating awareness through quilting is inviting people to look everywhere for resources. Not just past experience, but everything becomes fodder. I provide the environment where more resources are available and stick with it through the hard parts – letting go of old rules about what colors go together, what "good" means. My job was to challenge my client's rules about what creativity means, look in places she was not trained to look, and ask new questions of herself. She was using the images from a dream and was surprised to uncover new meaning. Dancing with her process was delightful – at one point she was stuck and asked for my recommendation. I suggested she cut it all up. That was not what she expected and a lot of doors opened. She started adding things that weren't in her nature to choose and left some ragged edges. She had many insights about how rule-bound she was, not just in the quilting, but in her life. She left with a lot more room to design a creative life for herself.

---

[82] Yalom, I. (2005). *The theory and practice of group psychotherapy*. Basic Books.

New to facilitating through quilting, I moved in and out of confidence. I had to continually let go of my self-doubt in order to be a powerful facilitator for my client's process. I kept consciously stepping into self-trust. When I'm a participant, I have a strong experience of trusting and letting go. I translate that easily by putting myself in the shoes of the people I'm facilitating. I shake people out of their expectations so that there's room for transformation and surprise.

My best work is when I hold the space for new possibilities. I make a conscious effort to energetically put my arms around the room. Not to keep it safe, just to create the container for courage. I don't want people to rest and lay back unless that's something they never do. I call on myself to be more radical, unconventional, and authentic. Participants find the courage to call themselves out and go outside business as usual. I step into deeper and deeper levels of trust – in the process, in each individual soul, in the way that Spirit has our back.

When transformation is flowing, I'm the vehicle or a channel. I'm not paying attention to me. I'm incredibly happy, moved, honored, jubilant, excited, but my attention is on the person, the container, the group, and on what's needed. [83]

To see the variety and details of Virginia's quilts, go to
http://www.kodakgallery.com/I.jsp?c=16fggb6r.31gdvi83&x=0&y=lpxy6h&localeid=en_US

As a vehicle or channel, we hold the space for transformation. Balancing taking the lead with calling people forth is an art form dependent on trust. When we've seen growth emerge from chaos enough times, we put a lot less pressure on ourselves to make things happen. Whether we're working with new or existing groups, we continually face the challenge of creating space for autonomous, shared leadership to emerge.

---

[83] Virginia Kellogg personal interview 2/28/08. http://www.LeadershipthatWorks.com

The Dance of Co-Facilitation

The beauty of co-facilitation is that we can model heart connection, shared leadership, openness, and receptivity to feedback. To paraphrase Gandhi, we get to be the love we want to see in the world. Every facilitator makes hundreds of mistakes, but as co-facilitators, we help each other recover from any missteps, not by covering things up or smoothing things over, but by creating an opportunity for learning.

Nobody models the heart of co-facilitation the way Campbell Plowden does. He balances both leadership and shared power by embodying a deep trust in the process and his co-facilitators. He leads 3-day workshops for the Alternatives to Violence Project where he takes risks, shows up authentically, and supports co-facilitators and participants as they step into their power. Here's how he describes a transformational experience in a maximum security prison:

> If they're not revealing themselves, as the facilitator, I take risks. I reveal more personal information, so that they take risks. I check in with myself and ask, "What's something personal for me, what's a story I haven't shared ever before?" so that when I share it, it has that ring of authentic risk-taking. I'm not talking about one of my top five personal stories. It gets harder and harder to do that because there aren't a lot of stories left that I haven't told. When it gets scary, and there's no magic, no spark, what do I do? I try to love or jolt the group back into synch. How? By being extra attentive, emanating compassion for everybody, and listening very carefully to people.

> In one workshop, the flavor and mood changed on day two because some people felt scared pushing up against their discomfort, low energy, or apathy, while others were deepening their trust. When Shaun, my inside (inmate) co-facilitator struggled with an activity, I intervened. A participant said, "You have a problem with control." Afterwards, privately, another co-facilitator, Derek, reamed me out. I took a step back and listened fully and thought about the feedback. I acknowledged his concerns. As an inmate, Derek took a huge personal risk to share negative feedback with me, an outside lead facilitator. Then I shared my perception: that it was not my intention to undermine Shaun, but I felt we were losing ground, losing their attention. As lead facilitator, I felt a deep responsibility for the entire group. I wanted Derek to understand the emotional weight I carried as lead facilitator, and that sometimes I make decisions to act on my own even if it may not be popular.

> As a result, Derek and I connected in a person-to-person way that hadn't happened before. The next day we were in synch and worked as partners, resolving what was happening in a natural, effective way, both feeling very good about each other. It was a breakthrough for him that both of us really understood each other. If I'd only listened, he may have felt patronized;

however, because I willingly accepted his feedback and offered a heartfelt explanation of my emotional state, we deepened our mutual respect.[84]

In another story, Campbell tells about relinquishing control and deepening his trust of his co-facilitator as they develop shared leadership:

> My early memories of Ken are about his way of being in the group by showing off his intellect. When he talked about his community service in the inmate community, tutoring, teaching chess, and even when he talked about his anger, he was in his head. Inmates saw him as a smart, tough guy who was respectful, but you wouldn't want to mess with him. I thought he was sincere, but it seemed he was trying to earn his place in the group through bravado.
>
> Finally we were on the same facilitation team of an advanced workshop. Day two felt a little flat, so we decided to do an exercise called "care-fronting." The exercise begins with partners putting their foreheads together while talking about an issue that they disagree on. Personal space is thrown out the window. Usually they start to really hear each other and come to a greater understanding of each other, but in this case, the exercise ended with a lot of disparate energy. Some people had come together and others had become extremely agitated – lots of mixed energy floating around.
>
> I wanted to do the next part of the exercise, a guided visualization, because I enjoy the power of my voice as a calming agent. But when Ken volunteered, I heard his sincere caring for other people, which was often deeply buried. So I said, "Go for it."
>
> We dimmed the lights and Ken started by saying, "Imagine you are walking in a warm sunny place and see someone you care about, but have an unresolved conflict. What are you thinking and feeling?" As soon as Ken started speaking, the room went quiet [Campbell paused, cried softly and then continued]. Ken had a hypnotic power of humanness that instantly pervaded the room. He put out his deep empathy for them and their turmoil, and he showed that it was in him to open up and show his caring, just in his tone of voice. As soon as he started speaking, I was able to let go of my tension of being lead facilitator, which I almost never do in the prison. I felt such complete trust for his control, his holding of the spirit of the group. I could release myself and fully engage in the exercise. This space allowed me to do some good, hard personal work related to a loved one.

---

[84] Campbell Plowden personal interview 2/28/08.

After another intense hour, it felt like we were all in an outdoor terrain where people were wandering around blindfolded and kept burning their feet on fires that were popping up from the ground. Ken concluded the exercise beautifully. Some facilitators just read instructions verbatim from the manual and with luck the process can still work. Since participants had just been through an emotional wringer, though, this approach would have fallen short. Ken had to deliver the message in a 100% honest way and he nailed it. When he started to speak, the random fires were absorbed back into the earth, and the blindfolds came off – they didn't need them anymore. As people sat in a circle, it felt like everyone had also gravitated toward each other around a small warm fire. Facing outward around the safety of the fire, they faced their unresolved issues with courage.

When I asked Campbell about his tears, he shared from a soul-wrenching place:

I think I'm releasing grief from Ken's dying. I miss him. I'm so deeply saddened by the cruel irony of fate. He struggled with his demons of violence. Abused as a child, he faced the pain of having taken other people's lives and the pain of being incarcerated over and over. Ken had just started to deeply connect with his humanity, in large part through the Alternatives to Violence process. But as he was getting out of prison, he found out he had incurable brain cancer. In spite of that, or perhaps spurred on by that knowledge, he tried really hard to make his life come together. I feel the loss of his developmental process having been short circuited. I can't help but speculate about how much more good he could have done in the world by sharing his light.

I don't want to over-romanticize his situation. Toward the end of his life, Ken got into trouble, jumped parole, worked in Mexico, and found some good people who cared for him when his cancer caught up with him. I like to think that he died with some peace of mind. I really wish I had been able to talk with him about the final phase of his journey. He left me with some big questions.

Ken was like a horse whisperer – except he was an inmate whisperer. But that doesn't quite capture the essence of how he connected with people in turmoil. Somehow he summoned the energy in himself to be the calmer. He helped people to build the courage to face hard issues.[85]

---

[85] Campbell Plowden personal interview 2/28/08.

What I appreciate most about Campbell's story is that through heart connection, he supports Ken's emerging awareness and comes to trust Ken so deeply that he surrenders the lead role and they complement each other's development as facilitators.

I came to know Ken through Campbell and was drawn to his authenticity and deeply moved by his exploration of what motivated his violence. Ken himself told me stories about carefully planning ways he could get into fights so that he'd come out on top. He would even pretend to be drunk to give the other person enough courage to start something. He was stunned to discover that all his violence came from his craving for respect. Fighting was the only way he knew how to get it. In prison, he'd started doing yoga and had done a lot of work on his emotions. He could name his emotions instantly. I was astounded by the depth of his self-compassion as he transformed his judgment into awareness of his intense needs. In turn, he inspired me to deepen my own practice of self-compassion.

Ultimately, Ken found a new way to get that respect, not from perpetrating violence, and not only from Campbell and me, but from the many people he touched with his deep compassion for turmoil.

Interactive Co-Facilitation

Most people who call themselves co-facilitators actually practice a tag-team approach where one facilitator works with the group at a time. Using a more collaborative, interactive approach where both facilitators work together simultaneously, almost like improv theatre, we demonstrate deep trust in each other and in the flow. With some practice, we learn to:

- Blend facilitation by building on each other's ideas
- Make changes in direction without refuting each other
- Model trust without checking excessively with each other
- Interrupt each other with grace
- Jointly hold the needs of the group and the needs of individuals as a gift
- Track time while giving each other space
- Stay aware of natural openings
- Share feedback openly and support each other's growth
- Empathize and celebrate success

If we co-facilitate as if we're doing improv on stage, we can rely on one of the most well-known of all improv activities, "Yes, and." We say "yes" no matter what our partner gives us, "and" we build upon their contribution. Instead of throwing bricks around the room, we stack them, building on the bricks that have come before. In addition to saying "Yes, and" to our co-facilitator, we do the same with participants. When a participant offers an idea, raises an objection, or shares an experience, instead of responding, "Actually I was going to cover that later…" or "Here's contrary evidence," if we say "yes" to whatever they bring, "and" leverage the value, we build trust and flow. Now sometimes a participant says something I find quite ridiculous and every cell in my body is screaming "NO," so I find it difficult for the word yes to come out of my mouth. For instance, someone says, "All the bankers should be hung," I can still acknowledge the opinion without agreeing by saying, "You are passionate about the banking system," or "I hear how upset you are." That's far different from, "Are you crazy?" or, "No, that would be illegal," which would stop the process cold. By building on what the co-facilitator and the participants say, we add to the trust and the flow. It might sound something like this:

> Facilitator A: Now let's move on to the activity and put these mediation concepts into practice.
>
> Facilitator B: Yes, I'm eager to get moving on the practice too, and before we do that, I want to say one more thing about mediation skills... if you want people to hear each other fully, slow the process down.
>
> Facilitator A: Yes, I'm glad you brought that up so that you can notice what happens when you slow things down in the third step of the practice.
>
> Participant: What do you mean third step? I've never heard about steps one and two!
>
> Facilitator B: Yes, it's kind of wild and crazy to start with step three. And since step three is the heart of the practice, we'll come back to steps one and two in a moment.

We can build on just about everything. In this way we help the group to trust that opposing opinions can co-exist. Through "yes, and" we can dialogue even when we disagree, and thereby co-create mutually satisfying outcomes. In addition to acknowledging our co-facilitators and participants, we can also incorporate extraneous events. If the flipchart crashes to the floor, or a bird pecks at the window, and we just ignore them and continue on, the participants perceive that we're wedded to a script. If we acknowledge the crash or the bird's frustration, that's a step up, but if we weave these seemingly unrelated events into the flow, as though they are meant to contribute to our understanding, we become jazz improv artists instead of individuals practicing our own riffs.

I especially enjoy the music I make when co-facilitating with Mary Kuentz because I value her playfulness and directness. Here she explores what makes co-facilitation work and what happens when it doesn't:

> I like having a common language and common understanding with my co-facilitator, finding what we're both passionate about and committing to alignment. Beforehand, we have a conversation about why we're here, what scares us, and what's important to us. We also talk about what we hope people walk away with, how they will be changed, *and* how we will be changed.

If we're not aligned, if we're going in different directions, it feels harder, and the joy and ease of co-facilitation is gone. We can either find the joy and ease or release ourselves into nonalignment and process the difficulty. Either way, there's plenty of learning available.

I once worked with a co-facilitator where we got along really well personally. He teased me, which was his way of connecting. That worked for me until he teased me about not knowing the material, which triggered me. During the break I said, "I would appreciate if you have some feedback that you tell me directly. The teasing isn't working because you're trying to tell me something without telling me." It felt rough. A participant came up during the break and said, "You're not in synch and it shows." I wanted to speak to it in the group, and let them know what was happening between us, so they could see how we work it out. But he didn't want to take us off the timeline. We needed to clean it up ourselves. So we did something half-way. By sticking to the time line, the workshop became generic – we lost the magic, lost the intimacy. Without self-disclosure and transparency, a lot of learning was lost. From that experience, I learned to stand my ground and trust what I know. Now I trust that we can stay on the time line, process what's happening in the group, and make sure that everyone gets more learning. Transparency works![86]

Occasionally one co-facilitator gets sidetracked or loses connection. Below are some of Mary's and my responses to some common situations that arise in co-facilitation.

What do we do when our co-facilitator:

Becomes animated about his own ideas when the participant runs out of ideas? *Acknowledge his excitement and ask where the participant is in the process.*

Loses the energy of the room by working with a participant who starts the process energized, but by the end of the session looks deflated? *Check in with the participant and others, articulate my observations, and go from there.*

Takes a participant back to the place he didn't want to go? *Check in, share my observations, connect empathically with where he's going and redirect to stay with the participant's agenda.*

Deflects feedback by explaining his reasoning for his choices? *Share what I'm noticing and ask how she would like to receive feedback in a way that connects.*

---

[86] Mary Kuentz personal interview 4/21/08.

191

Uses her authority in a way that detracts from individual autonomy? *Articulate what I see, empathize with the unexpressed needs (either mine, his or other's), and make a request.*

Invites powerful physical movement, but the participant continuously returns to a collapsed posture? *Assume that my co-facilitator and I already have an agreement that we can jump in and co-facilitate, so I articulate what I see and make empathic guesses about what's going on.*

Rushes through the process? *Articulate what I'm noticing and how people are impacted. If the participants are getting value, then rushing hasn't interfered. If I notice that participants look confused, I check in with them.*

Does not notice that four people in the room are either asleep or drowsy? *Acknowledge the drowsiness myself and ask what people need.*

Says, "We have more time, don't we?" but doesn't check for your response? *Interrupt and answer the question – we have about ten more minutes.*

Gets triggered and needs to leave the room? *Ask participants what's happening with them. Trust that my co-facilitator can take care of herself, get what she needs, and come back. Check in when she does.*

Doesn't hold time agreements and repeatedly wants to add one more thing? *Share my observations and voice my concern about keeping agreements, without judgment.*

Speaks in circles, often explaining what he just said? *Acknowledge his desire for clarity and check what need is he meeting with explaining? Give empathy and make a request that he notice his impact, and stop speaking* before *people drift away.*

Keeps talking even when participants disengage? *Check in with my interpretation of what's going on in me in terms of disengagement. Ask my co-facilitator what she's noticing.*

Disagrees with you? *Appreciate the differences.*

Uses more than her share of the airtime? *Check in with my own interpretation of her "share." Then self-empathize silently and tell my co-facilitator how I'm feeling and what I'm wanting.*

Establishes a hierarchical structure with either herself or yourself on top? *Get curious about what needs the hierarchy is meeting and request something else that meets my needs and hers.*

Rarely speaks and relies on you to give directions, debrief activities, and offer insights? *Ask for more participation. If this is his first time facilitating with me, he might be scared, so I'd offer empathy.*

Gives feedback to participants without being aware of the impact? *Share my observation of what was happening for him in giving the feedback and ask what he noticed. Check in with participants to see what's up for them.*

Doesn't make time to debrief the learning? *Redirect the conversation.*

Evaluates participants' contributions by saying, "Good question," or "That's great." *This seems harmless enough, but ask for specifics. What do you value about that question? What's great about it?*

Expresses a judgment about a participant? *Don't step over this. Share my need for connection. Support him in unpacking the judgment. Help him own his inner process by uncovering his feelings and needs, and then check in with the participant.*

As co-facilitators continuously build trust with each other, they have a ripple effect on the group. When I was co-facilitating with Kobi Skolnick, an Israeli activist with Combatants for Peace, things went beautifully the first day. It was our first time co-facilitating, but he had a knack for it and I'd come to trust him deeply. On the second day when he asked the group to take a vote on a side issue, I cringed. I didn't need to say anything, because the group refused to go along with his suggestion, insisting on more dialogue. Even though the process went on, I felt myself physically and emotionally pull away from Kobi, telling myself that I'd have to handle this rowdy group on my own. That night when we debriefed the process, and I explained how the suggestion of a vote seemed incongruent with the group's needs, I could see he really took it in. He had a gentle way of telling me what he wanted from me:

> You said that loving each other was the most important thing we could do as co-facilitators, so when we got disconnected, I was lost. I touched you with my foot, but you didn't look at me or respond. I lost all confidence.

His words woke me up! We stayed up past midnight talking about what *I* could do differently. Until that moment, I'd been thinking of what *he* could do differently, which was ridiculous. Instead of judging him or being disappointed in his skills, we brainstormed many options that would engage us both. I fell back in love with him and we came to a much deeper place of trust. We both have a sweet tooth for exploring new growth opportunities, and he knew how to call me into doing my inner work. That's the beauty of co-facilitation.

So how do we support each other as co-facilitators? We co-create learning objectives, plan the program, dance with whatever is alive, and build on what each other is saying. We also create plenty of time for mutual connection and share what each of us wants to get from the experience personally. Most importantly, we can *ask for what we want*. We can set agreements about what kind of support we want, so that we both get to play with our growing edge and know the other will be there for us. A few requests I've heard co-facilitators ask:

- If you see any discomfort in me, will you ask me to share with the group so that I learn to be more vulnerable?
- To help me track time, will you set a timer for 15 minutes and say, "You have about 2 more minutes"?
- Will you remind me during the debrief to celebrate insights and capture the learning?
- To increase alive engagement, can you support me in asking dissatisfied participants for their feedback live in the moment?

Sometimes I envy solo facilitators because they can do whatever they want. But they don't get the support or learning opportunities that co-facilitators offer each other. They have a lot of autonomy, but at what cost? Whether we work solo or in a team, self-care is crucial to our well being, so asking for and creating what we want is vital. We rely on our co-facilitators or our support network for brainstorming, designing, capturing the learning, holding our feet to the fire if we're procrastinating or getting us to take better care of ourselves. Without a support team I'd be lost.

Whenever we co-facilitate, there's a danger that we will rely too heavily on our partner or team and diminish our own value. Sometimes we don't prepare as rigorously, or we simply take a back seat. Brian Reddy says, "Curiously, the de-skilling phenomenon is most obvious and pronounced among Human Resource Development practitioners. As group members – talented as they might be when in the role of consultant—they resist using their skills for group effectiveness. When later queried, members offer explanations such as, 'I didn't want to look like the consultant…' or 'I didn't think of it; I wanted to be a regular member.' Often, just making the de-skilling observation can loosen up members and legitimize their using their skills."[87]

I've been in a few situations where I've de-skilled myself, and I don't find it that easy to shake it off. It's a curious phenomenon. I've tried to uncover the needs that would lead to this behavior, but the best I can come up with is that I want to belong, create a sense of harmony as we become one voice, and I want it to be easy. There's a reason we call it facilitation – the root word facile means flowing, moving effortlessly, easy to do. Up-front agreements about how we'll co-facilitate help us address tough issues when they arise. In my early days of co-facilitation, I almost always worked with people who had a similar skill set – we'd been to the same training programs, so we had a shared context, language, and understanding of ways to process. Later I would choose co-facilitators who had a different style and fresh ways of doing things so that I could learn. Today I want a balance – I want the ease that comes from shared understanding, *and* I want to enjoy learning new approaches to facilitation.

Criteria for Choosing Co-Facilitators

Over the years many people have asked to co-facilitate with me, and I know instantly whether I want to work with them, but occasionally I find it difficult to say why. So I made a list of all the things I look for in a co-facilitator. Some basic skills or ways of being are so important that they're non-negotiable. No one has the whole package of traits, but for the sake of learning, I want to work with facilitators who bring skills to the table that I want to develop, such as:

- Holding multiple agendas simultaneously
- Designing activities on the fly based on what the group needs now
- Synthesizing group desires
- Bringing out my humor and creativity
- Designing metrics for evaluating and improving the quality of the program

If you'd like to see the complete list of criteria I use for selecting co-facilitators, refer to the resource section on page 384 and then think about your own criteria.

Creating a Dynamic Training Team

When working with large groups, our first step is to create a dynamic training team. Our commitment is to holding the space and caring for everyone's needs. Some of the things we discuss up front:

- How will we create a learning community?
- What expectations do we have of each other?
- What agreements do we want to make?
- What is our growing edge as individuals and as a team?
- What kind of support does each of us need from one another?

---

[87] Reddy, W. B. (1994). *Intervention skills. process consultation for small groups and teams.* Pfeiffer & Company.

Exercises

Reflections:

1. What's unique about your personal style?
2. If people noticed one thing about you, what would give you the most joy?
3. What message does your body have for you right now?
4. How does you body express full self-empowerment?
5. What does your posture tell you about yourself right now?

Small Group Discussions:

1. In small groups, draw a mask and describe how your outer expression is different from your inner experience.
2. Collectively design a creative way to discover what the group notices about charismatic people in the room.
3. In pairs, tell a story about a time when you noticed your own charisma. How did people respond to you? How did you respond to yourself?

Activities:

1. Try John Heron's Experiential Presence activity described on page 242 of the Complete Facilitator's handbook and give each other feedback.
2. What can you do with your reclaimed presence?
3. What are *your* criteria for choosing your co-facilitators? Out of all the things you're looking for in a co-facilitator, what matters most?
4. Now co-design an ideal relationship with a co-facilitator. How can you ensure that you support each other fully?

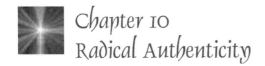

Chapter 10
Radical Authenticity

I did not know I was on a search for passionate aliveness. I only knew I was lonely and lost and that something was drawing me deeper beneath the surface of my life in search of meaning. There is a hunger in people to go to those deep depths; to know that our lives are sacred; that our hearts are truly capable of love. It is a yearning to be all that we can be. A longing for what is real. --
Anne Hillman, The Dancing Animal Woman

Honesty does not have to be brutal. Instead of equating authenticity with blurting out our cruelest thoughts, we can use honest dialogue to build awareness of what's needed. Facilitators that scold or reprimand the group or display even a hint of arrogance, only put the entire group in a defensive mode, because they want to protect each other from criticism. Instead of talking behind each other's backs, they'll step into authentic communication and create opportunities for mutual satisfaction. By talking about what matters most, people communicate transparently, become energized, and invite others to see their needs as gifts. When people feel understood, they open to new visions and develop team spirit that impact productivity and the bottom line.

In this chapter about radical authenticity, we'll unravel the myth of neutrality, expand openness and transparency, and explore ways to communicate more honestly. Using the language of the heart, imagery and e-prime, we'll learn to tell our truth without judgment. Open dialogue is not about determining who is right and who is wrong, or claiming higher moral ground. Openness includes pursuing what we want, but not at the expense of others. By listening to what others *really* want, we open up to new perspectives that lead to personal and organizational transformation.

Neutrality

When facilitators remain neutral, they help groups develop trust and think creatively, despite differences of opinion. In contrast, when facilitators have a stake in the outcome or an opinion about the direction, faith in the process diminishes. Neutral facilitators can help team members listen to each other by honoring the wisdom from all points of view. As a result, they're able to develop a plan that everyone trusts as fair and sustainable. The intention behind neutrality is to prevent the perception of favoritism or that the outcome is rigged.

The problem with "modeling neutrality" is that in many cases, we can only *pretend* to be neutral. Taken to extremes, facilitators who overuse neutrality appear cold, heartless, and disengaged. Distancing ourselves from participants doesn't serve anyone. Whether we're a news reporter, referee, judge, mediator, parent or facilitator, we have our personal reactions. As hard as we might try to portray neutrality, we can't separate ourselves from our visceral, emotional, authentic reactions. The problem with turning down the flame on our emotions is that we hide parts of ourselves and we become flat and lifeless.

Picture the facilitator sitting in the parking lot, the gear shift in neutral, the engine idling, waiting for people to get in the car, but meanwhile the car uses energy and goes nowhere. To get people into the car and start moving, we can do more than sit passively in neutral. We can offer them our hearts and our understanding. When they have a sense that they are seen and understood, they want to go for the ride. When they see that we extend our open-heartedness to *other* people, they soften and have more spaciousness to see and hold others as collaborators rather than adversaries.

The intention of modeling neutrality is to support *all* parties but we can do that best by fully receiving and honoring each person's emotions, including our own. That doesn't mean we take sides with one person – it means we take sides with every person, by really feeling into their experience and honoring all that they bring – their feelings, their passion, their longing. The concept of neutrality belongs in the same category of advice as "teachers should not have favorites," and "doctors should not get emotionally involved," or "bosses should not make friends with their employees." There's nothing wrong with favoring people—as long as we recognize that cultivating favor with *everyone* is a blessing, not a curse. And what's so great about not getting emotionally involved – we're afraid we might *feel* something? The only boss I'd ever want to work for is the boss that knows how to build friendships across the board. When we stonewall ourselves off from others, we miss countless opportunities. In our desire to foster inclusion and create safe space for people to work openly, we don't have to cut ourselves off from people to be effective facilitators.

Openness

Openness is all about keeping it real. That doesn't mean we reveal the details of our finances or our sex lives out of the blue, but we share what's relevant for the sake of building heart connection. Nothing contributes more to our personal presence than our honest expression in the moment. Many, many people have told me compelling stories about their vulnerability as facilitators, and I particularly enjoy the risk-taking and early vulnerability described by François Beausoleil from Montreal.

> On my way to working with a new group, I was thinking, "What can I do to open wide the vulnerability door? What is the level of vulnerability that I'm wanting? What is my role?" I didn't know the answer. As the group came together, instead of talking, I wanted to *show* who I am, so I started singing

Mother by John Lennon and doing percussion on my body. Music is important to me, and I was missing my mother and father, so my singing was full of emotion. People were clapping, but at some point, I noticed internal discomfort. I thought, "Are you crazy? This is a business setting. People don't know you at all. Percussion on my body? This is not a show – it's a training." A little later I shared my discomfort with the group – I was telling myself I should never do something like that. I asked their reaction to the singing and five or six people said they really liked it and found it meaningful. Then I could really relax and enjoy myself.

My vulnerability and transparency created an immediate level of trust in the group. I've done many days of training with them since. Last week one woman told me that my singing made a profound impression on her and helped her to bond and trust. I take a risk when I bring myself into the work, but it's proof that this work is meaningful to me. Whenever I share something deep, things shift in terms of engagement. When I show up, I'm not sure how I'll be received, but I do it anyway. Even if some people express that they are unhappy, we connect about that. [88]

They enjoyed his singing, but I suspect they valued even more when François shared his discomfort vulnerably. The singing opened the door, but they could really see his humanity when he opened up with his feelings. Everywhere I go, people crave transparency. They don't want our buttoned-up personas, they want our realness. What a misconception that we think "having it all together" will help us to belong, when the opposite is true.

Richard Michaels, my partner at Coaching that Works, doesn't plan vulnerability. He looks for natural openings.

My own vulnerability takes me to deeper places. Sometimes I get trapped, wanting to look a certain way, or appear smart, a good facilitator, masterful, whatever. So sometimes I miss the moment where I can be vulnerable. That's an edge. When I take risks, I get feedback from the group. Often they see my vulnerability as courage and strength which creates connection. It's important to take risks, but if I tell myself to take risks, then I feel afraid because I'm pushing myself, saying, "Oh, I should do this risky thing." Instead of creating a risk, I look for a natural opening and follow my intuition. Following the gut and following the moment without a plan. It's less of a performance and more authentic.

So I explore facilitation from the inside out. I actually share and step into the vulnerability. I go beneath the surface and use facilitation to connect to

---

[88] François Beausoleil – personal interview 5/21/08

authentic power and truly learn how to use myself as the experiment in a laboratory.[89]

Getting comfortable with our own vulnerability is a bit of an oxymoron, but the practice of sharing ourselves transparently is what helps people connect with our realness, which helps them get in touch with their own. People all over the world are hungry for transparency and sharing our inner world invites them into deeper, more intimate connection.

Transparency

In our culture vulnerability is often confused with weakness, but expressing ourselves transparently takes courage. Our readiness to express our internal emotions and explore our deepest needs gives people a sense of trust and an invitation to share their own vulnerability. Not every group is ready for deep disclosure which can provoke anxiety and loss of trust. But as people develop high awareness, when the facilitator holds the intention of the group and uses transparency for the sake of the whole, everyone benefits.

For example, a facilitator may say: "I want to share my experience to see if others feel similarly or differently. My energy has been dropping, and I don't feel as connected to what's going on in the group. I'd like to ask how many people would welcome a change in direction right now?"

If we have agreement from the group up front and we sense receptivity in the moment, some ways to share transparently and vulnerably include:

- Sharing why we've chosen a particular intervention
- Sharing our emotions, learning, and appreciations in the now
- Using a fishbowl technique of the facilitator team to model transparency
- Modeling receptivity to live feedback from co-facilitators and the group
- Choosing to do our own personal growth work within a supportive group

We choose our level of transparency based on our evaluation of the readiness of the group. We also evaluate our own readiness to disclose. Virginia Kellogg, my business partner since 1997, continues to inspire me. Here's a story from her early days as a facilitator about the power of being real:

> When I'm really receptive, I offer less guidance, and that's when I do my best facilitating. I used to think I needed to be dynamic, talk a lot, and then everybody would see my power. But that isn't how I'm most powerful. It's not about me. It's about the experience of the individual and the group of which I'm a part.

---

[89] Richard Michaels personal interview 3/20/08. http://CoachingthatWorks.com

As a new facilitator, I would bring an entourage of people to support me. On one weekend retreat, none of them could come. I was terrified of having no support. I set the participants up to have buddies and told them, "I want everyone here to be my buddy. That means that sometime during the weekend, I want each of you to check in with me on how I'm doing." I've never been better supported. Until then, I had such a pull to be an adored leader, but it's a huge trap. I was building circles of fans, but I never felt seen at all. But that day, I was seen and better supported than ever. When I told participants I was terrified, all of a sudden they could see me *and* love me. Afterward a participant said, "If you can lead this group as scared as you are, then I can lead!" I got it then that I had to get off the pedestal. That doesn't mean I abdicate leadership. Instead I become a peer - I got a hand with my needs and they stepped into a more powerful place as leaders themselves.

How do I balance being a leader and a colleague? By being a peer with the people I lead. I use examples of my own experience to bring people more deeply into their experience. I am more vulnerable about sharing my own stories. The challenge is to be in a real relationship with people I facilitate instead of being an invisible person. What makes our coaching training so heart-opening is that we create space for people to be themselves by being real as facilitators. The power of nourishment pushes people into their unique creative expression, to be more of who they are, and do their work in the world. [90]

When we're in the facilitator role and we get lost or we don't know what to do, the simplest and perhaps most-endearing approach is to ask for help. Even though it's our "job" or our "role," if we let go of our attachment to how things should look, participants are touched by our transparency, inspired to help, and empowered to explore options. Even if chaos ensues, that can give us enough space to re-ground ourselves in the group's desires and come back with a suggestion that takes the group forward.

Many facilitators hold a common belief that we should not contribute to the content or express our feelings. We want to work with the feelings that already exist in the group without overshadowing them with our own feelings. However, if we take that too far and don't disclose anything about ourselves, we erode trust. We can increase the level of transparency in the group by sharing ourselves transparently. Jan Blum from Springboard Communication describes how she learned to invite the whole person to show up:

My co-facilitator, Marti, suggested that we ask people to share something they'd just as soon others didn't know about them. I blanched. I imagined this

[90] Virginia Kellogg personal interview 2008. http://LeadershipthatWorks.com

would shut people down real quick. For some reason, I agreed to try it. I had the word "CHOICE" written on the whiteboard and before we ever got the questions, we talked about how we value choice and anyone could pass or decline at any time during the workshop. After Marti walked thru the questions we would like each person in the group to answer, I offered to go first (to set both the pace and to show equal regard by sharing something vulnerable about me). I was shocked by people's reaction. It seemed like they were eager to share these things that were unspeakable, relieved that anyone would want to know. It created a bond and an openness that I would have never imagined and set a tone of full engagement for the entire workshop.[91]

Few groups have enough safety and freedom for people to share their attractions and aversions authentically, and many people consider it off-limits because they want safety for everyone. With an imbalance of power and unhealed trauma present in almost every group, expressing attraction can feel scary and dangerous. But ultimately, I like to see people test the waters and learn to express their inner world with self-compassion and compassion for others. The assumption that attraction and aversion must be implied or kept secret puts limits on our authenticity. I would love to hear how other facilitators welcome expression of attraction and aversion in holistic ways.

Chris Argryis's work helps us explore our growth toward transparency by using the Ladder of Inference, pictured below. We all make meaning from our observations. Our inferences and assumptions help us decide how to respond. We diagnose situations because we want to understand. However, unless we test our inferences and assumptions, we run the risk of acting on invalid assumptions. Fortunately we can offer support by asking each other to test our inferences.

Collectively we can change the way we think by lowering our level of inference. When we share specific examples, we give people observations that they can validate. People often have different understandings for the same words, so sometimes we need to clarify what words mean.

That doesn't mean we say, "Juan, you're on the top of the ladder of inference, and I think you ought to come down a few steps." Our goal isn't to show Juan the error of his ways or to diagnose him. Instead we can share a practice of making our thinking process more transparent, reveal the impact Juan's action has on us and determine our common interests. Making our thinking visible reveals our inner process to others, and more importantly to ourselves, deepening our self-discovery process.

---

[91] Jan Blum personal correspondence 2009.

Figure 10.1 Climbing the Ladder of Inference

7. Take action based on conclusions or decide

6. Adopt beliefs based on conclusions or evaluate

5. Draw conclusions or diagnose

4. Make inferences or make assumptions

3. Assign meaning or interpret data

2. Select specific data or determine what is important

1. Experience raw data, words spoken or observations

Figure 10.2 Example of Climbing the Ladder of Inference

7. We need to find someone to take Molly's place.

6. We only need advocates for new technology on the team.

5. She can't keep up with changing technology.

4. She doesn't think the new technology is important

3. Molly was doing something that she values more than talking about technology.

2. Molly came 30 minutes late.

1. The group agreed to start the meeting at 10 am. Molly came at 10:30.

Figure 10.1 shows the path up the ladder of inference, while Figure 10.2 shows an example. Ideally what we think and what we say are the same, but to achieve this congruence of thoughts and words, most of us need to change the way we think. One way to become more transparent is a rigorous practice of coming down the ladder of inference and sharing our observations, feelings, needs, and requests.

The transparency test involves three steps:

1. Notice what you're thinking.

2. Imagine yourself telling other people what you're thinking and what your strategy is.

3. What is your reaction? If you're feeling embarrassed or uncomfortable you're probably not being transparent.

Transparency is the practice of revealing ourselves, which can include sharing personal stories or our reasons for making specific choices in facilitation. Expanded consciousness comes from practicing transparency. When combined with heart connection, transparency can contribute to trust, safety, learning, connection, and community. Because the facilitator's role is to focus on the group's needs, sometimes transparency is discouraged out of a desire to hold the integrity of the facilitator's role. In the article "The Gift of Self: The Art of Transparent Facilitation," Miki Kashtan describes the value of transparency, "…the benefits of transparent facilitation outweigh the risks and propose a practical approach for deciding when and how to be transparent while facilitating. Responsible transparency requires both a high level of self-awareness and internal mastery, as well as finely-tuned communication skills to convey to the group what we choose to share of our inner experience while sustaining the focus on participants' needs."[92]

A rigorous practice that helps us develop the art of transparency is to write about a difficult conversation using two columns. In the left-hand column write what you thought or felt during the conversation, and in the right hand column, write what was actually said. Figure 10.3 shows a case where the right- hand and left-hand columns are radically different.

Figure 10.3 Left-Hand Column and Right-Hand Column

Left-Hand Column Thoughts and Feelings	Right-Hand Column The Actual Conversation
I sort of like this guy, but all he ever talks about is Harvard. I hope he doesn't sit by me.	Guy: Can I sit here? Suze: Sure!
How annoying. I'll just ignore him if he talks about Harvard.	Guy: When I was at Harvard, we had chairs just like this. Suze: My niece just started at Harvard.
Argh! I can't believe I'm feeding into his talk about Harvard. He must have flunked out and never got over it. How can I get away from this guy?	Guy: Really? I could talk to her and introduce her to a few people. Suze: Sure, but I have an appointment in five minutes, so I have to run. We'll get together another time.
Yeah, right.	

All too often what people think and feel isn't even vaguely similar to what they say. Usually people can tell we're being evasive or disingenuous, but they don't know why. Mapping out a conversation using the right and left-hand columns helps us identify what's really going on (in the left- hand column) and choose to talk about our experience in ways that are real. If our

---

[92] Kashtan, M. (2005). *The IAF Handbook of Group Facilitation: Best Practices from the Leading Organization in Facilitation.* Edited by Sandy Schuman. Jossey Bass.

thoughts are full of judgments that we'd be embarrassed to reveal, then we first look at changing what we're thinking.

Honest Expression

Although many, many people claim they value honesty, few of us make it a rigorous practice. The primary reason? We're afraid of judgment – fearful that others will judge us or perceive that we judge them. In part that's because we *do* judge others and they *do* judge us. Even when things are going well, some of us suffer from the imposter syndrome – "If they only knew how clueless I am…" or "How come I can facilitate in war-torn countries when I can't even facilitate peace and harmony in my own family?" How do we use self-judgment as a stepping stone to compassion? We can turn the stone over, connect to the cynical harshness and allow the water to wash over our suffering and change our bitter judgments into a well of compassion. In addition to seeing ourselves with compassion, we need to empathically connect with the other person before we share transparently.

We can learn to think, act, and speak in ways that remove the shackles of judgment so that we can express ourselves without shame or blame. We can apply the simple model of self-empathy (reflection on observations, feelings, needs, and requests)[93] to the practice of honest expression. In this moment if I self-empathize using this model, it sounds like, "When I use the delete key more than any other, I'm frustrated, because I need some flow and clarity in my writing, so I request that I write without any interruptions for the next two hours." Applying the same model when I express myself to Dave, I say, "You have come into my office five times this morning, and I'm frustrated because I need more flow and clarity in my writing. Would you be willing to come only once and then give me two hours to write without interruption?" I find this process extremely useful because it helps me connect with what's *really* going on internally before I express myself to others. Until we have had a lot of practice with this model, we sound like a clunky robot. The language can feel so dry and wooden that it has the opposite effect of what we're intending – disconnection. I've heard countless people respond to the way beginners use the model with lines like:

- Do you know how stupid you sound?
- You've lost your spontaneity.
- What do you really think?
- You sound so clinical.
- Let's get real.
- Don't use that crap on me.

That's enough to scare anyone away. But when we practice Observations, Feelings, Needs and Requests (OFNR) like a musical scale, we increase our range so that we can develop beautiful connections regardless of differences. Ultimately OFNR is scaffolding for building our

---

[93] Rosenberg, M. (2002). *Nonviolent Communication: A language of life.* PuddleDancer Press.

relationships. Eventually we no longer need the scaffolding. If the technique becomes the goal, we shield ourselves from the possibility of deeper connection. As we're learning the technique, if we remember *why* we're using it – to open our hearts – then we can experiment, take risks, mess it up, and still maintain the connection.

I was at a conference with Sigal Shoham, a one-woman playwright who can improv anything, when a man asked for some time with her. Quickly she said not now, but when he said he didn't think she'd ever give him some time, she stopped and said, "Something about what you're saying is true for me, so let me check in with myself." After a few moments of silence she said, "When you asked to talk to me, I had an immediate fear that if I start a conversation with you, there will be no end to it. I want some reassurance that I'll get some value from it and that my time with you nurtures me too." His response was, "Wow! Thanks for that – that's very helpful for me because I get a similar reaction from a lot of people, but no one has ever told me *why* they don't want to talk to me." Clearly he found this short conversation very satisfying because he got some understanding about what was pushing her and possibly others away.

What I like most about Sigal's approach is that she agreed to give him feedback *before* she knew what she was going to say. Her response might be difficult for him to hear, but she was willing to explore anyway. She *owned* her experience, making it about her. She didn't say, "Your energy sucks me dry," or "you never stop talking;" she talked about *herself.* I find her spontaneity infectious whether she's facilitating workshops, performing her one-woman plays, or offering empathy at the Farmer's Market in San Francisco.

When people get honest feedback about their behavior, they may be baffled, hurt or delighted, but they invariably want to understand their impact on others. The skill of giving inspirational feedback is to share what we imagine they want and if they're open to it, possible strategies for getting what they want. During a workshop a friend said to me, "I have some feedback for you about your leadership if you'd like to hear it." His tone was soft, and I interpreted his facial expression as caring, so I said, "Sure." If you want to connect more deeply with the people you're talking to, try breathing with them." What I loved about his feedback is that he went straight for something he knew I wanted and then offered a suggestion. I find myself very receptive to people who take the time to understand what matters to me.

All too often, feedback stems from judgment instead of a vision of what's possible. One way to communicate our reactions to people's behavior is to translate our perceptions and judgments into awareness of our personal needs. It might sound like feedback I got recently, "When you speak so quickly, I find myself tensing. I'd like you to slow down so we can enjoy the moment." I enjoyed the invitation. Honest expression about what we want *for* others or *from* others is a practice that generates intimacy, even if the messages are hard to hear.

We all long for intimacy – it's a primal human need. If we open energetically to another person or the group, we can experience each other's deep mystical radiance. And yet many of us fear intimacy, including self-intimacy. To protect ourselves from pain, we withdraw or hide from intimacy even when we recognize that we're longing to melt into sweet connection.

Loving other people could lead to sex or we could get hurt; loving ourselves could lead to self-centeredness or insensitivity to others. So it's not uncommon for us to run away from intimacy whether it's with ourselves or others. At the same time, this primal human force keeps drawing us into deeper levels of intimacy so that we can experience each other's realness, open our hearts to each other, and generate exquisite connections.

Facilitating groups by helping people express their honest emotions openly and transparently leads to trust and intimacy. But when participants honestly express their judgments, they breed distrust and fear. Even thinking judgmental thoughts without expressing them leads to distrust because people can easily read the judgmental energy and body language. We can sense when people are withholding, either because they're afraid people will judge them or they don't want to open Pandora's Box. All they want is a little comfort and harmony. So how do we create an environment of honest expression without frightening people? As facilitators, it's not enough to speak compassionately; we need to think compassionately too. To build safety, any time a participant shares a judgment we translate it into a wish, a value, or a need. As a spiritual practice we see each person's divinity, not just in general, but in every moment.

When a large medical lab was going through a merger, the CEO intuitively knew that closeness in the senior team was important, so she arranged a retreat at a beautiful spot in a redwood forest. Our primary directive was to increase intimacy in the team, so we designed each activity to build on the last. Although billed as a team-building retreat, we weren't sure the Medical Research Director would show up because "his work was too important" and he'd complained in the past that retreats were "too touchy-feely." But in the opening circle, when we asked people to share one of their dreams, he said with a lot of emotion, "All I want is for people to love me." The room went silent. In that moment everyone could sense the shift in the energy. Most of the body language indicated that they were eager to join him in that place of transparent vulnerability, but one person pushed her chair back a few inches. As facilitators, we said a few words to honor the sacredness of the moment and create some safety for those experiencing discomfort.

Later in the day the group did a mask making activity where people created paper plate masks of their personae at work, and then described the purpose of that mask. The intimacy deepened as people shared from their inner world, including one participant who said his fear was that people thought he was incompetent in his new position, and what he really wanted people to know is that *he was way less competent than people could possibly imagine.* Much later he revealed how difficult that was for him to say. Most C-level leaders are afraid to show any vulnerability whatsoever, but this group found his self-disclosure endearing, since many of them were in tough jobs, in slightly over their heads, at least some of the time. Each time someone shared vulnerably, they invited the rest of the group to shatter the images they'd been portraying. The CEO shocked everyone by saying her blustery demeanor was an attempt to hide that she was shaking like a leaf inside. The only person who was not a doctor described her mask as astonishment caused by everyone's openness to her leadership of the expansion.

Another talked about gratitude for inclusion in the senior team despite a lack of research credentials.

Intimacy cannot be forced or planned, but as facilitators the three things we can do to support intimacy are create safe space for disclosure, model vulnerability ourselves, and acknowledge risk taking. The art of developing intimacy is about continuously pushing the envelope while creating a sense of safety. Getting the toughest nut in the group to open up usually takes *work*, so when it comes easily, I wonder about the contributing factors with this group of hospital leaders. Over breakfast a few of us had a brief conversation in which they guessed that I was an old hippy – not something I usually reveal within the first 30 seconds of meeting with executives. But in this case I went a step further and told them about our '55 Chevy that we made into an outhouse complete with the toilet paper hanging on the stick shift at Frog Run Farm in Vermont. When facilitators and leaders share transparently, everyone joins in. Openness is a two-way street, and only fear of judgment holds us back.

Sometimes when people reveal too much too fast, or the content is deemed inappropriate (for the age group, religious beliefs, purpose of the group), the group feels uncomfortable and doesn't know how to respond. Quickly someone changes the subject. To build safety, the facilitator can acknowledge the speaker's vulnerability *and* empathize with the group members who just want their discomfort to go away. We can rock back and forth between safety and calling people out. Nothing opens a group more than vulnerability from the leader, and nothing shuts it down faster than phony vulnerability for the purpose of manipulating the group into revealing themselves. Affirming what people share invites others to engage in the process and go deeper.

Language of the Heart

We use different language if we're talking to a child, recent immigrant, engineer, gang member, miner, executive, or minister. For the sake of meeting people where they are, we use *their* words. Minorities are experts in "coding" – changing language to match the dominant culture. But people feel most comfortable speaking in their native language. Every identity group has its own language, a way of letting people know they belong.

Emotions are universal, but the cultural norms for how we express emotions vary widely. In emotionally expressive cultures there's a greater range of acceptability in dramatic expression, gestures, animation, volume, and pitch. In emotionally reserved cultures, not only is the range more limited, but feelings are metaphorical rather than overtly expressed. Instead of saying "I felt scared to death," someone from a culture less comfortable with emotions, might say, "I almost shit my pants," or "I almost wet my pants," if the culture is even more reserved, or a poker face in cultures where any form of emotional expression is taboo. Generally profanity is more acceptable in emotionally expressive cultures, but in less expressive cultures, profanity is often used to mask vulnerability. When my mother had a stroke and lost the use of her right arm, she took great pleasure in swearing and enjoyed the shocked responses from people who had never heard her swear in her life. When I asked her about all the profanity, she claimed, "It makes me feel *strong*." In her weakened condition, emotional expression is a viable alternative that gives her a sense of strength.

When I'm facilitating in most corporations, I don't use the F word. Instead of feelings, I talk about reactions, or if I'm dealing with engineers, gut reactions. There are only about six acceptable feelings in most American corporations: disappointed, frustrated, concerned, happy, annoyed, and impatient. Eventually, once trust is built (which can take ten minutes or two weeks) I start adding feelings to their repertoire by asking if they're overwhelmed, hopeless, hurt, vulnerable, burned-out, tired, conflicted, bewildered, or uncomfortable. I interpret similar limitations when it comes to positive feelings; words like nurtured, tender, aroused, and sensitive can generate discomfort, but as awareness and connections deepen, people begin using the full range of feelings and needs. When working in corporations, I like to meet them where they are, which usually means adapting my behavior by picking up my pace and talking about values instead of needs to reduce the sense of desperation.

What if we're working with a mixed group where some people come from an emotionally reserved culture and others come from an emotionally expressive culture? One group wants the ground rules to include no interrupting, shouting or swearing, while another group insists on complete freedom of expression in order to get to the "real issues." The first group expects the facilitator to create a safe container where nobody gets hurt; the second expects the facilitator to create space for raw, unfiltered expression. One way to provide space for both safety and full expression is to name the cultural differences and provide some space for expression where people from each culture can thrive. We can also break them into self-selected small groups or pairs so that they can be heard in ways that meet needs for both safety and authenticity.

I want to meet any group wherever they are and also get a sense of where they are headed. I have no doubt that all people across cultures want full expression and they crave the opportunity to be vulnerable and understood. Ultimately I love working in multicultural environments because, across the board, people are hungry for real connection, authenticity, and loving support. Words have the power to resonate at the soul level, so instead of speaking in a foreign language, we're more likely to connect if we speak in their mother tongue, whether it's Marathi, poetry, rap music, or the language of the board room.

For example, Mario wanted more balance but struggled with making changes in his life. He had a strong desire for more freedom, wanted to accomplish his goals as a project manager, and was frustrated that he wasn't making much progress. Because he's a hockey fanatic, here's the language I used to describe his dilemma:

> So you are sitting in the stands. In one hand you have the puck, which represents freedom to go anywhere, choice, and possibilities. Notice how much you value that puck and all the choices it represents. In your other hand you have the stick which represents focus and drive and accomplishment. Hold onto that stick for a moment and connect with how much you appreciate focus and drive. These two sets of values are not incompatible. What has to

happen so you get out of the bleachers, get on the ice, and start moving your puck toward the goal?

Without generalizing or stereotyping, we listen first, and then start using *their* language, whether they talk about sports, gardening, food, or something completely foreign. Many times I've been the only American in a group, where people frequently speak in their native tongue and then translate. Once a woman spoke with great intensity and I didn't even know what language she was speaking, but I repeated her words verbatim with the same intensity. Everyone stopped. The man she was speaking to said, "Do you even know what she said?" I answered, "Not the words. But I sensed by the way she said it and your reaction that it was important and needed to be repeated." Before he could translate her words for me, I said, "I can translate just by watching her body language. She wants you to know that she cares about you and desperately wants to reach you." Incredulous, he asked her, "Is that what you were saying?" She nodded and he was able to receive her.

Despite this example, most of the time, the words help us connect powerfully with ourselves and others. Using empowering language means giving up pleading, apologies, appeasement, qualifiers, struggle, demands, justification, and self-deprecation. The trick is to catch ourselves using habitual, disempowering language in the moment and change our language simultaneously. We can transform rebuke, condescension, and disapproval by changing the way we're hard-wired. When we notice disempowering language or thoughts, we can immediately shift into curiosity. We can choose how we think and how we talk by replacing "should, ought, must, and have to" with unlimited options and choice. The possibilities expand as we change our language.

Labels have a static feel especially when applied to people. We brace against labels like "imbecile, racist, fat slob, boring, egotistical" because they don't resonate with us, aren't true for us, or at least don't seem true all the time. But positive labels can be just as deadening; "inspirational, courageous, compassionate" imply an unchanging nature. Rather than labeling people, it's far more informative and authentic to say, "I'm inspired by the way you…" or "Your work gives me the courage to…" Here's what I love about your deep compassion…" Although valuable as shortcuts, labels separate us from others. When we label ourselves, we disconnect from the rich complexity of our experience.

Imagery and Metaphors

The greatest thing by far is to be a master of metaphor. It is the one thing that cannot be learned from others; it is also a sign of genius, since a good metaphor implies an eye for resemblance. —Aristotle

If we really want people to get what we're talking about, and if we want to understand ourselves even more deeply, we create images that touch people's hearts. Sometimes the images resonate, and sometimes they provoke sharp discomfort. Here's an example of vivid imagery from Miki Kashtan at BayNVC, "In 1990, I saw a spray-painted message on a board in Berkeley: "American Dream; African Nightmare." These words have haunted me ever since." You can read the full story about her trip to Ghana on the BayNVC website.[94] The juxtaposition of metaphors and imagery generate fresh ways of seeing things and moving out of paradoxical dilemmas.

> Ralph Summy says, "Early in the second wave of the feminist movement its protagonists realized the importance of language in shaping and reinforcing attitudes of sexism and misogyny, and they campaigned relentlessly to make the language more inclusive and less exploitative. Today most males (and women, too) have felt the effects of this campaign, and many—despite the backlash against "political correctness"—take great pains to avoid gender-specific language. The proponents of nonviolence, it is proposed, should attempt to emulate the success of the feminists by substituting current violent expressions with imaginative **nonviolent** ones. This would constitute one important contribution (among others) in reducing the many acts of violence—legitimate as well as illegitimate—that pervade our society."[95]

Using alternatives to violent metaphors helps us renegotiate our use of language. Our words shape our thoughts and thus, how we perceive the world or "reality." Violent imagery permeates our everyday speech. If we continuously talk about killing two birds with one stone, spearheading initiatives, or taking a stab at something, we bombard ourselves with violent imagery. We can consciously shift our language to feeding two birds with one scone, planting the seeds of change, or setting our sights on a shining star, we alter our experience. In the resource section on page 425 you'll find an expanded list of violent metaphors and some alternatives.

As much as I'd like to remove violent phrases and imagery from everyday language, these phrases are so commonplace that there's a danger of overkill. I use that word intentionally because it can feel deadly to nitpick language. For instance "strike while the iron is hot" conjures up a blacksmith at the forge for me, but for others it's about a shooting iron. When I visualize doing something on the "cutting edge" I picture the sharp side of a "state of the art" kitchen knife, but other people see swords clashing. Keeping my eye on the big picture often means stepping over grating language. For instance, I sometimes tell people that I don't work with deadlines because I prefer "alive-lines" but if there's even a hint of judgment or correcting another's language, the energy falls flat, which is the opposite of my intention.

---

[94] Kashtan, M. Retreived from http://baynvc.org/new_announcement_details.php?announcement_id=191
[95] Summy, R. Nonviolent speech. *Peace Review*. Dec98 Vol. 10 Issue 4.

The people I most enjoy listening to use a wide range of imagery and metaphors that help me connect at the gut level. As an Episcopal priest, Maria DeCarvalho has been preaching for 20 years and has found that stories or images are the hook that helps people find the huge truth that's connected to their lives. When Maria speaks, people listen. We're riveted. Why? Because she's a metaphor mama – part motorcycle mama with her Armani scarf and part poetess, surprises bursting from her red lips. When she speaks, I hang on every word because I can visualize and viscerally experience everything she's talking about. Imagery and metaphors are vivid ways of expressing our inner world. Powerful metaphors resonate at the soul level.

When I asked Maria how she generates such exquisite metaphors, she said, "I don't try. They just come to me. Metaphors are a much more passionate way to express myself. I had a semi-boyfriend in high school, and I remember telling him that I felt like the child of a baker who brought home the broken cookies. I was tired of eating broken cookies. He wasn't happy, but he got it, and said, 'You always have a picture that helps me understand.'"[96] Metaphors aren't just a pretty dress that we put on our words to help them stand out. They're more of a window that opens to the essence of our experience. For most of us, metaphors don't just slide off our tongues. We have to roll them around in our mouths and chew on them before we're ready to voice them. I've heard many people complain that they just aren't any good at making metaphors. There's only one reason people judge themselves this way – it's because they don't *do* it. We can make our language more engaging if we just get off the fence, step into the corral, kick up a little dust, and put a rope around that wild metaphor. If fear comes up, we breathe into the horse's nostrils until we've made a friend.

I've heard several facilitators assert that needs awareness is more valuable than imagery, but either one can contribute to more aliveness. Particularly when I'm working with people from different cultures, imagery helps us share our experience. If we try to force-feed people feelings and needs, they'll reject them like a bad kidney transplant. I've seen people become completely transformed when they talk about the bird they're holding, the glowing gem in front of them, or the heavy stone that's rolling away. Imagery can connect us more deeply with our experience or can have the opposite effect if we use it to disembody our experience or hide behind the humor. "There's a cloud hanging overhead" puts a lot of distance between the grayness and tears forming in the corner of the eye. Alternatively if we put the metaphors in our body, we can help people connect with our visceral experience – the butterflies are looking for a way out of my belly; there's an icy shell protecting my heart; I'm shaking the bars of the jail cell; that's the sound of my jaw hitting the floor; or my antennae are picking up some mixed signals. In contrast, some metaphors can disconnect us from our experience by distancing ourselves from our bodies or using them to describe someone else: the helicopter hovering overhead wants to rescue me; my mother is driving my car off the cliff; my to-do list is growing faster than gossip in a trailer park. These point to people's thoughts, but eventually can open the

---

[96] Maria DeCarvalho personal interview 6/24/08. http://www.byanotherway.com/

gate to feelings. Imagery acts as a flag that helps people visualize our experience, but our feelings help them get a sense of our internal experience and deepen our connections.

My inspirational writing coach, Nancy Coco, director of the Lehigh Valley Writing Project at Penn State, has taught me a lot about writing and connecting my thoughts. To get rolling on a topic, I imagine I'm running rapidly down a creek bed, jumping from stone to stone, trusting that the next stone will appear, just when I need it. That works for getting me moving, but bringing a reader with me is a different story. Sometimes I need to place another rock between my thoughts, or if the water gets deep, I might provide a boat so the reader can get to the next rock without feeling stranded. So how about getting in the boat with me as we move into another tributary where we can look at how active voice brings clarity to our speaking and writing and helps us shift from judgment to observation?

Active Voice and E-prime

When we replace passive voice with active voice, our language comes alive and listeners and readers engage more fully. As innocuous as it sounds, the verb "to be" promotes abstractions, labeling, and judgments, which lead to disconnection. David Bourland coined the term E-prime to support language usage that reduces the possibility of misunderstanding and conflict.[97] Thinking and writing using E-prime involves eliminating any form of the verb "to be" including: is, was, were, am, been, am, are and the contractions, I'm, you're, he's, it's. The E-prime discipline forces us to write more coherently, and more importantly, think differently. Instead of confusing opinions with facts, practicing this linguistic discipline helps us communicate more richly and authentically.

"I am timid," sounds different from, "I feel timid in this moment," because the verb "to be" connotes a permanent, static quality; whereas, the active voice has an energetic quality that honors the flow and continual changes in and around us. When we eliminate "to be" and choose a language of active verbs, we avoid stereotypes, generalizations, and separation from objects.

A positive label, "I am smart," has the same sense of permanence as "I am stupid," and still connotes absolutism and rigidity. Using absolutes, (any, always, never, none, everybody, all) impacts us similarly. If I say, "You are dull," I imply that you have always been dull and always will be. That's very different from saying, "I feel bored right now as you tell your story." When I provide the context and specific details, I reinforce the sense that people change continuously.

Notice the difference between sentences with "to be" and without:
- It is so difficult to be vulnerable at work. → I have difficulty expressing myself vulnerably at work.
- He is so annoying and sexist. → I felt annoyed when he said, "Women don't know how to use the remote control."
- You are intoxicating because you are so beautiful. → I feel intoxicated by your beauty.

---

[97] Bourland, D. (1991). *To be or not: An e-prime anthology.* International Society for General Semantics.

- I'm a fat slob. → I ate three pints of chunky monkey yesterday and gained 5 pounds.
- You are so lazy. → You haven't gotten off the couch since noon.
- Kids today are so narcissistic. → My children have never participated in a community service project.
- I am a failure. → I failed my driver's test.
- That restaurant was fabulous. → I enjoyed the way they season the food.
- It was cold yesterday. → The thermometer went to 13 below zero and I felt cold all day yesterday.

I notice fewer labels, more ownership, more specifics, and more action in the second version, which not only contributes to better writing, but also better understanding. I find this practice much easier to do in writing than in speaking. E-prime doesn't roll off the tongue without a lot of practice. When I've used E-prime live, I've found it challenging at first, but the distance between me and other people evaporates quickly because we own our experience.

Exercises

Reflections:
1. Spend the next hour without using any form of the word, "to be." What did you discover?
2. Map out a recent dialogue, putting what you actually said in the right-hand column and what you were really thinking in the left-hand column. What needs to happen so that what you think and what you say are identical?
3. Every hour check in with yourself and ask, "Am I withholding anything, or am I in the flow of my own authenticity?"

Small Group Discussions:
1. How would you talk about a dilemma if you were talking to a teenager? Musician? Dancer? Banker? Soldier? Monk? Politician? Board President? Builder? Others?

Activities:
1. Choose a person you'd like to connect with. What words would that person find *most* connecting?
2. Scan your memory for metaphors. What metaphors or images have you found most moving?
3. Create three original metaphors to describe your past, present, and future journey of personal transformation.

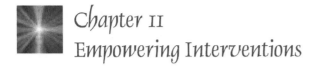

Chapter 11
Empowering Interventions

Want to feel more comfortable stepping into the fire?

Building on the last chapter about authenticity, in this chapter we'll explore interventions that empower individuals and groups. How do we build trust by offering direct feedback, confronting people with care, and interrupting discomfort? Going beyond questions, we'll look at the liberating practices of sharing observations, making statements, and giving directives, in ways that build trust. We'll also explore how we can transform diagnosis into compassion and express heart-felt appreciation.

Empowering Feedback

> *Consider that providing meaningful feedback is a life skill and receiving feedback is the highest honour. It means that person is invested in your growth and development.*
>
> —Ron Wiens

Giving empowering, developmental feedback is a caring way to invest in the future – both theirs and our own. Unfortunately, the old adage "praise in public, criticize in private" has spawned a movement that forces feedback behind closed doors. Consequently, very few people know how to give feedback compassionately because they rarely see it modeled well, and when they do, they're often triggered because they're in the center as the receiver. I'd like to start a new movement both at home and at work for feedback to be public whenever both parties are open to it. That way the giver can also get feedback on the way the feedback was delivered. I assert that when feedback is given without judgment, shame, or blame, everyone benefits. When feedback is based on observations rather than labeling or name calling, new awareness and interdependency can emerge.

The purpose of feedback is to inspire. Instead of using feedback to share judgments, we keep our focus on having the greatest positive impact. Rather than interpreting the feedback for them, we can give people plenty of space to explore their reaction. Clear observations delivered with love help people distinguish between reality and imagination. Often the observations are enough to inspire people to take action, but we can make the choice to be much more explicit about what we want people to *do* with the observation by adding our feelings, needs and requests. Figure 11.1 highlights the difference between judgment, pure observations and feedback that uses all four steps of the Nonviolent Communication model.

Figure 11.1 Transforming Judgment into Useful Feedback

Judgment	Observations	Observations with feelings, needs and request
That was the worst presentation of all time.	Three people were dozing during your presentation.	When three people were dozing during your presentation, I felt some anxiety because I value full engagement. Would you like to brainstorm some ways to engage your audience with your vision?
Our board meetings suck.	The board meeting went 30 minutes longer than stated on the agenda.	Since the board meeting lasted 30 minutes longer than we'd scheduled, I'm concerned, wanting predictability about future meetings and lively participation. Would you be willing to end on time or check in to see if people have energy for extending the meeting?
You're so defensive.	Your body slumped when I asked if you wanted feedback and you said, "Sure."	When I asked if you wanted feedback, your body slumped as you said, "Sure." I'm curious about your internal reaction to my offer. Can you tell me what you're feeling right now?

Care-fronting

The word "confront" raises alertness but is often associated with fear. Many facilitators never venture into confrontation for fear of being disliked. A sweet alternative is the practice of "care-fronting," or confronting with care. People *want* to know how they're perceived. They *want* to know the impact they have on others. The empowering experience of care-fronting wakes people up to something they are not aware of in themselves. The intention is to enhance their well-being or the well-being of others. But how do you do this without being presumptuous (judging what they are not aware of, determining what is in their best interest to become aware of, and raising consciousness about the matter without being asked)? To do this without bullying, nagging, or assuming a stance of superiority involves choosing the intention to support, selecting the depth that the receivers are open to hearing, and having confidence that they have the desire and ability to do something about it. For care-fronting to have an empowering impact, you first need heart connection, spot-on timing, and content that invites reflection and action.

Most importantly, when we care-front, we want to have the best interests of the receiver in mind. If we believe the person is doing the best he can at any given time (with whatever information and resources are available) and we are truly investing in his development, public feedback is a growth vehicle for all involved.

By definition, care-fronting is unsolicited because the person is unaware of what she's unaware of. Before launching into care-fronting, we can ask for permission, take a reading on their receptivity and energy, and pay attention to the ambience and timing. The purpose is not to take people down a notch, but to take them up a notch. Or better yet, we can take them *in* a notch, since reflection is deeply empowering. We can ask ourselves a few questions first:

- Could the person feel embarrassed, guilty, or ashamed?
- Do I think I am right and the other person is wrong?
- Am I trying to get other people on my side of the argument?
- Am I anxious, angry, judgmental, or blaming?
- Is the person unable to take action on the information I want to give?

If the answer to any of these questions is yes, don't care-front publicly, but don't give feedback privately either, until you've transformed your own judgments or distress into more useful, inspirational feedback.

On the other hand, if you're investing in people's development and believe they'll receive the care-fronting as a gift, then play on. If the team values care-fronting and you ascertain others can benefit from hearing the feedback, a deeper level of camaraderie can evolve. Likewise, it opens the door to receiving a high quality of feedback publicly because people find confrontation inspirational when done with full compassion. An example:

> The first time I co-facilitated with Richard, we were struggling to keep to the
> timeline, and the discussions went off-track often. When I tried to reel the

group back in to move on to the next piece, Richard said, "and there's one more thing I want to say about that…" and the conversation would go on for another ten minutes. During the break I started to realize how exasperated I was with skipping content and burdened by the task of adhering to the time line. So I shared my observations and described the tension that I felt in my chest. I also gave him a vague description of the support I wanted from him for helping me hold time. However I didn't have a specific request in mind. So I asked him to help me think of ways that he could participate more fully in holding time with me collaboratively. Excited by the challenge, he came up with several options, including how he would track the time for the next activity and keep us on schedule. Despite my anxiety and tension about the time, I didn't have any anxiety about my relationship with Richard. I trusted that he could fully hear the feedback, take it in, co-create new strategies and take action. Our assistant, Jan, listened to this entire interaction without speaking. Afterward she said, "Thank you for letting me witness this process. I appreciate the care and the way both of you interacted with each other."

As we've worked together over the years, we've built a lot of trust in each other's receptivity to feedback, so much so that we can share feedback publicly within the group so that everyone benefits from our process. When I have any doubt about my ability to deliver feedback with love, I feel it in my heart, and I get support about what's bothering me before proceeding. Invariably the feedback I want to give others is feedback I can use myself, so I put a lot of stock in looking in the mirror. Anxiety can lead me to put on rose colored glasses, walk on egg shells, or circle around the issue without ever coming to direct center. Coddling, pampering, seducing, and colluding are all common ways of avoiding confrontation. Out of a desire for shared love and shared power, confrontation can lose its power unless I can find a way to be both supportive *and* direct. People are hungry for an authentic, rigorous, powerful, loving approach to confrontation, so I make it a practice to ferret out any avoidance and take risks.

Cindy O'Keeffe describes her coaching style as "compassionately direct," She raises the bar on integrity by having clean, direct conversations like this one:

I work with a client who was repeatedly passed over for promotions and couldn't understand why. Like a lot of intense, successful people, he'd hit a bump in the road and didn't know how to get around it. Upset by the critical feedback, he wondered, "Wait, I work so hard – how can they doubt what I'm doing?" and felt betrayed. He saw it as a ding to his integrity and work ethic. So I acknowledged his dedication and that he felt bruised, and then we took a look at what might be hindering his effectiveness. I coached him to consider other's points of view and describe how they might be interpreting his actions. He then was able to see things differently and come up with new ways of approaching the team. I ended by summarizing what I really value about him, as well as what was getting in the way, and he felt seen and validated.

From there, it's very comfortable to explore. A complete absence of judgment can sometimes feel very vanilla, possibly even remote and sterile. By layering in recognition and compassionate directness, the process becomes validating as well as constructively vulnerable.

He was smart and collaborative, but he was been criticized for being too passionate, intense, and assertive. When he began to dial it down, he said he felt like such a pussy cat. Everyone was still intimidated, but no one on the team would tell him. I was the one to put out there the unsaid thing – that the pussy cat is still ferocious. He responded, "Really?" The gap between his perception and theirs was much bigger than he realized.

When I worked with him, I connected with the essence of his humanity – that place where we're all the same. Intrigued and connected, I honored the soft spots and recognized his desire to affect change. There were times I felt judgment, particularly if a third party might be negatively affected by my client's actions (or inaction). Rather than coach him to "my solution," I'm direct about what I'm thinking and say instead, "This is really your choice, and I have an opinion," which I share candidly.

I connect with so many different types of people, and so many parts of people. The exterior is how they're known – hard-driving professionals, but they're also dedicated parents, artists, pet lovers, or spiritual practitioners. They all have a softer side and are surprised that their colleagues don't see it.

A lot of this direct conversation comes fairly easily to me with a natural flow to it. Still, every day I ask myself, "How can I be fresh today? How can I dial the curiosity up right now?" This alignment of focus helps me connect to my intuition. What's provocative for me right now is the idea of slowing down to ramp up.[98]

Cindy describes a direct way of coaching that people crave. She invites people to own their softer side or whatever side of themselves they've closeted. What sweet relief people feel when a coach or a facilitator sees who they are, and invites them into becoming more of who they already are. As they reclaim lost parts of themselves they're thrilled to be received for who they really are. In addition to helping people see their blind spots and reclaim lost parts of

---

[98] Cindy O'Keeffe – personal interview 3/20/08.

themselves, another way we can support people is by stopping them when they are out of alignment, or unaware of their impact on the group.

Interrupting

What if we're working with people who like to tell long stories? They seem to go on and on… As long as we've already built rapport and have heart connection, there are plenty of ways to interrupt the storytelling. Telling the details is a strategy that people sometimes take when they want to be understood deeply or when they like their comfort zone and are avoiding taking action. Our job is to listen between the lines and discover what they really need. They might need clarity, information, self-trust, support, or any number of things that you can ask about.

Let me backpedal for a moment. Before we look at when and how we might interrupt, let's take a look at why a facilitator might encourage storytelling:

- Stretch the imagination to envision a desirable future. "Tell me a story about an ideal day in the future."
- Someone tells a series of stories that are connected to inner state of overwhelm. "You sound completely overwhelmed. What else is happening that is contributing to the pile up? As you think about all the ways you're overwhelmed, can you slow down and notice what you are wanting?"
- Use story telling to uncover the life force, innate power, values, and vision. "Can you share an experience of a time when your values were fully honored? How can you honor those values more fully this week?"
- Encourage enjoyment of the inner-critic to uncover the beautiful need. "You sound angry – can you voice that anger fully to see what sweet desire of yours is fueling this fire?"

Those are a few ways to encourage storytelling, but what about when we want to interrupt long, boring stories? When people tell stories, they are usually connected to the past or are projecting into the future, and often they do both at once, by connecting what *has* happened with fantasies about what is *about* to happen. Some stories are life affirming, but many cut us off from the flow of life, which is when facilitators intervene. I'm giving a lot of examples here because interrupting seems to be one of the most difficult facilitation skills for people who grow up in cultures where interrupting is considered rude. Out of a desire to be polite, when we don't interrupt, the session goes nowhere. Each of the examples below could be delivered judgmentally or with deep caring. I encourage you to connect energetically with the heart of each person portrayed and then read the interruption aloud.

- Paul tells the same story slightly differently several times. "I've heard you tell this story before. Will you relive the event one more time in silence and connect with what you need?"

- Shocked by someone's actions, Gregg explains all the contributing factors. After empathizing, you suggest, "It sounds like you're bewildered and want to make sense of this. Would you like to role play so you can understand where he might be coming from?"
- Nothing stops Kaylie from telling you *all* the details of the story and you're starting to feel flat. "I feel a little flat, but it sounds like you really want to be heard fully. When you connect with what you're wanting, can you give me the core essence of your experience in one sentence?"
- After identifying the needs and fully experiencing the energy of the need, Suzanne seems fully self-connected. But when asked about what actions or requests are likely to sustain the self-connection, she starts telling the story again. "Hold on. Are you sharing more details of the story because you really need more time to grieve before you can take action?"
- Giuseppe tells a story about someone's actions that left him feeling helpless. Sensing his desire to move out of helplessness, you empathize silently and ask, "So what do you want to do about that?"
- Your energy drops as Jacques tells a story. "I notice my energy is dropping like a rock and I'm guessing your energy is also dropping. Can you connect to what's missing?"
- By telling many details, you suspect that Carlos is avoiding the work of self-connection because of possible pain. "What are you not saying?"
- You want to express transparently. "It breaks my heart when I hear how much you value friendship, yet you explain repeatedly how impossible it is for you to have friends. When I hear how stuck you are, I want some relief – I'd like to connect to the energizing forces within you… You don't want to be alone, so what would you like to change?"
- Circling back to the story becomes a habit. "I hear how discouraged you are. Here's a challenge for you: What are five little things you can do to tap your courage and move you forward?"
- The inner critic is running wild. "Yes, you are so stupid… Or is it that your inner critic wants easy connection, and you also want to give yourself much more freedom to make mistakes and learn from them?" Or you can ask, "Would you like to reframe that story you're telling yourself?"
- You're overwhelmed by the details. "Can I stop you? That's a little more than I can take in right now. I'd like to reflect back to you what I'm hearing to make sure I'm getting you. Okay?"
- You're worried that the venting could go on forever. "Let me check something. It sounds like you've had a horrendous week and really need to vent. How about you take another two minutes to pour out all that's bothering you, and then we'll look at what you need and want to do about it.

- Ziggy complains about being wronged. "Hold on—let me see if I understand. You're frustrated and you care deeply about integrity. Are you trying to gain insight that you can use in the future?"
- Rico analyzes multiple options tirelessly. "It sounds like you really value analysis and want to make a great decision; what do you need to do to get the information you need to move forward?"
- Sunita takes great pleasure in entertaining you with her story. "Telling stories seems to be something you really enjoy. To help you stay focused on what you want, would you like to tell a story about how you want things to be different?"
- Joanne shifts from one issue to another aimlessly. "Wait… Can you check in with yourself and get clarity about your purpose in telling me this?"
- Dave is speaking very rapidly, trying to fit a lot of information in. "Slow down… Would you like to take this a little deeper? What's going on for you?"
- You start to wonder if all the details have any relevance. "What really matters here?"

When we create an alliance with a group, we can ask for permission to interrupt story telling so that our client expects us to intrude whenever our intuition moves us. When stories become a smokescreen, we can accelerate connection by helping people connect with two things: insight or movement. Continuously empathizing with the same story over and over serves no one. Likewise, being polite, holding back, or letting the story go on beyond your comfort level does not contribute to life. As Marshall Rosenberg suggests, "Interrupt as soon as you've heard one more word than you enjoy hearing." As long as you're self-connected and connected to the needs of the speaker, open your mouth before you know what you're going to say and trust that whatever transparent expression comes out will enhance your connection.

What are some other ways to interrupt that empower people? Take a look at the list of interruptions and create a few of your own. There are many ways to interrupt, but connection must be in place first. If we feel any discomfort about interrupting, it's probably because we have not built the connection. As long as we hold the essence of their agenda when we interrupt, and we tie our interruption to their need, value, agenda or goal, most people appreciate the interruption. If the person responds, "But wait a minute, I want you to know what she said and what I said so you can understand the context," then take the listening even deeper, tuning into their presenting agenda (what's on top), the deeper agenda (underlying needs), and the transformational agenda (emerging changes). Even if they don't respond immediately to the interruption, it can still have a big impact, although we may not know how until much later. We all get calls like the one I got last week, "Remember you asked me about my vision two years ago?" I didn't. "Well I had no idea, which bothered me. But I figured it out and now my book is published." In the same ways that I've had profound but delayed reactions to their comments, we're all impacted by each other, even if we aren't aware of it in the moment. Now we'll look at a few other ways of interrupting the process that can have a profound impact – sharing our observations, making statements and giving directives.

Empowering Observations, Statements or Directives

Facilitation is not a game of Jeopardy where we try to figure out the questions when we already know the answers. Question after question can become tiresome, so instead of relying exclusively on questions, we can expand our level of support by making statements. While we want people to have choice in every moment, we imply choice more with tone and receptivity, than whether or not we frame it as a question or a statement. Sometimes people need a break from empowering questions and welcome direct statements.

Behind most questions is a statement, so we can speak more transparently and directly by offering observations or statements, uncolored by judgment. A few examples of observations: people are sitting closer together after working in pairs; the volume just increased and people are speaking faster than usual. Some examples of statements are: an image of fast moving water is coming to me; there are no names or dates on the action items. Some examples of directives: amplify that last word; or make that into a request. Refer to the resource section on page 404 for some empowering observations, statements, and directives that help support awareness.

We take observations for granted because they are so obvious, but when people are deeply immersed in thought, they can miss the observations completely. By stepping out of the mind stream which disconnects us from the flow of life, we can become an observer, by simply noticing what we see or hear. When we just observe, without labeling our experience, we learn to see with new eyes. If we simply look without thinking, without attaching words to what we see, we have an entirely different experience. When we perceive directly, without thought, we become one with the objects in our environment. The same way we linger on our needs and savor them, when we give more spaciousness to our observations, we experience life more fully and become more present. The facilitation skill of sharing our observations becomes an art form as we determine *which* observation to share, and when.

Shifting from Diagnosis to Compassion

Diagnosing individual behavior or group process can feel intellectually stimulating and can give facilitators a sense of order and comfort. Diagnosis gives us the sense that "this is familiar territory" when in actuality, we're experiencing a unique moment in time. The practice of labeling individual or group behaviors can generate respect for the facilitator's intellect, but does it really help the group to build awareness? Often a clinical shroud falls over the group, the hierarchical divide widens between the person doing the diagnosing and those diagnosed, the group connection weakens, and deeper awareness of the needs of the group is obscured. For instance, I felt so sad when a fellow facilitator who struggled to connect with participants from another culture, diagnosed one after another. One was "competing with the facilitator" another "dominating the conversation" and another "hadn't dealt with authority issues," because none of these pronouncements led to trust, insights or connection. As a result, his desire to be seen as competent never materialized. As with most judgments of other people, the person doing the judging is usually the one who can benefit from unpacking the baggage, and discovering his own needs. When the facilitator's tone is didactic or dismissive, people brace against the diagnostic pronouncements or feel ashamed. Or worse, they buy into the diagnosis and rush into fixing themselves without understanding their underlying feelings and layers of motivation. Based on their desire to fit into the facilitator's expectations, participants often patch themselves up so that they can regain a sense of belonging.

The widely recognized drama triangle, a model originally developed by Stephen Karpman, describes three habitual roles: victim, persecutor and rescuer. The victim is treated as or accepts the role of damsel in distress, while the persecutor takes on the role of villain and the rescuer comes along to act as hero or savior to help the damsel or underdog. As the drama continues, people often switch roles or changes tactics. For example, the rescuer can shift their role by attacking the persecutor and becomes the new villain, by saying, "Your ego is getting in the way. How can you be so uncaring?" Or the victim turns on the rescuer by saying, "I'm not as weak as you seem to think. I can fight my own battles, thank you." As facilitators we have a choice of seeing each player in the drama as dysfunctional, unconscious, and selfish, *or* simply as people who are acting upon their desire to meet their needs in the best way they know how. To support awareness and clarity we can surface the needs by asking rather than telling:

- To the person I perceive as the Victim: You seem overwhelmed, wanting clarity about how to protect yourself and reclaim your power?
- To the person I perceive as the Persecutor: You seem outraged – do you need acknowledgement that your intention is to support the group and build shared awareness?
- To the person I perceive as the Rescuer: Are you a bit scared because you want to create emotional safety, spaciousness, and support for the whole group?

We can support the group by uncovering the wide range of needs in the mix, and seeing their positive intent. Excessive conceptualizing and categorizing behaviors reinforces an intellectual hierarchy that disconnects people from their hearts. As facilitators, when we compare an individual's or a group's experience to another's, we're communicating our own discomfort, desire for order, focus or stability, and our tenacious drive to make sense of it all. Facilitators who lack confidence tend to deliver brilliant interpretations, rather than helping people achieve self-awareness through their own efforts. Although diagnosis comes from the desire to contribute to awareness, there's another way to help individuals self- connect and groups develop a deeper understanding of their process. The alternative is to shift from diagnosis toward a compassionate discovery of feelings and needs. This cooperative exploration helps participants and facilitators get in touch with emotions and motivations in the here and now.

Instead of separating ourselves with diagnostic judgments, we can generate significant advantages by shifting to compassionate awareness. Exploring human feelings and needs is an energetic but gentle practice, with a very different feel from the cold, clinical, judgmental, "gotcha" approach that often accompanies diagnosis. Diagnosed participants often undermine themselves, sacrifice their autonomy, and lose their sense of equality. The diagnosis often fails if the person feels humiliated by the facilitator's perceptivity or lack of perceptivity. Facilitators can develop real heart-to-heart connection when we focus less on intellectual prowess and theory. Our interpretations are most effective when we offer them in the context of mutual caring. Since all humans share the same needs, when we connect with what's happening internally with others, we embark on a shared journey of trust, openness to exploration and healing.

Active, empathic listening and inquiry is a status-equilibrating process that leads to a sense of community. Participants can offer compassion more easily and quickly than diagnosis, which promotes less dependence on the facilitator. The whole group becomes a resource. A sense of equality emerges much sooner because hierarchical relationships shift when participants see the facilitators more humanely – as people who also have feelings and needs that they may need help discovering. As both participants and facilitators move away from solitude, the responsibility for healing becomes a shared group process, rather than each person getting a turn on the hot seat. Each little bit of healing contributes to the next bit of healing, and everyone experiences "being held" or nurtured. A life-enhancing process of "we're all in this together" replaces the "us" against "them" mentality. Open, genuine, authentic, supportive relationships are more likely to emerge when we shine the light on personal growth opportunities for both participants and facilitators.

Below are a few examples of traditional diagnosis, followed by alternative interventions in italics.

Acceptance Anxiety: *I sense some anxiety in the group. Perhaps you want to know that you are accepted, liked, or wanted?*

Orientation Anxiety: *Several people have not spoken. Could this be a need to understand? Perhaps the group wants clarity or a sense of shared-orientation.*

Performance Anxiety: *As the anxiety rises, I'm wondering if it's about a desire for mastery, personal power, or competence.*

Emotionally Frozen: *People in the group have not expressed their emotions. Do you want to protect yourselves from turmoil?*

Avoiding Pain: *Is the silence about unexpressed grief? Would you like to have your emotions accepted and to trust that people care about what's happening with each other?*

Repression: *Are you afraid to express your anger, wanting to protect your identity or sense of self? Underneath the buried rage, do you long for the freedom to explore?*

Projection of Anger: *The deeper the pain, the stronger the desire for healing. You may feel helpless, really longing for a way to step into your power and create mutually-satisfying relationships.*

Jocularity: *The jokes may come from a desire to relieve tension. What happens when you sit with the tension, feel it fully, and connect with what matters most to the group?*

Mockery: *When you say, "Awww, let's have a group hug," maybe you're afraid to trust the growing intimacy of the group?*

Avoidance through Complaining: *Focusing on the dislike of the temperature, the chairs, and the food may be a way to protect yourselves from intimacy or possible judgment if you express yourself openly and authentically.*

Collusion: *When two people distance themselves physically and emotionally from the group, they may need reassurance that the group values freedom and autonomy.*

Transference: (submissive, defensive, dependent, or approval seeking) *I sense some old pain. Would you like to feel safe enough to trust that you can get everything you want in a relationship?*

Scapegoating: (One person is blamed for lack of group progress) *By focusing on one person's behavior, this might be a comforting way to explore the changes you want to see in your own behavior.*

Competition: *Three people have interrupted each other within the last five minutes. I sense that agitation is rising and that people desperately want to be understood and would like to be seen for their competence and power. The group is not taking time to let each other know that they understand what has just been said.*

Retreat: *More than one person seems to be sad and alone; perhaps you want to trust that people care about each member of the group.*

Covert Processes: (racism, sexism. and homophobia go unchecked.) *When you say that, "Gay people are destroying marriage and morality," maybe you just really want to have a solid sense of belonging to a group of people who share your values and some reassurance that you can have the lifestyle that you love.*

Suppression: *After saying the words, "I feel," instead of sharing your inner feelings, you express what you think. Perhaps this comes from anxiety and a desire to create acceptance in these new relationships. I have more trust that relationships can be built if you express your emotions and share your inner world openly.*

Negation of Spiritual Presence: *I'm feeling uneasy, experiencing a shift in my energy and a desire for openness to the spiritual essence of each person.*

Past Distress: *Your distress may be coming from hidden pain of not giving or receiving enough love. If that resonates with you, would you like to connect with your pain and your desire for unconditional love?*

Domination: *Minaz and Paul speak more often than the rest of the group. Shirzad and Chloe have not spoken. I sense some discomfort in the group, perhaps because you want inclusion and shared opportunity to voice your internal experiences.*

Repression: *Are you afraid because you want to protect your identity? Maybe the desire for group acceptance keeps you from speaking, but underneath you are seeking the freedom to explore and express yourself fully?*

Power Struggle: *Everyone needs power. If we define power as the ability to meet needs, then shared power increases our ability to meet needs exponentially. I sense a lot of frustration in the group, with individuals looking for ways to get their personal needs met, but it's a struggle because you haven't conveyed that others' needs also matter.*

Authority Issues (seeking approval, compulsively attacking the group leader, rejecting suggestions, questioning authority, acquiescing, or challenging competence.) *Maybe your anger stems from a desire for partnership or equality. I'm unclear about whether the group wants to be led, or if you want freedom and a way to create shared leadership?*

Gender Issues: *Women were interrupted six times in the last hour; the men were interrupted only once. When a man was given credit for something a woman said, no one objected. When I see the men speak twice as often as the women, I'm concerned that women give up their power for the sake of harmony.*

Task Orientation: *Unscheduled time is filled with clearly-defined, familiar tasks. This may be a strategy for building relationships and trust. This could also be a way to protect yourselves from the discomfort of letting each other know that you care about one another or that your relationships matter.*

Confrontation: *The group seems to value peace and harmony over the values of openness and trust that come from dealing openly with conflict. Meeting both sets of needs could contribute to the well-being and development of the group.*

Dependence: *When you ask for permission to contribute, I see an intense desire to respect and learn from the facilitator. Without giving up on those values, you may also want to claim your own power and trust in yourself that you have something meaningful to contribute to the group.*

Fleeing: *The familiarity of talking about the past keeps us from being present to the opportunity to connect at the heart level right now. Repeatedly talking about the world outside the group means we avoid the emerging issues and miss the opportunity to connect right here and right now.*

Norms: *The absence of touch, intimacy, and emotional expression could stem from the group's collective values of efficiency, productivity, and progress. One of the strategies used to meet these needs is to focus on the task rather than the way people work together. Another strategy is to build stronger authentic relationships that contribute to the actual efficiency of the group.*

Ultimately, I want to eliminate labels, not just when I speak, but in how I think about people. I'm glad I know that the victim/attacker/ rescuer/ savior scenario is a classic pattern in group behavior because it deepens my awareness of our shared humanity. We may use a common language to explain human behavior, just as we use common language to describe needs, but individual motives are unique in any given moment. Some would say that "rescuing" is a perfectly valid way to describe a behavior, and I think there's some merit to that argument. Labels serve as a short cut to understanding behavior but detract from connecting with each individual at the heart-level in the present moment. If someone repeatedly interrupts another's process, it may be helpful to know that others perceive him as a rescuer *and* can see his positive intent. The richness of the group process is not in the labeling of the behavior but in exploring the motives of the behavior. As much as I would like to remove labeling from my thinking, when labels do come up, I want some compassion both for myself and the person I'm labeling.

The psychologist Irvin Yalom says, "The superego, the id, the ego; the archetypes; the masculine protest; the internalized objects; the self object; the grandiose self and omnipotent object; the parent, child, and adult ego state—*none of these really exists*. They are all fictions, all psychological constructs created for semantic convenience. They justify their existence only by virtue of their explanatory powers."

Although labeling is a convenient short-cut for describing familiar behavior, labels don't help us open our hearts to the people we're judging even when we're using positive labels. A practice that fosters inclusion is to transform labels as soon as they arise by connecting compassionately with the person we're labeling. By translating labels into compassion, we deepen our connection to what is happening now.

In addition to translating diagnosis into awareness of needs, I've learned over time to make my language more inclusive. When I've said, "The group seems to want inclusion," I've gotten push-back in the form of, "*I'm* part of the group and *I* don't care about inclusion right now. I want *freedom* to do what I want." So I learned to cherish the unique voices in the group the same way I cherish the inner voices of an individual by saying, "Ah, so some of you want inclusion, and now I'm hearing that some of you also want freedom." I liken the collective needs of the group to the collective needs of an individual. Each of us has a committee of voices that want to be heard. Even when the needs sound like polar opposites, I frame them as compatible needs. Likewise when people in the group take different positions, "We need to come back on time," and "We need to come back when we're ready," both voices can be heard if we connect with the needs of each position—one may want to honor the value of learning that's possible (when everyone is back on time), while another may need respect for each individual's freedom (by coming back when they're ready). But these needs are not incompatible: we can cultivate both learning and freedom simultaneously. Only the strategies are incompatible. A third strategy that might meet both sets of needs is to start the learning on time and still give people the freedom to come back as they are ready.

I've heard a few people claim that groups don't have needs – only individuals have needs. Since all human beings have universal needs, certainly groups of all sizes share those same needs. When we attempt to identify the *prevailing* needs of an individual or a group *right now*, we may get disagreement on which has priority, but we can still acknowledge that the group collectively has needs, as expressed by individuals. If Jane says she needs rest, Soledad needs adventure, and Alex needs action, I can validate their experience if I say the group has expressed needs for rest, adventure and solitude. It can sound jarring to say that an organization needs trust, communication and leadership, when in actuality, the people in the organization are the ones with the needs. In individualistic cultures people experience connection and feel understood if we identify their unique needs. In cultures where collectivism is valued, people feel understood if we talk about the group needs. As a facilitator, it helps me to see the group as an entity so that I can envision wrapping my arms around all their needs at once, instead of running around embracing each individual's needs separately. As long as we use language that comes from the heart, people will be able to hear our compassion and desire for inclusion.

Championing, Acknowledging, Appreciating

> *"The outpourings of intuition consist of a continuous, rapid flow of choice, choice, choice, choice. When we improvise with the whole heart, riding this flow, the choices and images open into each other so rapidly that we have no time to get scared and retreat from what intuition is telling us."* —Stephen Nachmanovich

Among the many ways we can empower people, the simplest but most neglected are: championing, acknowledging, and appreciating. Ideally these opportunities arise spontaneously, but it helps to offer these on a daily, if not hourly basis, since people long to be fully seen and rarely get enough continuous support.

Championing

When we champion people, we help them see things that might not be obvious. We can point to their strengths and core values, underscore their abilities and resourcefulness, and help them raise the bar on their personal expectations. Benjamin Disraeli said, "The greatest good you can do for another is not just to share your riches, but to reveal to him, his own." When sharing feedback, the greatest value is in expanding openness, which is a two-way street. When both parties ask for feedback and disclose their observations, the coaching relationship blossoms.

Too often, I go into organizations where the leader takes the stance, "I have it all together." Imitating the CEO's behavior, senior leaders and key players take the same stance, which trickles down throughout the organization. On the surface, everyone has stopped growing, and while they often point the finger at others who need to change, the desire to change themselves is nonexistent. The difference in growing organizations is that people at all levels share their vulnerability and learning in an open, supportive environment.

Marcus Buckingham, a researcher from Gallup, co-authored, First Break all the Rules: What the World's Greatest Managers Do Differently, based on studies with 100,000 managers in 400 different companies. Their research shows that leaders who get great performance from their people don't try to re-wire people or try to put in what was left out. Instead they try to draw out the gifts and energy that are already there, just waiting to be tapped.

He says, "When it comes to getting the best performance out of people, the most efficient route is to revel in their strengths, not to focus on their weaknesses." He adds, "Stop trying to change people. Start trying to help them become more of who they already are."[99]

We can champion people by helping them become more of who they already are, which gives them the support to take risks and take leadership.

Janice Hunter from the International Association of Coaching says, "We all need championing, especially when we're overwhelmed, down, or just plain stuck. We all need subtle reminding of the unique contributions we have to make to the world. So go ahead, champion your loved ones, champion your clients, and champion the world! And don't forget to champion yourself. Often."[100]

Championing isn't just for people who doubt themselves or question their abilities. When we really know people, we can act as their memory by reminding them of their core values, the change they wish to see in the world, and their chosen path.

Acknowledging

Acknowledging someone is different from complimenting, which implies evaluation and judgment and gives no specific information:

- Good job!
- You're great!
- Way to go!
- Outstanding!

Instead of vague slogans, we can be far more specific by acknowledging their growth, learning, and actions:

---

[99] Buckingham, M. & Coffman, C. (1999). *First, break all the rules: What the world's greatest managers do differently.* Simon & Schuster.

[100] Hunter, J. Retrieved from http://www.certifiedcoach.org/news/voice_may2006.html

- You're relishing your self-awareness and the balance you've created at work and at home.
- I want to acknowledge your courage in acting on what matters most to you.
- You sound very connected to your values, and you're honoring them fully.
- You've stepped out of your comfort zone, and I want to celebrate that.

Sometimes imagery or metaphors capture the essence better than anything else:

- You're on a quest for the holy grail
- The hummingbird in you sees beauty in every flower
- You surrender to wonder and awe, opening yourself to the sun's rays
- As the alchemist you see opportunities to turn lead into gold

When we acknowledge, we don't ask. We tell. Without attachment. We watch how they take in what we see. If it lands, they can sit with it or massage it. If it's off, we create space for the client to look for another expression that is closer to home: "I'm not a hummingbird. I'm a mountain lion!" Ultimately, we enable clients to see themselves afresh, to notice what is emerging in each moment, so that they can acknowledge their own gifts, awakenings, and power.

By taking the 'I' out of acknowledgment the focus is on the participant, not the facilitator. Instead of "I wonder if," or "I'm seeing," an acknowledgment usually starts with, 'you' or 'your.' which feels a bit static when our purpose is to identify the aliveness. I find the practice of labeling people awkward at best, because we're imposing our fixed view, instead of embracing their wholeness. Saying "You're brilliant, strong, or courageous" has similar energy to saying, "You are dull, weak or timid," in that we don't share how we came to that conclusion. We leave people in the dark.

Evaluative comments and labels like, "You have accomplished so much!" or "You are courageous," can melt people, but we can imply that they to be valued, approved of, positively labeled, cajoled, or given precious insights about themselves If we have a strong desire to support people, they may hear the patronizing sound of being patted on the head. If we climb into the pulpit to bestow congratulations or evaluate progress made, people can perceive a hierarchical element of the relationship. Similarly, if we're prone to cheerleading on the sidelines, participants may inadvertently attune to extrinsic rather than intrinsic motivators or our desire to shift the focus or energy away from what's present.

Even if a client identifies with or enjoys our label, "You are a fabulous writer," the static nature of the label doesn't allow space for the part of them that experiences writer's block. You are a workaholic, a good mother, so sensual, a gifted artist, are convenient ways of labeling people, but these acknowledgements don't honor the changing nature of the human experience.

Sometimes I cringe when I hear acknowledgment because I perceive it as manipulative when it focuses on who people *are*. As if we come up with acknowledgement in a vacuum and we're not part of the equation. The only way we can come to any conclusions about who people *are* is through observing their behavior, perceiving their energy, and then labeling *our* filtered experience of them.

In actuality, no one is fake or authentic, kind or mean, normal or abnormal. Labels, diagnosis and interpretations ultimately dehumanize and disconnect us from our experience. Claiming to know what you *are* alienates me from the truth about your inner experience. Ultimately we can have more intimate relationships with people if we share our inner experience as we witness their process. Any time we think of what someone *is*, we lose the opportunity to experience their aliveness, because the label limits the experience. Life isn't static; it's a process that changes continuously. Claiming "You're a dynamic person" is as useless as saying, "You're a boring person." Neither is the truth. Sure, we have moments when we can perceive people as "dynamic" but it's not something they *are* or *have*. A moment later we can see them as "wimpy." So any statement we make in static language of who people *are*, whether it's positive or negative, limits us.

Sure, positive labels feel much more innocuous than negative labels and can help people move into new ways of seeing themselves. But positive labels have a dark side – they depend on the euphoria produced, and prevent a deeper, more substantive interaction with their experience and the labeler. When we move into our desire to connect and understand, rather than analyze, label or lead them to deeper awareness of themselves, we open to a fuller experience of their process.

Ultimately, people have strong visceral reactions to being seen fully. So instead of drawing attention to the facilitator, we consciously facilitate the flow of life energy. We can do this without labeling, imposing, presuming, evaluating or doing the work for the client. Although acknowledging people for living their values is a step up from offering praise and compliments, acknowledgement coupled with evaluation carries inherent risks. Particularly if people want approval, positive comments, or praise, look carefully at *why* you acknowledge, *how* you acknowledge and what *effect* this has over time. Sometimes acknowledgement is more often about the giver than the receiver – we want to be liked or seen as wise. But assuming that our primary motivator is to support people, we typically acknowledge for several reasons:

- Reinforce values awareness
- Enhance insight
- Encourage new behaviors and choices
- Ensure the person is seen, heard, or understood
- Help the person feel satisfied about himself or herself

Telling people what we see, that they might not yet see about themselves, is a way of honoring their life energy. Instead of tentatively asking or guessing, we step into our own intuitive power when we name the life force as we see it moving through the group. We take in the wistfulness, sit with their labor pains and notice what wants to be born. As we hear their longing and flow with the living energy of their deepest desires, we come to that sweet resting place of meeting them fully. Sometimes they feel shocked to know that they embody the very thing they long for, whether it's courage, self-care, or joy. We move with them from the place of lack toward the place of fulfillment. Without leading them or jumping ahead, we acknowledge the flame within.

Appreciating

The way people live their values, develop new insights, or take action on what matters often impacts us as coaches. While acknowledgement focuses exclusively on the client, expression of appreciation enhances the interaction and connection. Acknowledgment is often used to steer human behavior; whereas, appreciation is a genuine expression of what's alive in the coach. The relationship deepens when we share what inspires us, how our thinking has changed or how our own growth or transformation is impacted by the work of the client. Instead of vague compliments like, "I appreciate you," we can deepen intimacy and empower the coaching partnership by sharing the specifics of *what* we appreciate:

- I appreciate the way you explored from the heart because…
- Would you like to hear how you've contributed to my well being…
- I feel tenderness and I'm connected to my own desire for…
- The most moving part of your work for me was…
- I'm touched by your vulnerability – are you interested in what opened up in me?

A full appreciation has three parts – the observable behavior of the client, the emotional impact, and which needs are satisfied. The specific components of appreciation foster transparency and give people a sense of their power and impact. The two-way street creates a more robust relationship, fostering intimacy and authenticity. When the client understands her impact on the coach, the relationship is further enhanced by a sense of equality, mutuality, and shared power.

Exercises

Reflections:
1. Facilitate a ten-minute session without questions. Use observations only. Debrief by sharing your insights with each other.
2. Choose three people you would like to give feedback to and ask if they're interested in receiving it.
3. After giving feedback to at least one person, ask for feedback on your delivery of the feedback. How did each person receive your feedback?

Small Group Discussions:
1. How do you let people know what's going on in you when you perceive them as:
   - Desperate to make contact, and you feel overwhelmed?

- Frantic about accomplishment, but you're troubled by the fast pace?
- Seductive and fun, and you notice caution arising in you?
- Filled with hidden, deep-seated anger, and you are scared?
- Oblivious to you, and you are baffled about the lack of connection?

2. Remember times when you've avoided confrontation – you've withheld your reaction, delayed having a conversation, or avoided potential conflict. Stop procrastinating – pick up the phone and practice care-fronting. How does it feel when you care enough to express yourself with full honesty? Get feedback from the people you care-front – what was their reaction?

3. How do you self-connect right now, without labeling yourself?

Activities:

1. With a partner, one person takes ten minutes to tell a story about something that happened in the past. Interrupts at least ten times in creative, heart-connected ways. Share what you learned about interrupting. What was empowering or disempowering about the interruptions?

2. Following is a list of common ways that participants are labeled along with one possible need. What other needs could these people be trying to meet?

Jokester: levity	Sniper: respect
Cynic: hope	Misogynist: belonging
Chatterer: understanding	Star: attention
Blocker: safety	Authority: connection
Debater: clarity	Steamroller: progress
Know-it-all: competency	Challenger: authenticity
Resistor: ease	Silencer: reflection
Side-tracker: making a contribution	Partyer: fun

There can be many, many needs connected to each behavior, and often people are unaware that their chosen behavior doesn't get them what they want. How do you intervene in each case?

3. Notice when appreciation is stirring in you and express it. Offer three appreciations a day for a week and check in with the recipient's response. What impact does appreciation have on the receiver? What did you learn?

Chapter 12
Personal Transformation of the Facilitator

Any transition serious enough to alter your definition of self will require not just small adjustments in your way of living and thinking but a full-on metamorphosis.

— Martha Beck

Now we'll explore personal transformation, looking at how self-awareness and self-love support our personal growth and improve the quality of our connections. Our ability to transform judgment of ourselves and others impacts our ability to facilitate groups. When we see ourselves more clearly, we can see others more clearly. We'll also venture into transforming limiting beliefs and dialogue with the shadow.

Self-Awareness

The quest for awareness and inner peace is a sacred journey. Rather than fixing our flaws, we discover that profound inner peace comes from the astounding revelation that we are already whole just as we are. Following the path with heart means taking the direct route home to oneself. What a relief to realize that everything we need is already inside. This flame of truth burns cleanly, leaving each of us with inner peace, the wellspring of happiness. If we perceive that the world is changing at the speed of light, instead of fighting it, we become the light. Expanding our capacity to deal with change and ambiguity in the world calls for self-awareness, including reflection and continuous personal transformation.

In modern culture, our thoughts predominate, so stilling the mind restores the balance. Accessing multiple forms of intelligence, going beyond using our brain, can expand our awareness. Intellectualization is a common way to circumvent feeling. To avoid pain, we think and analyze to create paths for diversion and evasion. Full awareness helps us contact our life energy so that we come closer to our deepest urges and full potential.

Five Steps for Deepening Self-Awareness

1. **Notice the Breath**

    Sit, close your eyes, and focus your attention on your breath without trying to change it. Notice the expansion and contraction of your body and the subtle sensation of the air flowing in and out. What effect does focusing on the breath have on your body, mind, and spirit in this moment?

2. **Notice Physical Sensations**

    Now turn your focus to whatever sensations are in your body. Do not try to change the sensations, judge them, or create a story about what the sensations mean. Simply notice. What effect does focusing your attention on physical sensations have on your body, mind, and spirit in this moment?

3. **Notice Emotions**

    Now shift your attention to whatever emotions you feel. Accept your emotions without evaluating them. You may notice contentment or restlessness, joy or sadness, fear or love. What effect does focusing your attention on your emotions have on your body, mind, and spirit in this moment?

4. **Notice Your Heart**

    Pay attention to the connection between your emotions and your heart. Listen to your deepest values. Simply notice any needs that surface. What effect does focusing your attention on your heart have on your body, mind, and spirit in this moment?

5. **Notice Subtle Energy**

    Notice the energy that's alive in you. Accept all of it. Release any judgment by paying attention to the beautiful, internal energetic quality of your soul. What effect does focusing your attention on your energy have on your body, mind, and spirit in this moment?

Without fighting the mind, we can shift our attention to the breath, stay with the body and give attention to our feelings, which opens us to the heart dimension. The heartache becomes an innocent longing. Something elusive beckons and we consciously embrace the yearning. Whether we're called by a vague hunger or a persistent desire, when we respect our longing, we experience a release from the struggle. Following our energy is a journey into a new relationship to ourselves, honoring our deepest yearnings and uncovering a guiding wisdom. Focused attention helps us notice what is happening in us, in nature, in the environment, and in other people. The practice of simply noticing engages our awareness and brings us into the moment.

Self Reflection

Reflection and deep inner work results in whole-person transformation that integrates energy, body, emotion, intuition, intention, and spirit. Working on ourselves helps us gain inner awareness and keeps us open to the growth and awareness opportunities available to individuals and groups. Reflection alerts us to issues and options, and gives us access to strategies that foster transformation.

Whenever I ask people about their personal purpose or unique contribution in the world, many, many times it's about being of service, helping others, or making a difference. But when I ask, "What is it that you want to help people do more than anything else?" the response can be very revealing because what we want for others is what we want for ourselves. For me, my desire to serve is about increasing my own awareness and creating close relationships with people who support connection and transformation.

Here's an example of a time when I wanted to serve others, but didn't have the faintest idea that my own lack of awareness prevented me from being an effective facilitator of the group's process.

> After facilitating a workshop with a leadership team at a college, I called to talk to the sponsor about his evaluation of the process. He hemmed and hawed and finally said, "One of the participants thought you were condescending." Sheepishly I asked for specific details. He didn't provide them but clarified that *he* didn't think I was condescending, yet he could understand how *she* might.

> Me? Condescending? I was devastated. I tried to contact the participant by phone and by e-mail but got no response. What struck me was that my experience felt so different from hers. So I did some soul-searching, came up lacking, and asked for help. I called Jean Handley, a facilitator from New Orleans, whom I admire for her candor, inclusion, inner peace, and ability to move groups forward. When I asked her where she got her facilitator training, she named four places, and then said, "But my staff and I have been reading Nonviolent Communication (NVC) by Marshall Rosenberg, and that's where I'm going next." So off I went to study with Marshall. NVC has been the most liberating practice of my life, both personally and professionally, because I learned how to transform judgment into compassion. Every spiritual practice recommends non-judgment, but only NVC has shown me *how* to make the

shift. It started out as something I'd use occasionally and has become a way of life.

With self-reflection and a bit of hindsight, I could see how my words and actions at the college could have been interpreted as condescending. It's not enough to be careful about what words come out of my mouth; my judgments have a way of seeping out through my pores. It took me years to change the way I think about people and change my energetic response to them. One of the beautiful practices of NVC is the emphasis on doing my own work, and the focus on empathic self-connection as a precursor to connecting with others. We are each a work in process. We all have our stories. The beauty of falling short of our own expectations is that we get in touch with our own yearning and we're drawn into the healing process. We all face many opportunities to facilitate healing, starting with our own.

Personal Growth

Let him that would move the world, first move himself. — Socrates

We all need the same conditions to grow. Besides basic sustenance, we want understanding, respect, and authenticity. Carl Rogers, a founder of humanistic psychology, developed the person-centered approach and found three emotional conditions needed for growth:
- Congruence (outer expression matches inner reality)
- Acceptance (unconditional positive regard)
- Empathy (fully present focusing on what is alive in another)[101]

Being genuine without denying our feelings, appreciating each other's full humanity, and sensitive awareness all contribute to opportunities for personal growth. We must have these three conditions to grow ourselves and we can provide them for others. As part of our innate desire to contribute, we learn multiple ways to create the conditions for growth. The high-road to transformation is a rigorous path of discovery and truth. Although many of us have a strong desire to help others, we don't become very adept at it until we do our own deep inner work. When we follow our own unique path, we remember and reclaim our core aliveness. The three components of personal transformation are:

1. Follow your Heart
   - live in the question
   - embrace passion and self-intimacy
   - answer the call and surrender to your path

---

[101] Rogers, C. (1961). *On becoming a person.* Houghton Mifflin.

2. Be the Change
   - listen to the tremble and embrace the fear
   - dream big and express your creativity
   - lighten up enlightenment with laughter

3. Contribute Freely
   - shine the light on your gifts
   - give what you want to receive
   - ask for and offer support

When we follow our hearts, we choose love, which connects us with our inner joy and light. To be the change, we learn to trust our inner teacher and expand our comfort zone. By saying no to anything that doesn't serve life, we can step into the fullest expression of our gifts. What better way to take action than to serve humanity and experience gratitude more fully?

Cultivating Self-Love

> We wait all these years to find someone who understands us, I thought, someone who accepts us as we are, someone with a wizard's power to melt stone to sunlight, who can bring us happiness in spite of trials, who can face our dragons in the night, who can transform us into the soul we choose to be. Just yesterday I found that magical someone is the face we see in the mirror: It's us and our homemade masks. — Richard Bach

Sometimes we wear our self-criticism like a badge of honor, but all our relationships suffer as a result. The way we treat ourselves is nearly identical to the way we treat others. Many of us are afraid to appear narcissistic or selfish, but self-compassion is the foundation for holding others with compassion. A practice of unconditional self-love opens us to offering our unconditional love to others. If we struggle to respect and love ourselves, it is that much more difficult to respect and love others.

When we remove the thorny crown of self-destructive labels, we can hold ourselves more tenderly and creative forces can move through us. Every self-judgment we've held about ourselves can be transformed into a burning, loving compassion. We can hold our precious needs passionately but gently. John Heron offers both professional and personal definitions of loving:

Professional definition of love: "To love a person is to help to provide the conditions in which that person can, in liberty, identify and realize his or her own true needs and interests – wherever possible in association with other persons similarly engaged." This definition is basic to all forms of professional helping, to parenting, and indeed any kind of loving care.

Personal definition of love: "To love a person is to delight in, and take pleasure in enhancing, that person's uniqueness." Both definitions cover loving oneself as well as other people.[102]

So how do we create the conditions that bring more love into both our professional and personal lives? We can start by creating a practice of unconditional love for ourselves, really enjoying our uniqueness. Every time we berate or judge ourselves, we can transform that thought into compassion, delighting in our positive intention, taking pleasure in understanding our deepest needs. The absence of love is a serious deficit that feeds the scarcity mentality and disconnects us from life's current. Because negating love is a learned behavior, it can also be unlearned. We can give our love to the world much more freely if we have a practice of giving love to ourselves. In this way we can restore human dignity and deepen our connections with each other.

Leslie Karen Lobell, a therapist from The Art of Loving Institute, says:

Learning to love yourself may be the greatest love you ever experience and achieve. Self-love is not "selfish" or bad. When you love yourself, you will feel good about yourself, and you will feel better about the world. This will make it easier for you to give love to others. Especially if you are a parent or any type of caregiver, you must not forget to take time out to care for yourself. When you take time to re-energize, you will have more energy both for yourself and to share with the people you love and those in your care. The person who feels self-love is generally happier and much more pleasant to be around than the person who lacks self-love and self-esteem. Embodying self-love is the greatest example we can set for our children, for our loved ones, for our friends, and for all those we encounter in our lives.[103]

The practice of transforming self-judgment is profound because it impacts us at the soul level and has the power to impact everyone in our lives. To really know nonviolence, we need to trust that our hurt, anger, and pain are not our enemies. To transform violence towards ourselves we choose unconditional love for every judgmental thought and offer absolute compassion for every part of ourselves.

Radical Self-Care

Sometimes we're so intent on serving others that we forget to take care of ourselves. We're more able to be present for others if we treat ourselves the way we want to be treated. I'm happy

---

[102] Heron, J. (2001). *Helping the client.* London, Sage Publications. pp 154-5.
[103] Lobell, K. Art of Loving. Retrieved from http://wwwartofloving.com/love/loveyourself.htm

if I swim three times a week, garden every evening, and write from 6-8 am daily. Some of my friends truly inspire me with their practices of radical self-care:

- Star gaze for 10 minutes each night
- Get six hours of empathy per week
- Try a different form of artwork every day
- Meditate 11 minutes for a thousand days
- Work no more than ten hours a week
- Practice daily sunrise yoga
- Take three 20 minute workouts a day
- Create a five minute morning check in with a buddy

The list could be endless, but the important thing is to choose something outrageous and give yourself a gift. Paula Kellogg, a coach at Leadership that Works, shares how she takes care of herself:

> I think meditation is essential to my well being. I feel the same way about reflection. It isn't something I check off my list, or tell myself, "I better do this" It is *essential* to being, to bring myself into focus is essential for me to be present.
>
> If I notice I'm not present, my first celebration is noticing that I'm not present. I spent 30 years thinking that multitasking was the goal. When my monkey brain is going and I'm in the pinball machine, and I notice that, that's the celebration. Then I might breathe, or I have some rocks that I grab, and that tactile activity of rubbing some rocks, which I do every time before I coach, connects my mind and body and brings me to center.
>
> If I'm not alive or present, I can't provide that spark. My internal shifts ignite my fire. I feel it in my belly. Noticing the shifts affirms that I'm present. I ran away from conflict as a child, but now it revs my engine. The hard places are a magnet, almost like dancing a jig.[104]

Self-care is key to our personal well-being and the people we care about. We can choose to be in a continuous state of feeling overwhelmed, or we can take care of ourselves and make choices that allow us to have a life we love.

---

[104] Personal interview with Paula Kellogg 2/22/08.

Transforming Limiting Beliefs

> There is only one cause of unhappiness: the false beliefs you have in your head, beliefs so widespread, so commonly held, that it never occurs to you to question them.
>
> — Anthony de Mello

Where do limiting beliefs come from? What is the limit of human potential? Spiritual masters, poets, philosophers, artists, and business innovators all tell us our only limits are those we ascribe to ourselves. Just as the answers to our needs and desired outcomes are within, our limiting beliefs are also inside.

Working with limiting beliefs moves us toward radical holistic self-acceptance, helping us open to more freedom, aliveness, and effective action. Loving ourselves includes loving that part of ourselves that condemns. When we decide there is nothing to reject, our inner warmth is here to stay. To loosen the stranglehold of limiting beliefs, we face them with awareness. Seeing what is happening alters the landscape. Without judging our limiting beliefs and without forcing ourselves to change, we can build awareness of our limiting beliefs in the present moment. Identifying a limiting belief and noticing what needs we're attempting to fulfill allows us to make friends with our past behavior, give thanks for our attempt at self-care, and choose new beliefs and behaviors to fulfill those needs. The interaction between our inner sense of limitations and our desire for something more fulfilling is the opening into the great mystery. Our longing is not our enemy and neither are our limiting beliefs. Instead of distracting ourselves or suppressing the desire, if we honor both the desire and the block, we open to an intriguing fascinating hint of something more. Acknowledging our hunger, acknowledging the voices that protect us or try to keep us safe put us on the pathway to self-acceptance and inner freedom.

One of my core limiting beliefs is, "I'm not smart enough." This is something I've told myself over and over. After an IQ test, I started kindergarten a year early, so my limiting belief doesn't even make sense. Ignoring or suppressing the voice has no impact. Finding plenty of evidence to the contrary did nothing for me. It's only when I made friends with my limiting belief and really tried to understand her positive intention that I've been able to find some relief. Going through a process of uncovering my needs, I discovered that I tuned out "big words" and avoided talking to PhDs because I wanted language that fostered inclusion that people of average intelligence could understand. With this awareness I can thank my limiting belief for passionately holding my value of inclusion, and now I can find other ways to create inclusion, without the ridiculous strategy of tuning out words I don't understand or avoiding people who might use them.

There's something very healing about understanding, even appreciating my limiting belief. Once she's been heard, she doesn't have to keep repeating herself. Oh, that's what you've been trying to tell me – thank you!

Transforming Judgment of Others

Everything that irritates us about others can lead us to an understanding of ourselves.

– Carl Jung

One way to cultivate self-love is to transform judgment – both the judgment we have of ourselves and of others. But how do we shift from judgment to compassion? Every spiritual practice suggests eliminating judgment, but only Marshall Rosenberg's Nonviolent Communication model has shown me *how* to transform judgment. The practice of translating judgment into observations, feelings, needs, and requests has been the most liberating practice in my life.

In many organizational cultures authenticity suffers because people think they have to check their feelings at the door, but in actuality, everyone is always feeling something. When people equate emotions with being needy or weak, they often avoid expressing themselves fully. In cultures where feelings are off limits, I sometimes show a tape of Martin Luther King trembling during his "I Have a Dream" speech so that we can see how full emotional expression helps us connect with the speaker. Feelings reveal our needs, wants, and desires, which lead to understanding, collaboration, and team work.[105]

Building on Marshall Rosenberg's work, Jane Connor who teaches Compassionate Communication at Binghamton University, gives *Trigger Translation Journals* to her students to carry with them for the semester. Anytime they're triggered, they translate their judgment into self-empathy and empathy for the other person. Included in the 3 x 5 spiral bound notebook is a list of feelings and needs. The four steps are:

1. Judgment: What judgment do you have or what are you telling yourself?
2. Observation: What observable behavior or words triggered the judgment?
3. Self-Empathy: What are my feelings and needs?
4. Empathy: What are the other's feelings and needs?[106]

This practice helps us build the muscle of continuously transforming judgment into awareness of feelings and needs, both our own and others. Martin Luther King Jr. said, "You

---

[105] Lasley, M. Difficult conversations: Authentic communication leads to greater understanding and teamwork. *Group Facilitation Magazine.* v7 13-20 2007.

[106] Jane Connor, author of Connecting Across Differences, created Trigger Translation Journals in 2004.

can have no influence over those for whom you have underlying contempt." Even more important than having influence, this practice of transforming judgment leads to inner peace and peace with others.

The International Association of Facilitators created a list of core competencies for certification and there is no mention of feelings or emotions. I'm flabbergasted because I consider awareness of feelings and emotions vital to the facilitation process. I once attended a training where the facilitator never shared a single feeling in four days of what was billed as "Expanding Emotional Intelligence." Her demeanor was steady and calm although she was more animated and spoke more passionately about the amygdala – the part of the brain that processes emotional reactions. Just thinking about his experience I start to form some judgments, "She's dispassionate, clinical, and boring." But I can transform that into compassion, for myself (I want to deepen my understanding of real, felt emotions) and for her (she values intellectual stimulation and inner calm). This practice of transforming judgment into compassion is where facilitators and alchemists become one as we turn hearts into gold.

When the Facilitator is Attacked

If you think someone is attacking you, stop and breathe deeply. If you defend yourself or go on the counter-attack, you'll only amplify the distrust and escalate the conflict. If you're physically threatened, by all means protect yourself, but in all likelihood the person you see as a monster is simply trying to get what they need. Accept them unconditionally and you'll gain allies; deny them their full expression and you'll pay for it dearly. So how do we make the most of it when we're shaken or troubled? The first thing to do is to stop labeling them or their behavior and start connecting with their positive intent. What do they really want? What do they care about? Just shifting our thinking in this way can open the door. When people are heard and understood, their behavior changes. They open if we open. When we're triggered, this isn't as easy as it sounds, and that's why self-empathy practice is so vital to the facilitator and to the group. Even when we're steeped in loving consciousness and can see the positive intent behind the anger, many of us lose the ability to stay connected when we're triggered. Sometimes words of retaliation spill out before we've had a chance to think, but even if we have control of our mouths, the daggers from our eyes can be just as damaging. At times like these we can name it: "I'm not happy about what I just said." Or, "I need a moment of silence to self-connect." As strange as it sounds, we can build trust by asking for help, "I want to ask the group to support me for a moment…" But we only take a break as a last resort. There's nothing that will flatten a group more quickly than saying, "Let's take a stretch break," right in the heat of the conflict. Even when full-blown anger is directed at the facilitator, that doesn't mean the group wants you to disappear or smooth things over. It means they're engaged and care deeply, so don't squander the moment. Move toward the pain instead of away from it. I find this extremely difficult to remember in the moment, and that's why I work with a co-facilitator who can remind me to step into the fire to burn through the pain.

When a person's wrath is directed right at us, empathy helps us connect to ourselves and to the person expressing anger. A few examples of empathic responses when people are upset:

- *This is a ridiculous way to spend our time.* So you're frustrated because you value efficiency and want to focus on things that really matter?
- *You don't know our industry so I don't see how you're qualified to run this team meeting.* I hear your concern – you'd like some reassurance that our meeting will be valuable and productive?
- *She's dragging the rest of us into her soap opera and you're encouraging her!* Sounds like you're upset and you want some choice about how we spend our time?
- *Can't you do something about the people who can't ever get here on time?* Are you angry because you need some consideration? Or maybe you want respect?
- *I can't believe you haven't noticed that Toi has been trying to speak. Is this intentional?* Are you mortified because you really value inclusion and want to trust that everyone here will be heard?
- *You are the most sexist, racist facilitator of all time.* You sound totally appalled. Is it because you need respect for all people and you want to reach me about the impact my words are having on you?
- *These examples are silly. We aren't children.* I hear your frustration and wonder if you want some respect and understanding? Maybe you want some examples you can relate to and see yourself using?

As participants deepen their awareness, they begin to feel safe enough to do deep work. That safety gives them the confidence to recreate their family of origin, so that they can work through healing the old pain from their relationships with parents and siblings. Or sometimes they use the facilitator to work through their broken relationships with teachers or bosses. When the facilitator becomes the lightning rod, I take that as a sign of deepening trust. If a participant says, "You are just like my father," instead of saying, "I am *not* your father," we can support healing by saying, "Let me be your father now so you can say what you've been holding back." Then we can empathically connect with the father, step into his shoes and say, "The part of me that is just like your father wants to tell you that I regret talking to you the way I did. Back then I was suffering so much that I didn't know any other way to speak to you." I've seen people literally reel backwards in shock when the facilitator says the words they've been dying to hear.

Shifting Assumptions

> *Forget every idea of right or wrong any classroom ever taught you, because an empty heart, a tormented mind, unkindness, jealousy and fear are always the testimony you have been completely fooled.* — Hafiz

If you're like most facilitators, when you get stuck, you start making up stories about the group, but you can shift these stories into compassion. First notice the story you're telling yourself, then move into self-compassion, naming your needs either silently or aloud, and then you'll be more open to express compassion for others.

My dear mentor, Miki Kashtan, a social activist from the Bay area says, "There's no such thing as difficult people; only people beyond our current skill level." We can stop thinking of people as "difficult" by recognizing their humanity. To take this a step further, we can stop labeling people, starting by translating our stories and labels into compassion and a desire to understand.

Figure 12.1

Shifting from Assumptions to Compassion

Your Story	Self-compassion	Compassion for others
They have no intention of making a decision; they're just going through the motions.	I'm lost and want to know what's more compelling than this.	When I see the energy in the room, I'm sensing that we're not focused on an issue that everyone values. Is that so? What's the real issue that you *do* want to discuss?
They're too hostile towards each other to work together.	I'm disturbed, wanting more composure to help them connect.	Several of you seem crushed and want to reclaim your dignity. Can you share what is important to you?
There are too many personality disorders in the group – they need therapists.	I'm tired; want more energy to be with the things that I find painful.	I hear a lot of pain in the group and people want to be understood. To ensure people get *heard*, let's reflect what the other person says before you say your own piece.
The real decision will be made at the top and everyone knows it.	I'm frustrated and want all of us (including me) to connect to our desire.	Even if the decision is made at the top, what needs do we want them to consider, and how can we influence the decision?
It's all political maneuvering; everyone is grabbing for power.	I'm baffled and want shared understanding that we can all have power simultaneously.	I want to open the space for all needs to be on the table and trust that they aren't mutually-exclusive. We can hold them collectively, but first let's get them out.
I'm not a strong enough facilitator to handle this volatile group.	I want mastery, ease, and a sense of centeredness to stay present with intense emotions.	I hear your passion. If you're angry or frustrated, take a minute of silence to check in with yourself – what does your intensity really want?
They're forced to be here. I can only work with people who want to be here.	I'm frustrated because I value autonomy and freedom.	I'm sensing that you want to use your time well. What would make our time together invaluable?
I've tried everything; nothing works!	Argh! I want this to be easier! I want to trust the process and get things moving.	I'm struggling with how to move forward. What's needed here?
They're personally attacking me – how crazy is that?	Ouch! I want to help!	You're concerned about my skills and want to trust that I can support you in resolving this conflict?
There's a black hole in the corner – a cluster of people who aren't on board.	I'm confused; I want to understand how it serves them to sit silently with arms crossed.	I notice that I'm curious about your opinions, and I'm imagining that you have some concerns. Is that right?

Working under Pressure

If we do everything perfectly, participants never have the opportunity to see how we grow and learn. We all learn more from mistakes than from anything else. Many, many participants have told me that what they appreciate most is watching how we operate under pressure. Sometimes it's of our own making, like the time I mentioned that Marshall Rosenberg learned to embody empathy by having imaginary conversations with Hitler. I stimulated a lot of pain in the group by advocating for compassion for every one.

"But what about child molesters? They're scum."

I knew I was entering dangerous waters because if there's one thing people can agree on, it's the horror of child molestation. I consider compassion for molesters an advanced practice, and we were only an hour into the program, but I didn't want to avoid a direct question. So I said, "As an advocate for victims of sexual assault, I have no doubt that sexual abuse of children is traumatic. As part of their healing process, one of the things people wonder is 'How could you do this terrible thing? Why me?' When Marshall Rosenberg describes working with a victim and a perpetrator, he empathized with the victim until she felt fully heard about the devastating impact on her life and the pain and suffering she still experiences every single day. After hours of empathy, she eventually became curious about what could have possibly motivated her assailant. The rapist started by saying, 'I'm a horrible person. I'm dirt." But Marshall insisted on uncovering the needs he was trying to meet. After a lot of exploration, he said, "You know why I did that to those children? When I looked into their eyes and saw how terrified they were, that's the only time I felt that someone else understood what it was like when that happened to me when I was a child.' He seemed stunned by this new awareness of his need for understanding his pain, and Marshall helped him explore the hundreds of other strategies available for getting understanding for his pain and suffering.

As I was telling the story, I scanned the room and was afraid I'd awakened a lot of pain. So I asked for responses. One woman found it helpful because she'd always wondered how anyone could do such a thing. Another woman said tearfully, "I'd like you to change the subject." Taking in her suffering, slowly I responded, "Thanks for asking for what you want. I ask the rest of you to listen for her needs. She may want emotional safety or protection or she may care deeply about others in the group." She nodded and my co-facilitator changed the subject.

I was shaken and didn't speak for a couple of minutes, but when my co-facilitator suggested a break, I said, "Before we go on break, I'd like to share what is going on for me right now. I have a lot of self-judgment right now and would like you to help me empathize with myself. I'm telling myself that I should know better than to bring in a challenging topic so early. The last thing I want to do is stimulate pain in the group." My co-facilitator supported me in identifying the needs I was *trying* to meet... supporting leaning about empathy, wanting to make a contribution, and the needs that were *not* met: care for everyone, a sense of safety, emotional support.

Sensing that I wasn't complete, my co-facilitator asked if there was anything I wanted back from the group. I responded, "Yes, I'd like to see a show of hands if anyone found what I shared just now meaningful or useful." About 50 out of 55 people raised their hands. I felt happy to see how many got something from my sharing, and told them so. I also shared that I noticed that not *everyone* raised their hand. So I offered, "If anyone is troubled or concerned about anything I've said, please come see me at the break."

Lots of people wanted to talk to me at the break, sharing a wide range of responses and requests... Where can I get support for my child who has been molested... I had a very different response and wish we could have stayed on the topic because I found it extremely helpful. I estimate that 2/3 of the women in this room have been victims of sexual assault, so we need a lot of individual support.

I was deeply moved by every response, including one about me, "I think you shared this with us because you *trusted* us." The sponsor thanked me for demonstrating the process of compassion for others and myself live in the moment.

In our debriefing session at the end of the day, my co-facilitator and I talked about what we loved about the day, what we learned, and what we'll do differently in the future. I had an odd sense of satisfaction with how the disappointment in myself led me into a vulnerable place that created sweet connection and live opportunities for learning. "The most challenging moment is what they'll remember," said my co-facilitator. The deepest learning cannot be planned; it arises from real issues in present time.

Transforming Anger in Three Breaths

Have you ever been told to "Stop being so angry," which only fueled your anger? Most anger management techniques focus on squelching the anger, but if we really want to have an impact on our anger, we need to get to know it a little better. When we're angry, we've lost connection with life, but we always have a good reason for behaving this way. Underneath the anger is an unmet need crying out to be heard. Gail Taylor, founder of The Integrated Approach[107] offers a practice for working with an emotion that many people are afraid to explore – anger. Her practice, "Transforming Anger in Three Breaths" may take longer than three breaths to master, but this rigorous practice builds awareness and relieves suffering like no other. Whether you learn it in a day or over hours of practice, eventually any emotion can be released and you can feel better in just three breaths.

This is not to say emotions are "bad" or to be avoided. On the contrary, emotions carry invaluable information. In this practice, when we put our attention on our emotions and extract the unconscious information, it gets us in touch with the primary emotion, which is likely to change in as little as 90 seconds or less.

Practicing awareness of needs in slow motion is the precursor to doing it quickly. At any moment we may slow the process down or speed it up. For instance if we want deep awareness for ourselves, we can take time to unpeel the onion and discover the underlying need. But if someone else is in pain, and we want to be more available to them, we can speed it up. Either way, the purpose of the process is to generate self- awareness and self-love right now. One way to keep ourselves in the self-love zone is to work with transforming our old beliefs.

Two Ways of Processing

Some people process their experience by looking at similarities while others look at differences. We compare our present experience with something similar, or we compare it with what's different. Someone who tends to process through similarities says, "Yes, that's almost exactly like…" whereas if we tend to look for differences, we say, "No, it's not like that – it's like this…" Because I look for differences, many people find it difficult to empathize with me. Hearing the "no" can feel disconcerting especially if you hear a no as, "I'm wrong." When I teach empathy, using myself as client, I intentionally leave off the "no," or add a buffer of, "It's a little like that, but it's more like…" Ultimately I want everyone to feel comfortable with the "no," so I eventually ramp it up so that they can hear the gift underneath the "no." The key to developing comfort with the "no" is in realizing that when our guesses are off, we're still helping our partner get closer to what's actually going on internally.

Because I process quickly, even when the empathy guess is right on, I'm usually in a slightly different place by the time I hear the response. As a result, sometimes my empathizers try to stay one step ahead of me. When I told my long-time empathy buddy, Jane Connor, that I was torn between the breakthroughs in my writing and working on my relationship with my son, she said, "Is that because you don't think you'll find it energizing to work on your relationship?" I detected a preference – I told myself that she wanted me to do the more vulnerable work. I said, "I think you're leading me to what you want." She agreed, thanked me for naming it, and gave me a more accurate reflection. When she asked if I wanted to be

---

[107] Gail Taylor. Retrieved from www.TheIntegratedApproach.com

understood that I'm torn – wanting to work on something that's energizing and also wanted some healing with my son – that resonated with me. That led to some hopefulness that I could work on both at once. A moment later she said, "I'm worried about interrupting your flow, but because I'm judging myself, I'd like to know if you are not trusting me to be present for you after what just happened. "I responded, "Not at all. I'm inspired by your response and your ability to become even more present with me when I ask for it."

Dian Killian, the director of Brooklyn NVC says, "Transformation and healing are almost synonymous – not the same, but connected. Often transformation occurs when we receive empathy because of the sense of being heard or understood. We have a different experience when we tell our story and receive empathy because it's juxtaposed with the original painful event where we experienced unmet needs. It's almost like going back to the dog that bit you, and instead getting licked affectionately. Re-wiring the original experience or stimulus leads to transformation and healing."[108]

Transforming Self-Judgment

> *Simple kindness to one's self and all that lives is the most powerful transformational force of all. – David R. Hawkins*

When we hear our inner critic saying things like, "I'm so selfish… I'm such an idiot… Nobody really cares about me…" instead of judging our inner critic, we can connect with the need behind the judgment. Imagining that our inner critic is motivated by some positive intent, we can ask ourselves, "What does my inner critic want for me right now?" This is the first step in holding the inner critic a little more gently, rocking it like a baby who is crying out for something. Instead of hushing the voice of the inner critic, we can empathize. To uncover the needs behind the judgment, we can ask, "What is the opposite of the judgment?" A few examples are shown in Figure 12.2.

---

[108]Dian Killian personal interview with Lynda Cowan Smith 3/13/08 http://bnvc.org

12.2 Transforming Judgment to Awarenss of Needs

Judgment	Opposite of Judgment	Need
I'm so selfish...	I'm so giving...	Serve or Contribute
I'm such an idiot...	I'm so thoughtful ...	Consciousness
Nobody really cares about me...	Everybody cares deeply about me...	Deep Caring

We can transform our self-talk by holding the needs of each voice with care. Harsh self-judgment is merely a wakeup call that our needs aren't met and are calling out for our attention. Offering ourselves loving compassion helps us expand our sense of self-acceptance which opens us more easily to accept others. This practice of self-connection leads to inner peace. Peace really does begin with me.

Befriending the Inner Critic

When you change the way you look at things, the things you look at change.

— Wayne Dyer

The inner critic is the inner voice that judges, blames, and labels us. It may seem counter-intuitive, but befriending the inner critic empowers us. Also known as the committee, head trash, old tapes, monkey mind, inner mugger, loyal soldier, or gremlin, the inner critic spews out a familiar refrain. The message varies, but the inner critic usually reinforces inaction with lines like, "You are so stupid," "They won't like you if you do that," or "You'll never succeed." The louder the voice, the closer you are to what matters most.

When your inner critic comes alive, you can get curious about the inner judgments and their positive intent. The author of *Nonviolent Communication*, Marshall Rosenberg says, "Judgment is the tragic expression of an unmet need." Underneath every judgment is something we want. Whether I'm criticizing myself or someone else, it's because I don't know a better way to express my needs. A few examples:

I'm ugly: My need is for a sense of esteem and belonging to the group.

He's crazy: I need safety and peace.

I'm so fat I can't stand it: I need health and energy.

You're stupid if you don't get what I'm saying: I want understanding between us.

252

I'm so judgmental: I'd like more self-care and care for others.

The inner critic evokes pain, anger, sadness, and fear, the emotions that are connected to unmet needs. The basic human needs are called different names by different people but are universal: connection, expression, adventure, freedom, security, and belonging.

Identify the unmet needs of the inner critic and we can tap our deepest longings. Often the inner critic wants something important: familiarity, comfort, or calm. Or it might want mastery, security, or confidence. Exploring the inner critic's underlying desires deepens awareness of the polarities within. Helping people embrace their inner polarities gives them freedom to see and experience emotional baggage and helps them develop more trust in their intuitive self and awareness. The process transforms people as they gain access to inner wisdom and create effective action based on their deepest values.

Dialogue with the Shadow

What is Evil, except Good tortured by its own thirst? —Kahlil Gibran

No matter how wonderful our intentions or how much we practice compassion, a few hours with our family of origin, and we slip back into unconsciousness behavior. Even someone who reminds us of our mother, father, sibling or ex can stimulate behaviors that seem to come out of nowhere. The process of transformation comes to a screeching halt unless we consciously integrate the shadow – those hidden, disowned parts of ourselves. Everyone else seems to be very familiar with our shadow, but we keep it hidden or really have to crane our neck to see it. Any stimulus can be a portal to dialogue with the shadow. Whenever we're triggered by another person, whether we're angry, hurt, attracted, disgusted, or obsessed, chances are high that we've just caught a glimpse of our own shadow. If we can't stop complaining or gushing, we can learn to appreciate the charge by shining a light on our emotions and having a dialogue with our shadow. Not only can we reclaim lost aspects of ourselves, but we can also unburden others of our projections and release ourselves from all the work it takes to keep our shadow outside our awareness.

Embracing the Shadow Practice:
1. Choose someone who stimulates a strong emotional charge in you, whether you're outraged, infatuated, appalled, or madly in love.
2. Talk about the person. Place an empty chair in front of you and imagine the person sitting with his or back toward you. Talk about the person out loud, letting your

judgments fly, speaking in the third person e.g. He's controlling, ridiculous, and horribly abusive.

3. Talk to the person. Turn the chair around and imagine the person facing you and talk as if she or he is in front of you, speaking in the second person. Tell him or her what disturbs you or ask whatever you want to know, e.g. How could you do this to me?

4. Become the person. Sit in the empty chair and embody the traits of the imaginary person. Talking in the first person, describe your thoughts, feelings, and needs, e.g. I am lost; I am hurt; I need power. Stay with it until you feel compassion for what it's like to be the person.

5. Integrate as one. Return to your original chair, bringing with you the qualities of the other person and allow yourself to integrate the other's experience as your own. Experience the part of you that is exactly like the other. Re-claim the lost part of yourself and fully integrate your emotions and desires. Journal about your experience.

Exercises

Reflections:

1. What change do you most long to see in the world?
2. If you knew it would be well received, what would you contribute?
3. What healing do you yearn for?
4. What limiting beliefs would you like to release? What needs were you trying to meet by holding those beliefs? What other ways can you meet those needs?
5. How will you cultivate self-love?
6. What parts of yourself are calling out for self-love?
7. How does self-love help you open your heart to others?
8. What judgment would you most like to transform?

Small Group Discussions:

1. In small groups, brainstorm ways to create opportunities for self-reflection throughout the day?
2. Use a trigger translation journal for a day and discuss your learning.
3. Brainstorm ways you can give yourself the gift of radical self-care. Each individual finds which are compelling and puts a start date on at least one line item.

Activities:

1. What would you say in response to these "difficult people"?

- A former professor in the group takes many opportunities to share her intellectual knowledge. She says she knows that lecturing the group is not the most effective strategy, but she keeps going back to this default behavior.

- A sociology student frequently asks, "Aren't you projecting?"

- A woman sits outside the group with arms crossed and looks frequently at her watch.

- A man speaks four times more than anyone else and doesn't seem to notice whether people are listening.

- A psychologist analyzes the behavior of group members, preceded by the comment, "Don't take this the wrong way…"

2. Fill out the Balance Wheel in the resource section on page 380 and get a sense of what a balanced life would mean to you.
3. Watch a movie. Track the feelings and needs on a two column list and pay attention to any changes in feelings and needs being expressed. Also notice the level of connection you experience. When do you become more connected? What contributes to disconnection?
4. Remember five times that you've labeled or diagnosed people (whether or not you voiced the label) and translate each label into compassionate connection to their needs.
5. Now connect to your own needs in choosing to label them.
6. Spew out all the most common lines you hear from your inner critic. What is the underlying positive intent of each line from your inner critic?

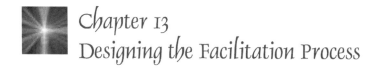

Chapter 13
Designing the Facilitation Process

Everything we do is either an act of love or a cry for help. - Marianne Williamson

Most people want nothing to do with contentious meetings. That's why the greatest call for facilitators is to help groups resolve conflict. We also get asked to facilitate groups that want to develop new competencies, solve problems, develop facilitation skills, increase personal awareness, or initiate full-blown systemic change. Regardless of the scope of work, we start by designing the process. In this chapter we'll identify the desired outcomes, then set the learning objectives, sequence the learning, design a variety of activities, debrief the learning, create follow up support, and develop an evaluation plan. Later on we'll deal with the logistics of facilitation, including working with groups by phone.

Desired Outcomes of Facilitation

After establishing connection, the first step of facilitating any group is to determine their desired outcomes. The facilitator's hopes and dreams for the group are not nearly as important as the hopes and dreams they have for themselves. Some outcomes that clients repeatedly ask for include improved communication, conflict resolution, leadership development, facilitation skills, team building, behavioral change, problem solving, and managing resistance to change. Each group is unique and measures progress and success in its own way.

Before we create strategies for improving group effectiveness, it helps if we understand their needs. We can do a formal needs assessment, hold focus groups, send out a survey, or simply observe the way groups work together. Of the many ways to evaluate the condition of the group, my favorite is fast and engaging. Everyone gets to participate and we can see the results immediately. The assessment is based on group satisfaction in seven important areas. On a scale of 1-10, how satisfied are you with each aspect of your relationship with your work group?

Figure 13.1

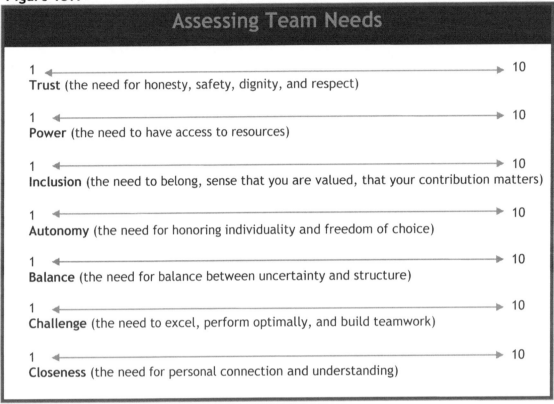

Assessing Team Needs

1 ⟵⟶ 10
Trust (the need for honesty, safety, dignity, and respect)

1 ⟵⟶ 10
Power (the need to have access to resources)

1 ⟵⟶ 10
Inclusion (the need to belong, sense that you are valued, that your contribution matters)

1 ⟵⟶ 10
Autonomy (the need for honoring individuality and freedom of choice)

1 ⟵⟶ 10
Balance (the need for balance between uncertainty and structure)

1 ⟵⟶ 10
Challenge (the need to excel, perform optimally, and build teamwork)

1 ⟵⟶ 10
Closeness (the need for personal connection and understanding)

Any group will have a wide range of responses. Although we can use the continuum activity to rank the importance of each aspect, the real value comes from observing how people interact during this process. When people start talking about what would improve their scores, they open up to their collective hopes and dreams and find ways to create supportive work groups where everyone can contribute fully.

Working with intact work groups has its own challenges and rewards. Team members can enter the room with a lot of despair or a lot of hopefulness. One of the ways we can develop trust from the beginning of the relationship is to consider the entire group as our client. We hold the needs of the sponsor, the leader, the entire organization, and the person who hired us, but we pay particular attention to the needs of the group. We contract with the entire group and get agreement with all of them before beginning in order to prevent surprises. Outsiders may have an interest or a stake in any outcomes of the group process, but the client is the entire group, which means we hold the values, needs, and interests of each person in the group. To follow is my view of my responsibilities as a facilitator, but I adapt this based on the needs of the group:

- Encourage dialogue and create opportunities for inclusion and choice.
- Create an environment of empathic reflection to ensure people are understood.
- Get the needs on the table before exploring strategies.

- Elicit diverse opinions and tap the group's resourcefulness.
- Expand options by helping the group explore new ways of doing things.
- Move the group through stages of decision-making and build a sense of shared direction.
- Expand shared facilitation and leadership skills within the group.

Designing Experiential Activities

Crafting Learning Objectives

Learning objectives start with an active verb and allow us to measure progress by observing specific behaviors, as shown in figure 13.2.

Figure 13.2

Crafting Learning Objectives	
Vague	**Specific**
Understands the four step process.	Demonstrates the four steps of the process.
Knows how to influence others well.	Makes specific doable requests.
Is non-judgmental when appropriate.	Identifies judgments and translates into empathic connection.
Has high emotional intelligence.	Identifies and articulates internal emotions in self and others.
Makes good decisions.	Uses consensus-building skills to make shared decisions and generate ownership.
Knows how to communicate effectively.	Listens actively and reflects the speaker's message with clarity.
Learns how to analyze systematically.	Diagnoses issues, analyzes alternatives, and engages in methodical problem solving process.
Develops strong relationships.	Demonstrates perceptiveness to people's feelings and honors their contributions.
Encourages openness.	Encourages diverse input from the group before making a decision.
Is perceived as honest, authentic and acting with integrity.	Honestly expresses personal values and internal emotions.

Sequencing the Learning

The five elements of effective personal growth training in sequence are understanding, modeling, practice, feedback, and application. We start off by supplying a context for the learning activity, which helps people understand the purpose, the desired outcomes, and the rationale. Then we model the new skill or desired behaviors using descriptive stories, videos, or live demonstrations, to help participants understand the nuances of skill set, including the language, the timing, and the interactions. Practice is probably the most important, and often most neglected, piece of training. Without it, people do not have the confidence to use the skills that were modeled, seen, or talked about, and they leave without assimilating the learning. They think they'll practice when they leave, but they don't. Learning is not just about taking in knowledge; it's primarily about changing your behavior. Feedback that comes from the self, peer participants, and trainers helps validate that participants master the desired skills and identify opportunities for development. Taking a moment to journal, to visualize transferring the learning back into their lives, both at home and at work helps ensure that the training has a lasting impact. Follow-up is vital to making sure the learning sticks. Any training program that does not incorporate a follow-up structure is a waste of time and money. When participants know that we'll be checking on their progress a month later, they're more likely to engage in their action plan.

Learning Cycle

1. Conceptualizing the skill – verbal description of the skill, anecdotes can portray the value of the skill
2. Modeling the skill – live demonstration or video
3. Describe the activity – purpose, structure, sequence, timing, expectation of learning
4. Practice – in pairs or small groups
5. Feedback – first from self, then from others. (Repeat practice and feedback until desired level of mastery)
6. Reflection and review – first in small groups and then in the large group capture the learning through discussion (can also give feedback on the design of the activity)
7. Follow up structure to expand the learning through practice

In optimal learning environments, the learning activities are sequenced to build on each other so that participants develop confidence. To develop new competencies, the following progression gives people the reassurance they need to actually use new skill sets when they leave the workshop. We start by letting them know why the skill is of value, followed by a demonstration or a video that deepens understanding. Then they practice by trying parts of the new skill to decrease apprehension. By offering feedback, we share observations and suggestions about building the skill further. Repetition allows them to use the new skill until confidence is built. The purpose of reflection is to capture the learning through journaling, or sharing in the large group the intention of using the skill in the future

When we vary the topic and vary the activity, we help people maintain their desire for learning. When people are tired of one activity, it doesn't mean they need a nap or even a break – doing something different taps the reserve energy of the group.

Working with intact work groups has its own challenges and rewards. Team members can enter the room with a lot of despair or a lot of hopefulness. One of the ways we can develop trust from the beginning of the relationship is to consider the entire group as our client. We hold the needs of the sponsor, the leader, the entire organization, and the person who hired us, but we pay particular attention to the needs of the group. We contract with the entire group and get agreement with all of them before beginning in order to prevent surprises. Outsiders may have an interest or a stake in any outcomes of the group process, but the client is the entire group, which means we hold the values, needs, and interests of each person in the group. To follow is my view of my responsibilities as a facilitator, but I adapt this based on the needs of the group:

- Encourage dialogue and create opportunities for inclusion and choice.
- Create an environment of empathic reflection to ensure people are understood.
- Get the needs on the table before exploring strategies.
- Elicit diverse opinions and tap the group's resourcefulness.
- Expand options by helping the group explore new ways of doing things.
- Move the group through stages of decision-making and build a sense of shared direction.
- Expand shared facilitation and leadership skills within the group.

Giving Instructions for the Activity

- Even if you've done the activity many times, write out your instructions, so you know exactly what needs to be said.
- Practice saying your instructions using as few words as possible.
- Give instructions only once.
- Use "you" to describe what they'll be doing so they can imagine themselves in the process.
- Put them into groups AFTER all instructions are given (if you give directions in two parts, you'll have to get the group's attention again.)
- Once they get started, only interrupt their process if you've forgotten a crucial piece of information.

Setting Context - Framing the Learning

Depending on the maturity and skill level of the group, you can set the context for learning in advance so that people know what to look for.

1. Front-loading the learning: tell them what they will learn up front so they know what to look for. *This is what you should learn from this activity based on experience of others…*
2. Back-loading the learning: Tell them at the end what they might have learned. This *is what you should have learned from the activity based on the experience of others…*
3. Offering the activity without context and then debriefing the experience by determining the focus and guiding people to what they *may* have learned, mining the learning afresh. *What did you learn from this activity and how can you apply it in your life?*

Designing on the Fly

We can create activities on the fly based on group needs in the moment. Experience with a wide range of group activities leads to blending traditional activities with innovative new ideas. Experiential learning activities may be incorporated in the design of the program or used spontaneously based on issues that arise in the group. We can design activities in the moment based on our intuition of what the group needs. What follows is an example of an on-the-fly design that has since evolved into a regular activity that we use to teach intervention skills.

Figure 13.3 Layout for Intervention Skill Practice

Intervention Skill Practice

Directions: Ask for five volunteers who are willing to meet in a fish bowl in the center of the room. Their task is to determine the five most important facilitation skills and prioritize them. The purpose is to help determine which skills to cover in a one-week program on facilitation skills. Arrange the fishbowl with the five volunteers in the center of the room, with clusters of 3-4 observers around the outside in a flower shaped-configuration, as shown in Figure 13.3

First Round
10 minutes to prioritize facilitation skills: the group in the center fish bowl lists the five most important facilitation skills, and if you have time, prioritize your list.

Simultaneously, observers take notes in two columns:
*   individual needs of the people in the fish bowl
*   possible interventions you would make if you were the facilitator

10 minutes to determine interventions: the observers (in small groups of 3-4) discuss the intervention options and come to a consensus. What intervention would be most helpful in this moment? Simultaneously, the fish bowl group reflects in silence on the group experience and makes their own list of needs and interventions (they don't continue to process or move toward their goal).

Then one member from each observer group shares his/her intervention out loud, but the group in the fishbowl does not respond or offer their own interventions. The facilitators coach the observers, as needed, helping them get clarity about their intention, change questions into statements, use fewer words, or shift to empowering language.

Second round: the group repeats the first round: the fish bowl group takes another 10 minutes to continue with their task, and the observer groups again take notes, come to consensus, and share the most useful intervention.

Third round: same as the other rounds.

Closure: After the last round, each person in the fishbowl group shares one insight in one sentence. Simultaneously the observer groups do the same. Debrief the learning in the large group.

We can easily change this basic activity by shifting the task so that participants practice skills in making requests, sharing observations, offering feedback, building consensus, making decisions or resolving conflict.

Structuring Learning

As developmental facilitators, we not only facilitate the group's process, but we provide opportunities for group members to develop their own facilitation skills. Going into the process, we need to have clarity about learning objectives, sequencing learning opportunities, framing the learning, and debriefing the process. Paula Kellogg retired from teaching but kept her hunger for learning and developing people when she shifted her profession to coaching and facilitating. With a reputation for bringing people together, she wasn't surprised when the State Department of Education asked her to facilitate a contentious meeting between the six largest school districts, some wealthy, some poor. Their goal was to complete a project that had stalled. Here's how she describes her experience:

> I never knew why I chose to become a teacher – I thought of it as a quick way to get through school and get summers off. Much later I learned that working with children was a way for me to heal my sadness as a child. Likewise, I didn't really know why I chose coaching and facilitating as a second career. I

263

thought, "I can work from home, set my own hours," and only afterwards realized I want connection and deep reflection. As a result, I am more careful about the work I accept, which allows me more time for reflection. I've kept a journal since I was 17, but more recently I've started using my journal very differently. Every night I ask myself, what am I learning? Each morning I ask, what are my opportunities? My learning and my opportunities have exploded.

When clients call, I wonder what exciting things they will put at my feet. Right by my phone, I have criteria for saying yes. Does my gut say "whoa!"? If there is a compelling outside-the-box reason to say yes, I'll find time on my calendar. Training myself not to say yes just because someone wants me leads me to balance. Reflection, really noticing what I say yes to, is a fairly new phenomenon in my life.

Right away I wanted to work with the Department of Education because I knew we'd all learn something. They came with a lot of baggage – the people representing the poor districts were on guard and people from the rich districts seemed to want others to know how much they could do with all their resources. So I started with an Appreciative Inquiry[109] question, "Describe a time when you knew you had picked a career that made you come alive." They were shocked, but all started sharing. The whole room started softening. They were a room full of suits, but they became a room of people. Talking about aliveness brought some commonality.

Another shift occurred when I pulled an empty chair to the table and said, "This chair represents the students. I would like to have them be part of the conversation." I usually like to sit in the center of the long side of the table, not on the end. Even with me in that position, they were talking to me and not to each other. As we started through the preliminary agenda, I took my pad and sat away from the table. They began speaking to each other, identifying problems, which I translated into questions we needed to answer. They began to answer them randomly, so I stood behind the chair of the student, brought the attention there, to point them toward the answers.

After I invited the non-talkers to share, from there they continued on their own. Occasionally I'd steer them back to questions that hadn't been answered until all were ultimately addressed. They worked together and felt a sense of accomplishment and were surprised when I asked, "So what? What does that mean? Now what shall we do?"

---

[109] Appreciative Inquiry is described in more detail in Chapter 14.

After some dialogue, they set up a think tank to meet regularly to discuss how they were alike and how they could work together to support the children. They got some dates on the calendar (which is usually next to impossible) to develop and organize think tanks.

They seemed complete, but I asked permission to process the work. They talked about what they learned from the Appreciative Inquiry questions, changing the geographical position in the facilitator, and the power of the empty chair. At the end of the meeting, as I reflected, I thought, "Whoa. They got along, stepped into new relationships, and they also learned about facilitating a meeting." Not that bells went off, but people experienced true transformation.

I hold a deep belief in the brilliance of children. They're born that way. As a teacher it's second nature for me to look for brilliance in adults. The facilitation process affirms my belief that people are brilliant and that I don't have to be the fixer. All I did was help set the atmosphere, turn their problems into questions, and got the hell out of the way. I brought attention to the true purpose of the meeting: the children, and I noticed who wasn't sharing. I gained confidence in my ability to set the stage to move groups. My belief in myself takes away some fear which allows people to breathe. I love my job because I contribute to people's growth. They deepen their connection to themselves, and it's not about me.

Another piece of learning is that I don't have to be such a planner. I didn't need to know much about the issue. If I listen, particularly to what's unsaid, I can do it. People want to get along. They don't want to be territorial. Given the opportunity, they choose harmony.[110]

Paula's willingness to get out of the way comes from confidence in the group process and years of experience. What I admire most about her experience is her commitment to developing the facilitation skills of her clients. Instead of doing all the work for them, she transfers her skills to the group, despite limited time. Some facilitators would see this as making themselves obsolete, but Paula sees it as giving added value.

Logistics of Facilitation

Facilitation done well looks so simple! There's a lot that goes into developing the skills and setting the environment. The logistics are minor but so important to the quality of the experience.

---

[110] Personal interview with Paula Kellogg 2/22/08.

Face-to-Face Facilitation

To maximize the physical capacity of the group, comfort is essential. Refreshments, lighting, fresh air, temperature, seating, sound, and space all contribute to comfort. I tend to take all these things for granted until challenges arise, but careful planning can contribute to the quality of the experience.

People wilt when they are dehydrated, so water pitchers and glasses should be within everyone's reach. To promote a sense of abundance, plenty of healthy, visually-appealing food reduces the scarcity mentality. Fresh fruit, vegetables, cheese, nuts, whole-grain crackers, yogurt, or high-protein snacks build lasting energy. If we can avoid sugar and caffeine, groups are more alert, but some people might leave to visit the nearest coffee shop.

Natural lighting is a high priority for me – otherwise I spend a lot of time keeping the group energized. Even if people are used to fluorescent lighting, the natural light from windows allows people to see each other more easily and read documents without straining.

Fresh air always contributes to people's sense of well-being, and the suggestion often comes up to move the meeting outside. Outdoor meetings can be refreshing, but glaring sunlight, gusty winds, wet grass, uncomfortable chairs, outdoor noises, and bothersome insects may all detract from the group experience.

The biggest complaint is that the room is often too cold or too hot, even if people remember to dress in layers. Heat can really sap the energy, but so can a room that's too cold. In groups over 30, acoustics vary, but sound doesn't carry as well, and even if participants can hear the facilitator, they struggle to hear soft-spoken members of the group. Whenever possible, I forego microphones because language becomes more stilted, people feel intimidated, continuous reminders are needed to get people to hold the microphone closer, and running the microphone around the room takes time. Without microphones, we continuously remind people to raise their voices – asking them to speak to the person across the room or farthest away from them.

If people are used to sitting in a comfortable chair daily, they won't be very comfortable in a plastic chair. Even if people are seated in ergonomic chairs with lumbar support, a couple of hours in a chair is often too long. Scheduling breaks every 90 minutes is standard, and so is building in movement. We can get people moving by breaking into small groups, taking a straw poll by standing, writing on wall charts, creating an art gallery to walk around and see what people have written, mingling to discuss an issue by switching partners every minute or so, using a floor continuum to assess where people stand, voting with dots or switching the seating. Naturally, we don't offer these movements randomly but in conjunction with the group's objectives.

Tables protect people and allow them to hide, so I prefer no tables unless people are doing a lot of writing. In some cultures people want the formality, safety, and the distance that tables provide, but that doesn't encourage creativity or emotional expression. Although the amount of space people want around their chair varies in each culture, I prefer plenty of square footage, so people don't have to move their chairs for others to get by them. If we have a small group in a large meeting room, we can create a sense of coziness by blocking off a corner of the room with tables. On the flip side, if the room is too small for the size of the group, not much can be done to increase comfort, except to create break-out space in other rooms so that people can hear each other. Consider that rectangular tables are more formal than round tables; whereas, couches provide a social atmosphere for small groups. In the resource section on page 402 you'll find a checklist for arranging meeting space. All too often we take comfortable chairs, room temperature, and sound quality for granted, only to find out when it's too late to do anything about it.

Facilitating Groups by Phone

One of the obvious advantages of facilitation by phone is that it saves time and money because everyone can call from any convenient location. Initially some people may be reluctant to work on the phone. Once they experience it, most people love the flexibility it affords. Despite initial reluctance, many people report that they are more open and vulnerable over the phone than in person.

For the facilitator, working over the phone increases your sensitivity to voice, tone, pace and inflection. You become adept at reading the energy and develop more access to intuition. Even experiential exercises translate to phone facilitation. In the same way you might guide a visualization or an awareness exercise with individuals face to face, you simply create the experience by giving instructions over the phone.

Some tips for creating powerful experiences over the phone are:

1. Guide the experience as if you were face to face. For instance you can ring a bell, tell people you're lighting a candle, do some guided breath work, co-create an agenda, or invite people to step over a line. Even though you can't see them, assume people are joining you.

2. Invite people to stop multi-tasking, imagine you're in one room together, and give the group the gift of listening deeply.

3. Encourage playfulness when you co-create experiential exercises remotely. Consider it an experiment and encourage stepping in wholeheartedly. You can model playfulness, break through the tension with a listening game done in gibberish, or use Marshall Rosenberg's line, "Anything worth doing is worth doing badly."

4. Flow into the experience by directing attention to the body, imagination, or feeling, as a natural part of the dialogue. With body awareness or emotional awareness exercises, this may mean speaking more slowly or softly (but still loud enough for everyone to hear).

5. Leave plenty of time and silence for people to do what you ask. Avoid the tendency to rush. Err on the side of giving more time than is needed so that you send the signal that there is time to really drop into their experience. You may preface the experience by explaining the purpose of the silence or why you are slowing down the pace.

6. Protect the space you have created and guard against side conversations or jumping out of the experience prematurely. Letting people know in advance when they'll have a chance to talk, asking people to check in to see if there's more to explore, and encouraging people to pay attention to what you'll ask them to share later helps them stay engaged.

7. Use your intuition and share what you sense or feel as you guide the experience. Assume your intuition is useful, even when it doesn't resonate perfectly.

The phone has its challenges. We can't smell the fear or see the furrowed brow, but listening to the intricacies of each voice on the call can be exceptionally revealing. Paying attention to the breath, the tone, cadence, volume, pitch are all illuminating. And when we're unsure about what's going on, we can check simply by asking, "What's going on?" The challenge of facilitating phone meetings is that it's easy for people to tune-out or multitask. The social bonds are weaker, and it's harder for the facilitator to keep everyone involved. But the advantages are clear – not only is it more convenient and less expensive, but also people are more direct, meetings are shorter, and including diverse groups can be easier.

Some of the ways we can create safe space online or on a conference call is to ask people to imagine that they're all sitting in a room, paying close attention to every word, and not doing anything they wouldn't do in a face-to-face meeting (clip your fingernails, leave without saying anything, talk on another line at the same time). Some facilitators use visual imagery – imagine that we're at a roundtable or draw the seating arrangement so we can go around and hear everyone. Silence is less effective on the phone but can still be used sparingly. Sending out a list of questions for the discussion ahead of time helps people come prepared and stay engaged. Some participants really miss all the visual cues and find it difficult to rely exclusively on words. But it doesn't take long to become adept at hearing the vocal nuances. We may check in more often, by summarizing, raising questions, asking people for their contributions, and moving the group towards conclusion.

Webcams have challenges of their own. They help us to see what people are busy *not* saying, but we're often distracted by technical issues that range from blurred movement, to eye contact that's off- center, to poor visual quality.

A lot of people *think* they can't facilitate by phone because they rely so heavily on visual cues. However more and more learning experiences rely on the phone. If you'd like to see a 60-

page powerpoint on leading teleclasses and telecircles, that includes sections on designing your own teleclass, creating an inviting learning environment, developing facilitation skills, leveraging the energy, and eliciting feedback, go to www.leadershipthatworks.com/leaderskills

I enjoy facilitating groups on-line because I find the Internet becomes a quasi-spiritual space. The subtle energy paired with autonomous energy creates an intimate shared space for freedom of expression. Many people feel more comfortable in an online environment because they can edit and revise before they post. This can be annoying to people who value spontaneity and flow but freeing for people who are reluctant to speak in the group. In an asynchronous environment the learning is streamlined, and everyone has the space to communicate.

The sense of anonymity provides some safety which invites trust, deeper vulnerability, and intimacy. People more willingly talk about their fears, "I'm *still* scared," and their regrets, "For 15 years I was the leader of a Mormon group that helped gay kids become straight until I realized I would never be straight," and their dreams, "I've always wanted to create a recovery center to help victims of sexual assault reclaim their power." These comments all come from MBA students in a coaching course that helps them uncover their vision, values and goals. Even the most skeptical end up saying things like, "The characteristic that I treasure most is the forum in which to express openly....Having attended both traditional and now online settings, I had been concerned that such interaction would suffer in the online classroom....couldn't have been more mistaken...I count with warmth the friends that I've made ...ones that I trust will be close for a long time..."

It still surprises me how much on-line participants appreciate my vulnerability, and one wrote, "Each time I hear you relate personal experiences, you become more human to me and more accessible—I guess it's that powerful need for inclusion and trust. It was particularly helpful for me to hear you say that when you don't know what to do you return to feelings and needs. Just reading that, I let out a sigh of relief—partly to hear that sometimes you don't know what to do and partly that there is a ground to sit upon at those times." Another wrote, "I deeply appreciate the transparent honesty that underlies the intention of your post. I repeatedly enjoy how your honesty models for me the courage and willingness to expose your truth and the potent vulnerability that must create for you. This is true leadership to me – to model a behavior that so clearly stretches the edges of our comfort zone. One that I find encourages and inspires something I have always yearned for more of: to be more willing to be more fully myself."

Managing Break-out Groups

Break-out groups change the dynamics and allow more reticent people to speak, which contributes to intimacy, disclosure, and trust. Most people bring more energy to small groups and they feel more comfortable raising difficult issues. Because they get to contribute anonymously when they report back to the large group, many people are more honest. Each group can be working on different tasks simultaneously and the size lends itself to efficient decision-making and problem-solving. But the disadvantages include the time it takes to divide into groups, give instructions, settle into the small group, reconvene the large group, and report out. Then the full group faces the daunting task of integrating the work of the small group. This process can be boring or unsettling unless we design the reporting out in ways that inspire connection.

Several ways to divide into small groups:

- Count off by the number of groups you want to create (not by the number of people in each group).
- Cluster with people sitting nearby.
- Offer a variety of topics and invite people to self-select based on their interests.
- Have people line up based on level of experience, then group by experience level or count off (to disperse the experience among the groups).
- Select randomly.
- Tell people to get into groups of three and raise their hands until they have a group of four or five.

Give participants complete instructions before asking them to move into small groups. Novice facilitators give part of the directions, get members up and moving into small groups, quiet the group, give the rest of the directions, and when they notice confusion, they stop them part way through the activity to re-explain. We can avoid this type of confusion by writing out directions in advance, practicing giving directions, and saying them with as few words as possible. Train the group to listen fully by asking for complete silence before you start explaining. Encourage them to listen by saying things like, "I'd like to give directions only once. Instead of relying on others to listen to the directions, listen closely enough so that you can explain to others."

If the directions include multiple steps, put the directions on handouts, a flip chart, or a power point display. If you give participants questions to answer, don't expect them to remember the question word for word. You probably won't remember it exactly either, and when they ask you to repeat it, you'll create confusion.

The purpose of having small groups report back to the large group is to share the collective wisdom discovered in the small group and to build community. When breakout groups report back to the large group, I'm often bored silly because they distill their experience into buzzwords that gloss over the beauty of what happened in the group. You can avoid this drivel by asking people to share the highlights or nuggets of their experience rather than a summary.

Setting up Role Plays

Whenever possible, instead of role plays, I like to design activities that are real. Working on real issues is far more powerful than any imaginary scenario. However, there are times when role plays help people ease into difficult situations – helping people deal with intense anger or deep pain. Sometimes overused, sometimes underused, role plays can unleash new ways of learning. When we play other people, we get to experience others more deeply which can deepen our empathic capacity. In Thailand, Kanya Likanasudh used puppets to demonstrate a role play that observers experienced as healing:

> I gave deep empathy to a couple of people before this workshop and some people were calling me a healer when to me, what I was doing was listening to what their hearts are yearning for, a basic skill in NVC. Using a jackal puppet on each hand, I did a role play between a rapist and the victim. I had giraffe ears on myself representing the facilitator. The victim puppet shared her experience of how difficult it's been since the rape, suffering every single minute of her life. The guy was saying, "I'm sorry," but I interrupted him and said, "No, don't say you're sorry yet. Really feel the impact of what she's saying to you."
>
> At the next workshop, a woman came running up to me, asking if she could walk home with me. We took the ferry boat and the sky train. She said, "Those words that you spoke through the puppets were the same words I've said to myself so many times." She was moved when she heard what the victim puppet wanted from the rapist...to have him know how much suffering she has been going through. When she saw how the rapist puppet had such a difficult time getting in touch with his feelings as he heard about the consequences of his actions, she felt some compassion seeing that he was terrified by his own behavior. She herself had been raped and had never been able to voice her feelings to anyone. She felt the weight lifted from her shoulders and said, "I want to help other people heal like you did." I was bawling on the sky train because I felt such a deep connection with her. I had no idea the role play would have such profound effect on her and other women.[111]

One of the things I love most about role plays is that they unleash parts of ourselves we didn't know we had. Valuing authenticity and presence, some facilitators insist on no role plays, but then we all miss out on exploring hidden parts of ourselves. By playing others, new parts of ourselves get to come out and play. Keeping it real is an art. Role plays can actually enhance authenticity because we invite people to expand their range of experience and empathize deeply with another by embodying the way they move, speak, and choose their language. We can reduce the distance between two people when we open our hearts to their feelings and needs. When we take on a role, we embody another's inner experience, which leads to deeper understanding at a visceral level. Role plays help us develop empathic connection when we truly take on their personae and act from our intuition.

---

[111] Kanya Likanasudh personal interview 4/28/08.

To develop empathic presence, we can choose from four types of role plays based on the level of empathic consciousness in the person or group. In each role play, both people step fully into the role, one as authentic and one as empathic. When you're in the *authentic* role, spontaneously respond to whatever is said, including judgments, honest expression, or whatever matters to you. When you're in the *empathic* role, connect with the heart of the other's experience and reflect back whatever they might feel or need. These role plays are listed in the order of difficulty, from low to high. Starting at level one can help the person more easily move to other levels. We can make suggestions or simply give people a choice of which role to play. For example, if a participant wants to reconnect with her brother who repeatedly beat her up as a child, she has the option to:

1. Play her authentic self, saying whatever lives in her, while her partner plays an empathic version of her brother who really understands her experience.
2. Play her authentic brother, saying whatever might be true for him, while her partner plays an empathic version of herself, who really understands her brother's deepest needs.
3. Play her empathic brother reflecting back the needs of her partner who is playing her authentic self.
4. Play her empathic self while her partner plays her authentic brother, sharing whatever lives in him.

If a participant is highly-charged, starting at level one can help to relieve the distress before trying the other role plays. If participants have already done a bit of work on themselves regarding this issue, trust your intuition and start wherever you like. After several rounds, participants will lose track of who is empathic and who is the authentic and enter into a more genuine dialogue based on the shifts that occur as people feel heard.

Flip Charts, LCD or White Boards

You can't change the world without markers and paper. Flips charts can enhance or detract from the ambience of the group. Make them too accessible and people rush into scribing to relieve discomfort or move into solutions prematurely. If you have more than 30 people, some of them will strain to read the flip charts, no matter how large you write. Here are a few tips for creating readable flip charts:

*   Create pre-written flipcharts so you aren't rushed
*   Write no more than six to seven lines per page
*   Use lower case for readability, making each letter at least 3" tall
*   Stand behind the flip chart, writing around the corner, so people can see as you write
*   Use no more than three colors per page to keep charts aesthetically pleasing
*   Alternate colors for each line

I like to bring my own markers because I have *strong* preferences for:
- Dark-colored markers – black, dark green, dark blue, purple or brown (avoid yellow, orange, or pink, which are too light to easily read)
- Unscented markers to avoid complaints
- Chisel point markers for bold lettering

Flip Chart Tips
- Use post-it flip chart paper, or pre-tear the tape for easy hanging
- Make a 1" tear on each side of the paper, then pull straight down to hang on the wall
- Create a wall plan for how you're going to hang your flip charts
- Tab your pre-written flip charts with post-its or masking tape to find each one easily
- Use sturdy flip chart easels that you can press on
- Ask for help in hanging completed flip charts

Scribing

- Choose an experienced scribe (not a participant) so you can stay connected to the group
- Put a header at the top of the page as a banner to differentiate charts
- Ask for headlines when people say a lot
- Capture the essence of what people say in their words, not yours

LCD Projector

In general, I don't recommend using power point presentations because they are overused. Generally they aren't engaging, even if you use all the bells and whistles. Unless you're in a high-tech environment, the lighting seems to subdue the group, and the focus is on the wall instead of each other. If you facilitate at a conference, where participants see one power point presentation after another, they'll cheer if you do something more enlivening.

With that said, there are times when an LCD projector is my friend. In a large group, people in the back can't see flip charts, so a power point presentation can keep visual learners focused. With so many distractions in a large group, simple instructions projected on the wall can serve as a reminder.

White Boards

For small groups, white boards can be used to take notes that help people feel understood and ensure they're all on the same page. It can be particularly helpful during a conference call to help keep participants engaged visually. When all the participants have access to the white board, the scribe can capture the essence of what's been said, and then participants can add to it which helps them feel more deeply understood.

Sound

Nothing is more annoying than inability to hear the speakers in the group. In most groups over 40, your can continuously ask soft-spoken people to repeat themselves, speak louder, or use a microphone. Many people find a microphone intimidated or repeatedly forget to hold it next to their lips. In larger groups, support people can run the microphone from one section of the room to another to foster a sense of inclusion. This can be annoying if you only have one microphone and the runner passes by people without acknowledging their desire to speak. Two microphones can help runners include voices from many directions. Setting up stationary microphones and getting speakers to stand in a queue is another alternative that eliminates the annoyance that arises when people start to talk without a microphone and then have to wait for the runner. In many groups there are more people queued up to speak time will allow. Letting people know we're only going to take three more questions helps manage expectations.

Debriefing the Learning

The debriefing process begins with supporting each other to be present. Connecting with where we *are*, not where we *want to be,* helps others to do the same. Instead of a stale didactic approach of telling people what we already know, we can speak about what we're discovering in the moment. Sharing our own fresh insights moves us out of the realm of teacher/ student relationship and into the realm of impacting each other's awareness and learning. A variation of the NVC model offers a simple process for capturing the learning:

Observations
- What did you notice?
- What stands out about your experience?
- Where is your attention now?

Feelings
- What's your reaction?
- How did your emotions change during the process?
- How are you feeling now?

Importance
- What was significant?
- What did you learn?
- What needs were met or unmet?

274

Application
- How will you take the learning forward?
- What will you do differently in the future?
- How will you apply what you learned?

Debriefing is the process of capturing and integrating the learning from activities. I liken it to going fishing, where facilitators:
- Observe what happens when everyone is swimming freely – flowing in the experience.
- Take charge of netting the learning and getting the fish into the boat.
- Move on to new fishing grounds before harvesting every single fish.
- Reel in the learning when participants want to extend their experience and run the line outward.
- Keep the lines of learning separated and cut loose tangled lines.
- Help people focus on this fishing trip, not old stories about previous fishing trips or old learning, but what they are learning in this moment.

Using the same model, I like to create space to debrief the facilitators' learning right after the event while names and incidents are still fresh. When we wish we'd done things differently, we can do a "post-hearsal," a term coined by Inbal Kashtan that involves role playing dissatisfying interactions, recreating it in ways that are more enriching for everyone involved.

Personal reflection and journaling help participants get clarity about their learning and can be used before sharing out loud or in lieu of speaking. Nancy Coco, director of the Penn State - Lehigh Valley Writing Project says that when facilitators journal along with participants, they not only model the behavior they expect from participants but they also get clarity about their own inner process which leads to shared insights. A few additional reasons why Nancy advocates journaling:
- Writing is discovery – you may *think* you know what you have to say, but the act of writing can move you into the unknown and reveal insights if you are open.
- Journaling enables you to track the flow of the experience, noting emotions, judgments, insights as they arise in the moment and engaging you in the group while enabling introspection.
- Journal writing can also be mined post-session to surface themes for further reflection or work for self, coaching partners, or group.
- Journaling can be prompted by what is said, what is not, a desire to engage but not share aloud…it's a means to capture, shift, and/or release energy to move the group.

Our thoughts can become jumbled and confused. Writing helps us gain clarity as we download our thoughts and put them in the light of day. Writing without censoring ourselves opens the heart and the brain, unleashes our innate creativity, and helps us tap into the unknown, the collective unconscious, and the universal mind.

Peer Support Follow Up

Without follow up, the benefits of most programs don't last. Setting up peer support groups, learning partners, or practice buddies helps people build on the learning and excitement generated in the group. You can allow people to self-organize or create a process for them to create their support system. Some people don't want follow-up support – they have enough on their plate already. They can journal to create their own internal support. For the others, here's a simple way to help them organize continuous support:

- Get into small groups of 2-5 to design your support team.
- Each person shares what an ideal support team would mean to them.
- Collaboratively design the alliance.
- Agree on logistics (dates, times, venue, roles).

Over the years I've started or been part of many support groups. They focused on learning more about leadership, coaching, empathy, consulting, and facilitation. The most beneficial group met every Monday morning for 90 minutes for a year. In the beginning we set aside about 20 minutes to share new learning, but we often skipped this. We allowed 10 minutes for check-in (which included whether we wanted to receive empathy), and spent the bulk of our time offering group empathy, with a five minute check-out at the end. Occasionally we'd use the group to talk about our relationships and ways of working together, tweaking our process.

Exercises

Reflections:
1. How can a support partner or group help you?
2. Describe your perfect support group.

Small Group Discussions:
1. When using a developmental facilitation process with a group for the first time, what facilitation skills do you want them to have when they leave?
2. How do you continue to develop your own facilitation skills?

Activities:
1. Create your own list of responsibilities that you want to take on as facilitator. Delete anything that doesn't feel life serving.
2. Take part in a group phone call or teleclass and take notes on what you think people are feeling based on their voice.
3. Offer a teleclass before you think you are ready—today!
4. Design a role play to help two people who have been friends from childhood who have avoided each other ever since one was promoted to be the other's boss.

Chapter 14
Fives Phases of Organization Development

The real voyage of discovery consists not in seeking new landscapes, but in having new eyes. — Marcel Proust

Too often facilitators get asked to come in and do a half-day process because the client is skeptical or their budget only allows for a dry run, when a complete cultural change is called for. Sometimes we're tempted to get a foot in the door, but if we give them what they ask for without looking at the entire system, they end up wasting their time and money because no real transformation takes place. We may have lost an opportunity or taken a step backwards if they see us as the flavor of the month or we look like warmed up leftovers from the programs that have gone before us. In the grand scheme, a systems approach to organization development helps is more life-serving and contributes to human evolution and global consciousness.

In this chapter we'll go behind the scenes of a growing company and explore organization development through the eyes of both the consultant and the CEO. They candidly share their struggles and successes in each phase of the organization development process: Entry and Contracting, Sensing and Discovery, Diagnosis and Feedback, Planning Interventions and Action, and Evaluation and Closure.

We'll also look at some models and tools for supporting organization development, including Appreciative Inquiry, REAL conversations, questions for diagnosing the organization's needs, suggestions for getting a signed contract, managing the change process, and evaluating the OD initiative. First we'll start with an overview of the five phases of the organization development process and then look behind the curtain at how the process impacts the people. By supporting people in organizations to open their hearts, they learn to deepen personal awareness and create more fulfilling relationships, which allows work groups to thrive and ultimately their organizations contribute to making a better world.

Five Phases of Organization Development
1. Entry and Contracting
2. Sensing and Discovery
3. Diagnosis and Feedback
4. Planning Interventions and Action

5. Evaluation and Closure

As organization development consultants enter organizations to collect data, share their diagnosis of the organization's needs, design interventions, and evaluate progress, we can also build internal organizational capacity to do the same. Each phase of the OD process serves a distinct purpose. So let's see how this works.

Entry and Contracting

Authenticity, presence, and empathy are the vital components of the entry process. During the initial conversations, we build trust by listening non-judgmentally and offering support. Rather then glossing over or censoring the issues, this approach allows the underlying concerns and opportunities to surface. By listening deeply, understanding the client's issues, and establishing the alliance, we uncover the goals and deeper desires. Now there is a word you don't hear much in organizations...I said desires because we want to go much deeper than goals. By tapping people's passions we get clarity about personal and organizational expectations. Once we're connected with their hearts, we co-create desired outcomes, determine roles and responsibilities, and establish business terms.

Sensing and Discovery

While relying heavily on our intuition, we also collect information based on hard data. Dialogue, surveys, interviews, assessment tools, and focus groups are used both to collect information and build relationships. Throughout this process, the emphasis on building relationships means we're much more likely to generate trust which helps us get to the heart of the matter.

Diagnosis and Feedback

We come in looking for what works and what we can leverage. Instead of a pathological approach to diagnosis, we can help members of the organization identify the life-giving energy in their work experiences, and then discover their needs and wishes. A summarized report of the information and shared analysis acts as a catalyst for deepening awareness, inviting choice, and stimulating action. Many organizational cultures have a preference for hard data, a scoring system for analyzing the current situation, and a way to measure progress. When accompanied by anecdotal data, the impact can be very moving, heart-connecting, and inspirational. Analyzing the data *for* the client can be highly informative, but isn't as empowering as a joint analysis. Collectively we can explore a gap analysis between the current situation and the desired situation.

Planning Interventions and Action

We end up with one-way communication and minimal buy-in unless we intervene with authentic feedback. Feedback leads to a blueprint for change and collaborative action planning.

Action plans are broken down into small steps, with accountability structures, including who is taking responsibility and agreed on dates for completion. Implementation of the action plan can include a wide range of OD interventions: individual or group coaching, training, leadership development, team building, diversity dialogues, and conflict resolution are some of the processes used to support the change initiative.

Evaluation and Closure

The measures of success established at entry are derived jointly. Evaluation can include financial measures such as the bottom-line impact (profitability or return on investment) or stakeholder satisfaction (quality-of-life or employee retention). OD work is an intimate process that calls for an empowering closure. Instead of celebrating once a year at the company Christmas party, we advocate for continuous celebration. We not only celebrate successes; we also celebrate new insights gained from disappointment or failure. Both provide opportunities for heart connection and stimulate dialogue that leads to new opportunities.

Case Study

To give life to these concepts and practices, I offer a case study that illustrates the beauty and hazards of the organization development process. Both Sushma Sharma, the CEO of Resonant Consulting, and Evan Harris, the managing director of Optimaz[112], described the impact of the organization development process in a large outsourcing business in Mumbai, India, which grew from 50 to 1,000 employees in three years. They both openly shared the high and low moments of the process, and explored three aspects in detail: the cultural divide, power dynamics, and the change process. Keeping this case study in mind, let's explore the five phases of organization development in more detail.

Entry and Contracting

Entry is the most vital phase of the collaboration. Sushma Sharma, from Resonate Consulting, compares this phase to, "going on a blind date, where both sides experience anxiety and anticipation." The first meeting can fall flat, or can lead to co-creating a great future together. Entry is all about heart connection, building trust, and communicating authentically. Sushma led the OD process at Optimaz. She described her initial meeting with managing director Evan Harris as, "very sensitively and tentatively connecting with one another, and honestly sharing who we are." In the first meeting, they looked at expanding his leadership and his dream. She coached him for several months on a personal level and said, "Trust was built over time as I confronted him about his views about India, attitudes towards people, impatience with the pace of change, and dissatisfaction with the competencies of the people." He quickly

---

[112] The name of the company has been changed for this case study.

changed his leadership which inspired his senior leaders to ask for coaching. Soon after expanding the coaching process to the senior leaders, they began the system-wide OD process.

During the entry and contracting phase, Sushma learned about the historical background of Optimaz.

> Evan: The chess pieces were already on the board when I came into Optimaz. The UK parent company had been extremely successful for 20 years. They had 20,000 employees, were #1 in their industry, and financial growth was exponential. Until 2004, they had only operated in the UK, with an absolute focus on profit. Most corporations have growth strategies, set goals for penetrating new industries, and at least talk about corporate responsibility, but Optimaz focused only on profit.

> When Indian competitors entered the industry, they undercut the first-world cost base structure, which threatened the UK business model. On the cusp of India's taking over the Business Process Outsourcing industry, our customers demanded the work be outsourced to India.

During the initial conversations, the vast differences between UK and Indian cultures surfaced and the underlying concerns and opportunities emerged. Sushma listened deeply as Evan explained the cultural divide, roles, social norms and the exponential growth rate of the outsourcing industry.

> Evan: People from the UK neo-imperialist culture thought of India as a smelly, backward place you go to get diarrhea, and they didn't want to touch it with a barge pole. I was the only one who recognized the opportunity and wanted to experience a completely different culture and live and work in Mumbai.

> As managing director, my job was to build the business in India and make money. It was a huge battle to get the executives in the UK to take India seriously. Our competitors in India were going crazy—doubling or tripling in size every year, while our efforts at Optimaz were inching forward. The Indians were baffled that we were moving so slowly. I'd recruited a team away from successful companies, had pitched the great opportunities, and then we sat there stagnating. People with experience could go anywhere; if they left, the mass exodus would ricochet downwards.

Sushma asked questions and shared the nuances of Indian culture which helped Evan understand his employee's perspectives.

> Evan: I saw both sides of the enormous cultural chasm as I shielded Indians from the disdain from the UK and tried to bridge the canyon. To understand the culture, I had to remove my Western hat. Instead of focusing on

competency, I joined the Indians who focused on relationships. In the West people walk in with competency, but in India they trust that focusing on relationships will lead to the competencies.

With no social safety net, Indians are fixated on security and each person understands their place in the larger system. I didn't understand this. I was the white guy sent in to ensure an Indian business was operated like a UK business, which was suicide. The classic imperialistic paradigm meant we had to impose our world view on people who didn't share or even understand our world view.

Another glaring cultural difference was that people in India never say no. No doesn't mean no. Yes doesn't mean yes. That's infuriating for people from a task-based world. This behavior wasn't a reflection of incompetence; it was a reflection of social norms. Their Western response was dismissive – any deviation from the UK paradigm was seen as feminine. They expected everyone else to accommodate, merge, assimilate, accept, and submit to the masculine conqueror.

During the entry and contracting phase, the consultants listened, connected and built the relationship. The historical background provided context and helped the consultants understand the values and concerns. But what's happening currently is what really matters in the entry stage. "Why are you calling us *now*?" is the underlying question that brings all the hopes and fears to the surface. Evan described the current crisis with rising alarm.

Evan: One of our teams complained they weren't getting enough money and their manager told them to try to get more money somewhere else. She never checked out the data or suggested we'd pay market rate, which I consider a fundamental obligation. At that time, the industry pay rates were doubling every year. Our competitors were opening up shop two miles away and paying 50% more. We were dependent on this team of 12 guys. The reputation, the stability, and continuity of the organization were at stake. If those 12 guys left, many more would leave en masse. We wouldn't have even known they were going until they were gone.

On the brink of disaster, one person came to me in tears and the whole story tumbled out. I freaked out because I didn't know anything about it. In Indian culture no one goes over their boss's head, so it took a lot of courage for her to come to me.

Throughout the *entry and contracting* phase, the consultants built trust and developed a preliminary understanding of the needs of the organization and desired outcomes. After establishing the scope of the work and business terms, they moved into phase two of the OD process.

Sensing and Discovery

With rapport and trust established, and the contract in place, the consultants began the *sensing and discovery* phase of the process. They collected information from a variety of sources and continued to build relationships. Three modes of discovery that helped create deeper connection and understanding are observation, dialogue, and surveys. They watched how people interacted, talked to them about what matters most, and collected raw data as the basis for analysis and interpretation. Facilitating transformation requires sensitive inquiry to discover the hidden potential of leaders and teams. Real conversations in the here-and-now helped uncover the authentic issues. For instance, Sushma and her team held one-on-one meetings with the senior leaders at Optimaz, led focus groups, and attended their open-house meetings to get a feel for the ways people interacted with each other.

Relying heavily on their intuition, the consultants started collecting information by interviewing the leadership team and talking to them about their concerns, fears, hopes and dreams. The consultants at Resonant helped the senior team uncover the power dynamics which emerged as one of the most challenging issues. Evan described the power structure and codependency at Optimaz:

> Evan: Working with a team on the other side of the world, the foundation of the work relationship had to be trust. The Indians were willing to trust – they had to accept the UK as the conqueror and deal with the cultural inferiority complex. They were very open to doing things differently, operating under the belief system that the West knows how to do things better. The problem was that openness was not reciprocated. The rigid world view from the UK couldn't accommodate another way of thinking.
>
> The other dynamic was the underground backlash against the imperialistic way of operating. The power-under mentality fueled resentment of the domination system. India is an extremely hierarchical, patriarchal society. Individuals do not have power. To be part of the culture is to submit. It starts with being born into an extended family where the parent's rule of law is absolute. Shame is the weapon used to enforce conformity.
>
> When they go to school, at age three, Indians are forced to submit to indoctrination. The guru talks. The student listens. They absorb, memorize, and regurgitate the information right up through their MBA. Critical thinking and innovation are not encouraged. Submission is in the air they breathe. There are exceptions, such as the first son of an industrialist who is bred to

rule and knows he's entitled. The rest are bred to be worker bees. The hierarchy is absolute. The CEO makes *all* the decisions. The others gain security and power by going along. They learn to suppress their resentment, but their rage leaks out in destructive behaviors. Those higher up the chain crush those without power because it's happened to them. For instance, drivers and cleaners are treated cruelly. Many, many people were shocked when I made the drivers permanent employees with benefits.

By bringing egalitarian principles to Optimaz, Evan expected people to become competent, self-actualizing, and innovative. Because they understood the culture, he anticipated they would be better qualified to make decisions. Evan valued autonomy and assumed everyone wanted more. For him, autonomy was like food, a basic necessity, but the employees saw it differently.

With few exceptions, the Indians thought it was unnatural to make their own decisions. They wanted me to show them what to do. They thought I was speaking Martian when I suggested they create their own work processes. I didn't even have the awareness that I was doing anything unusual. New employees would come in very confident, with great track records of success based on doing what they were told. Because I expected them to create, their confidence would collapse. There were some exceptions, but most of the time, I wondered why people weren't able to get on with it.

Only later did I realize I was sticking them on a motor bike before they'd learned to ride a bicycle with training wheels. Emotionally I'd have to hold them during the period of collapse as they abandoned their old identities. The whole world loves the idea of autonomy until they get it.

Despite formal processes for gathering information, some of the most valuable information comes through informal conversations. Sometimes they asked directly, "What is your high dream?" and other times they kept their ears to the ground, listening to people's hopes, fears and dreams. After several days of meetings, the consulting team had enough observations to identify patterns and get clarity about what was needed.

Diagnosis and Feedback

In the third phase of the Organization Development process, the consultants diagnose the organization by identifying both individual and organizational needs and present the feedback to the client organization. Some consultants present their diagnosis of organizational needs in writing, use a power point presentation. Others collaborate with members of the organization to co-create a presentation of the needs that are driving the organization.

I've heard many people share their belief that members of an organization cannot be effective diagnosticians because they have overt or covert vested interests. Naturally, we all have vested interests, even as consultants. Part of a collaborative diagnostic process is to surface the needs beneath the interests, trust that people can hold their own needs as valuable, and still identify the needs of the entire organization without seeing one set of needs as more important than the other.

Sharing the Diagnosis

A traditional approach to Organization Development diagnoses all the problems: conflicting goals, restricted information, ill-defined roles, autocratic leadership style, rebellion against authority, action based on rumors, low energy, suppressed creativity, absence of long-term plan, and disruptive ways of addressing conflict. However, there is another way. Resonate consultants shared their diagnosis by tapping their intuition and discovering what people want. Using an Appreciative Inquiry approach to diagnosis, they identified the life force of the organization and desires of the people based on the stories told and data collected. They talked about what's missing in terms of what people want or need:

- Cross-cultural understanding and competency
- Balance of autonomy and direction
- Shared access to clear, factual, information
- Authentic communication and bi-directional feedback
- Creative approaches to managing conflict
- Clear, shared goals with dated action plans
- Co-created vision with well-developed long-term and short-term outlook
- Well-defined, adaptable roles and responsibilities

Another option Resonate sometimes uses is to offer a diagnostic workshop to facilitate articulation of team climate and team processes. As the organization joins in the quest along with the OD consultants, the co-discovery enhances the process of ownership. The diagnosis needs to be rapid and responsive to the needs of the teams and the new challenges they are facing.

At Resonate Consulting, dialogue is the primary tool used for sharing diagnosis and feedback. Sushma Sharma has a gift for helping people openly receive the feedback. She described part of the *diagnosis and feedback* process with Evan Harris:

> Sushma: After talking to the senior team, I gave Evan the feedback about his leadership. I shared their perceptions – both negative and positive – his impatience with change, quick decisions, openness, honesty, perfectionism, and teaching style. He wanted a high quality environment with zero defects. He was very receptive to the feedback and changed his behavior quickly. Evan

was extremely committed to the coaching process, meeting every 2 weeks for 3-4 hours, even if he was in London.

The second step came because people saw a lot of change in Evan. They became committed because they saw him walking the talk: he really listened with more patience and communicated more sensitively with people. He changed his style of working, allowing himself to be vulnerable and lead with honest directness.

He wanted them to be self-actualizing, but that only happened when he began to partner and place trust in them. In the beginning he couldn't understand why people didn't want autonomy and freedom, but he started understanding the culture sensitively. He was able to build the organization, build himself into a leader, and fully committed himself to developing the next level of people.

We started coaching his direct reports because they asked for it. The emotional insensitivity was intensely prevalent. Several relationships weren't working at all. They had stopped talking to each other, so we supported them in working with their interpersonal issues and conflicts, and building trust with each other. Most of the employees were very young—in their twenties—and needed a place to belong. During these 3-4 months of coaching the top team, they started believing in the process, so I suggested we do a total OD process.

The diagnosis of the organization focused on interpersonal relationships, rapport, communication patterns, and inter-departmental issues. The organization had only one leader - the rest of the senior team had no presence as leaders. When we shared the feedback with the top group of 40 people, it came as a shock. They knew it intuitively because the culture didn't really engage people, but they were still stunned.

Awareness of the developmental needs of individuals became a driving force at Optimaz and people became deeply engaged in supporting each other's professional growth. After looking at themselves as individuals, they were able to look at the organization as a whole.

Evan described the *diagnosis and feedback* stage of the OD process a little differently:

Evan: The overall feedback was really positive—people felt like they mattered. We had strong core values, but our identity was unarticulated. We had a leadership vacuum beneath me, low trust between teams, lack of cohesion in the senior team, poor communication, and operations weren't getting along with other teams.

Planning Interventions and Action

Soon after the *diagnosis and feedback* stage, the OD consultants designed *interventions and action* to improve the working relationships, develop leadership and improve communication. Evan talked about a few of the interventions:

> After talking to everyone on the senior team, the consultants designed a two-day off-site workshop with 33 of the top managers. We started with a values process to determine what makes us who we are. In one of the exercises we lined up based on length of service. On one end of the spectrum, a few of us had more than two years of service, on the other, six days. Each group created and acted out a play based on our perceptions of Optimaz. The newcomers, who thought everything was great, went first. With increased level of service, the enthusiasm dwindled and all but died in the most senior group. We were clinging for survival because we knew what we were up against.

> We interviewed each other about moments that meant something to each of us. In another activity, in teams of five, we wrote statements that reflected our values. "Optimaz is like a family," was one value. Each person was given 3 stars to choose our top values. Then we broke into teams and did a play to depict values in action. The whole process was fun, upbeat, and brought people together. We ended with a party and left feeling cohesive and hopeful.

Back in the workplace, awareness expanded and everyone opened to the value of the OD process, which gave more people a voice. Emotional insensitivity was replaced with deep exploration of emotions. But Evan felt overwhelmed by the intensity and weight of the process:

> We learned to hold someone during an emotional opening: when one person expressed deep emotions, the rest of the group held them. During the off-sites, we could manage this carefully and sensitively. But doing it all day long while we were trying to run a company was more difficult. Our business became one big group process. We had a lot of cohesiveness, a lot of light coming in, and the company was prospering. In hindsight, I realized we didn't really know what we were getting ourselves into. We weren't prepared for the emotional onslaught.

The OD practitioners were focusing on the positives, telling us to dive off the board, but they didn't understand the level of fear the managers were experiencing. The enormous pressure to hold it together took its toll on me emotionally. When people were on the floor shaking, I was in agony, wondering if the company was going to spin out of control.

Transformation requires a period of letting go. The whole senior team collapsed at once. They had accepted the power-under dynamics for so long that they didn't know how to take responsibility for their side of the relationship. They couldn't see the person in power as a human being, only as a dictator. The Indian model is that the leader holds it together. Leaders cannot open themselves as human beings – if they do, they get crushed by the people underneath. I didn't know this going into the process.

Throughout these interventions, Evan was not only developing the organization, but doing his own personal and spiritual growth work. He describes his discomfort in dealing with the level of fear and the speed of change:

In my spiritual process, I was dismissive of the weaker parts of myself that were scared. My internal model was to override them. So I was insensitive to other's fear and extreme discomfort. We didn't respect people's safety thresholds. I had cut myself off internally from my feminine side. People were faced with their own self-inflicted disempowerment. They were choosing the power-under position of safety, so it felt like a cricket bat slammed in their heads when that safety net was taken away.

I overruled the sensitive, gentle parts of myself so that I could have more action, adventure, and risk taking, always questing even when I was scared shitless. What I really needed was safety, stability, and close loving relationships, but I was completely blocked. In hindsight I would have been much more sensitive, slowed things down, and given people space. I would have let people go at their own pace, and they would take the risk only if they knew their vulnerabilities would be respected. I didn't have the awareness that accelerated, forced change doesn't hold space for people to evolve at their own pace in their own way.

Through all this, I had a support team. I would come home on Fridays and collapse on the couch for two days trying to recover. My wife Kylie was going through transformation of her own, but she held it all with me. Her spiritual caring grounded me. It was enormous to have her share the burden. My coach lives in an untouched haven where the natural earth forces give her a lot of internal strength and substance. And our consultant also helped me out a lot.

As an example, Evan repeatedly wrestled with the parent company in the UK who wanted him to fire people just because they were no longer needed.

> I started a project that employed 15 new people. To get them on board, I'd sold them a dream, assured them of security and offered them opportunities to build relationships. Three months later the UK pulled the project. They expected me to fire them, which you can do in the UK, but not in India. No one understood the consequences—not only would it impact the 15 people, but the reverberations would result in losses throughout Optimaz. It was tough to get the parent company to shift their world view and see the organization as a whole.

> The Indians who liaised with the parent company had to deal with the imperialist judgments that they had screwed up, were incompetent, or were not making sense. I fought the fires, explained the context in which Indians were operating and why they'd made a particular decision.

All that support gave Evan the courage to expand the OD initiative, but the high-speed of change was difficult for the organization to absorb.

> After a Christmas break at home in Australia, we widened the scope of the OD work to include all the employees – 600 at the time. In hindsight, I realized the senior team needed to go through transformation first to become cohesive in our message and outlook before expanding to the whole organization.

> Creating a non-hierarchical organization in India was like climbing Mount Everest. Maybe you could do it in Silicon Valley, if you have a bunch of self-starters who are genetically programmed to self-actualize, but in India where everyone thrives on control, it was a death march.

> One of the lowest moments of the OD process was when 25 mid-level managers went off site for a couple of days and got in touch with all that they'd been suppressing and then got together with the six of us on the senior team. When the two teams came together, the rage saddened me, but we all condoned it because they were expressing themselves authentically. I pushed back, challenging them around sensitivity. I wanted them to treat everyone with compassion, but they wanted the authority to die in order to give life to the suppressed. All six of us were lambs at the slaughter. The second tier team was liberated, without any awareness of how they'd speared the authority or the wider dynamic. People got in touch with their own colonization and domination within themselves, and then confronted it in the

organization. I wanted all of us to hold each other during this process, but the rage was overwhelming.

Once people got on the other side of our difficult process, we had fantastic new levels of awareness and bonding. Wonderful things were happening. People were engaged. We all loved working at Optimaz and had a lot of respect in every direction. People were treated like human beings. Performance was awesome and we gave enormously better service. Attrition was only 20%, which is unbelievably low for the BPO industry. We had a beautiful, huge open-plan office on one floor where we were all visible to each other. We encouraged people to celebrate and acknowledge success. Something would happen and one group would start clapping, and the whole floor would join in, as if there were angels in the room. Then everyone would laugh at once.

In hindsight, Evan evaluated the OD process and shared what he learned and what he would have done differently:

Had we realized what we were dealing with, we would have held each other. I have some grief because I got sacrificed. We had built a fantastic organization and were producing amazing results. We removed the boundaries on a massive scale.

However, when I opened up emotionally, all their issues with their parents, society, and school system came slamming back at me. It was traumatic for everybody. We wanted to change authority without understanding the dualistic relationship hierarchy provides – power at the top, protection at the bottom. We had put all our effort into changing authority without understanding how to change submission.

Evan also shared his evaluation of the challenges and opportunities that the OD profession faces:

OD practitioners think their job is to nullify authority, but it's not that simple. Everyone recognizes the destructive elements of hierarchy. The assumption that people on the bottom are being crushed is real, but they also have an unbelievable panacea of safety. They can wallow and bitch without making any decisions, so they feel supported, safe, and comfortable. We made a deep spiritual contract on both sides.

We pointed to the hierarchy and noticed all the suppression and emotional violence, but ultimately I came to believe that people *wanted* to submit. Unconsciously they sought out the dynamics of their birth family. When we take away the crutch that people *think* they need, we create a lot of turbulence because people are terrified that we're taking away their protection. It's unconscious for everybody. People are terrified and they don't even know why.

As an outsider, the OD practitioner isn't part of the hierarchy; so she is not emotionally connected to the fear. The consultant isn't going to lose her livelihood, but the people in the organization face the real risk of being sidelined, losing their status or losing their job.

Most OD practitioners don't understand power dynamics. They go into the field in the first place because they love empowerment and autonomy, and want to see it linked to business success. But why aren't hierarchical structures flattened? Because the intricate web of safety and security connects people deeply to their childhood experience.

It all seems naïve, dangerous and destructive to me now. I got the benefit of the OD initiative, so I'm grateful for the experience and don't want to dismiss the blessing. Now I want to proceed more gently.

Though dressed up in corporate catch-phrases, everything revolves around power and violence. I could join a supposedly-progressive organization and try to lead in a non-hierarchical manner. However, who am I to force someone to go through that process, knowing now that most people don't want to embark on that transformation in the first place?

Somewhere there has to be a gentler environment in which people can seek their own transformation and progress at their own pace, rather than having an organizational hierarchy ram 'change' down their throats.

Right now I want to find the gentle environment that I believe is necessary for a new paradigm of positive change. There must be a way to act as a positive force without using violence.

Sushma Sharma described some of the interventions used in the OD process at Optimaz:

The entire culture changed within 6 months because we used a range of interventions. We worked with the top team one day a month because they were not talking to each other. During a two-day off site retreat, we spent a day creating our dreams and another day we started an Appreciative Inquiry process where 150 people were interviewed. After that we worked on choosing our values. Through the collection of data on values, some beautiful, hair-raising stories about sensitivity came out, which were almost 180 degree opposite of first diagnosis.

A year later we did an organization-wide intervention, which went beautifully. We were all taking a big risk, but the top team of 33 people co-anchored the process. Evan worked on his own despair of what was happening in London. He was showing them a brave front while feeling vulnerable inside. The employees were looking up to him so much, that they had no ability to support him or extend their leadership back to him. His desire to transform himself, actualize himself, earned him the absolute trust of the people. The love they had for him came as a result of his nurturing leadership. I've never seen such favor given to anybody. Totally out of love, they created an egalitarian culture. Some people brought their whole families on stage to thank him, reading something beautiful in Hindi, and dancing. It was a beautiful experience of love flowing in all directions.

Evaluation and Closure

How do we evaluate success? How do we measure the value of transformation? How do we know what matters? What factors contribute to transformation? Can we replicate results? Can we even measure what really matters, including the generative ripple effect of transformation? In her paper, "Dancing the Measures of Transformation,"[113] Jill Moscowitz explores the ambiguity of transformation and cautions against using benchmarks or fixed indicators, calling instead for participatory experience where storytelling enriches the shared knowledge of effectiveness. She says:

> When we do social assessments in order to understand who will benefit from a project or intervention, we are not only creating some sort of baseline, but we ideally will be outlining the conceptual maps and willingness for involvement among participants. WEP [Women's Empowerment Project] illustrates the value of building on existing local groups in part because the local groups already share and invest in the common good. The current concerns with 'sustainability' often ignore the point that existing local groups are more committed to the sustainability of their own worlds than are the external experts who believe they bring an answer to issues of sustainability. WEP has also shown that it is possible to avoid the sadly common effect of external intervention of replacing one elite [system] with another by ensuring

---

[113] Ion, H. W. Dancing the measures of transformation. 2002. Retrieved from http://www.givingspace.org/papers/may2002/Heather1.doc

that the local group keeps its own accounts, monitors individual participation, and reports on its own activities to other groups of similar purpose. Trust, reputation, and the intimacy of proximate and involved members are mutually-reinforced.

Instead of outsiders measuring the value of transformation, when the people who experience the transformation share their stories of excellence, they deepen their shared understanding of best practices and naturally co-create the criteria for measuring success. Meaningful measures of transformation contribute to the long-term stability of the change and foster true redistribution of power. Empowered conversations that take place in a transformational community build trust. Rituals that celebrate accomplishment are a means to create a tradition of transformation.

In the evaluation of the OD process at Optimaz, Sushma Sharma described her perspective:

> By any measure the performance at Optimaz was awesome. People who hadn't been talking became close. The culture was filled with dynamism and celebration. People held their own meetings without the presence of senior people, and took their learning to the rest of the organization. The open dialogue between junior and senior people resulted in inclusion, belonging, responsibility and accountability. Feedback was welcome in multiple directions.

> I work with so many organizations where there is no support from the top and people resist the change, but at Optimaz, the commitment from the top to grow and change was tremendous. Evan realized his own vision and dream of autonomy of people taking charge. People were afraid to embark on the process, yes. But they could see where it was going, and the energy sustained them.

> Originally Evan was extremely impatient with the stagnation and slow rate of change. In hind sight, he thought we had rammed the change and demanded too much too fast. In my experience, changes don't happen if they aren't quick and fast. A lot of work happened because of the fast pace.

> On one level, it was a very successful, happy experience. As I look back, I don't think I diagnosed the emotional capability well. Evan needed more support to deal with the fragmentation inside. I don't think he ever fully acknowledged the positive role he played and the kind of leadership he provided. The deep heart connection helped them improve and transform themselves. The culture shifted from command and control and micro-managing to letting go, and including and involving people. In that environment, I did not experience violence nor mollycoddling, but love and

care. In the final evaluation, the trust that got built was tremendous and the business prospered.

Facts and figures such as change in income, number of people reached, and projects completed give us a left-brain picture of tangible results. But the question remains: how do we measure the value of transformation that impacts self-confidence, gives people a sense of belonging and purpose, and enhances the larger community? In my experience, stories are far more powerful than spreadsheets. Anecdotal evidence has the power to stir hearts and inspire new action, exponentially increasing the opportunities for additional transformation. A sense of optimism leads to new explorations, connections, and renewed hope. Facilitating successful change initiatives at the organizational level inspires us to tackle the larger challenge of sustainable social change.

Additional Organization Development Tools and Models

Organization Development builds on many practices, providing a systems approach to change that leads to grand scale transformation. Some of the ways that OD enhances the change process:

- Appreciative Inquiry taps the life force and builds on the strengths of the organization
- REAL conversations invite vulnerability and discovery
- Vision and purpose deepen connection through creating shared values.
- Cultural change reinforces multiple opportunities for empowerment.
- Transformation in the context of production of goods and services provides built-in support.
- Large group process work changes organizations rapidly.

What does it mean to intervene? We define intervention as coming between two entities—the current reality and future possibilities, but designing interventions is an art. As technicians we tend to follow our favorite or tested interventions, but as artists, we use our intuition, self-awareness, and sense of flow to design empowering interventions. Our design is deeply connected to the diagnosis and the data we have collected. We continuously adapt by learning from what is working and what is not working, observing the shifts of energy, and creating safe space for people to explore. We have a wide selection of interventions to choose from, each with its own advantages and challenges:

Adaptable Dialogue
Appreciative Inquiry
Open Space Technology
Dynamic Facilitation
World Café
Dialogue and Deliberation
Conversation Café

Planning
Future Search
Vision Process
Scenario Thinking
Visualization

Leadership Development
Leadership Training
Coaching Individuals or Groups
Management Development
360 Degree Feedback
Feed-Forward

Conflict Management
Nonviolent Communication
Transformative Mediation
Restorative Circles

Interpersonal Relations
Team Building Activities
Process Consultation
Sensitivity Training

Change
Cultural Change
Change Management
Complex Adaptive Systems

Multiculturalism
Diversity Dialogues
Spiral Dynamics
Emotional Intelligence

I'm only going to describe a few of these interventions in this book; the rest you can Google, or if you want a great resource, look at the Change Handbook[114], where 90 international contributors describe some of these practices and many more.

Developing Cultural Understanding

Culture represents shared values that support the way people communicate with each other, coordinate their work, deal with change, and reach their goals. Some elements of organizational culture are observable, but many aspects are unconscious. Geert Hofstede has done extensive research on the world's cultures and intercultural cooperation. He identified five dimensions of culture: power distance, individualism, masculinity, uncertainty avoidance, and long-term orientation.[115] An understanding of multiculturalism helps us connect with diverse people and facilitate across cultures. Some of the multicultural dimensions I find useful in understanding people and facilitating in diverse groups are:

- Power Distance or Shared Power
- Individualism or Collectivism

---

[114] Holman, P, DeVane, T & Cady, S. (2007). *The Change Handbook.* Berrett-Koehler Publishers.
[115] Hofstede, G. (1997). *Cultures and Organizations.* McGraw Hill.

296

- Domination or Partnership
- Directness or Indirectness
- Tasks or Relationships
- Certainty or Change
- Long-Term or Short-Term Orientation

Power Distance or Shared Power

The acceptance level of the distance between people with more power and people with less power varies across cultures. Inequalities exist in all cultures, but the expectations and acceptance of how power is distributed contributes to the level of endorsement. Hofstede states that "Acceptance of inequalities by the people with less power contributes more to the power distance than by the people with power."[116]

Individualism or Collectivism

In *individualist* cultures, people value independence, personal freedom, and think in terms of "I." Individuals are expected to look after themselves and take pride in not asking for support. Individuals freely share their opinions. In *collectivist* cultures, people are integrated into cohesive groups starting at birth and think of themselves as "we." Social harmony, consensus, loyalty, and collective obligation are valued. Opinions are determined by interest groups which take priority over individual interests.

Domination or Partnership

In domination cultures people value competition, ambition, and achievement. People care about status and materialism. Gender roles and values are sharply different, often expressed as men acting more assertively and women more caringly. In partnership cultures people value community, mutuality, and warm relationships. Men's and women's roles overlap and they share similar values. The gap between genders is smaller, and both men and women express tenderness and use their intuition. Both genders collaborate, enjoy mutuality, and find fulfillment in connections.

Directness or Indirectness

In *direct* cultures, participants openly confront facilitators, disagreeing with the approach or questioning the method. Comfortable with expressive forms of communication, they enjoy confronting each other and often miss subtle cues and body language. In contrast, people from *indirect* cultures carefully craft what they say to each other out of care for each other's well being. They exhibit embarrassment if comments are made in the group that could be construed as even slightly critical. They express more candidly in private during the break rather than in the group. Rarely do they challenge the facilitator's suggestions or guidance. Their body language may suggest concern, but they keep their thoughts to themselves rather than express a contrary opinion. Facilitators can conduct individual interviews to draw out participants'

---

[116] Hofstede, G. (1997). *Cultures and Organizations*. McGraw Hill.

concerns, or we can solicit written suggestions and then give a presentation that describes themes or patterns. Typically they appreciate coaching to help them frame their concerns diplomatically.

Tasks or Relationships

In *task-oriented* cultures, getting things done matters more than building relationships. Participants thrive in a fast-paced environment, make decisions quickly, have a low tolerance for processing interactions, and despise meetings. In contrast, *relationship-oriented* cultures value connection and enjoy meetings that address everyone's concerns. Tasks are of secondary importance.

Certainty or Change

In cultures where *certainty* and predictability are valued, people try to minimize uncertainty through strict rules, shared beliefs, or religious conformity. People freely express their emotions and their discomfort with unstructured circumstances. In cultures where people accept *change* and uncertainty, they want as few rules as possible, tolerate a wide range of opinions, and enjoy religious freedom. As people who accept ambiguity, they enjoy contemplation and are less likely to express their emotions. In certainty cultures, people have *found* the Truth, while in change cultures people are *seeking* the Truth.

Long Term or Short Term

In *long-term* cultures, people respect tradition, value thrift and perseverance, and are more sensitive to ethical issues. In contrast, *short-term* cultures people react to pressing problems, fulfill social obligations, and protect themselves from shame.

We all see the world through the lens of our own culture, and we are more comfortable with people who share similar values, behaviors, and customs. Most of us have at least a drop of ethnocentricity running through our veins, often believing that our culture is intrinsically *better* than other cultures. We grow up absorbing the values of our birth culture, and we experience discomfort when our thought patterns, values, and viewpoints don't align with another culture. As facilitators who help people transcend ethnocentrism, we need to continuously explore our own biases.

Facilitators who come from egalitarian cultures find it difficult to honor contrary cultural norms. We're a bit baffled when everyone straightens their posture when an authority figure comes into the room, or changes their tone when speaking to people of higher or lower status. We're baffled that requests downward are so direct, while requests upward are indirect at best. Higher ranking people can take all the time in the world to speak, but lower ranking people use as few words as possible. We can tell where anyone is on the chain of command because they nod their heads in approval going up the chain of command and give stern looks when going down the chain of command. In contrast, facilitators who come from a high deference to authority culture who find themselves working in an egalitarian culture have difficulty accepting when a lower-ranking person questions authority or challenges the facilitator directly. When the participants don't take the subtle hints that they're out of line, the facilitator develops judgments that participants are disrespectful, insubordinate, competitive or power hungry. To overcome our cultural biases, we can immerse ourselves in other cultures, and try new behaviors to expand our capacity to understand multiple perspectives.

When Shridhar Kshirsagar from Mumbai visited America for the first time, half way through the visit, I asked him what he liked most and least about the country. He loved the warmth and openness of the people but was disturbed by the "throw-away" culture, citing the wasted plastic plates and forks in the cafeteria, but even more disturbing, he sensed that relationships in America are discarded just as easily. He compared it to the relationship maintenance styles in India's "elite" communities, in contrast with the majority of communities, where children are socialized to care about other's needs, to know their neighbors, and build long-term relationships. He was troubled that in communities where people keep in touch electronically instead of through visiting, where parents have to ask permission from their children to see them, the flow of relationships is missing. Because he values closeness and community, he's sad to see India's relationship-based culture deteriorate from the influence of American culture. I was startled to hear him liken American relationships to trashing the environment. I think of our high divorce rate as "recycling" relationships, but I'm also troubled by the tragedy of broken relationships.

When I've done values clarification work with mixed cultures, people often are very exited and passionate about discovering their own unique values and genuinely bewildered by other's values. An Asian man was deeply disturbed and could not understand how anyone could have anything other than "family" as their top value. I made the mistake of explaining how that could be so, and in hindsight realized I could have learned so much more by hearing why this value was so precious to him.

In addition to these formal, structured ways of collecting data, we also rely on felt sense and intuition. Our innate curiosity and desire to understand people at all levels can be the most revealing process of all. As we listen deeply, we discover what matters most to the organization. Although our curiosity can go in a thousand directions, we can use the REAL model to hold a wide range of questions in the back of our minds.

Understanding the essence behind the data, without getting hooked by the content, means we listen for the feelings and values behind the words. To transform leaders and leadership teams, probing interviews provide an opportunity for understanding and heart connection. The Appreciative Inquiry process creates new energy and helps people to discover themselves, starting with a simple inquiry, and pursue the concerns and needs authentically raised by the respondents.

To facilitate the collective group process, we expand the experiential learning capabilities. Observing some business meetings serves us well for understanding the subtleties of the underlying team processes. Some widely-used assessment instruments include:

- 360° Feedback Survey
- Change Preference
- Cultural Climate Survey
- DISC profile
- Fundamental Interpersonal Relations Orientation-Behavior (FIRO B)
- Leadership Style Inventory
- Myers Briggs Type Indicator (MBTI)
- Situational Leadership
- Team Management Skills Assessment
- Thomas Kilman Conflict Assessment

We can also create our own questionnaire based on the leadership competencies that need to be developed. The Appreciative Inquiry Commons[117] web site offers an internal protocol for interviewing that can be adapted for any organization.

Real Conversations

During her 30 years in the organization development field, Sushma Sharma developed the *Getting REAL* model to capture the art of building authentic connection. The four components include Relating, Exploring, Adapting and Learning. The questions asked at the beginning of the OD process set the tone and shape the relationship. Some of my favorite questions for each phase of Getting REAL at the *entry* phase are listed in the table.

---

[117] Appreciative Inquiry Commons. Retrieved from http://appreciativeinquiry.case.edu/ 2009.

Figure 14.1

	Getting Real
Relating	**Getting to know the client as individuals and as an organization** • What is your passion? • What is your highest dream? • What values do you hold dear? • What keeps you awake at night? **Sharing myself authentically** • What are my passions? • What are my deeply held values? • What motivates me to do this work? • What is my growing edge?
Exploring	**Discovering the potential of working together** • Who are the sponsors, clients, stakeholders? • What are our dreams for this relationship? • What are the leadership challenges? • What will make our relationship honest and ever evolving? • How do we support each other's growth and transformation? • What end results do you expect to co-create?
Adapting	**Deepening connection with flexibility and openness** • What are the natural openings? • What are the possibilities for transformation? • What is emerging? • How can we shift the focus of inquiry to what's needed? • How will we tap new energy and enthusiasm?
Learning	**Learning about changes in self** • What am I learning in this moment? • How do I model vulnerability and openness? • What changes do I want to make? • How can I be more assertive or authentic? **Learning about changes in the other** • What challenges is s/he facing now? • What excites me about the other person? • What connects us with our shared dreams? • How do we foster a power-with relationship? **Learning about changes in the organization** • What are people collectively eager to learn? • Where is transformation possible? • How does shared learning impact the organization? • What's fun about what we're learning?

Contracting

Over the years, hundreds of people have asked me to help them write a proposal. Unfortunately I have to tell 90% of them they're wasting their time. If a prospect asks for a proposal before you have full agreement, new practitioners sometimes think this means they have the job. They don't. "Send me a proposal," is often code for, "I'm not going to work with you but I don't know how to tell you." Proposals take a lot of time to write, so don't be fooled by the friendly tone. On the other hand, if the prospect says, "Will you put our agreement in writing?" we know we're on track.

The contracting part of the entry process is hammered out through dialogue, not through writing a proposal. The contract solidifies the intention, direction, and desired outcomes. We establish agreements at entry and only put them in writing when both parties have full understanding of the contractual agreement. Roger Schwarz, author of *The Skilled Facilitator* has a saying at his firm: "No bad contracting goes unpunished." He adds, "Most of the problems we've faced with our clients have stemmed from key missteps in the contracting process. I've seen the same thing with thousands of leaders, facilitators, consultants, coaches and trainers over the last 25 years. They miss or avoid key issues as they start to work with groups, and pay the price later in credibility, work performance, wasted time and stress. I've come to believe that the most important and powerful intervention we can make with a group is to build a high-quality agreement on how to work together."[118]

Suggestions for Getting A Signed Contract

- Get all the decision makers in the room (or on the phone)
    - Who else will help you make the decision?
    - Can we all meet together?
- Establish rapport
    - Are we experiencing a loving connection and a mutual interest in moving forward?
    - Do I sense the potential for creating a magical relationship?
- Uncover the client's pain (what needs are they trying to meet?)
    - What keeps you awake at night?
    - What would you like to see change around here?
    - Why are you contacting us *now*?
    - What's at stake?
- Get their budget (even if they say they don't have one)
    - What would it be worth to you to resolve this?
    - How much do you have budgeted for this?
    - Off the top of my head, that would cost about $X
- Explore solutions to relieve the pain
    - Starting with a needs assessment…

---

[118] Schwarz, R. Retrieved from http://www.schwarzassociates.com/facilitator/67/The-Skilled-Facilitator-Teleclass-Series---The-Most-Damaging-Mistakes/ 2009.

- Based on what we've talked about, my recommendations are…
- There are several options: coaching, leadership development, team building, or a systemic approach to Organization Development – which seems like the best fit for you?
- Determine the scope of the project
  - Let's explore the desired outcomes
  - What are the measurements of success?
  - Phase I looks like… Phase II could include…
  - Let's define our joint responsibilities and determine the deliverables.
  - We can facilitate the OD process *with* you instead of *for* you.
- Agree on the logistics
  - How many people will be involved?
  - What is the duration of the project?
  - When do you want to start?
  - What venue is most conducive for learning?
  - What are the business arrangements?

Diagnosing the Needs of the Organization

In addition to the personal needs of every employee, each organization itself has eight basic needs, all of which contribute to the sustainability of the organization. At any moment, high awareness of needs informs our direction and fosters heart connection.

Eight Basic Organizational Needs
1. Purpose
2. Impact
3. Identity
4. Direction
5. Relationships
6. Structure
7. Energy
8. Communication

1.   Purpose
- Contribution to the greater good, service, results
- Increasing the wealth of shareholders
- Enhancing the well-being of all the stakeholders

2.   Direction
- Compelling vision, creating a more desirable future
- Focus on what matters most
- Sense of what's emerging, what's needed

3. **Identity**
   - Collective sense of who we are, clarity about what we stand for
   - Shared values, sense of meaning
   - Passion and shared inspiration

4. **Structure**
   - Access to resources, information and shared power
   - Order, effectiveness, efficiency, accountability, sustainability, continuation
   - Clarity about roles and responsibilities

5. **Energy**
   - Stimulation, challenge, vitality, inspiration, and flow
   - Harmony, order, peace, aesthetics, beauty, security, safety, stability, protection
   - Fun, humor, play, balance

6. **Impact**
   - Progress, improvement, accomplishment
   - Proficiency, competence, success
   - Mastery, growth, and development

7. **Relationships**
   - Connection, collaboration, consideration, caring, compassion
   - Respect, empowerment, integrity, trust
   - Inclusion, acceptance, community, belonging, interdependence, and mutuality

8. **Communication**
   - Comprehension, clarity, shared understanding
   - Openness and authenticity
   - Full expression, autonomy, freedom, creativity

Although corporations are mandated by law to maximize profits for their shareholders, and accumulating wealth is a favorite activity for many, many people, everyone I've ever worked with has deeper needs that drive their behavior.

I'm more interested in helping people connect with their organization's higher purpose because I believe in every fiber of my being that profits will follow if we're producing meaningful, useful products and services that the world needs. I know how naïve that sounds. After all, what purpose do derivatives and hedge funds serve except to make people rich? Ultimately, when businesses exist only for profit, they buy and sell the rope that hangs themselves. In contrast, organizations that are also contributing to make the world a better place add value, both in terms of human evolution and profits.

Too often organizations develop complex strategic plans with no awareness of what the organization really needs to prosper. Making shareholders rich is not the first priority of most people who work, even when they own the company. Accumulating money itself is only a strategy for getting recognition, having freedom, or making a difference. Likewise in nonprofits, where the primary purpose is to make the world a better place, financial sustainability is a key ingredient but not the *only* ingredient. Many people work so that they can generate enough income to live their *real* lives outside of work while others find deep meaning and a sense of purpose by working in an organization that improves the quality of life. By deepening our awareness of the eight organizational needs, we help people take responsibility for creating the kind of organizations that engage people's hearts.

Appreciative Inquiry Diagnosis

Instead of diagnosing an organization's needs by determining what's wrong, we can start with a needs diagnosis that leverages the energy of the organization. We identify what people *want*, not what they don't want. Connecting with life-giving forces and people's dreams gives us all hope. By doing needs analysis in partnership, the ownership of the process stays with the client. The beauty of Appreciative Inquiry is that people within the organization ask the questions to help each other articulate organizational needs.

Purpose
- What is the organization's raison d'être?
- What do we do that is life-affirming?
- How do we improve the quality of life?
- How do we engage all the stakeholders?
- How do we keep shareholders happy short-term and long-term?

Direction
- Where are we headed?
- How do we communicate a shared vision that continuously expands us?
- How do we stay focused *and* expand the possibilities?
- What inspires people about where we're going?
- Where do people direct their energy?

Identity
- What stories do we tell that reveal the heart of our organization?
- How do we express our passion?
- How would a newcomer describe our culture?
- What images or metaphors describe us?
- What criteria do we use to hire employees who flourish in our culture?

Structure
- How do we share power?
- How are our accountability structures life-serving?
- How do we structure our work so that it nurtures us?

- How do we ensure access to resources and information?
- How can we facilitate emerging new structures?

Energy

- What is emerging or evolving?
- How do we empower each other?
- What are the life-giving forces?
- How do we sustain harmony and productivity?
- What enlivens us?

Impact

- How do we maximize our contribution?
- What do we offer that people find valuable?
- How do we continue to grow and develop?
- What impact do we have or want to have?
- What end results do we value?

Relationships

- How do we build trust?
- How do we create sustainable relationships?
- How do we foster openness and respect?
- How do we develop heart connection?
- How do we balance relationships with tasks?

Communication

- How do we disseminate information?
- How do we express ourselves?
- How do we deal with conflict?
- How do we foster compassion?
- What do we do to encourage authenticity?

Exercises

Reflections:
1. What aspects of your culture do you cherish?
2. What aspects of your culture do you wish to change?

Activities:
1. Conduct a needs assessment of your own organization by evaluating each element of the eight needs on a scale of 1-10. (1= completely dissatisfied, while 10 = deeply satisfied)
2. Which organizational needs are most important to you personally?
3. Diagnose your own organization using an Appreciative Inquiry process to determine organizational needs.

Chapter 15
Facilitating Social Change

Does this path have a heart? If it does, the path is good; if it doesn't, it is of no use. Both paths lead nowhere; but one has a heart, the other doesn't. One makes for a joyful journey; as long as you follow it, you are one with it. The other will make you curse your life. One makes you strong; the other weakens you. — Carlos Castanada

Human trafficking and child sex tourism are on the rise. The United States and 37 other countries have yet to ban landmines.[119] Each day 27,000 children die from preventable, poverty-related causes.[120] More than 60 million girls do not go to school.[121] One in nine Black men between the ages of 20-34 is incarcerated in the USA.[122] In the last decade more than 200,000 farmers have committed suicide in India.[123] So many social injustices. How do we channel our outrage? Finding people to blame or identify as our enemies never solves the problem. However, practicing radical self-care generates greater sensitivity to ourselves and to others, which inclines us toward social responsibility. But doesn't empathy placate our passion and make us less willing to fight for justice? How do we transform our anger, tap our courage, and release the forces for social change?

Deliberately improving the quality of life requires leaders to transform on the inside in order to create meaningful change in the world. Our personal transformation enhances the well-being of our families, which impacts the quality of our communities and organizations where small successes build momentum and empower people to create synergistic change. New behaviors, new ways of thinking, new alliances, all contribute to sustainable social change initiatives that improve the human condition. In this chapter on leading social change, we'll

---

[119] Land Mine Crisis. Retrieved from
http://www.unausa.org/site/pp.aspx?c=fvKRI8MPJpF&b=1419173&printmode=1
[120] Unicef. The state of the world's children 2007: Women and children - The double dividend of gender equality. December 2006.
[121] Stewart, V. & Kagan, S. L. Conclusion: A new world view: Education in a global era conclusion, *Phi Delta Kappan,* Vol.87, No. 03 (November 2005): pp.241-245.
[122] Aizenman, N. C.. New high in U.S. prison numbers. *Washington Post.* Friday, February 29, 2008; Page A01
[123] Davis, R. Interview with Vandana Shiva: Environmentalist extraordinaire. *New Internationalist.* April 1, 2008.

look at creating a culture of shared power, social action, cultural change and social entrepreneurism.

By definition, social change is systemic – impacting not just individuals, but communities, cultures, and society. Because social change shifts the power structure, some people think conflict with those who hold power is inevitable, but if we can bring people with power and access to resources to the table, they become part of the solution. Empathic connection helps us bring diverse voices into the mix so that all the people who have a stake can develop and implement creative solutions to social problems. Honoring values of inclusion, shared access to resources, and care for all people, we can collectively change the way we think, behave, and make policy. Empathic presence helps us mobilize people to develop community-based responses that address the underlying social issues.

There are hundreds of thousands of social change initiatives. A few that I'm especially inspired by:

- A former mountain climber, Gregg Mortenson brings people together to build schools in Pakistan to alleviate poverty, improve education (especially for girls), and reduce Islamic extremism in the region.[124]
- Social activist Shridhar Kshirsagar restores dignity to marginalized groups in India by building community toilets so that Untouchables can stop carrying human waste through the streets.
- An activist and playwright, Eve Ensler stops violence against women by getting them to break the silence and change their relationships with their bodies.[125]
- A trainer and consultant, Dominic Barter offers Restorative Circles in Brazil that help victims, offenders, and communities to create their own healing process and collectively decide on restitution.[126]
- The Pachamama Alliance works with indigenous people to save the rain forest and their way of life.[127]
- A comedian and puppeteer, Marc Weiner uses the e to helping kindergarten students in Israel empower themselves to resolve their own conflicts.[128]
- A doctor at Harvard for half the year, Paul Farmer works in Haiti to transform medicine, where understanding the culture is crucial to effectively reaching people in need of health care.[129]
- The Michigan Peace Team provides trainings in active nonviolence and deploys peace teams into places of conflict, both domestic and international.[130]

---

[124] Mortenson, G. & Relin, D. O. (2007). *Three cups of tea*. Penguin.

[125] Ensler, E. (2007). *Insecure at Last*. Villard.

[126] Dominic Barter. Retrieved from http://www.stthomas.edu/justpeace/nvcrj/

[127] Retrieved from http://www.pachamama.org/

[128] Marc Weiner. Retrieved from http://theempathylabyrinth.com/

[129] Kidder, T. (2004). *Mountains Beyond Mountains*. Random House.

[130] Retrieved from http://www.michiganpeaceteam.org/

When many organizations work together toward social change, we have a movement. From the outside, social change movements look like a spontaneous rising up of outraged people who have reached a tipping point and are energized to make a change. People on the inside know that a great deal of organizing, educating, and collaborating drive a movement. Sometimes social change starts with a crisis, but not always. Many people think the Civil Rights movement got started when Rosa Parks' feet got tired, but it actually started decades before. Educating black Americans to read, hosting discussions and bible study in homes, and bringing in the teachings of Gandhi all planted the seeds of change. But momentum was really gained when leaflets were passed out in beauty parlors and women and children were engaged in the struggle. By the time young, charismatic Martin Luther King led the March on Washington, Catholics, Jewish, Orthodox Greeks, and the United Auto Workers were all included in the Civil Rights movement. Inspired collaboration cuts across race, gender, and class. Every movement needs courage, energy, and brilliance, but we also need personal connection.

Transformational social change empowers people to connect with their inner power. Instead of holding power *over* someone, social change leaders discover that power *with* others comes from deep connection. Shared power helps us unleash our collective creativity and contribute to human evolution. By connecting with our common values that lay just beneath our conflicting strategies, we can transform ourselves into more loving, peaceful states. The best way to lead people to transformation is not by trying to get *other* people to change, but by exploring *our own* inner landscape and seeking our own opportunities for shifting *our* perspectives and paradigms. In the process, many people are impacted by an opening heart, which has a ripple effect, helping everyone involved awaken their hearts and hold deep compassion for themselves and for others.

Peaceful Social Change

> Let me say, at the risk of seeming ridiculous, that the true revolutionary is guided by great feelings of love. — Che Guevara

I have always admired my social activist friends who avidly march, write letters to the editor, and take a stand for what they believe in. They inspire me to think differently. But my own involvement in activism is clouded by tense experiences, like the time I went to Washington for the Women for Peace Rally, just before the outbreak of the Iraq war. Amy Goodman from the radio show "Democracy Now" and the poet Alice Walker had beautiful things to say about women, peace, and change. But when a few women walked on the cordoned-off park in front of the White House, they were arrested. When they resisted being touched, the level of force increased. Amy Goodman claimed exemption, "You can't arrest me. I'm with the press. I'm covering this event, not part of it." They took her away anyway.

As the anxiety and tension rose, Natasha, a young mother, said, "We need to get these children out of here." We all sensed the danger for the children and for ourselves as the shouting and pushing surged into the crowd. I loved being there, but in that moment I knew I wanted a new way to express my desire for peace. I want to live and work on social change from a place of love and harmony, not from a place of fear or anger. It isn't always easy, but I still want to model the kind of peace that I want to see in the world.

Everything changed when I learned about nonviolent communication. Intense practice of compassionate consciousness has improved my coaching, facilitation, and leadership skills. The challenge for me as a peacemaker is to fully honor my experience, yet do it from a place of curiosity about what I'm learning now. Not as a sage on the stage or someone who has all the answers, but as someone who is hungry for shared discovery of new ways to live the Gandhian philosophy and be the change we wish to see in the world.

Daily I recommit to generating opportunities for transformation at the personal, group, and ultimately at a global level. By blending nonviolent communication with the best practices in coaching, facilitation, and leadership, we can establish new opportunities for social change, and together we can create cultural change so that we all share power.

Power Dynamics

> The most common way people give up their power is by thinking they don't have any. — Alice Walker

Imagine my shock when John Heron told me his three top values are autonomy, cooperation, and hierarchy – in that order. Hierarchy? I was bewildered until I learned his personal definition of hierarchy: "a state of being in which someone takes responsibility in doing things to or for other persons for the sake of future autonomy and co-operation of those persons – this is part of parenthood, education, and many professions."[131] The origin of the word hierarchy does not mean oppressive, autocratic use of power. Opening to spiritual presence while honoring each individual's autonomous expression, we can generate extraordinary connection to self, others, and spirit. The role of hierarch moves around the group. Each person has access to his/her inner leader, and by following that spiritual impulse can take the lead for the sake of empowering the autonomy and cooperation of others.

Why do most organizations, even those committed to egalitarian principles struggle with power dynamics? My understanding of the value of hierarchy helps me have compassion for the people who contribute to the imbalance of power. For instance it's easy for me to have

---

[131] Heron, J. (1999). *The Complete facilitators guide*. London: Kogan Page. p. 335.

compassion for people who advocate for partnership; my challenge is to see the humanity of those who are proponents for the domination paradigm as developed by Riane Eisler.

Figure 15.1 Shifting the Domination Paridigm

Domination	Partnership
Power Over / Power Under	Power With
Independent/ Dependent	Interdependent / Autonomous
Leader as oppressor, approval figure, star	Leader as resource
Authoritarian	Co-creation
Unilateral Control	Mutual Learning
Submits/ Rebels	Collaborates
Experience fear, guilt, shame	Experience mutuality, connection, fulfillment
Punishment, reward, coercion	Free choice to contribute
Win : Lose or Lose : Lose	Win : Win
Loss of choice	Acts from choice and self-empowerment
Loss of personal responsibility for needs	Takes personal responsibility for needs
Depletion—Short-term gain	Sustainability— Long term balance
Fear of appearing weak	Freedom to be vulnerable and open as part of humanity
Establish who is right or wrong	Appreciate different perspectives
Advocate for my strategy	Advocate for all voices to be heard and understood

*This chart is adapted from the work of Riane Eisler[132]

We all need power. Without it, we can do nothing. The scholar Kenneth Boulding said that power is "the ability to change the future."[133] All over the world people strive to attain power in order to do some good in the world. We use power to build community and to create a better future. I define "power" as the ability to fulfill needs. There are three kinds of power:

---

[132] Eisler, R. (2003). *The power of partnership: Seven relationships that will change your life.* New World Library.
[133] Boulding, K. (1990). *Three faces of power.* Sage Publications.

- Power-over
- Power-within
- Power-with

As skilled practitioners we recognize and creatively balance all three aspects of power. As individuals, we choose how we use each form of power. In many organizational cultures, the most prevalent form of power is *power-over*. When we dominate others, we have power over them or have the ability to get them do what we want. The obvious forms of *power-over* are violence, force, or threats, but there are much more subtle forms of *power-over,* including rewards. We have power over others when we hire, fire, and control salaries. Whenever we force others to submit, regardless of their wishes, we have power over them, which usually leads to submission or rebellion, neither of which contribute to empowered relationships.

Power-within refers to the true strength associated with courage, faith, and self-discipline. Self-confidence comes from knowing ourselves intimately and being grounded in our power within.

Power-within arises from deep connections: to ourselves, to others, and to the environment. While *power-over* promotes fear and aggression, *power-within* awakens love, peace, and contentment. Reclaiming personal power is a life-sustaining process. One way to multiply our *power-within* is to develop *power-with*. When we rely on empowerment to develop *power-with*, we express our faith that people are able. *Power-within* and *power-with* augment each other. We experience exhilaration in our own unfolding and in the unfolding of others.

Power-with reflects the ability to work with others to accomplish results through collaboration. Our ability to listen, empathize with, and understand others helps us to cooperate with others to achieve shared ends. When we have *power-with,* we're aware of both our own interests and others' interests—their feelings, hopes, and needs.

By seeking the inherent power in any relationship, the whole is greater than the parts. Synergy is achieved when we recognize every stakeholder's interests—everyone's needs are important. Power is inherently fragile. When people lead through *power-over*, they tend to hide their weaknesses, ashamed to reveal their shadow side. People who lead through *power-with* explore their darkness and embrace their aliveness and truth. By sharing their vulnerability, they reveal the source of their inner power—their willingness to grow and change. A *power-with* style of leadership recognizes every person's unique gifts, which uplifts and inspires people, helping them to become the best they can be.[134]

The myth of scarcity says there isn't enough power and we each have to fight for our piece of the pie. Actually, there is plenty of power – enough for everyone. Although many people associate power with domination and oppression, power is simply the ability to meet needs. If we're powerless, we focus on our own needs, but real power means we mobilize resources to meet the needs of all. The common assumption that my strength is based on someone else's

---

[134] Lasley, M. (2004). *Courageous visions: How to unleash passionate energy in your life and your organization.* Discover Press.

weakness is absurd. If we both work out at the gym, we both become strong. In the same way, getting my needs met doesn't mean that someone else's needs go unmet.

A power-over structure requires collusion; someone has to accept powerlessness. When we choose to obey absurd rules, do meaningless work, and let other people control access to resources, we accept the power-over dynamic. Oppression requires consent. But why do we consent? Usually it's because we're blocked from heart connection. When we armor ourselves or separate from our emotions, life energy, and deepest desires, we no longer have access to our courage, we don't take initiative, and we disempower ourselves.

We do not *have to* give away our power. Instead of power-over relationships, we can intentionally create power-with relationships. In a healthy world, we hold power at the personal level and don't have to give that control away to "experts" who tell us what to do. We aren't so easy to control when we have deep personal awareness. Why? Because we don't get stuck in guilt, shame, or greed when we're aware of life-giving forces such as love, connection and collaboration. Because our energy is flowing, we don't have to get ourselves into relationships or jobs that don't honor life. The natural forces within empower us at the personal and global level.

As sweet as it all sounds, shifting away from our familiar, habitual ways of giving away power can be a painful process. It's not easy, but personal growth work helps us get clarity about our motives. What happens when we delve into *why* we choose complacency, demand our rights, or insist on being heard? The answers uncover our own hidden desires. To step into our individual power and fully honor the power of others, awareness of inner needs is vital. With that awareness we can see the humanity of people in authority roles, re-design our relationships and ensure that pleasure and fun are values that we honor on a daily basis.

Personal awareness is the key to empowering ourselves and others. Even if we have support networks that validate and foster deep change, it can take a long time to change the world through individual personal awareness. Since we work on ourselves only after our basic survival needs have been met, personal growth work tends to be a middle-class activity for people with privilege. That doesn't mean it's not worth doing. On the contrary, when we transform ourselves, we move into new areas of transformation and create environments where everyone has power.

Creating a Culture of Shared Power

Power is generally viewed as the mobilization of human and material resources in order that a person or a group of people can exercise control over others, and thereby prevail in any conflict affecting wants or interests. It is assumed that behind every conflict ultimately resides the question of "power over" or who will be the dominator. Although win-win approaches can be found for resolving a conflict, it is uncritically accepted that the most effective way, when every other means has been exhausted, is to resort to a power-based or win-lose approach. The ultimate sanction in any conflict situation is to possess superior resources of power which will be manifested in violence or the threat of violence, and this will bend the opponent to one's will.[135] — Ralph Summy

How do we cultivate a power-with culture where all needs matter? Traditional problem solving usually means identifying the problem and using unilateral control to create the solution. One person makes the decision right away but without getting buy-in. As a result, the problem-solving time is short, but without buy-in, the decisions take a long time to implement.

A more efficient approach is to explore the problem in terms of interests and needs *before* designing a solution. Facilitated agreements take longer to create solutions but result in faster implementation time and ultimately save time overall. The process means that we "Go Slow to Go Fast."

---

[135] Summy, R. Nonviolent speech. *Peace Review*, 10402659, Dec 98, Vol. 10, Issue 4.

Figure 15.2

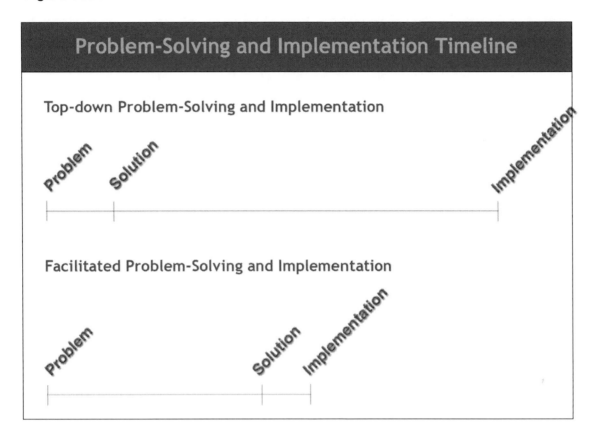

Problem-Solving and Implementation Timeline

Top-down Problem-Solving and Implementation

Problem   Solution   Implementation

Facilitated Problem-Solving and Implementation

Problem   Solution   Implementation

Anyone can make quick decisions, but when the team reflects on values, needs, and interests, they make quality decisions that they're eager to implement. As facilitators, we can level the field by helping people talk to those who have more power and authority, which invites shared leadership.

Shared Leadership

The old command-and-control model of leadership is based on fear and does not honor people's full potential. Based on the misconception that domination is efficient, people hold onto old styles of leadership. I've heard many people say, "I would never treat people that way," but continue to model their behavior after their predecessor simply because they don't know a better way to get things done. In contrast, shared leadership honors everyone's desire to make a difference. We share ownership of the problems, decisions, and implementation. Changing from a domination to a partnership culture takes more than time. Ironically, people don't shift from a hero-leader culture to shared leadership without a strong leader taking the initiative to make the change. People need leading into freedom. To liberate autonomy and collaboration, we need a leader with charisma and vision who believes in people to change the culture. To fully utilize ourselves and others, we need a delicate balance of initiating new ways of working together, empowering others to take initiative, and receiving inspiration from others. Shared leadership provides support and stability for taking risks and experimenting with new ways to practice power. Decision-making is best done by those most impacted by the decision – full participation and transparency contributes to effective decision making. To avoid disempowerment, we develop mutual awareness of power dynamics so that we can interact as equals.

Social Activism

> *The great thing in the world is not so much where we stand, as in what direction we are moving.* – Oliver Wendell Holmes

Sacred activism is the fusion of inner spiritual wisdom with wholehearted action. Instead of pointing fingers, we can open our hearts, love every part of every human being, and engage with healing the world's trauma. Unconditional love fuels transformation. Not blame and judgment. Embodying passion for justice means giving voice to our hearts that cry out for change, our souls that crave recognition, and our awakened bodies longing to take action.

There is no point in engaging in social change work unless we open ourselves to be changed by others' experience. Doing our own inner work allows the grace to emerge. We can't begin to support the change in others, groups, organizations, or cultures unless we're open to changing ourselves. Cultivating openness to experiencing people fully is the essence of embodying social change activism. That's how we develop awareness of the power in our core. From that unwavering place of willingly, eagerly opening to other's experience, we can collectively apply resources, ideas, and action to social problems, and generate momentum for social change that promotes the dignity and development of humankind.

Social action comes in many flavors. I used to believe that activism only took place in street protests, political campaigns or public policy changes. In my experience, soft revolution that is rooted in the land has a power all its own. I resonate with the sentiments of Michael Abelman, director of the Center for Urban Agriculture, "I'm coming to believe that my quiet time on the land, rebuilding soils, engaging in community life, and providing food for my neighborhood is as political and powerful as all of my years of more frantic public life."[136] Barefoot in my garden, I feel my mind slow down to the blissful rhythms of nature. I enjoy the fresh food and comfort of living in a house we built ourselves on a dirt road in rural Pennsylvania. Although my organic garden isn't going to save the earth or end world hunger, it adds enormously to my sense of well-being. Our compost pile is probably my most prized possession – nothing makes

---

[136] Abelman, M. (2005). Fields of plenty: A farmer's journey in search of real food and the people who grow it. Chronicle Books.

me feel wealthier, except perhaps the know-how of living off the land. Sometimes I eat a quart of raspberries before breakfast, but our alternatives to toilet paper feel even more decadent because I'm not talking about scratchy corncobs or crumbling dried leaves – I have a fondness for silky peonies in the spring which offer great coverage, marigolds all summer which leave a lasting scent, mums in the fall for their stunning color choices, and snowballs in winter for the most sensual experience of all. With options like these, it's a wonder I ever leave home. But my heart cries out for people in distress, so I appreciate the variety of ways that social activism blossoms in every nook and cranny of the world, pollinating creative approaches to change.

Kanya Likanasudh claims she's not a social activist, but I see her differently. Clearly she's changing people's lives. She talks about her experience facilitating a workshop in the South of Thailand:

> There is a violent conflict between Muslim separatists and the Thai government. The separatists see teachers as representatives of the central government—teaching or "brainwashing" their kids with ideas that do not align with their values. Central government wants everyone to live according to the Thai belief system. In the past three years, 91 teachers have died from being shot, bombed, or decapitated. Over half of the participants in our workshop were teachers, and many of them attended because they "had to."

> On the first day, many participants asked quite challenging questions about NVC. It was really hard for me to understand, let alone give empathy because they were speaking in metaphors. Was the sauce of this morning's breakfast dish the government, and the different vegetables the separatists or the NGOs? I was totally confused. To add to the difficulty of the situation, the whole workshop was being videotaped by the government. I sensed people did not feel so free to express themselves.

> That evening, I histrionically said to the training team that I didn't want to be a trainer ever again. Another trainer/translator on the team said she was leaving it up to God to take care of the situation. The next day was National Teachers Day. Teachers from three provinces where violence was occurring the most gathered to mourn their friends and co-workers who died.

> We woke up to a scene of soldiers, police, and tanks below our window. To add to the situation, the King's sister died on Jan 2nd. The whole country was in mourning. Commemorating her life was the first event on this Teachers Day. At lunch time, I began to hear rumblings about another event that some of the teachers wanted to attend. The organizer was getting frustrated because she wanted to make sure participants received the training, so we came up with a solution: Ple, the other translator and I would offer the same material at the long break in the afternoon. This way participants would have

a choice to attend both. A participant asked, "What does the majority want to do?" I responded, "At this moment the training team wants to hold everyone's needs with care, be it the majority or minority. So we are offering you choices to do what you like."

I imagined the Muslims at our lunch table who are the minority in Thai culture were having a taste of another way of being in community—one that would value their needs no matter how small their numbers.

That evening everyone showed up to the workshop on time, a feat for Thais...to be on time. They were ready to learn NVC! At the end of the workshop, four or five of the participants asked Lin, the trainer/translator, to come back and give NVC intros to their school or organizations. In their feedback, most of them mentioned how much they enjoyed the sense of friendship and connection with each other and the training team.

A Muslim teacher shared something that practically moved me to tears. She said, "Islam means peace. NVC is what Islam is trying to teach—how to be compassionate to another human being." She also shared the Buddhist theological concept of "making merit" where you accumulate good karma by doing good deeds so in your next life you will be reborn into a better situation. She said, "Kanya, you know it's soooo easy to make merit now. I don't even need to spend money on donations anymore and I could make merit starting this minute! In a conflict-ridden zone like the one we are in, people want to be understood and they want genuineness and sincerity. I now know how to give them that. I can give them empathy!" I returned to Bangkok with a smiling heart. [137]

Holistic Activism

An activist from Eugene Oregon, Tom Atlee wrote *The TAO of Activism* because he wants activism to be more productive and meaningful, shifting from adversarial power struggles to basing our activism on heart, humanness, spirit, wholeness, and life. He suggests we direct our inquiry toward:

1. **Activism that is more human, personal, and alive** – that has more art, community, story, friendship, spirit, aliveness in it for the participants.
2. **Activism that integrates all of who we are** – feelings, thoughts, bodies, spirits, citizens, etc.

---

[137] Kanya Likanasudh personal interview 4/28/08

3. **Activism that focuses on process, dialogue, listening, relationship, questions, learning, weaving** - that has no agenda of its own, but which enables, frees, links, enlightens, and empowers all energies towards a better world.

4. **Activism that focuses on the "life energy band" in ourselves and others** – the values, needs, visions, missions, purposes, things that matter or have juice for us, etc. – that evoke self-organizing, self-motivating energies and help prevent/resolve conflict.

5. **Activism as a spiritual practice** that exercises compassion, service, mindfulness, acceptance, trust, courage, faith, recognition of the sacred in everyone/everything, connection to a higher power, participatory/co-creative awareness, evolution of a sangha, or whatever our particular spiritual focus may be.

6. **Activism that focuses on higher-order (contextual) factors in society**, such as co-intelligence, democracy, story fields, cultural assumptions, etc., that give greater leverage for deep change than the usual issue-oriented activism.

7. **Activism that is more strategic and long-term** - that looks beyond the next demonstration. Each action fits into a larger whole. There's a plan and a logic to it that magnifies the relevance of each piece and adds up to a particular vision of society.

8. **Activism that works with patterns uncovered by "the new sciences-"** What would activism look like if it took seriously the dynamics of wholeness, complex adaptive systems, self-organization, evolution, and non-linear aliveness?[138]

Social Sector Challenges

To lead in the social sector takes gutsy compassion. We're energized by our vulnerability and passion for making a better world, but sometimes we're drained by the slow pace of change. A lot of people make the mistake of thinking that "real leaders" work in business, but how long would corporate CEOs last in the nonprofit world? Anyone can put products on the shelf. Leaders in the social sector take on far more difficult challenges. We take a stand for human evolution, working to end racism, war, poverty, sex trafficking, or whatever breaks our hearts. Putting ourselves on the front lines of social change requires heart and a different set of competencies than those needed to sell the products and services of the corporate world. Many people refer to this half of the world's operations as the "nonprofits" or "non-government organizations" but I find these phrases sadly inadequate, referring to what it is *not* rather than what it *is*. The social sector is an empowering force that represents half the world's operations.

As facilitators, when we support social sector leaders, we need ways to address their unique challenges, including burnout, internalized oppression, internal conflict, scarcity mentality, lack of succession planning, founder syndrome, and the long-term approach to change.

---

[138] Atlee, T. The Tao of activism. Retrieved from
http://www.activistmagazine.com/index.php?option=content&task=view&id=224&Itemid=146

Burnout

Do not think that love, in order to be genuine, has to be extraordinary. What we need is to love without getting tired. — Mother Theresa

If social change were easy, the struggle would be over. The challenges and the demands placed on nonprofit leaders are intense, and burnout is a major issue for nonprofits. When leaders sacrifice themselves, neglect their spirit, or abandon part of who they are, they destroy the morale and the effectiveness of the organization. The sacrificial burnout system is so endemic to nonprofits that leaders actually believe their *work* is more important than their *well-being*. The prevalent belief that they have to give their whole life to have social change succeed is compounded by the adoration they *think* they get from being martyrs.

As facilitators we can help leaders see themselves as linchpins and understand that their self-care and vitality are even more important than the work. Why? Because *they* make the work happen. Taking a stand for their personal self-care makes a real difference in the quality of their decisions. If they're burned out, ready to quit, and we can help them change to a more empowering leadership style, set limits, and create a nurturing support system, then they are bolstered enough to stay on to do the transformative work of social change.

Figure 15.3 Demands on the Executive Director

The stressors come from all directions. Executive directors sit at the pinch point of an hour glass responding to the demands of the board and employees. Juxtaposed on top of that is another hour glass where the executive director is also at the pinch point between funders and clients served. In addition to leading their employees, attracting funders, and serving the public, many executive directors have no choice but to develop leadership in their board of directors. Ideally board members come

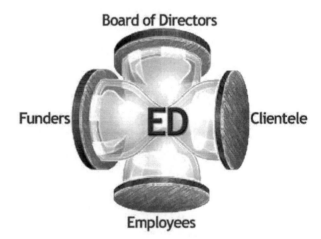

with a wide range of skills, the ability to provide oversight, and the motivation to raise funds. But how do we get high caliber people on the board? We tend to beg them to be on the board and downplay the amount of work it takes, so guess what we get – figure heads who contribute very little. A bolder way to get people on the board is to negotiate up front what we want, co-designing the expectations. Ideally we only want people on the board who could potentially serve as board president. It's a two-way street, so they also want to know what's in it for them – how being on the board meets their need to contribute. It's so difficult to get rid of ineffective board members, so we need to make it at least as difficult to get them on the board as it is to get them off. As stewards of the organization, the board recruits willing experts as though it's a courtship. With a rigorous, compassionate process up front, we can enroll real talent which attracts other movers and shakers. So we choose board members the same way we choose employees – we interview them. We ask, "What passion do you have for the cause? What expertise do you bring? What do you want to learn here? How do you want to develop?" If we ensure we select only people who want to be part of an evolving, learning team, then the impact of the organization will expand.

Like leaders of non-profits, facilitators tend to identify with servant archetypes. We need to take a stand for ourselves as well as those we serve and those they serve. We can't just give lip service to putting the oxygen mask on ourselves first; we need to live in the full experience of loving self-care. Can we push that to the next level and really look after each other while at the same time addressing the worst in human nature? We all need support for the long-term, tough challenges of supporting human evolution and organizational consciousness. We're moving beyond change and into more sustainable transformation and evolution.

The challenge for facilitators is to live our own lives on purpose, in balance, and to help individuals create and live their dream life and their dream organizations. From there we support them in creating communities where every individual can have that same opportunity, not just those who can afford it.

Rescuers Syndrome

Charity after a disaster is a legitimate rescue that offers immediate relief, but chronic societal ills require a long-term approach. When people wrestle daily with painful issues like rape, homelessness, or land mines, the suffering reaches deep into the human psyche. Getting art into schools is very different from working to eliminate racism or advocating for gay and lesbian rights because we face setbacks again and again before we make progress. Witnessing others' suffering often results in internalized pain. When activists work in toxic territory, such as sexual assault or human trafficking, they need support in recognizing how they internalize others' pain so that they can release the suffering they hold. It takes special courage to work in the realm of social change. Everybody wants to stop child abuse, yet it can be difficult to face all the people who don't even see the ways that they disempower children.

The co-dependent rescue mentality combined with the sacrificial culture can be challenging to transform. It's a long term process to get people to give up their default roles of servant, martyr, or savior because these archetypes are so embedded in organizational culture. While we continuously offer compassion, we can also help people recognize that their chronic response – to rescue anyone who has any pain whatsoever—doesn't always serve the larger organization. The "say yes to every request" culture is no match for the difficult decisions that need to be made—for that we need a resilient culture so that people and movements thrive. As facilitators, we can challenge leaders rather than judge or rescue them. It's so easy to go there—to save the rescuer—but when we're really present, right there with them, coming from our heart, and they know we're an ally, then they can redirect their energy toward taking the movement forward.

While leaders have a tendency to be overly-nice to the detriment of the organization, Joe who coaches nonprofit leaders, has forthright, nonjudgmental conversations. When he smells trouble, he directs his clients to be more assertive, "I'll love you no matter what, but here's the reality. You cannot put that person on your board just because you want to be nice. Do you hear what you're saying? You will go through two years of hell. Find the place in you to say no." He helps people find the moxie, take the lead, and make the tough decisions so that they can sleep at night.

Afraid to hurt people's feelings and afraid to say no, many nonprofit leaders don't set boundaries or even negotiate for what they want. When someone pays $25 to be a member of the organization, they think that entitles them to call the shots. Tragically, the nonprofit leader goes along with their demands, even if it's not remotely part of the organization's mission. We can support leaders by helping them say no with compassion. For instance, if an employee isn't performing, leaders need to have the tough conversations and let the employee go after two weeks, not six months. The same problem exists on the board of directors. Unless the executive director steals from the organization, most boards never take a stand, refuse to let an under-performing leader go, and the organization is torn apart by the soap opera. Leaders need a lot of support in the beginning until they can fly on their own, but when the board knows the executive director isn't working out and does nothing, it takes years to repair the damage. A responsible board makes use of the ripple effect by setting high expectations of their leader. In turn, the ED sets high expectations of the staff and immediately addresses the first sign of performance drifting with full compassion, creating an alliance with the staff to become better leaders and develop a more- effective organization. Instead of seeing the board, the ED, or the donors as saviors, we create partnerships, recognizing that we all give because it meets our needs to contribute to the community.

Leadership Capacity

Leaders of sustainable nonprofits are learning to depend less on charismatic methods and start relying more on systematic methods. Instead of using their leadership to cultivate followers, they're building capacity by empowering other leaders. Traditionally nonprofits have little or no budget for professional development of their leadership team. Many nonprofit leaders are so focused on helping their clients, and they're so deeply immersed in a sacrificial way of leading, they wouldn't dream of spending money or time on their own professional development. As martyrs, they believe they can only give, not take. Breaking through that mindset is the challenge. Sometimes the only way to get them to believe that they deserve support is to remind them how wonderful they feel when they *give* support and question why they would want to deny anyone else that pleasure.

To compound the lack of professional development, funders tend to look for programmatic results rather than take a long-term approach to developing leaders on the front line. Slowly over the past decade, the social sector has shifted its focus to developing leaders and building organizational capacity to expanding their impact. Many nonprofit leaders have delivered programs more efficiently by modeling successful businesses, but since the private sector is not in the business of creating social change, a new way of thinking about nonprofits is emerging.

The nonprofit sector faces serious questions about the next generation of leadership. A 2006 survey of 2,000 nonprofit executive directors by the Meyer Foundation and CompassPoint, revealed that 75% do not plan to remain in that position in five years. Some of their reasons for leaving include: burnout and a lack of work-life balance, low pay, the strains of fundraising, governance struggles with boards, and more attractive private sector opportunities.[139] Few have succession plans in place. Before baby boomer executive directors retire, they need support to develop, empower, and challenge their staff. Without micromanaging, they need to hand over the reins on a daily basis. The truck factor (what happens if you get hit by a truck) may sound pretty morbid, but I can't tell you how many nonprofit executives I've coached who refuse to take a vacation, actually believing the place will fall apart without them.

The values held by many Gen X and Y employees are a bit different from their seniors. They are tired of feeling invisible, want the opportunity to lead, and they can do so without the frazzled 60-hour work week. If there's inter-generational tension, it's because GenXers are outraged that boomers have destroyed the work/life balance by reversing the accomplishments of the older generation who fought tooth and nail for a 40-hour work week. Workers of any age in every sector could do with a little more work-life balance, but a whole lot of boomers value making a meaningful contribution so much that any other way of life is unfathomable.

One of the reasons there aren't many leaders waiting in the wings is that many organizations haven't confronted the dilemma of "Founder's Syndrome" or even recognized that the traits of the founder are both assets and liabilities. These same visionary, charismatic, driven, decisive leaders can be lone wolves who don't know how to take their organizations to the next level. We can support the development and transition of founders by helping them recognize the value of planning and policy- seeking input from others to improve organizational structures and decision-making. We can encourage them to relinquish old strategies that worked during the start-up phase. They can explore staffing selections based on future organizational needs. They may need a lot of support for developing an exit strategy and succession plan. Part of the process includes identifying and nurturing young leaders, especially leaders of color, and increasing intergenerational dialogue. To make that shift, they can start by creating more work-life balance for themselves and their staffs.

Meanwhile, we can also coach the leadership team to become less dependent on the founder and develop their own capacity to lead. We can facilitate cultural change much more quickly by creating an empowered coaching culture, where everyone breathes fresh life into the organization. The spirit of coaching acts as an antidote to the rescue culture. People at all levels become more trusting, engaged, collaborative, creative, and more alive. The beauty is in the alchemy of transformation—a very organic, magical process that changes people and organizations at the core.

---

[139] Compass Point http://www.compasspoint.org

Scarcity

Nonprofit leaders are drawn to social change work because of their passion. They have high dreams that they can only accomplish if they break the cycle of poverty. Otherwise they become embittered old-timers who resent the personal cost and lack of progress. Younger leaders start down that same path, and the only way to turn around the culture of scarcity is to develop the leaders and shift the fear that drives most nonprofits. Securing funding is a huge challenge, especially as politicians change every 2-4 years, along with the changing mission and turnover in foundations. As facilitators in nonprofits, we need to address the scarcity mentality about money just to get paid a living wage.

Social change organizations in the progressive world have a special culture that few outsiders understand. Many advocacy organizations have disgruntled staff because they lack the political savvy it takes to make headway in Washington, and in frustration, they fight their internal comrades. Activists need to build strength internally, at the personal and organizational levels, to support each other in the heart-breaking and heart warming work of social change. For that we need explicit boundaries and team building skills to stop the bullying and in-fighting.

Mission creep, or expansion of the organization's mission beyond its original purpose, is a common problem as organizations shift their goals to match the goals of their funders. The fear that funds will be cut becomes the driving force, and organizations spend the bulk of their time seeking funding, which is a travesty. Nonprofit martyrdom doesn't serve the organization or the clients because the poverty mentality gets transferred to the people they help. Low income people don't need more poverty mentality—they need economic empowerment. Recently foundations have recognized how they promote the poverty mentality by providing aid instead of empowerment. Instead of hosing down problems with cash and insisting that their dollars be used for direct services, philanthropists are looking at long-term results. For instance, funding for leadership development and capacity building within grantee organizations has been almost non-existent until recently. Grantmakers for Effective Organizations is a coalition of grantmakers that promotes strategies and practices that contribute to nonprofit success. In their GEO Action Guide: Supporting Next-Generation Leadership[140], they address the looming baby boomer retirements, the "war for talent", and the urgent need to identify and cultivate young and capable leaders for the future.

Solutions

Crutchfield and Grant believe the next leap is to see nonprofits as "catalytic agents of change."[141] They researched nonprofits and found six practices that helped these organizations magnify their impact (not necessarily their budget) to eliminate the root cause of social problems. The organizations worked on a variety of social change issues including hunger relief, youth leadership, environment, housing, public policy, education reform, economic

---

[140] GEO action guide: Supporting next-generation leadership. 2008. GEO. geofunders.org/geopublications.aspx
[141] Crutchfield, L. & Grant, H. M. (2008). *Forces of Good*. John Wiley and Sons.

development, and Hispanic interests. The six practices that helped them create sustainable change:

1. Work with government and advocate for policy change, in addition to providing services.
2. Harness market forces and see business as a powerful partner, not as an enemy to be disdained or ignored.
3. Create meaningful experiences for individual supporters and convert them into evangelists for the cause.
4. Build and nurture nonprofit networks, treating other groups not as competitors for scarce resources but as allies instead.
5. Adapt to the changing environment and be as innovative and nimble as they are strategic.
6. Share leadership, empowering others to be forces for good.[142]

Community Building

I am of the opinion that my life belongs to the whole community, and as long as I live it is my privilege to do for it whatever I can. I want to be thoroughly used up when I die. For the harder I work, the more I live. I rejoice in life for its own sake. Life is no brief candle to me. It is a sort of splendid torch, which I've got hold of for the moment, and I want to make it burn as brightly as possible before handing it on to future generations.

— *George Bernard Shaw*

How do we build thriving communities? Anke Wessels, the executive director for the Center for Transformation at Cornell University, actively supports transformation in her local community. After years of debate, community opposition, protests, and legal wrangling, Wal-Mart opened a store in Ithaca. Members of the Religious Task Force for a Living Wage were outraged by unreturned phone calls and wanted to write an op-ed piece condemning the low wages paid by Wal-Mart. When Anke asked the group to look at what they wanted – to ensure a living wage for workers – they determined that an op-ed piece might not be the best way to achieve their goal. Here's how Anke describes what they did instead:

> We wanted to discuss the high cost of living in Ithaca and propose a living wage. The Ithaca Wal-Mart general manager, Dave Jacobson, agreed to meet with us because he saw some value in reaching out to the community. Instead of condemning their corporate wage policy, I asked Dave what he was already

---

[142] Crutchfield, L. & Grant, H. M. (2008). *Forces of good.* John Wiley and Sons.

327

doing to contribute to worker's well being. As a single dad, Dave was aware of the stress of single parents, so he went the extra mile because he cares about each employee. During a snow storm, he gave stranded employees rides to and from work. He knew every worker by name, as well as their spouses and children. He was proud of the health care offering. Eventually he disclosed that he didn't think it was fair that protest groups were only targeting Wal-Mart, since their pay scale was based on what local retailers pay.

Meeting every couple of months, we got to know each other, and we learned what it was like for Dave to receive horrible letters about the evils of Wal-Mart, deal with a bomb scare, and feel unsafe when so many people in the community respond to him with disdain. Dave also talked about Wal-Mart's community efforts, but some organizations refused to accept money from Walmart because it would look bad.

When we told him how the living wage of $9.17 an hour was determined, Dave explained why he thought that was far too much to give to someone with no experience. In the next meeting, Dave revealed that it made him mad when employees worked fewer hours just so that they could get government assistance. I responded, "Let's take $9.17 off the table. If I came into your store willing to work full time but had no work experience, do you think I could afford to live in our community if I worked 40 hours a week?" Silence followed. Finally Dave said, "I never heard you say it that way before." He agreed that people could not live on that wage. In that pivotal moment, liberal and conservative politics came together because we cared about the same thing – that people could live on what they earned. In that moment of quiet, we were on the same side.

After that, Dave invited other managers from the community to join the next meeting. I was touched by Dave's words of introduction, where he discussed his initial fear of the task force, how he'd brought in someone from outside for protection, but he'd come to know, respect, and trust us. We had started out as enemies, but now we know each other's families. Dave told the group of managers, "We don't always see things the same way, but the conversations are meaningful." At that meeting Dave announced that Wal-Mart was considering a new pay scale system based on the local cost of living. Most of the managers present don't have a lot of power; the pay scale was determined from above, but they all agreed to explore the options. The process is continuing.

When I tell this story, many people are skeptical. They say, "Yes, but Wal-Mart is evil. You're collaborating with the enemy. You can't really trust them." For us, Wal-Mart is no longer the faceless enemy. We don't demonize the opposition. Conversations are a slow process which activists find very frustrating. It feels better to write a scathing letter to the editor, but that changes nothing. People need another framework to encourage understanding and explore ways to find common ground. They're so used to us vs. them, that they have no way to address challenges.

To really champion the rights of the poor or the underprivileged, we need respectful, transformative dialogue. That means we talk about what we're *for* instead of what we're *against*. We use vision as a guiding principle. Instead of thinking about humiliating or ousting someone or making a person see how horrible they are, we look at how we can *inspire* people. So the transformation occurs internally. I ask myself, what am I really looking for? How do I see the humanity of this person? In that way I can shift out of angry resistance, move toward uncertainty, and liberate myself to look at what we're working toward collectively. [143]

Taking on Wal-Mart, the largest retailer in the world, seems daunting, but the persistence of a few people inspires me. They embody a living example of Margaret Mead's directive, "Never doubt that a small group of thoughtful, committed citizens can change the world. Indeed, it's the only thing that ever has." Instead of choosing hopelessness, they continue to work on the most pressing problems, and their influence stretches way beyond their local community.

In American culture where almost everything is reduced to its commercial value, we assume the economy and the market are beyond our control. We've come to expect economic institutions to make decisions for the benefit of the privileged, not for the downtrodden. In a world where the market rules, we start to believe there is no alternative. The most harmful aspect of unfettered capitalism is that we've lost our capacity to imagine humane economic and social relationships that benefit all the people. We've lost our sense of hope that we're all in this together. CEO paychecks are on steroids, even when their companies are hemorrhaging from losses. Pay for performance has opened the floodgate of accounting discrepancies, but the beat goes on. Do we watch helplessly as globalization undermines local communities that result in food riots? Passivity and protest are not the only options. But what are the viable alternatives to an unfettered market economy that widens the gap between the rich and the poor?

People who believe that a more humane world is possible are creating alternatives. We're hungry for new ways of establishing an economy based on reciprocity and cooperation. When people decide to exercise their own economic power, they turn abandoned factories into employee-owned factories, run collective farms, reform health care enterprises, and create cooperatives. When investors don't get the huge returns they expect, viable enterprises shut

---

[143] Anke Wessels personal interview 7/1/08.

down, but when workers take over, they revitalize their communities by providing jobs, goods, and services. Owned and operated collectively by workers and consumers, these enterprises contribute to the economy and meet the human needs of sustainable communities.

Peer Support Groups

Mobilizing change can be irresistible and overwhelming; we all need support to create change. A peer support system helps us navigate rough waters. Whether we use our support team to boost confidence, extract learning, debrief failures, celebrate successes, or practice new ways of being, if we're clear about our intentions, we can both give and receive what we want through conscious design of the relationship. Here are a couple of support groups that have changed the way I think and act:

- Early in my career I met by teleconference with a group of nine coaches and consultants, where we used each other as an advisory board. I acted as convener, co-facilitator, and participant. Each week one of us was in the spotlight, sharing our financial reports, challenges, opportunities, and requests for support. Participants claimed they learned as much when they were giving as when they were receiving. Each consultant earned more than $100,000 a year, but one made twice as much as the rest of us. She claimed her success stemmed from her commitment to her own professional development. She spent 25% of her time, or one week per month, going to training. The immediate impact on me was that I doubled my budget and time for my own professional development, which catapulted me into a huge network and increased my income. More importantly, my work life was more aligned with my values because my learning increased exponentially.

- About two years into my study of nonviolent communication, I joined a phone practice group of people on the certification track, a process that can take several years. We used our time to share new learning, give and receive empathy, and facilitate our process. I've been to many intensive trainings, but this weekly 90-minute practice group deepened my awareness and learning in ways I would never have predicted – the rich field of chaotic interaction yielded sweet learning and closeness.

So I'm a big believer in the value of intentional co-created support groups. Below are a few suggestions to consider:

Logistics
- Meet 2-3 hours weekly, bi-weekly, or monthly
- Open the group to a membership of 8-10 people, so that an average of 5-7 attend each time (phone groups ideal size is 4-6, meeting for 1.5 hours)
- Agree that each person who wants support suggests a timeframe e.g. 10-15 minutes
- Divide the remaining time among those who would like to receive support
- Request that one person keeps time, giving two-minute warnings if desired

- Adhere to time agreements or re-negotiate as you go
- Review the process and make modifications on a regular basis – every 8 sessions

Start with an opening ritual, such as:
- Check in briefly about where you are *now*
- Read a poem
- Share a moment of silence
- Name your present feelings and needs
- Share a piece of your dream

End with a closing ritual, such as:
- Needs met or unmet
- Celebrations
- Learnings
- Next steps
- Song or Poem
- Requests for the next call

Coalition Building

If you want to make peace, you don't talk to your friends. You talk to your enemies.

—Moshe Dayan

Successful change requires organized, broad-based coalition building. We can build a power base by bringing together people representing different organizations and interests who work to create innovative solutions to complex social problems. How do you recruit people, involve youth, tap the private sector, overcome resistance to change, communicate your vision, and get results? Often one person provides the impetus to mobilize a community to solve a common problem or reach a common goal. Ideally that person understands the importance of shared leadership and can work with diverse cultures to bring about systemic change.

Margaret O'Keeffe, the co-founder of Curious Leaders in the UK, describes the interdependence of facilitating change on multiple levels:

> When I was working with a team of six other people co-creating the business version of the Pachamama Symposium (an organization protecting the Earth's rainforests in Ecuador and the indigenous people who live there), we were talking about the importance of big business acknowledging its role across the interdependence between environmental sustainability, spiritual fulfillment, and social justice.

The team included writers, coaches, people in leadership development, lawyers and business owners. Our challenge was to help bring duality thinking to an end. We wanted to help corporations embrace the fact that there is no real difference between our business and personal lives. Or Africa and Europe. This planet is completely interconnected. All systems impact each other. This is what we aimed to communicate. The international team met for weekly conference calls on a voluntary basis over a 1-½ year period even though we hadn't met in person.

I realized that, despite all of my coach training, spiritual practice, and learning development, I still had a lot of duality thinking in me. We all did. During some rocky conversations, we knew that we ourselves represented a microcosm—a petri dish, for what we wanted to shift. Ultimately we knew we couldn't shift anything if we couldn't shift ourselves.

On one call, we talked about getting support from a representative of the Pachamama alliance. As an NGO, the focus is primarily on grassroots efforts to reach the general public. Somebody said, "I don't think it makes sense to get support from him because he thinks it's a waste of time to speak to big business about this." I said, "That's duality thinking, and if this organization is standing for the end of that paradigm and talking about how all is one, then from a systemic perspective, isn't this included in the oneness? Wouldn't it be a good idea to have a conversation with him about just that?"   After a few discussions between his team and ours, we started to share and he wholeheartedly supported our work. They invited us to present an executive summary of our business version of the Symposium at a global gathering for Pachamama Alliance initiative as a result. I experienced a string of transformational moments, starting with myself, the group, and then outside the group. By engaging this gathering, the founders of the Pachamama Alliance formally acknowledged our contribution and gave us some financial support to finish production of a beta version of our multi-media presentation.

It felt tremendously connecting when we recognized that we were part of the system that we're trying to change. With compassion for the situation, we recognized that this is very challenging stuff. We couldn't force this on people; it would have to be an invitation. This 'aha' came not in a moment of joy but at a time when we were feeling quite hopeless. We wondered if the seven of us couldn't work together in a non-dualistic way, how in hell could we expect others to join us? It wasn't fun. There was no eureka – it was more like, "God, we actually don't have the answer." We knew we needed to shift ourselves but found it really difficult. On many occasions I wanted to give up and thought, "This is turning into an encounter group." I had a love/ hate relationship with the journey. I felt compelled by an absolutely universal force to complete it. The drive came from the heart, not from a logical place. It was a compulsion because we didn't want the human race wiped off the face of the planet. Big stuff.

Through this struggle we realized the answer lay within. By walking our own talk and through compassionate dialogue, our own sense of transformation emerged. We had been talking about putting this business symposium out into the world for critical impact, but we didn't feel that there was congruence around what we were saying. To judge the very business community that we each formed part of was actually absurd. We are all on this planet together.

When we ask questions and create meaningful dialogue, we acknowledge the challenges we face. How might we handle this differently? Would you be willing to consider a different way of looking at this? As within, without. It's one thing to talk about this intellectually, but having it in your bones, living it, is an entirely different story.

The experience was like a big block of ice melting. It's separate, stands on its own, melts, gets absorbed. Semi-thawed, sometimes I'm icy, melting, not a fait accompli. When I feel fearful, I'm like a little ice block; when I'm in the love space, I melt. When I melt, it's much more likely that people are going to start melting around me. I'm much more likely to be heard. I become a catalyst for the conversation through compassion and understanding.

Shifting from fear to love is a big emotional part of me. I used to not really share what was in my heart, but now I'm engaged with that process because I want things to transform. The process for us all was about going from fear to love.144

Margaret's path is unique but similar to many coaches and facilitators we interviewed who continuously seek opportunities for transformation. Whether we're changing ourselves or changing the world, we direct our attention both inward and outward.

---

144 Margaret O'Keeffe personal interview 2/29/08.

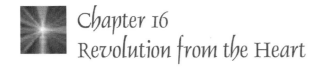

Chapter 16
Revolution from the Heart

In our time, we workers are being called to re-examine our work; how we do it; whom it is helping or hurting; what it is we do, and what we might be doing if we were to let go of our present work and follow a deeper call. — Matthew Fox

Imagine radically change the world without coercing, dominating, or converting. We don't have to stand in front of a podium, pound our fists, or shout down our enemies. Sometimes we don't even have to use words. Soft revolution starts from within. When we're heart-connected and rooted in our personal power, we can acknowledge the humanity of others by meeting them as equals, without pity or condemnation. When we express ourselves honestly, with full emotion, without blame or retribution, we can meet people energetically. Expressing our full humanity while simultaneously seeing other's full humanity builds trust. In this chapter we'll start with a story about the heart of change and explore unlearning "isms", addressing inequities, and cultural transformation. We'll also look at two phenomena that are gaining traction around the world – restorative circles and social entrepreneurship.

Amy Gilmore Cairns of Portland, Oregon, has developed conflict intervention trainings and coordinated international team support for work in Palestine and Israel. She's been part of the Michigan Peace Team, whose main mission is to support people to bring about peace and justice using nonviolence. The group trains volunteers to go into countries where there is violent conflict and act as a nonviolent presence and teaches people how to use nonviolence in their daily lives. One of the ways they are trained to stop violence is to physically put their bodies between conflicted people, without grabbing or forcing them. When she was a trainer for the Michigan Peace Team, she helped facilitate a peaceful outcome even though she broke her own rules:

> The Michigan Peace Team was asked to attend a Michigan State football game because violence was possible. During the pre-game tailgate parties I was riding my bike around, wearing my Peace Team shirt, so that people would recognize us if violence broke out. It was a beautiful day and everyone seemed cheerful. But then I noticed two guys squaring off, and I couldn't tell if they were joking around or about to fight, until one of them took a full can of beer and chucked it full force at the other. From the top of the hill, I yelled as loud as I could, "HEY!" They looked up at me, and so did many other

people, which reminded me why we do not yell – it can increase alarm. Then I broke another rule – I ran full speed down the hill toward them. By now a lot of people were watching me, including the two guys. When I reached them I stood between them, pointed to my Michigan Peace Team shirt and said the only thing I could think of, "You guys are making me look bad." Startled by this, one guy said, "I'm sorry," and shook my hand. The other guy did the same. When they hugged each other, the crowd burst into applause. I think the reason it all worked out was because I put forward my own vulnerability before asking anything of them. It pulled the focus from them and allowed them to help me as well as save face by discontinuing the physical conflict.

Although not tall by any standard, Amy commands a strong physical presence and communicates her peaceful intention with her body language. She may have deviated from the practice of staying calm under pressure, but her desire to keep the peace is palpable and moving. Her compassion and wisdom are inseparable.

Coaching Across Differences

Do we have to do anything special when we coach people who are different from us? In any coaching relationship, the client chooses the agenda, so how can our differences possibly matter? We're all human beings, right? So can't we just focus on the similarities?

Differences don't matter, unless you're the one who is different. Let's start by looking at the micro-inequities experienced by people who are not part of the dominant culture – white, male, straight, Christian, or able-bodied. From MIT, Mary Rowe has been studying micro-inequities since 1973, and defines them as "apparently small events which are often ephemeral and hard-to-prove, events which are covert, often unintentional, frequently unrecognized by the perpetrator, which occur wherever people are perceived to be 'different.'"[145]

Some examples of micro-inequities that impact women:
- people are more likely to interrupt women, roll their eyes, look away, or cross their arms.
- women tend to get left out of the information loop, aren't introduced, or don't get invited to lunch.
- even when a woman speaks with confidence, her idea is frequently ignored until a male repeats her idea verbatim and then the rest of the group gets on board.
- people often attribute women's ideas to men, completely unconsciously.

All of these inequities are meaningless as single events, but the cumulative impact takes its toll. Heightening their sensitivity to the subtle ways that men are more valued, women begin to

---

[145] Rowe, Mary. *Journal of the International Ombudsman Association*, Volume 1, Number 1, March 2008.

doubt their capacity to lead and internalize the oppression by believing in their own inadequacy. As a result, their performance diminishes and their sense of self worth erodes.

Of course, women aren't the only ones who experience micro-inequities. Every day an Asian is mistaken for another Asian, even though they don't look alike. A Mexican American goes out to eat and is assumed to be on the wait staff. Out of the blue, a gay man is asked for fashion advice. Over and over again, people from the dominant culture make little or no attempt to pronounce an immigrant's name. A teen is regularly asked, "How do you wash those dreads?" The person in a wheel chair doesn't get invited to the dance. Or the white man is overlooked for a senior position in a Japanese-owned company. Wherever people are perceived as different, micro-inequities run rampant.

So how do we coach people who experience these inequities? Rowe believes the only way to deal with micro-inequities is to bring them to the forefront to discuss them. As coaches, we can support clients in addressing these well-known inequities that lead to low productivity, impaired performance, low morale, absenteeism and turnover. The coaching process can help clients who question their abilities stemming from continuous, hurtful micro-messages. As unfair as it seems, employees who think they are excluded are expected to take responsibility for addressing the issue. However, when they do speak up, people of color are frequently told by white people that they "think everything is about racism" or feminists are told, "You're taking things too seriously; that's not what I meant."

We can miss big coaching opportunities if we assume organizations are gender-neutral, or that racism no longer permeates institutions. Ancell Livers from CCL says, "White coaches who do not perceive inequitable treatment or are unwilling to investigate if it exists may miss a key element in their coachees' experiences and thus set a coaching direction that misses the mark. In addition, white coaches who are reluctant to explore their coachee's perception of their environment may irreparably harm the coaching relationship."[146] The difficulty in coaching clients to confront bias in the workplace is that we also need to know when to challenge their assumptions of racist, sexist behavior.

To start with, we can challenge our own skepticism about our client's claims of bias and let our clients know we're prepared to look inward. For instance, we can ask for further clarification, find ways to deepen shared awareness of power and privilege, and unlearn our own biases. When we dive into the complex world of unlearning "isms" our word choice determines the level of candor and intimacy with our clients. Our voices and body language send subtle, nuanced messages that impact the quality of the relationship, and if we aren't actively working on dismantling our judgments, anyone can tell from the way we look, gesture, speak, or don't respond at all.

When we listen deeply to our client's stories, we help people find their voice. Instead of challenging our client's perceptions, we can say, "Tell me more," and get curious. Ancella

---

[146] Ting, S & Scisco, P (2006). *The CCL handbook of coaching: A Guide for the leader coach.* Jossey Bass.

Livers from the Center for Creative Leadership suggests six coaching strategies for working with leaders of color:

1. Inspire trust.
2. Find similarities.
3. Appreciate the social context.
4. Understand the organizational context.
5. Name the difference.
6. Challenge the coachee.[147]

Trust comes first. The coaching relationship doesn't go anywhere if the coach behaves in ways that contribute to perceptions of inequity, by making assumptions, reinforcing stereotypes, or not seeing the client's full potential. Some ways to mitigate these tendencies are to do the inner work to build awareness of how we as coaches use power and privilege, listen fully to the client's story, ask curious questions about cultural differences, and request feedback on the ways the coach empowers or disempowers the client.

After establishing trust by acknowledging our clients' experience as real, we can deepen the awareness of what they can and cannot change. If we ask for permission to discuss differences, the client often responds with a sigh of relief that they can finally open up about the real issues, and they say things like, "It's about time," or "Bring it on." When we bring up the topic of differences with sensitivity, we have the potential to deepen trust and intimacy. The masks come off. Only then does it make sense to coach people to identify what *behaviors of their own* they wish to change. If a woman asserts that she wants to be heard more fully, the coach can listen as she describes the exclusionary behaviors of colleagues, recognize what is outside her locus of control, and then help her look at how she can address the issue by changing *her* behaviors that will lead to the desired change.

Awareness of gender issues and solutions helps us offer meaningful, personalized challenges to our clients. Let's take a look at some of the behaviors that influence how we coach men and women differently. Eddie Erlandson and Kate Ludeman have been coaching male and female executives for decades and provide an overview of gender differences.

Women are more inclined to:

- seek help as well as give support
- partner and collaborate
- express appreciation of others
- value relationships and networking
- pay attention to how people feel
- be consultative and inclusive
- like endorphin-producing activities such as conversation

---

[147] Ting, S & Scisco, P. (2006). *The CCL handbook of coaching: A Guide for the leader coach.* Jossey Bass.

- underestimate their capabilities

Men are more inclined to:
- feel comfortable giving orders
- value analytical systems thinking
- feel comfortable with conflict and competition
- delegate and influence upward
- be directive and task oriented
- like the adrenaline of rapid-fire, high risk situations
- see themselves as exceptionally competent[148]

These differences are not absolute – many of us don't come close to fitting the mold. And yet, many cultures strongly reinforce gender differences, so how do we coach men and women differently? Kate Ludeman says, "I encourage my clients to shift from blaming to claiming and step into a higher level of accountability. The most powerful step in taking responsibility is assuming that whatever gets created out there is the direct result of something I have done or failed to do and is not somebody else's fault."[149] To change the power dynamics, women need to increase their visibility. Peggy Klaus suggests women break out to their cultural norms by learning how to toot their own horn and share authentic, meaningful stories about themselves.[150] Some other ways we can expand awareness or create a shift in women are by asking:
- How can you choose confidence?
- What choices can you make to break the pattern?
- How can you take responsibility for making the change?
- How can you look at this more systemically?
- How can you influence upward?

When we coach men we can expand awareness or create a shift by asking:
- What emotions have you avoided feeling?
- Who can you ask for help?
- How can you express appreciation of your team?
- How can you create a more inclusive culture?

As coaches, we listen, attune to the aliveness, and support clients in understanding what they want and getting their needs met. Inevitably, trust gets broken in any close relationship, but that only gives us the opportunity to rebuild trust and deepen shared awareness. For instance, I felt discouraged when an African American coach said, "How white of you…" in response to a project I was proposing that I *thought* would support coaches of color. But I'm very, very happy

---

[148] Passmore, J. (2009). *Diversity in coaching: Working with gender, culture, race and age.* Kogan Page.

[149] Passmore, J. (2009). *Diversity in coaching: Working with gender, culture, race and age.* Kogan Page.

[150] Klaus, P. (2004*). Brag!: The Art of tooting your own horn without blowing It.* Business Plus.

that we have that level of trust where she feels free to confront me. In their book about challenging racism in organizations, Tina Lopez and Barb Thomas explore issues like "capping", when the person from the dominant culture repeats what the racialized person said, even though she spoke with perfect clarity.[151] They devote an entire chapter to how they deal with their own racialization in both their professional and personal relationship. I find their transparency bold, refreshing and inspiring.

Several models have contributed to my awareness of coaching across differences, including Rosenberg's Nonviolent Communication, Rosinski's four steps for Coaching Across Cultures, Hofstede's Five Cultural Dimensions, and Trompenaars and Hamden-Turner's research on the Seven Dimensions of Culture. I share an overview here, and recommend a deep dive into all these books for anyone interested in multicultural coaching.

Using the Nonviolent Communication approach, we can support clients to connect with their hearts, and translate assumptions about racism, sexism, or homophobia into *what actually happened* and what they want to *do* about it. The process sounds like this:

- What happened?
- What are you making up about that?
- What did the person actually do or say?
- How do you feel?
- What do you want?
- What requests can you make of yourself or others to get what you want?

The NVC process, developed by Marshall Rosenberg shifts the way people think and offers critical skills for communicating with compassion that change the culture. Instead of stereotyping some leaders as "clueless white guys who need to be changed" we can use NVC coaching to connect. Rather than judging them, we start by assuming that all behavior is an attempt to meet a need. As clients learn NVC skills and measurable diversity models are put into place, they begin to appreciate the steepness of the learning curve that results from a team approach to cultural change. Because they feel heard and understood, they co-own the change process and become effective allies for cultural change. Even people in positions of power want to shift from the domination to the partnership paradigm, when they come to realize they ultimately have more power when leadership is shared.

Another model that contributes to our collective understanding of multicultural coaching is from the work of Philippe Rosinski. He suggests four steps in his book, *Coaching Across Cultures*:

1. Recognize and accept differences – acknowledge, appreciate and understand that acceptance does not mean agreement or surrender.

---

[151] Lopez, T. & Thomas, B. (2006). *Dancing on live embers: Challenging racism in organizations.*

2. Adapt to differences – move outside one's comfort zone, empathize (temporary shift in perspective) and understand that adaptation does not mean adoption or assimilation.
3. Integrate differences – hold different frames of reference in mind, analyse and evaluate situations from various cultural perspectives, and remain grounded in reality; it is essential to avoid becoming dazzled by too many possibilities.
4. Leverage differences – make the most of differences, strive for synergy, proactively look for gems in different cultures an achieve unity through diversity.[152]

Exploring Hofstede's Five Cultural Dimensions helps us move away from ethnocentricity and toward curiosity of other's cultures:
1. Power Distance – the extent that power is distributed unequally and expected and accepted by both leaders and followers.
2. Individualism/ Collectivism – the degree to which a society values individual or collective achievement
3. Masculinity/ Femininity – the degree to which a society reinforces a gap between men's values and women's values.
4. Uncertainty Avoidance – the level of tolerance for uncertainty vs. structure.
5. Long- term Orientation – the degree to which a society embraces, or does not embrace, long-term devotion to traditional or forward-thinking values.[153]

Trompenaars and Hamden-Turner have expanded on Hofstede's work and have researched Seven Dimensions of Culture:
1. Universalism vs. Particularism – rules vs. relationships
2. Individualism vs. Communitarianism – self vs. society centered
3. Specific vs. Diffuse cultures – analytic vs. holistic
4. Affective vs. Neutral cultures – emotion vs. cognition
5. Achievement vs. ascription – active vs. passive status seeking
6. Sequential vs. synchronic cultures – singe vs. multi-tasking
7. Internal vs. external control – self-determinant vs. cooperation[154]

Going beyond models, when we step out of our comfort zone, we support the growth of our clients and ourselves. Coaching diverse groups, when we do our own inner work about biases, develop curiosity about other's experiences, and unpack our assumptions, we accept life's

---

[152] Rosinski, P. (2003). *Coaching across cultures: New tools for leveraging national, corporate, and professional differences.* Nicholas Brealey Publishing.

[153] Hofstede, G. & Hofstede, G. (2005). *Cultures and organizations: software of the mind.* McGraw-Hill.

[154] Hampden-Turner, C. & Trompenaars, F. (2010) *Riding the waves of innovation: Harness the power of global culture to drive creativity and growth.* McGraw-Hill.

challenge to deepen awareness, connect across differences and change our behavior so that everyone shares power.

Unlearning Isms

> *The ultimate end of all revolutionary social change is to establish the sanctity of human life, the dignity of man, the right of every human being to liberty and well-being.*
>
> — Emma Goldman

At the heart of social change is transforming both the way we think and the way we act. No one is born racist, sexist, or homophobic. These learned behaviors can be unlearned. But it takes commitment to a life-long journey of unlearning. We absorb racist, sexist images and messages early in life: in places of worship, schools, books, television, advertisements, and the neighborhood. It takes time to clear out the distorted images and stereotypes, particularly in America.

People of color are frequently told by white people that they "think everything is about racism" or feminists are told, "you're taking things too seriously; that's not what I meant." When we can really hear each other's voices, instead of challenging each other's perceptions, we can say, "Tell me more," and listen deeply.

White fear of black violence is almost a reflexive response. A 1989 Nightline broadcast showed white pedestrians recoiling with visceral fear when black high school students asked them for change for a dollar, even though they were neatly dressed and the street was full of people. Most Americans barely blink when hearing that jewelry store owners bar black men from their stores, that whites avoid black gatherings as they did in Washington DC during the Million Man March. When a Washington Post poll asked whether it was common sense or prejudice for whites to avoid black neighborhoods because of crime, 75% answered common sense.[155]

In the US, we learn at a young age that talking about race is inappropriate. In my graduate classes on diversity one of the assignments is to ask two white people and two people of color, "What does it mean to be white?"[156] The responses range from, "It doesn't mean anything," to "It means you're *right*, and you have all the power and privilege." I encourage people to listen empathically, regardless of the response. Occasionally people refuse to participate in this activity, but many people find it eye-opening as they open themselves to talk about race. James Baldwin said, "Not everything that is faced can be changed. But nothing can be changed until it

---

[155] Helfand, J. & Lippin, L. (2002). *Understanding whiteness: Unraveling racism.* Thomson Learning Custom Publishing.

[156] Sue, D.W. (2003). *Overcoming our racism: The journey to liberation.* Jossey-Bass. Retrieved from www.uwm.edu/~gjay/Whiteness/WhitePrivilege.ppt

is faced." People who *have* access to resources like to think they deserve what they receive and prefer to believe in a just world based on meritocracy. Many white people feel more comfortable thinking of racism as individual prejudice than seeing racism as a system of advantage based on race. The system of advantage is perpetuated when we don't acknowledge its existence.[157]

We often think of racists as name-calling hooded Klansmen who blatantly, intentionally act from bigotry and discrimination. But what about passive racism? Laughing at racist jokes, accepting exclusionary hiring practices, and avoiding race-related issues are more subtle forms of racism. Because unconscious, passive racism often goes unchallenged, it is self-perpetuating. I question which is more harmful: overt racism or covert racism? At least when racism is overt, we can discuss it. When whites build their awareness of the advantages of racism, some find it painful. White people commonly respond to racism with irrational guilt or shame and lean toward seeing themselves as wrong in interracial conflict. Guilt can lead to a sense of self-hatred, while romanticizing the oppressed. White shame sometimes mobilizes people to act as change agents, but white shame and guilt denies the humanity of individuals, is self-indulgent, and benefits no one.

How often do whites consciously *think* about being white? When asked to complete the sentence, "I am..." the word "white" never comes up, but Black, Latino, and Asian are common. The same is true for other positions of dominance. Being white, male, heterosexual, or able-bodied is simply taken for granted. Rarely do dominant groups understand the experience of subordinate groups. Right-handed people have very little interest in finding out what it's like to be left-handed; they simply enjoy the privilege of being in the dominant group.

How do we dismantle 'isms'? It's easy to dismiss people we believe are racist, sexist, or homophobic, and use "moral justification" to push our agendas. But the real challenge is to accept the humanity of people who seem destructive, arrogant, or foolish and create opportunities for people to understand one another. People differ in their readiness to explore diversity issues, and I find it counterproductive to label people or their words as "ignorant" or "politically correct", because the dialogue stops. I'd rather see people explore their unconscious "isms" by talking about them sensitively. In discussions about "white privilege" I often hear comments like, "I'm white but not privileged," or "This sounds like you're bashing white people." Especially if people of color are present, we may have a tendency to protect them from pain by educating them, "Do you get followed when you go into a store because of your skin color?" If we defend out stance by saying, "We're just trying to deepen our awareness," that can also put a damper on the dialogue. Instead of shutting people down, we can encourage them to speak by empathically responding to each person. Here's an example of a discussion about white privilege:

---

[157] Tatum, B. (1997). *Why are all the black kids sitting together in the cafeteria?* Basic Books.

Mary: Because I'm white, I get sunburned more easily – that's not a privilege – that's painful.

Tom: But Mary, being white, we have greater access to education, more job opportunities, and we aren't as likely to get arrested.

Kiara: When something gets stolen at school, my son is the first person questioned because he has the darkest skin.

Tyreck: White people can get away with speeding. The rest of us drive about 5 mph slower so that we don't get pulled over.

Tom: I read the other day that whites pay lower interest rates – a full percentage point on average. We have access to capital and other resources just because we network with people who have power.

Mary: This is beginning to sound like all white people are alike. I grew up dirt poor – on a good day we had a rabbit for supper, so don't tell me I'm privileged just because I'm white.

Tom: But you are! Do the security people follow you when you go into a store in a white neighborhood? No.

Facilitator: Hold on. Let's slow this down a bit. It sounds like Tom really wants some shared reality and Mary really wants to be heard. Is it that you want to be seen as an individual, not just 'white'?"

Mary: Yeah. I'm not rich. Not even close. And I'm not responsible for security people who follow people who look suspicious.

Tyreck: What do you mean – look suspicious? I'm outraged by that comment. Do you realize how oblivious you are?

Facilitator: Tyreck, would you like some understanding for your rage and shared awareness of how skin color impacts us all?

Tyreck: Damn right. Mary, I'm scared to go into your neighborhood after dark.

Mary: That's ridiculous. My neighborhood is perfectly safe.

Kiara: For you maybe. For us, we might as well be wearing a sign that says, "Arrest me."

Mary: This is beginning to sound like white bashing. The best way to end racism is to stop talking about it. This is going nowhere.

Facilitator: Mary, I hear your frustration and you want this conversation to go somewhere – bring people together... Before we look at that, would you be willing to let Kiara know that you heard her concern about going into your neighborhood after dark?

Mary: But she has nothing to fear. We aren't racist.

Facilitator: Even if you don't agree with her, if you want to support connection and deepen the dialogue, I ask you to let her know that you understand that she's scared and needs a sense of safety.

Mary: I guess I can understand that you might not feel safe in a white neighborhood.

Kiara: That's important to me that you acknowledge my experience.

That's a snapshot from a longer conversation that gives you a glimpse of how to engage everyone by acknowledging them, whether we agree with them or not. It's tricky because every time you empathize, you run the risk of infuriating the people who don't agree. That's why I advocate for reflecting back feelings and needs rather than content, to help people connect. If we reflect back the content, we tend to amplify the conflict.

Part of the challenge is keeping people engaged in the dialogue of change. For instance, how do we engage white men as full diversity partners? I'm not asking this question from the context of, "How do we get white men to conform?" but rather, "How do we create opportunities for white men to fully engage in diversity initiatives?" When it comes to change, the onus of responsibility has traditionally fallen on minorities, so white men are often left out of the process or even stereotyped as people who do not advocate diversity initiatives. One of the drawbacks of most diversity initiatives is not including white men. For instance, most Fortune 500 corporations have affinity groups. To name a few, at Johnson and Johnson they have:

- African American Leadership Council
- Gay and Lesbian Organization for Business and Leadership
- Hispanic Organization for Leadership and Achievement
- South Asian Professional Network & Association
- Women's Leadership Initiative

Personally, I find it a challenging opportunity to honor each individual's heritage and unique cultural differences, *and at the same time*, create opportunities for inclusion, community, and a solid sense of belonging. Although white men traditionally have plenty of opportunities to honor their collective experience on the golf course or at the club, white male affinity groups working on their unique challenges and opportunities are rare and relatively new. Michael Welp, a principal at EqualVoice, believes that for the diversity movement to reach the next level of effectiveness and change in organizations, white men must know a lot more about diversity. He and his partners offer workshops called, "White Men as Full Diversity Partners," which give white men the opportunity to contribute fully to social change. He says, "If the goal of engaging white men in diversity is to succeed, the attitudes of white males will not be the only things that will need to change. One of the most troublesome concerns I have is that, as we continue to do 'white men's work,' there is still much work for women and people of color to do on themselves and their beliefs about white men."[158]

Despite our desire to act as vigilant change agents, sometimes we are seduced into looking the other way and slip back into business as usual. To keep paying attention to how we dismantle "isms" is vital. Although I understand why so many practitioners recommend that white people work on themselves privately to prevent re-stimulating people of color, I've also found that people of color are eager to engage in the dialogue. I advocate for mixed groups working together because we can come up with better solutions together than we can alone.

How do we challenge derogatory comments about class, race, sex, orientation? I've heard many facilitators use the phrase "zero tolerance," which sounds like an oxymoron. We won't tolerate intolerance! Why go beyond tolerance and understand them deeply?

> Intolerance slams doors and keeps them bolted tight shut. Empathy eases those doors open, to reveal, to make real, the wider possibilities that come with illumination. Intolerance clings to the sense of safety and reassurance that comes with sectarian certainty. Empathy supplements that certainty with the ease, the heartening confidence that comes with the clarity of broader understanding. And with that understanding, a more inclusive willingness can be persuaded to emerge. – Ciarmicoli and Ketcham[159]

When I think of all the times in my life when I've reacted with repulsion and then softened, I want some spaciousness for exploration and understanding of our initial reactions and desire to see each other's full humanity. Empathy helps us understand our own intolerance and others.

A friend of mine told me that when she hears a sexist, racist, or offensive joke, she responds with, "I don't get it." Invariably the teller explains the joke, and she says, "I still don't get it." As the teller starts to explain again, the joke teller begins to realize that it isn't that funny. I've tried this a few times, found it very effective and I'm pretty sure the joke was not told again. But when my daughter tried this approach with a guy who told "dumb blonde" jokes, he made her a t-shirt that said, "Should have been blonde." Since then, I've been a proponent of the direct approach, "When you tell dumb blonde jokes, I'm disturbed because I want respect for all people."

When we respectfully confront we can create safe space for learning and growth. Moralistic judgment of others' behavior does not foster an environment conducive to change. Deep caring

---

[158] Atkinson, W. Bringing diversity to white men. *HR Magazine*. Sept 2001.
[159] Ciaramicoli, A. P. & Ketcham, K. (2001). *The power of empathy: a practical guide to creating intimacy, self-understanding and lasting love.* Plume.

and empathic listening foster inclusion and creates opportunities for personal awareness and transformation.

When asked how he's able to be respectful when someone expresses a racist sentiment, Stephen Schwartz said, "Absolutely. Until you respect it, there's no room for change. Until you actually come to that person, acknowledging their stance, acknowledging why it arose and where it came from, there's no way that person is going to trust you enough to get into that more marginal, vulnerable space."[160]

It's one thing to take another into that vulnerable space; it's another to have the courage to go there on our own. Here's a personal example of my own naiveté and lack of awareness. Vikram, who leads diversity workshops for HR directors in India wrote to me, "Just back from Hyderabad from an ISABS event where Sushma and I facilitated a theme lab on diversity and inclusion. You would be thrilled with the lab. We had two transgender persons (eunuchs), a guy who had converted to Islam, a lower caste Hindu man and woman, an upper cast Brahmin, and a divorcee whose divorce is not legitimate. Can you imagine the complexity and beauty of the process?"

I'm embarrassed to admit that my first reaction to the word "eunuch" was repulsion. What? I thought eunuchs were from ancient history and that castration was forced on slaves to get them to build the pyramids or forced on sex offenders to prevent sex crimes. But after a bit of dialogue I learned that in some parts of the world eunuch means the same as transgender, and there are many millions of eunuchs throughout the world by choice. I share this story because I would like to live in a world where we do not condemn ourselves or other people who experience repulsion, but rather we work to understand the needs under revulsion. I want to appreciate each other's differences and see people compassionately even when they are uncomfortable or repulsed by differences.

One cultural difference I find uncomfortable is not making eye contact. While eye contact conveys confidence in Germanic, Nordic, Scandinavian, and European cultures, in Asia Pacific, Chinese, and Japanese cultures, the same behavior is usually considered disrespectful. In comparison, I find the practice in Romantic language cultures of a warm handshake accompanied by two or three light kisses on each cheek exceptionally enjoyable to assimilate.

Years ago, when a Native American friend, Yellow Arrow, told me that in his culture the Crow Indian considers direct eye contact a sign of disrespect, I found it *very* difficult to honor this custom because looking someone in the eye is such an ingrained habit for me. I tried to look at the table, but my eyes kept drifting up toward his. So I can only imagine how hard it is for people from other cultures to change their habits and begin looking people in the eye or firm up their handshake. Yellow Arrow told me about the time he was in a store speaking his native language with an elder of the tribe. A young boy came into the store and said to the old woman, "Speak English! This is America!" Yellow Arrow crouched down to speak at the boy's level

---

[160] Safransky, S. The prayer of the body: An interview with Stephen R. Schwartz. *The Sun Magazine*. October 1992. Retrieved from http://www.thesunmagazine.org/archives/1233?page=1

and explained, "The language you are hearing was spoken here long before English was ever spoken here."

While sexism and racism are more overt, classism is one of the most covert of all the "isms." Yet socio-economic biases permeate our lives. In western culture we use dress, how people talk or eat, their profession, the car they drive or don't drive, and many other factors to determine class. In dialogue on multiculturalism, I find people readily talk about race, gender, and sexual orientation issues, but are most reluctant to talk about class. Here's an activity that helps get the conversation started:

> Divide into three teams and define "multiculturalism." Make a mobile that represents your group's definition. The group who makes the most creative mobile wins a prize. (Each group gets a different set of materials: A) white paper and string; B) that plus stars, glitter, glue, scissors; C) all that plus brightly colored paper, ribbon, doodads, markers, etc.)

> Naturally, the team with the most materials wins the prize. The debrief is very revealing and generates a lot of discussion. Typically members of group C say things like:

> - I never noticed that we had different materials from the other groups.
> - When I saw their mobiles, I thought they just chose not to use all the materials.
> - If they had been more creative, they still could have won the prize.

> Typically group A members say things like:

> - Right away I noticed that we didn't have the same materials as the other groups.
> - Well I knew it wasn't fair, but I still felt really dumb that we couldn't come up with a better mobile.
> - You're not really going to give them a prize are you? (When I say yes, the real discussion about fairness and access to resources begins.)

> Additional debrief questions include:

> - Did anyone consider leveling the playing field or redistributing the supplies?
> - What stopped you from joining a different group?
> - What stopped you from forming one group so that all of you would receive the prize?
> - What did you learn?

This activity gets people thinking and talking about overcoming socio-economic biases. Collectively we have plenty of resources; our challenge is to distribute those resources in ways that honor the needs of all people. My biggest personal challenge as a change agent is to develop more empathy for my perceived enemies, including those whom I deem racist, sexist, or homophobic, and I can start by not labeling them. Curiosity and dialogue are the best tools I've found for combating my internal prejudice. To bring about social change, gaining access to the people with whom we want dialogue is much of the challenge. We first need to get rid of any images of them as enemy – those images will prevent anything positive from happening when we do get access. Enemy images are any judgments or thoughts that separate us from others, and I believe the only way to dissolve enemy images is to develop an empathic response. This means listening at a deep level of acceptance to where people *are*, as opposed to where I want them to be. In my experience, when people are seen, heard, and fully understood, they are more open to change and so am I.

Cultural Transformation

Why do so many people go to bed hungry when we have the resources and technology to feed everyone on the planet? With more than two million organizations working for social change, how come global injustices are spiraling out of control? Most of our efforts are geared toward solving specific problems rather than whole systems. Cultural transformation is a radical form of systemic change when we build on the positive energy that already exists. Instead of condemning past values, norms, beliefs, and practices, we identify what is already serving the culture and find ways to expand the life force. We identify the aliveness and collective wisdom by looking deep within and discovering what is already effective in terms of economics, ecology and humanity. We face the challenges of our times by generating solutions that tap collective wisdom.

I'm a big fan of Lynn Twist's work as a social entrepreneur with the Pachamama Alliance. My favorite story from her book, *The Soul of Money* is about the women of Dharmapuri who practiced female infanticide because they believed that "life was so horrible for a girl, and she would become such a financial burden to the family, that it was cruel to let a girl child live and more kind to kill her." After sharing their secrets, shame, and grief, they vowed to end the cycle forever. Lynn was stunned when they said, "We could not have taken this courageous step without your outside ears and eyes." After several days of intimate conversations, they asked if there were things in Lynn's culture that overwhelmed her. Lynn shared her deep upset with the violence portrayed in American media, and how the horrible messages are exported all over the world. Looking deep into her eyes, they told her to remember that they would be there for her, to encourage her to speak out.[161]

Wham! The women of Dharmapuri turned the tables, didn't they? Until that moment, I had considered violence in movies mild compared to the horror of infanticide. Gratuitous violence has become so accepted in our culture that I see it as a given, and feel quite hopeless as the profits from the media industry feed the appetite for violence. I can imagine people from a peaceful culture would be as horrified by media violence as I am by infanticide. As much as I appreciate the valiant efforts to end female genital mutilation, human trafficking, and wars in other countries, the women of Dhamapuri inspire me to look for opportunities to change my own culture. All of this points me to the value of sharing our stories of inner and outer

---

[161] Twist, L. (2003). *The soul of money.* W.W. Norton and Company.

transformation as we deepen our awareness and explore new ways of creating life-serving cultures. Beyond the ripple effect of personal transformation, taking a stand for change and leading a cultural change initiative can have a profound impact on society.

Seven Steps for Leading the People-Side of Change

1. *Assess Readiness for Change*

   Take the long view and explore your organization's history of change. Find out what made past changes successful and look for evidence that the organization can handle more change. If necessary, develop additional capacity for change.

2. *Build a Case for Change*

   Discover the urgent crises and opportunities that get people's attention. Study the market and competitive forces that drive the change process. Explore the implications to the bottom line. Imagine what happens if you don't make the change.

3. *Enlist a Team of Change Agents*

   Start by finding your highest-level change sponsors. Look for other key influencers from all levels of the organization to enlist. Recruit people who have the power to lead the change initiative and get others on board.

4. *Develop a Change Communication Plan*

   Design the best ways to communicate the benefits and the drawbacks of the change. Describe your vision so that you empower others to contribute. Incorporate the vision of how the change serves the highest good and helps the organization thrive.

5. *Manage Resistance to Change*

   Identify the people most likely to oppose the change and determine how you will address their needs. Anticipate the obstacles and create a plan to overcome resistance to change.

6. *Build Momentum*

   Pay attention to the pace and tone so that people can easily absorb the changes. Build short-term wins into the process. Define the milestones you will celebrate along the way.

7. *Sustain a Culture that is Receptive to Change*

   Manage your continuous personal change process and model openness. Establish expectations, desired behaviors, and competencies that people need to develop to support the desired changes. Sustain a culture of continuous improvement and keep the energy alive to ensure future success.[162]

---

[162] Lasley, M. (2004). *Courageous visions: How to unleash passionate energy in your life and your organization.* Discover Press.

Restorative Circles

Restorative Circles have developed within the Restorative Justice movement, a peaceful process for dealing with crime and human rights violations that honors the needs of the victims, offenders, and the community. Collectively communities have created a de-centralized justice system that builds on indigenous practices, where people develop their own healing processes, unique to their culture. Trained facilitators support the process to ensure understanding, safety, and dignity.

In Brazil, Dominic Barter uses Restorative Circles the justice and education systems to promote understanding, co-create solutions, and rebuild relationships. The forum empowers people to reach satisfying agreements that heal relationships, promote responsibility and build community. Instead of punishment, restoration practices foster a systemic response to reconnecting people, building community and creating a culture of peace.

The facilitators start by convening three pre-circles, where they listen empathically, meeting first with the authors, then receivers, and then the community, so that all the people impacted by the act have the opportunity to be understood. Instead of calling them criminals, perpetrators, or victims, Barter uses neutral language to describe the people and their actions. The facilitators convene the first pre-circle with the "receivers" or the people who have been harmed by an act and want restoration. The purpose of this meeting is to help people be understood, determine the "action" that they find objectionable, determine the authors of the act, and find out who else to invite to contribute to the restorative circle. In the second pre-circle we bring together the "authors" of the act, or the people who have acted in ways that others find harmful, to understand their reasons for acting as they did and determine who else needs to attend. We hold the third pre-circle with the "community" which can include anyone impacted by the act. The community members come not as spectators, but as people who can contribute to restoration.

In the actual restorative circle, the receivers speak first, then the authors, then the community. The receivers describe the impact of the action, their feelings and their unmet needs. The facilitators support the group by reflecting back the feelings and needs of the receivers until they feel fully understood. Only when the receivers have been empathized with fully will they be ready to listen to what the authors feel or need. Receivers often ask tough questions to gain understanding, "How could you have done this to us?" As authors tell their story and share their thoughts and feelings before and after the crime, the facilitators reflects the feelings and needs.

Community members also share the impact that the action had on their lives, and all involved parties share mutual responsibility for creating restorative resolutions to repair the damage or reconcile the harm done. From playground bullying to war crimes, the process is used to rebuild relationships in many arenas, from schools and communities to International peacemaking tribunals such as the South Africa Truth and Reconciliation Commission.

When the authors of the act share their plan for creating a better future for themselves and their community, they have the opportunity to repair some of the damage through some form of restitution. This can take the form of expressing remorse, financial compensation, community service, or education to prevent recurrence. Even more important than restitution, victims want to understand *why* the crime occurred, and they want to be understood for the depth of their pain and suffering. The purpose of the plan is to gain mutual agreement on how to heal the damage, prevent future crimes, and create community support for carrying out the plan.

Dominic Barter from Rio DeJaneiro shares this moving story about restoring faith in humanity:

> A couple of 16 year olds saw a lone man reversing his car out of a tight parking spot and decided then and there to "flash kidnap" him. Surprising him at gunpoint, they frisked him for arms, put him in the back seat, and began driving to the nearest cash point, where they planned to have him take out as much money as the ATM would give him and then leave with his car and belongings. However, they failed to find the small gun he had hidden on his body or to realize that he was an off-duty military policeman. In the resulting confusion, one young man escaped. The other was shot three times in the leg and had since begun an 18-month sentence in youth prison.

> In the Restorative Justice Circle, the policeman spoke of how his daily life has changed since he was kidnapped, how he worked years to buy his car – without stealing from others, how a feeling of paranoia has affected his family, and how he has been ostracized by his peers for not "doing the normal thing" and shooting both of the adolescents dead on the spot. The adolescent spoke of recovering for weeks in a hospital, of wishing he were dead when he sat on the cell floor, of missing his recently deceased mother, of being locked up, of studying in prison, and of being separated from his family.

> The adolescent's father, then his grandmother, then the policeman's son, and then his stepmother – in turn, each member of the community present spoke about the time since that day. This first phase of dialogue only ended when each person present had been heard and it had been demonstrated to them the sense their words had made to those they spoke to. "You are like a mirror to me," the adolescent said when asked if the policeman had heard him accurately.

> In the next phase of the dialogue, the policeman spoke in graphic detail of sitting in the back of the car, deciding who to shoot in the head first, and how to do the least damage to the upholstery of his car. He described this as a way of protecting himself, of valuing his property, of doing his civic duty. Then he described how the adolescent had turned his head, and something about his face reminded him of his son. He had thought then of his parents, of families losing loved ones, and decided instead to scare and arrest them.

The adolescent spoke of his life at the time of the crime, of the moment of deciding to commit the kidnapping, what he and his peer hoped to do with the money, his thoughts about the police, his panic at discovering his victim was armed and a military policeman. At one point, speaking of his life since his mother's death, he was interrupted by a community member, offering to explain his actions as the result of the emotional confusion and pain he had been through. He was quick to reply that this was a profound loss, and he was beginning to see, as the dialogue of the Circle unfolded, that it would not serve him to believe that one caused the other. His mother was not responsible for his actions that day, he was.

Amongst the many action plans made in the final agreement of this Circle was the father taking his son on a journey to the coast (once he was released); the grandmother visiting the prison to share stories of her daughter with the son; the policeman giving a talk to the inmates in the youth prison; and the adolescent giving a talk to the police officer's colleagues. They agreed to set study achievement levels for the adolescent while in prison, support him in finding a school on release, and share a record of the Circle agreement with the sentencing judge for consideration at the time of parole.

These actions sought to repair harm, restore dignity, security, and justice, and to reintegrate all into their respective communities. Sharing this work and accompanying others as they use it is a powerful way for me to contribute to a world where communities enjoy peace, security, and the satisfaction of taking self-caring action.[163]

Social Entrepreneurship

Your life's work, the work you love, is what awakens within you when you are reminded by your compassion, your desire to give. It will not come to you by focusing a desire to be better than others, by thinking about how you will survive, or by wishing everything in your life were easy. It will come when you hear the call of your innate compassion for all of humankind. — Lawrence G. Boldt

Social entrepreneurs recognize social problems and use entrepreneurial principles to create a venture to make social change. Instead of measuring success only in terms of profit, social entrepreneurs focus on their impact on society. This new sector of the economy focuses on a

---

[163] Dominic Barter. Adapted from http://www.wordsthatwork.us/site/13.65.0.0.1.0.phtml and hearing Dominic speak in December 2007.

triple bottom line (people, planet and profit), employs 40 million people and engages 200 volunteers estimates Charles Leadbeater, author of The Rise of the Social Entrepreneur.[164] There's a lot more to being a social entrepreneur than using business skills to generate revenue to achieve social ends. They have a completely different mindset. Undeterred by naysayers, they have confidence in themselves and trust in the human spirit. Anyone can see the problems, but social entrepreneurs are crazy enough to think they can do something about them. Instead of trying to save the whole world, these changemakers choose *one* area of focus and they persist. Often it takes many years for their ideas to bear fruit, but nothing stops them. They have the courage and vision to recognize opportunities, generate resources, and create organizations that drive social change.

Famous social entrepreneurs include Florence Nightingale who developed modern nursing practices; Margaret Sanger who developed family planning practices; Maria Montessori who revolutionized early child education; and Gandhi who empowered a nation. But one of the most influential social entrepreneurs of our time is Muhammad Yunus, founder and manager of the Grameen Bank and winner of the Nobel Peace Prize in 2006 for his lending program that has reduced poverty throughout Bangladesh. They have given over 7 million uncollateralized loans to the poorest of the poor and have a 95% repayment rate. This program has been widely replicated around the world and has huge ripple effects on communities.

In Nepal 100,000 women have benefited from the Women's Empowerment Program in just four years. Instead of paying interest to a bank, their micro-credit program builds equity for themselves in micro-enterprises. Their investment in themselves and the program changes their sense of self-worth. Since their core funding dried up last year, these women have taken the initiative to expand the program to more than 15,000 other women, despite civil unrest in Nepal.[165]

Ben & Jerry's and The Body Shop are widely known for their products and taking a stand for social responsibility. They demonstrate their care for the environment, their workers, local communities, and donate to progressive causes. A few other less known, but inspirational social entrepreneurial ventures:

- The Women's Funding Network developed the "Good Deeds" brand, a product line similar to Newman's Own, whose profits will go toward projects that empower women and girls world-wide.[166]
- Economic alternatives to human trafficking (modern day slavery) have been successfully applied in Southeast Asia. Livelihood alternatives specially-tailored to

[164] Leadbeater. C. (1999). *The rise of the social entrepreneur.* Demos.
[165] Odell, M. J. Save & build: Scaling-up and reaching the poor, a field trip to explore potential habitat and women's empowerment links. *Habitat for Humanity International.* February 2002.
[166] Retreived from http://www.gooddeedfoundation.org/poverty

survivors of violence include: livestock raising and rice packaging in Bangladesh; book binding and dance movement therapy in India; and handicrafts in Nepal. [167]

- Homeboy Industries helps former gang members become contributing members of their community. In addition to counseling, tattoo removal, and job training, job placement helps young people redirect their lives. Income producing ventures like Homeboy Bakery, Homeboy Merchandise, and Homeboy Maintenance give them hope for the future.[168]

- Denise Cerreta founded One World Everybody Eats Café in Salt Lake City, Utah using a new business model that is being replicated in five other cities. Customers pay whatever they think the meal is worth or whatever they can afford.[169]

- Aurolab produces and distribute lenses, sutures and hearing aides in developing countries. Started by David Green, they use a sliding scale model where some pay nothing, and others pay well above cost, which allows them to maximize distribution and remain sustainable.

- Potters for Peace build local factories in the global south, to make terra-cotta water filtration systems that provide safe drinking water. They have produced about 300,000 low-cost filters, that are used by 1.5 million people.

The contemporary movement for social entrepreneurship arose in the 1980s in the Bay Area of California, arising from a combination of new wealth, social consciousness, and entrepreneurial spirit.[170] Foundations like Hewlett and Packard along with nationally renowned nonprofits including Delancey Street and The Bridgespan Group have shaped the movement. Now more than 30 universities around the world have social entrepreneur programs and Stanford has been a hotbed of activity. The Ashoka Foundation seeks out and funds social entrepreneur's projects and is led by Bill Drayton who describes the social entrepreneur sector:

> This is by far the fastest growing sector; this is where you'll have a big impact, and this is where the energy in society is and will be for a long time. This is where the real opportunities are to make a mark, because there is so much catching up to do. There are no glass ceilings if you start your own thing. If you go to a dinner party now, people are much more interested if you say you are a social entrepreneur than an investment banker.

---

[167] Successfully tested livelihood programs in south asia: a guide for the rehabilitation and reintegration of survivors/victims of violence including trafficking. Retrieved from http://www.ungift.org/docs/ungift/pdf/knowledge/south_asian_resource_book.pdf
[168] Retrieved from http://www.homeboy-industries.org
[169] Hawn, C. The Gospel According to Adam Smith. *Ode Magazine*. June 2008. p 47.
[170] McHugh, L & Stone, A. R. An education with a mission: A guide to social innovation at Stanford. *The Stanford Daily*, 1/25/2005.

Economics of Social Change

In American culture where almost everything is reduced to its commercial value, most people assume the economy and the market are beyond our control. We've come to expect economic institutions to make decisions for the benefit of the privileged, not for the downtrodden. In a world where the market rules, we start to believe there is no alternative. The most harmful aspect of unbridled capitalism is that we've lost our capacity to imagine humane economic and social relationships that benefit all people. We've lost our sense of hope that we're all in this together. CEO paychecks are on steroids, even when their companies are hemorrhaging from losses. Wall Street is flooded with accounting discrepancies, but the money is stored in off-shore accounts, and the beat goes on. Do we watch helplessly as globalization undermines local communities that result in food riots? Passivity and protest are not the only options. But what are the viable alternatives to an unfettered market economy that widens the gap between the rich and the poor?

One of the leaders in the growth of social entrepreneurship is Ashoka founder Bill Drayton who says, "Right now we have one of the rare instances where we can really impact the long-term architecture of half of society — for generations going forward. Every leading social entrepreneur is a role model. The result is that in community after community, each entrepreneur is encouraging someone, or several people, to become local changemakers. And that leads to everyone being a changemaker."[171]

People who believe that a more humane world is possible are creating alternatives. We're hungry for new ways of establishing an economy based on reciprocity and cooperation. When people decide to exercise their own economic power, they turn abandoned factories into employee-owned factories, run collective farms, reform health care enterprises, and create cooperatives. When investors don't get the huge returns they expect, viable enterprises shut down, but when workers take over, they revitalize their communities by providing jobs, goods, and services. Owned and operated collectively by workers and consumers, these enterprises contribute to the economy and meet the human needs of sustainable communities.

Exercises

Reflections:

1. What power issues do you need to deal with as a facilitator?
2. Since facilitation evokes intense vulnerability, how do you avoid emotional exploitation?
3. How do you create empowering relationships when power is thrust on you because people need leadership and feel comfortable with authority and obedience?

---

[171] Drayton, B. & Wang, T. Finding the next social entrepreneur. *The Stanford Daily*, 2/8/2005.

Small Group Discussions:

1. Take a look at your local community and other communities you belong to. What do you love about being part of each?
2. How can you improve the quality of life in each community?

Activities:

1. What is the one social change that you'd most like to see in your lifetime?
2. Out of all the places you can put your energy, what are you passionate about and what contribution would you like to make?
3. How can you design your peer support system so that you both give and receive the support you want?
4. Ask two people of color and two white people, "What does it mean to be white?"
5. Have a dialogue with someone you consider racist, sexist, or homophobic and explore their values. If you find yourself thinking judgmentally, get curious and connect empathically with their deepest needs.
6. Journal about your own "*isms*" and get clarity about how any lingering or entrenched beliefs help or hinder connection.
7. Break in to seven groups and flip chart behaviors that help or hinder inclusion for each identity group: Women; People of Color; Gay/Lesbian/Bisexual/Transgender; People with Disabilities; White Men; Youth; New Employees. Each group focuses on one identity group. Debrief by sharing similarities and differences of each group.
8. Take the Race IAT at www.implicit.harvard.edu and dialogue about your results and reactions.

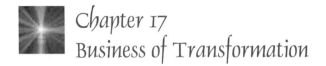

Chapter 17
Business of Transformation

When we are pursuing our Right Livelihood, even the most difficult and demanding aspects of our work will not sway us from our course. When others say, 'Don't work so hard,' or, 'Don't you ever take a break?' we will respond in bewilderment. What others may see as duty, pressure, or tedium, we perceive as a kind of pleasure. Commitment is easy when our work is Right Livelihood. —
Marsha Sinetar

Developing a sustainable coaching, facilitation, or organization development practice takes time and courage. Facing our fears transforms us in the process. All the skills in the world are for naught if we don't utilize them. Although it would be wonderful if we could make coaching, facilitation, and social change skills available for free, I have the most faith in spreading these life-serving skills through developing a practice. If many of us find ways to make this work sustainable, we'll attract more practitioners to the field, which will go a long way toward generating the ripple effect. In this section, we'll look at developing a practice, asking empowering selling questions, creating collaborative measures of success, viewing money as an ally, and generating abundance.

Both the coaching and facilitation professions are still in their infancy, but there are many opportunities for applying transformation skills throughout the world. Whether you plan to begin a business with private clients, integrate coaching or facilitation into your existing profession, or work as an internal change agent within your current organization, you can use the resources in this section to get started. So how do we start to build our practice? How do we build a business, market ourselves, and create structures for success? We can start by looking at what we most want.

Facilitating in Organizations

It is a rare organization that hasn't experienced the stress of workforce reductions, budget cuts, and streamlined operations. In developing countries, rapid expansion can prove equally challenging. People everywhere want a sense of meaning, satisfaction, and respect for the work they do. Coaching empowers individuals to develop their leadership potential\ so that they engage in their work wholeheartedly and affect the bottom line. Rather than fearing the consequences of change, coached employees embrace change and collaborate to create a better future.

The command, coercion, and control model might work in emergencies, but it doesn't tap human potential. Today, when empowered employees resolve problems, continuous performance improvement becomes a way of life.

In addition to collecting a paycheck, employees want work to serve as an important source of human fulfillment, a way to develop one's potential, and an outlet for creative expression. Coaching can encourage employees to bring their best ideas and efforts to the workplace, increasing commitment to the organization and its overall success.

Different from traditional mentors or consultants, skillful facilitators and coaches rarely provide solutions or advice. Instead, we facilitate the process by asking rigorous questions. We help people focus, connect with what's important, explore new possibilities and develop action plans. Attuned to values and vision, we help organizations build capacity, develop leadership, and maximize their contribution to the world.

Facilitation is a collaborative rather than an authoritarian relationship, with a focus on solutions rather than analysis of problems. We don't need to be an expert in their industry; the emphasis is on fostering awareness, setting and realizing rigorous goals, and facilitating sustained personal and organizational growth.

Benefits of Facilitation in Organizations

- Increases job satisfaction
- Builds morale and trust
- Promotes focused professional development
- Facilitates career advancement and succession planning
- Attracts, develops, and retains talented leaders
- Fosters creativity, innovation, and team spirit

Figure 17.1

Changing the Mindset	
From Boss	To Facilitator
Invokes fear to achieve compliance	Shares power to stimulate creativity
Looks for problems to solve	Looks for strengths to leverage
Makes demands	Makes requests
Controls through power	Facilitates by empowering
Knows the answer	Seeks answers
Points out mistakes	Celebrates learning
Delegates responsibility	Establishes accountability
Believes knowledge is power	Believes vulnerability is power
Issues directives	Engages in dialogue
Sees people as "costs to minimize"	Sees people as "assets" to develop

Changing the Mindset

Even though many work cultures are used to the boss/ employee relationship as shown in Figure 15.1, the change to a facilitative culture is simpler than it might seem. People buy in easily because a facilitative culture makes the manager's job so much easier and rewarding and employees take far more responsibility.

An event management company hired us to help them create a coaching culture. The CEO gave us only one directive, "My people work too hard. They need more balance in their lives. Your job is to get them to go home at night." I probably don't have to tell you how unusual that is – we usually get hired to get more out of people, not less. I thought it was a plum job, but never have we worked harder. They didn't want to go home at night. And finally we figured out why. The boss, whom they adored, wasn't going home at night, so why should they? It's not enough to want a balanced life for employees if you don't want it for yourself. Unfortunately, it was his child's life-threatening illness that got the CEO to put family ahead of work. When he cut back on his hours, everyone else picked up the slack for a while, but then they all chose to balance their lives between work and families. Although they went through a tough period after 9/11 when companies were not celebrating with events, the team was highly successful in creating a coaching culture – because they cared about each other.

Designing Multiple Relationships

When an organization contracts for coaching services, they rightfully expect clarity on their return on investment. They need to know what progress is being made through the coaching intervention. You as coach can create structures to honor the confidentiality of the coaching relationship. Some ways you can handle this:

- Design reporting structures that come from the person being coached. The client can report directly to the manager, or you can have a three-way conversation about the impact of the coaching process. The last thing you want is to be the middleman.
- Design a meeting where you are present, but the client and their sponsor or manger talk about the client's progress. You can be a silent witness or the facilitator of the conversation.

However you design this reporting, be clear with all involved that you will not breech confidentiality. This is the only way to hold the integrity of the coaching relationship and allow the clients to do their best work. If the sponsor wants to know how the coaching is going, be clear that you will not have private conversations about progress.

Sometimes people leave the company as a result of the coaching work. It is so much better to tell them about this possibility upfront. It is a common by-product of coaching that once employees (especially whose having problems) start to look deeply at what they want and how their current work supports their needs and desires, they choose to leave.

Another common pitfall in organizational coaching is the confusion between coaching and consulting. Most organizations have used consultants (subject matter experts hired to bring their expertise to bear on a problem in the company), but most have not yet used coaches. Be clear with your organizational clients about what coaching is and what it is not. Do not fall into the trap of giving advice which doesn't empower people. Advice-giving is a slippery slope, and you eventually get into a hole from which no amount of expertise will pull you out. Be clear from the beginning about the benefits of coaching and the benefits of drawing out the expertise from the client. Train your clients to see the value of coaching and how it differs from consulting.'

Your discovery session is the best place to make sure your client understands the differences between coaching, consulting, mentoring, and therapy. In your first coaching session, you can model what coaching is and is not.

Complimentary Coaching Sessions

Many coaches offer complimentary coaching sessions so that prospects can experience the power of coaching before buying. A personal experience of coaching is by far the most effective way for a prospective client to understand the power of our work. We can use the 4-Fold Way to make sample sessions powerful and effective:

- Show up! This means bring all of you and engage fully with transformational listening skills.

- Pay attention to what matters to the client on the deepest level you can access. Call them forth to create from their deepest longings.
- Tell the truth as you see it. Dare to act from your personal power. Sample sessions are not the place to withhold or play safe.
- Stay unattached to outcome. People naturally gravitate toward finding the best coach for themselves. Stay unattached to making the sale, and instead help them uncover whatever is alive.[172]

Enrollment is the art of helping people connect with new possibilities for their lives or their organizations. We go beyond communicating authentic interest in another person. Simply put, enrollment is linking what prospective clients want in their lives with what we have to offer, without gimmicks or manipulation. But it's a two-way street. Sharing what we're passionate about and being vulnerable about our own growing edges also contribute to connection and enrollment.

An empowering way to get the business is to enroll your client. Instead of memorizing a 30-second elevator speech about yourself, you connect with what's most alive in each other. Enrolling clients comes through authentic self-expression, not a separate marketing activity of selling ourselves. From a spiritual perspective, coaching, facilitation, and enrollment are the same. We create sacred space for growth and transformation, both through our work and in the enrollment process. How we energetically hold and present ourselves is our main source of attracting clients.

When we offer a sample session, the prospect will understand what we have to offer and hire us, right? It doesn't happen like this! Not only do we explain what we have to offer, but we connect our offering to what our prospect needs. Our value may be obvious to us, but if we don't spell it out for them, they'll never learn how our power and vision connect to *their* needs. Straight out, we tell them why we want to be their coach or what part of their vision we find inspiring.

A few enrollment statements that highlight the energetic quality of the connection:

- I feel connected to your quest…
- Coaching you would be special because…
- I love what you are creating with your life and I want to partner with you to make … happen.
- I would be honored to work with you because…
- I know you will find the right coach for yourself and if that person is me, I would be thrilled to work with you because…

---

[172] Arien. A. (1993). *The four-fold way: walking the paths of the warrior, teacher, healer, and visionary.* HarperOne.

Whatever words you use, make them authentic and from your heart. Just because you create a marvelous, magical connection doesn't mean the prospect will say, "Where do I send the check?" If you want to work with a client, *ask* for the business! The main reason people don't get clients is that they don't ask. We can simply ask, "Will you be my client?" or "Do you want to work with me?" or "When would you like to start?" It's like getting married though; we don't usually ask that question unless we already know the answer. A few things you can say to get clarity about their intentions at the end of a sample session:

- What is next for you in your process of looking for a coach?
- How was this sample session for you?
- Where do you want to go from here?
- What else do you need to choose the right coach?
- Would you like to move forward with coaching?

Discovery Sessions

Once you get a new coaching client, start with a Discovery Session of your own design. In co-creating an intentional relationship, find out as much as you can about what your client needs as you begin the journey together. Do not skip this step, as it provides an important foundation to the relationship. Discovery sessions vary widely but include these common elements:

Creating a conscious relationship: Design how you will create your relationship and work with each other based on mutual respect, trust, openness, and honesty. How can you be the best coach for your client, and what do you need in order to step into the most powerful relationship?

Making an Empathic Connection: Learn all you can about your new client, connect with their deepest desires, ask empowering questions, and give them the space to tell you all they want you to know about themselves.

Clarifying Values: Determine what really matters to your client so you can help them stay aligned with their deepest needs.

Establishing Desired Outcomes: Determine the direction and agenda of the coaching relationship by visualizing the future and establishing personal and professional goals.

Making Agreements: Talk about your agreements and how you make and break them with care. Get clarity about logistics, scheduling, payments, missed sessions, and vacations.

Questions to Build the CoachingAlliance

- What would a great coaching relationship look like?
- What do you want to get out of this relationship?

364

- How will we build trust and confidence in each other?
- What do you need from me?
- Would you be willing to give me feedback in the moment instead of saving it?
- How do you want me to give you feedback?
- When you become blocked or stuck, what works best to get you moving?
- What kind of accountability structures work best for you?
- I am not relaxed when clients come to the coaching session late. Will you agree to be on time?
- If something isn't working in the relationship, will you tell me?

Coach's Role

The coach's role includes creating a safe, supportive environment where the client can prosper. The way we do that is by truly, deeply believing that the client can have the life they want and respecting the client's perceptions, learning style, and needs. We offer support for new behaviors and learning and challenge their limiting self-beliefs. We also go beneath the surface, interrupt story telling to get to the heart of the matter, and offer accountability structures to support the client.

Client's Role

Coaches work with clients to create their own sense of power in the coaching relationship. We can ask them to take responsibility for the content of the sessions, express honestly what's working and not working, make requests to redesign the relationship, and step wholeheartedly into the process.

Holistic coaches create opportunities for transformation by giving people opportunities to be seen, heard, understood, and recognized for the gifts they have to offer. At first glance, the business of coaching and the spirit of coaching don't belong in the same sentence together, but the two are intrinsically related. When we're connected to soul and spirit, developing a business and generating sales are a breeze, simply because we're in our element and people are attracted to our essence.

Unlike coaches, facilitators and OD practitioners rarely give away free sessions – when an entire group's or organization's time is at stake, the client needs to have enough confidence to buy before they try. The enrollment conversation has a lot of similarities, but facilitators and consultants go further into the relationship-building process by determining duration of the engagement, desired outcomes, and measures of success.

Empowering Sales Process

An empowering sales process is a collaborative approach to needs analysis and designing satisfactory outcomes. You may be tempted to skip one or two of the seven steps because you know or trust each other, but each step contributes to creating a dynamic alliance. Each piece builds on the other, and I've found that skipping any of the steps comes back to bite me.

We start with creating an up-front agreement that we'll deal authentically with each other; otherwise people are reluctant to tell you the truth, whether they're completely sold or have no intention of buying from you ever. Sometimes this involves getting them to practice saying, "No, I'm not going to buy from you," or helping them uncover what they're saying "yes" to instead, "I have more confidence in another consultant because they're offering us a three-year program."

In step two we uncover their objectives or desired outcomes, which is often different from what they initially present. How will their lives be different if they buy? In step three we do the vital work of uncovering what needs they hope to meet by buying. This crucial part of the process helps us focus on *what they really care about*, not the bells and whistles of the product or service.

Once they feel understood about what really matters, before we go any further, we want to know their budget. Even if they say they don't have a budget, most people actually do, even if they aren't aware of it. They truly haven't thought about what it would cost, but they almost always have a ceiling – somewhere in the back of their mind, there's a limit. And you can find out their limit by throwing out a wild guess, "In ballpark figures, it sounds like what you want will cost about $200,000," If they respond, "Oh no, we couldn't possibly spend more than…" you know their ceiling, but don't take it at face value. I've found that many people willingly spend about 25% more than their ceiling, if we uncover and meet additional needs. Or they may respond, "That's very reasonable," which probably means we've left money on the table.

Once we understand their budget, we look at the options in step five, where we brainstorm some possibilities and co-create the solutions that fits best for their culture in step six. Lastly, we arrange for the follow-up so that both parties have clarity about what we've agreed to so far, what our next steps are and when our next meeting will take place.

To follow are a few empowering questions that are divided into sequential sections of the selling process.

1. Upfront Agreements – engage authentically in the dialogue

    Do we have about an hour to talk?

    If for any reason you decide not to work with us, or we decide not to work with you, we'll be honest about it, rather than waste each other's time. Okay with you?

2. Objectives – define the ideal outcomes

    If you had a magic wand, how would you use it?

    What do you want to see change?

3. Connect with Needs – empathize with their pain

   What keeps you awake at night?

   Why are you calling me now?

4. Budget – determine the investment

   How much would it be worth to make the changes we've talked about?

   What's your budget for this project?

5. Options – explore ways to move forward

   What alternatives have you considered?

   If you don't go with us, what will you do instead?

6. Solutions – establish commitment and create action plan to move forward

   How would you like to move forward?

   Based on what you've told us, would you like to hear our recommendations?

7. Follow-up – build in next steps

   Shall we review our next steps?

   When would you like to talk again?

For a more comprehensive list of empowering selling questions, refer to page 414 in the resource section. Both lists are only examples. Like learning a set of musical scales, these questions just get you started. Allowing the conversation to flow and using *their* words takes the relationship deeper. Creating an empowering alliance is vital to both parties, since the sales process is just the beginning of the relationship.

Responding to Objections

You can help your prospects come to their own conclusions about whether or not to hire you by asking a series of questions that help them explore their desired future. High pressure sales tactics are the antithesis of co-creating a coaching relationship based on choice and trust. Whether they hire you or not, you can still deepen the connection by hearing the "no" and empathically connect to the probability that they are saying "yes" to something else.

How would you respond to the most common objections?

Figure 17.2

Responding to Objections	
Objections	**Empathic Responses**
I'm too busy.	So your time is really valuable and you want to use it for things that are meaningful to you?
I can't afford you.	It sounds like you want to feel energized about how you use your money.
I don't think you can help me.	Ah, so you really want some help and you want to have confidence that you can get what you need?
I've already got several people who coach me informally.	You like the feel of an informal, friendly coaching relationship?
I'll have to ask my partner.	Are you a bit worried and want some reassurance about your intuition?

Create Collaborative Measures of Success

How do we practice inspirational diagnosis and evaluation to tap the organization's life force? How do we create collaborative measures of success? Success is measured based on criteria that are tied to organizational goals. The steps for creating collaborative measures of success include:

1. Tie the initiative to organizational goals
2. Set observable objectives that are directly tied to the initiative
3. Specify how coaching, facilitation or organization development will be applied to achieve these objectives
4. Isolate the effects of the initiative by collecting pre-and post-data or using a comparison

Objectives start with verbs. Sometimes our objectives are vague but can be measured with a 360° feedback assessment, where observable behavioral changes are rated by managers, peers and direct reports. To improve on vague objectives we articulate observable, actionable objectives that we can easily measure.

Figure 17.3 Clarifying Objectives

Vague Objectives	Measurable Objectives
• Improve communication skills • Collaborate with cross-functional teams • Improve team productivity • Deepen personal awareness • Develop decision-making skills	• Reduce employee turnover • Streamline feedback process • Increase market penetration • Improve response time to complaints • Reduce litigation costs

Not everything needs to be measured. Some of the objectives are best left as intangible benefits of organization development, but others can be converted into monetary benefits For instance, if turnover is reduced, customer complaints are decreased, or if a new product is launched ahead of schedule, this translates into bottom-line impact. The challenge is to take intangible results and make them measurable, e.g. strengthening communication skills, building internal leadership capacity, or improving the quality of life for employees.

Money as Our Ally

Is money our friend, an addiction, or a tool for making life easy? Wouldn't life be simpler if money didn't change hands? Or is money a way of simplifying our transactions, expressing our gratitude for goods and services, or relieving us of feeling continuously indebted to others? John Heron says, "There is clearly something odd about turning human helping into a profession, with training, accreditation, status, case conferences, and institutional politics. Does the wise flow of love from person to person require all this apparatus of paternalism?"[173] What if we just gave our work away? The world could become a better place faster if we practiced our craft freely, without remuneration. But when people in the helping professions *are* paid, more practitioners are attracted to the field, and that's a more concrete way of increasing the opportunities for transformation. I want structures that support the flow of money, contribute to ease, help us choose how we use our time, and provide clarity about where to focus our energy to be mutually beneficial. I want to prosper, I want my clients to prosper, and I want to contribute to the greater good in ways that are sustainable for all of us.

Because clients bare their souls, employ us as facilitators, and give us their money, the relationship can be burdened by power issues. Acknowledging the power issues helps us move

---

[173] Heron, J. (2001). *Helping the Client.* London: Sage Publications. p. 11.

away from 'power-over' and towards 'power-with' relationships. When we consciously design our relationships up front, self-empowerment becomes a choice.

I want to work with people regardless of their ability to pay, and at the same time, I want to earn a reasonable amount of money to sustain a modest lifestyle. The work I do in larger organizations in some ways subsidizes my pro-bono or reduced-rate work. Ideally I'd like to see clients pay whatever amount brings a smile to their face, and one of the reasons they're smiling is because they enjoy contributing to my well-being and supporting the continuation of my work. I also want to be paid an amount that *I* feel happy about – an amount that allows me to continue doing work that I love and contribute to projects that inspire me.

The old, tired adage that clients "don't value the work if they don't pay for it," is convenient but simply not true for many people. However, a modest monetary investment on the part of the participant increases my confidence that they value the work and will follow through on their commitments.

I'm eager to find new ways to bring the practice of *Facilitating with Heart* into every family and every organization. I focus my practice on the workplace because that's where I have the most hope about generating social change. The opportunity to reach and impact people is far larger than working with individuals. I also get excited imagining facilitators all over the planet spreading this work because organizations receive benefits and are willing to pay well for added value.

Pricing:

I hesitate to share information about money because it becomes dated so quickly and because many people use it as a way to rank themselves. I can imagine each reader placing me somewhere on a ladder, with yourself either above or below on the financial ladder. I'm deeply grateful for the money I make and know that it's a lot more than many people even dream of yet a lot less than others would find tolerable. I hope this doesn't sound like I have it all together because I don't. I have some savings set aside for retirement, but my financial stability and my sense of well-being is dependent on my next contract. I worry about being vulnerable because I want understanding. I have both a lot of ease and some disappointment about money. Sometimes I feel shame because I have so much, and other times I feel shame because I don't have the ability to mobilize resources to really have the impact I long to see in the world – not yet anyway.

In the early 90s I learned the hard way that most corporate buyers will not consider a training program that costs less than $3,500 a day because they perceive that the provider lacks credibility. The most important thing to the buyer is that you don't make them look bad. I predict you won't get in the door by offering a free workshop or telling them to pay whatever they'd like to contribute. You won't meet their needs for reliability. Smaller businesses want to pay a lot less, nonprofits and government agencies even less. In the nonprofit arena, I find that budgets range from $900 to $2,500/ day per trainer for workshops, and only rarely do I see small nonprofits pay more than $2,400/ day, but it does happen. I know some trainers who offer a 25% discount to nonprofits and others who do pro bono work because nonprofits just don't have the budgets.

In 1998, after our first year at Leadership that Works, when our rates were all over the map, we set our standard rates at $5,000 per day for two facilitators, but occasionally people offered to pay us $8-10,000/day. We asked for $3,000 for a half-day workshop because the rest of the day is not billable. Surprisingly, our highest paying clients were not corporations but universities and charities; their higher payments allowed us to do a lot of pro-bono and reduced rate work. For some of our favorite clients we would charge $1800/day for two of us – we give them a break for many reasons – we are deeply inspired by their vision, their ability to initiate social change, and their contribution to human evolution. Does $5,000/day sound like a lot? It wasn't! When we divided up the money, here's a rough idea how we disbursed it after expenses:

- 25% for the facilitators
- 25% for the design team
- 25% for the sales team
- 25% for administration (includes logistics, registration, professional development, and 10% for profit)

New collaborators sometimes ask why the sales team gets so much. Nothing happens without the sale. We all put in a lot of time developing relationships that sometimes sputter out and sometimes really ring our chimes. The sale can take a few minutes or it can take years.

Eventually our pricing structures evolved so that we aren't charging an hourly or daily rate but a rate for the value received. Instead of leaving money on the table, we want clients to pay top dollar, so we set our rates high enough that we can also do plenty of pro-bono work for causes that we care deeply about. We tell people what we would like to receive, but we also want to know what they want to contribute. Often we can work within their budget or refer them to someone who can. I recently told a social activist client that I wanted both of us to be happy about the fee and she was delighted to collaborate to reach a joint decision. Sometimes we make similar offers to nonprofits or small businesses with low budgets, but most corporate clients just want to know we'll get results and won't embarrass them, so the fee is secondary. The value of participants' time is so much higher than our fee that our pricing structure carries little weight in their decision. When organizations go out shopping for the best deal before they've built a relationship with us, I'm highly skeptical about working with them.

Sometimes organizations want to cut costs by using only one facilitator. We simply explain that we don't work that way. We almost always co-facilitate to meet needs for support and so that we can model vulnerability, equality, conscious connection, and love. Many consultants never raise their rates. Consequently, younger facilitators often charge more than their experienced, seasoned counterparts. For that reason alone, I encourage people to start their practice with a rate that will sustain them for many years to come.

Whether you're working with an individual or the entire organization, one guideline I recommend is to get their budget. Most prospects claim they don't have one saying, "Just tell me what you charge," but in reality, they always have a ceiling even when they are not aware of it. Years ago, my sister taught me how to find out their budget – you guess. This might sound like, "Off the top of my head, this looks like a $100,000 dollar project." But you don't guess low, you guess high enough that they say, "Oh no, that's way too much; I was thinking more like $75,000." If you add 25% to what they say their budget is, you're probably pretty close to their ceiling. I like to see people stretch just slightly out of their comfort zone so that they're invested in the project – it's a strategy for building relationships.

Reflection Activity:
1. How do you talk about your pricing strategy transparently in ways that are completely aligned with your values?

Proposals

I've written way too many proposals. Over the years, I've learned never to write a proposal until we already have a verbal agreement about the money. The proposal merely validates the oral agreement.

When someone in an organization asks for a proposal, I used to think that meant they were ready to move forward. It doesn't. It means they are fishing or blowing me off or considering someone else and want to show they've done their due diligence. I can spend a lot of time writing a great proposal, but unless I have the agreement first, I'm wasting my time. I assert that after you make a strong connection, get in touch with their pain, offer a program that will relieve some of that pain, and—come to an agreement about money and logistics, *then* you're ready for the proposal.

Most of my proposals depend heavily on using the client's language and have several sections that might look like:
- Situation Summary – the needs of the organization
- Desired Outcomes – the results they want, measures of success
- Recommendations – description of the program, methodology
- Value and Investment – costs and what they pay for
- Timing and Scope of Project – logistics
- Acceptance – authorization to proceed

If you want to know how to write a great proposal, I recommend Robert Middleton's online book, *The Marketing Guru*,[174] which is full of useful marketing information.

I am thrilled that I get to work with a lot of social activists in nonprofits, but I also love working with the cut and thrust, masculine energy of corporations. I feel at home in that

---

[174] Middleton, R. *The marketing guru*. http://www.actionplan.com/

environment, but part of what I love is that I get to impact the softening of the work place and bring in some balance with nurturing, compassionate energy.

I enjoy companionship with people who can see beyond the evil empire stereotypes and truly enjoy working with organizations. Business drives the economy and has incredible power to mobilize resources for personal development and social change. Organizations provide jobs that sustain people and offer products and services that make life easier.

That doesn't mean I endorse the dark side or the atrocities committed in the name of business. Despite deep despair about how some businesses operate, I have great hope that infusing compassion in the business world has the power to unite us, offering global communion that crosses ethnic and political boundaries. I long to partner with a cadre of sensitive, vulnerable, visionary leaders who embrace the business and nonprofit world and choose to serve by helping them evolve.

Fund Raising

Most people hate fundraising. Even if we have a great cause that we love, asking for money is painful. Some fundraisers follow rules, offer gimmicks, or invoke guilt to get people to give, but there is another way. By doing the inner personal work, we can ask from our core, from the place within that longs for an enlivening interaction. Unscripted. Real. Authentic. Heart connecting. When we come from a place of knowing why we're moved to ask, and we're open to their response, and willing to be moved by their response, we can create the quality of connection that is conducive to giving. Rich Snowdon from Nonprofit Hearts leads workshops on fundraising. If you want an inspiring approach to fundraising, read his moving piece, *Asking Kindred Spirits for Money.*[175]

Here's an excerpt from a fund raising email from Inbal Kashtan that touches me deeply because she writes so intimately, with such loving consciousness and hope:

> Subject: We're married, and asking for your support
>
> Dear family and friends,
>
> When Kathy and I chose to get legally married in August, I assumed that the legality of our marriage was likely to end on election day this November. A ballot measure (proposition 8) is aiming to make it so. And given the history of opposition to same-sex marriages, I was not feeling hopeful. But then I heard that polls were showing that the passage of this proposition was not certain, and I started to hope. That maybe, just maybe, Kathy and I – and millions of people in our situation – could have this level of equal access to resources, legal protection, recognition and acceptance. Wow.
>
> I'm still shaky in that hope, but it's there. And as Nov 4 comes closer, I'm finding that my heart is breaking! I've gotten attached to the legality of this

---

[175] Snowdon, R. *Asking kindred spirits for money.* Retrieved from nonprofithearts.net/rich/money.html

marriage, even though I didn't expect to. I've gotten attached to calling Kathy "my wife" without feeling ridiculous about it. Even though we've been married for TWELVE YEARS (we did the legal marriage on the anniversary of our very traditional Jewish wedding), I've always felt silly calling Kathy "my wife" because the context just wasn't there for it to make sense to most people. Today I said to a doctor "my wife" and she didn't even blink at it. So simple. Yet nothing I take for granted.

When I see how this legal marriage is affecting ME, someone who didn't even think this issue was so important, I realize how vital it is that this segment of society that I belong to - of people in same-sex relationships - gets to really belong in society. It's not even so much for me, for us, for our generation, that I find this so important. What really, really gets me is thinking about the young people who grow up without hope for full belonging, full choice about what to call their relationships. It's for them. I believe that this very symbolic label of "marriage" will go much further than domestic partnership, even when domestic partners have the same rights, in the direction of full acceptance of gay/lesbian/etc folks. That's what really gets me.

That, and the thought of Yannai, our 10-year-old son, who is very actively involved in trying to defeat this proposition (and passing proposition 2, and electing Barack Obama - he's been making calls, leafleting, researching, emailing, and more!) - it's the thought of *his* disappointment. Oh, I want to howl with the heartbreak of that. I want him to believe that this state - and this country, and this world - is ready for his mothers, his family. And for him, whomever he chooses to partner with.

So, would you help our family defeat proposition 8? Would you make it a gift for our wedding, if that appeals to you?

Inbal's vulnerability touches me – she writes from the heart and for the sake of a more humane world. Among the many ways to raise funds, the personal ask has the most power to move me. Letter writing is a great place to start, but most of the time we have no idea of the impact. In contrast, the phone or face-to-face ask gives us immediate feedback. Phone banking, or raising funds as a group, helps build momentum. We can empathize with each other when the calls that don't go so well and celebrate the calls that inspire us.

Generating Abundance

The *law of attraction* has been known for millennia and states that your thoughts determine your experience. Gautama Buddha said, "*What you have become is the result of what you have thought.*" We manifest our predominant thoughts by attracting both what we want and don't want. The film *The Secret* popularized the concept but attracted opponents who claim there is no proof that the law of attraction is anything more than a pseudoscience. Theories rooted in quantum physics assert that thoughts have a magnetic energy that attracts like energy. To harness this energy we can practice four things:

- Know what we want and ask the Universe for it
- Focus on our longing with enthusiasm and gratitude
- Behave as if our desires have already manifested
- Open our hearts to receiving what we want

Attracting what we want can be a *narcissistic* practice, or we can open our hearts to generating fulfilling lives not just for ourselves but also for the world. When it comes to suffering, none of us can truly stop suffering until all of us stop suffering. In the same way, reducing our own personal suffering is a pathway to reducing suffering everywhere. One of the ways we can generate abundance is through giving, whether through giving money, time, or other resources.

I'll always remember going to the Women's Funding Network, a group of philanthropists who fund projects that empower women and girls. One woman told me that 20 years ago it used to be a big deal for a woman to write a check for $200 because "she had to ask her husband." They didn't even think of their money as their own, but now hundreds of women are willing to write checks for a million dollars or more. One of the most moving stories came from a woman in Nicaragua who said she always saw herself as someone from a third world country, who receives charity, but doesn't give it. Her stereotype of philanthropists was that they were all old white men. That all changed when she worked with high school girls who gave pennies toward projects that would improve the lives of Nicaraguan girls. When those girls saw themselves as philanthropists, they became empowered leaders, creating their own projects. The Fondo Centroamericano de Mujeres primarily fund projects that are led by young women who support innovative and creative initiatives, which are replicable and relevant to the Central American context. The girls have evolved from receivers of charity to leaders of social change projects who generate resources that enhance women's human rights, including economic autonomy, gender-based violence, education, health, sexual rights, participation, and leadership.

Social change philanthropy focuses on the root cause of social problems whether they are economic or environmental. By including the people who are most impacted by those injustices as needs assessors and decision-makers, philanthropy becomes more diverse and available to all. Success is measured not only by dollars raised, but by the process of how money is given. Inclusive processes shift the power dynamics. Peace Development Fund Executive Director John Vaughn says, "It is more than teaching people to fish. It's supporting their efforts to get a company to stop polluting the lake they're trying to fish in."

Organization development improves the performance in both the for-profit and not-for-profit sectors, and becomes the vehicle for social change. We can use OD concepts and practices to strengthen social-change organizations and expand their impact. In the next chapter we'll look at expand the principles of organization development and look at how we can heal social problems and catalyze social change.

Exercises

Reflections:

1. How will you respond in your own words when asked, "What's the difference between coaching, therapy, facilitating and consulting?
2. Go out and get a new coaching client and consciously co-create a relationship that nurtures both of you.
3. How do you connect at the heart and soul level with the business of coaching?

Activities:

1. Design your ideal practice by finishing the following sentences:
   My ideal clients are…
   My specialty niche is…
   The unique benefits my clients receive from me…
   As a result of my work, my clients can…
   My clients are referred by…
   I partner with…
   My intentions are…
   My ideal business has…
   Number of clients…
   Hourly Rate…
   Day Rate…
   Hours per Month…
   Days per Month…
   Monthly Revenue …
   Other Income…
   Total Income…
   Monthly Business Expenses…
   Monthly Net Income…

2. Think of a few clients you'd like to work with and go after them. Without planning your enrollment statements, tell them why you'd like to work with them.
3. What empowering selling questions would you want to be asked?
4. What other empowering selling questions could you ask that would give your prospect an *experience* of transformation?

Conclusion

Once social change begins, it cannot be reversed. You cannot uneducate the person who has learned to read. You cannot humiliate the person who feels pride. You cannot oppress the people who are not afraid anymore. We have seen the future, and the future is ours.

— Cesar Chavez

It's with great sadness and trepidation that I bring this book to a close. I don't want it to be over. Jumping out of bed every morning to write has been a wonderful process, and I'm not ready to stop – nowhere near ready to tie a ribbon around this package. Like a squirrel, I've danced along the branches of each section, cracking open the nuts of insight and storing some for later, knowing that I'll be nourished all winter. As part of the cycle of transformation, I want to keep coming back to this treasure trove that so many people have contributed to, adding structures, models, and stories that support my learning and yours. Perhaps a time will come when I'm worn out, or complete, preferably in a state of joy, but that time is not now. I want to keep going, diving into new practices, *and* I want to put this evolving piece of work out there for people to use and improve upon.

So please, please send me stories about what works, what doesn't work, and what emerges as you immerse yourself in the process of *facilitating with heart*. Whether you're seeking personal transformation or social transformation, or anywhere in-between, I want to hear about your experiments, successes, and disasters. A lot of people don't like good-byes, but I actually enjoy them. Farewells are the springboard to something new. I have full trust that we will continue to open our hearts to the tears, laughter, and insights, and help each other evolve as individuals and as society.

Resources

In this Resource section of the book, you'll find worksheets, lists, activities and handouts. If you'd like to contribute your favorite resources for others to use, send them to me, and if they're a good fit, I'll include them with gratitude! –Martha

Balance Wheel of Fulfillment

One way to explore self-care is to use a life balance wheel. This tool gives you a snap shot of your life today and allows you to see how satisfied you are in different areas of life. With the center of the wheel as 0 and the outer edge as 10, rank your level of satisfaction with each life area by drawing a curved line to create a new outer edge.

Career
- My work stimulates and fulfills me
- I am excited about my career path
- I am proud of my contribution at work

Money
- I have enough money to meet basic needs
- I regularly contribute to a savings account
- I am free of money worries

Health
- I exercise and take vacations regularly
- I eat well and I'm happy about my weight
- I manage stress easily

Friends and Family
- I enjoy my friends and family
- I have a strong support network
- I have meaningful relationships with people I care about

Intimacy
- I enjoy romance with my partner or spouse
- I connect with people I care about
- My partner and I resolve conflict caringly

Spiritual Growth
- My spiritual practice supports me
- I live according to my values and principles
- I am living the life of my dreams

Fun and Recreation
- I regularly enjoy leisure time
- My hobbies and activities stimulate me
- I laugh deeply and often

Contribution
- My contribution to others is fulfilling
- I enjoy serving others
- I spontaneously and regularly give to people in need

Reflection Activity:
After rating your satisfaction with each area of your life on a scale of 1-10, determine what actions you will take to improve your satisfaction levels.

380

Bodily Sensations

achy	flutter	relaxed
airy	frozen	restless
bloated	fuzzy	shaky
blocked	goose bumps	sharp
breathless	hard	shivery
bubbly	hot	shudder
buzzing	heavy	smooth
chills	intense	sore
cold	itchy	spasm
cool	jumbled	spinning
congested	jumpy	sputter
constricted	light	still
clammy	mild	strong
damp	moist	suffocating
dazed	moving	sweating
dense	nauseous	tense
dizzy	numb	thick
dull	paralyzed	throbbing
electric	pounding	tight
energized	pressure	tingly
expanding	prickly	tremble
faint	puffy	tremulous
flaccid	pulsing	twisting
flexible	quaking	twitch
fluid	queasy	vibration
flushed	quivery	warm
	radiating	wobbly

Capturing Group Memory

Ned Ruete is a big believer in Group Memory. He even tells people he's not really a facilitator; he's just a good enough recorder that he can work without a facilitator. His practice of capturing the value of what people say is the essence of his facilitation style. Here are Ruete's ten rules of facilitation:

1. Write it Down and Hang It on the Wall.
2. Work on one issue at a time. Let the group choose and word the issue. Write it Down and Hang It on the Wall.
3. Agree on how to work on that issue. Tap the group wisdom for how to work before offering your own process. Write it Down and Hang It on the Wall.
4. When someone offers an idea, Write it Down and Hang It on the Wall. If they offer it repeatedly, point to where it is written down and hanging on the wall.
5. If someone attacks a person for a "dumb" idea, ask them where the idea is written down and hung on the wall. Move to it. Move the discussion to the idea, away from the person who offered it. If additions, qualifications, clarifications, or pros and cons are offered, Write it Down and Hang It on the Wall.
6. When the group is discussing, voting on, or coming to consensus around a solution, Write it Down and Hang It on the Wall.
7. When the group moves away from the agreed-to issue, go to where you wrote it down and hung it on the wall, call their attention to it, and give them the choice to change the issue, go back to the one they agreed to, show how this one affects the one they agreed to, or put a time limit on the digression. Whatever they decide, Write it Down and Hang It on the Wall.
8. When the group moves away from the agreed-to process, go to where you wrote it down and hung it on the wall, call their attention to it, and give them the choice to change the process, go back to the one they agreed to, show how this one affects the one they agreed to, or put a time limit on the digression. Whatever they decide, Write it Down and Hang It on the Wall.
9. When someone says, "We ought to _____," find out who will. Write it Down and Hang It on the Wall.
10. Before breaking up, find out when the group will get back together. Write it Down and Hang It on the Wall.

And mostly – if someone is running on about something that is not germane, don't write anything on the wall. Pretty quickly they'll learn to focus their comments. This is Jack Ryan's Grandmother's Rule: if you don't write it down, it didn't happen.

One of the most powerful impacts of group memory is that it shakes people out of their "usual meeting" mode. When there are large, visible artifacts of things being done differently, when functional behaviors get rewarded by being *Written Down and Hung On the Wall* and dysfunctional behaviors are not, you can quickly make a quantum leap in meeting effectiveness. That leap may only be from a total waste of time to 50% or 75% wasted time, but it's a start.

These simple, basic strategies pull people out of the mode of intelligent-but-aimless, about-the-topic-but-leading-nowhere conversation that makes so many meetings unproductive. Usually we talk about things but nothing gets done. Talking about things is important – it's the most common form of divergent thinking, and the other way to kill a meeting is to stick to the agenda and never talk about things. But after the talk has gone on awhile, say, "How do I capture that in group memory?" and start bringing people back to the objectives and process. Move them towards position statements, action items, report or proposal outlines, or bullet points, whatever work product they are there to produce.[176]

---

[176] Included with permission from Ned Ruete

Criteria for Choosing Co-Facilitators

Awareness and Tone
- Demonstrates high needs consciousness, holds all needs as valuable
- Recognizes self-judgment, can self-empathize and shift to generative thinking
- Demonstrates openness to trying new ways of doing things
- Believes in the resourcefulness, courage, and inspiration of each individual
- Reads the energy, voice, and body language of each person in the room
- Shares vulnerability and is open to learning and growth
- Offers presence and comfort with group process and conflict
- Values own learning as much as participants; dances on the growing edge
- Solicits developmental feedback and continuously works on self-improvement

Facilitation Skills
- Offers empathic reflections
- Elicits learning from the wisdom of the group
- Dances with aliveness, stays present, and changes course
- Holds multiple agendas simultaneously
- Demonstrates tracking skills and weaves in the threads
- Creates activities on the fly
- Exudes passion for making learning fun, bold, playful
- Elicits creativity using collaborative approach
- Creates aesthetically-appealing flip charts
- Adds to co-facilitator's learning, leveraging each other's personal growth
- Dances spaciously with co-facilitator: blending, taking the lead, covering, tracking, holding the container for learning

Modalities
- Experienced designer and facilitator of Organizational Development interventions
- Visioning Process
- Strategic Planning
- Appreciative Inquiry
- World Café
- Future Search
- Open Space Technology
- Sociocracy
- Board Governance
- Diversity Dialogue
- Non-Profit Leadership Development
- Restorative Circles
- Organization Development

Other Skills
- Synthesizes group desires
- Demonstrates wide range of skills: design, coaching, consulting, mediation, negotiation
- Articulates the observations that inform intuition
- Creates space and encourages playfulness, humor, wackiness, and love
- Makes requests that are connected to needs awareness
- Diagnoses stage of organizational development and creates appropriate interventions
- Designs experiential training using NLP to match different learning styles
- Practices spiral wizardry and uses language that resonates in different cultures
- Ties design to learning and organizational objectives
- Holds the details and ensures logistics are covered
- Creates handouts with appealing lay-out and design
- Knows or can find subject matter experts to collaborate
- Leads engaging teleclasses

Expression
- Expresses transparently, vulnerably, and authentically
- Reflects back feelings, needs, and implied requests
- Assists people in making doable requests
- Communicates concepts and directions with clarity in 40 words or less
- Interrupts as soon as people stop listening, demonstrating care and understanding
- Debriefs learning on four levels – observations, feelings, needs, action
- Vocalizes appreciation without generalizing or labeling
- Gives caring, honest, inspirational feedback
- Authentically shares mourning, celebrations, and gratitude for contributions

Timing
- Establishes connection, inclusion, tone, trust, intimacy, and engages participants immediately
- Ensures that every voice is heard within the first 15 minutes
- Meets needs of both fast and slow-paced participants
- Shares consciousness of time and can hold agreements
- Slows down to do deep work and holds silence during transformation
- Sequences learning activities that build on each other
- Creates closure that captures and transfers learning
- Starts and ends on time, yet generates a sense of spaciousness

Results
- Balances process and task so that everyone is heard and the group get results
- Captures salient points on flip chart
- Builds consensus and gets agreements
- Creates action plans with accountability structures

- Designs metrics for evaluating and improving the quality of the program
- Hears the emerging needs of the client and can design/sell the next phase of the program

Sales

- Leverages networking skills, brings people together, recognizes opportunity
- Can get in the door, connect, and sell programs that delight clients
- Hears the clients' pain fully before offering strategies for easing the pain
- Creates ease, helping clients share their budget along with hopes, dreams
- Articulates program options that meet client needs
- Elevates client relationships to see new possibilities
- Generates enough money to sustain future work and contribute to underserved communities
- Writes proposals that resonate – in the client's language
- Develops sustainable support systems and builds community

Disempowering Reponses

Agreeing with Judgments: Yes, that guy is obnoxious.

Asking for More Information: So she insulted you. Who else was there and what did they say?

Consoling: It wasn't your fault; anyone else would have done the same thing.

Denying Feelings: You shouldn't feel that way. He was only trying to help.

Disagreeing: How can you say that? She's so smart!

Educating: I hope you learned your lesson from this. You have got to be more assertive if you want people to listen to you.

Giving Advice: If I were you, I'd go to the beach.

Judging: You have no people skills.

Moralizing: That was a really insensitive thing to do. You need to apologize.

Reassuring: You'll be fine. By tomorrow this will all blow over.

One-upping: That's nothing; something much worse happened to me…

Shifting Away from Concerns: You sound pretty riled up. Let's focus on next week's meeting.

Solving the Problem: All you have to do is cancel the contract and move on.

Sympathizing: Oh, you poor thing…

Telling Someone What to Feel: Cheer up. You should be happy that you still have a job.

Telling Your Own Story: Something very similar happened to me…

Explaining it Away: You did that because…

Correcting: That's not what happened…

Blaming: You're the one who…

Investigating: Why did you …

Educating: If you'd stop being so defensive…

Analyzing: You're projecting your own problems…

Empowering Responses

Instead of offering judgment and advice, we can connect with their inner experience to help them uncover their own solutions:

Approval and Disapproval: Instead of sharing your evaluation, reflect the needs.

Comparing Yourself: Instead of thinking about who is smarter or how your experience is different, stay focused on the uniqueness of their experience.

Evaluating or Analyzing: Instead of interpreting or psychoanalyzing, reflect the observations so that the person can make their own meaning.

Ignoring Nonverbal Cues: Listen to the essence of the content, but also reflect what you observe about body language, tone of voice, rate of speech and energetic cues.

Leading the Speaker: Instead of reflecting where you think they are going next, reflect where they are right now.

Long-windedness: Simple, short reflections are most effective.

Multi-tasking: Instead of cleaning off your desk and trying to listen at the same time, give 100% attention. Show that you care by suspending all other activities.

Pointing out Contradictions: When someone contradicts something they've said earlier, instead of pointing out the discrepancy, reflect the most recent comment and acknowledge the change, progress or new clarity.

Pretending You Understand: If you get confused, say so. "I'm not following you. Could you say that another way?"

Suggesting a Particular Response: "I think you ought to go in there and tell him you want a raise," doesn't honor their sense of self-direction or resourcefulness.

Understating or Overstating: If the person expresses mild annoyance, instead of saying, "You sound really angry," reflect with the same level of intensity and energy. Likewise if the speaker is loudly expressing outrage, she won't feel understood if you quietly reflect, "You sound a little annoyed."

Emerging: Practicing Awareness of Emergence

By Jim and Jori Manske

An understanding of the concept of *needs* in nonviolent communication usually includes the following basic distinctions:

1. Needs are universal
2. Needs are the resources required to sustain or enrich life.
3. Needs make no reference to a particular person doing a particular thing.

An underlying presupposition that I've never heard discussed is that, "Needs are met or unmet," and that the feelings we experience arise are based on the "binary" state of our needs.

For me, I've noticed that it is not so black and white. I have found it useful to fine tune my own awareness about the state of my needs and the feedback I receive from my body—my feelings. This has resulted in contributing to my needs for autonomy, presence, creativity, and fun.

I have identified four stages in the "Need Cycle":

1. Fulfilled: This is what is traditionally referred to as a "need met and typically results in feelings of satisfaction, contentment, joy, appreciation, happiness, etc. It is a transient state.
2. Emerging: Sometime after every meal, we can learn to notice a subtle shift from satisfaction to a feeling of slight discomfort, a niggle of the feeling of hunger. Although we may recognize that we can still go for awhile without eating again, we nevertheless feel less than comfortable. As time goes on, and the need is not addressed, the level of discomfort will increase until we feel pain. Then, the need has become...
3. Urgent: Here our need has "fallen off the shelf." The pain motivates us to move toward fulfilling the need, sometimes without regard for the needs and feelings of others or our own best interest.
   Although it often seems to happen in an instant, I wonder as I become more mindful if I will begin to notice the subtle shifts sooner? Once a need becomes urgent, there seems to be less choice about strategies that might meet the need. It becomes easier to move from request energy to demand energy.
4. Satisfying: Somewhere along the journey between fulfilled and urgent, I can make a choice to move toward satisfying a need. The sooner I connect with the need (through the awareness of the feeling), the more choice I have about finding life-affirming

389

strategies to contribute to fulfilling the need.

By the way, chronically ignoring the pain of an unmet need can stimulate a cycle of addiction and violence as one tries to address the pain by masking it (with addictive behavior) rather than contributing to the fulfillment of the need. The addictive behavior "works" because the pain seems to disappear as we become temporarily distracted by the pleasure stimulated by the behavior. Since the underlying need is not addressed, the addictive behavior must be repeated, often with ever-increasing dosage and frequency, in order to continue masking the pain. This can cause serious, even life-threatening consequences without an intervention that addresses both the underlying need and the seemingly-positive benefits of the addictive behavior.

How to Practice
Consider your need for sustenance right now. Notice the feelings in your body. Connect and identify where you are in the Need Cycle. Remain mindful of the need for sustenance as you move through the cycle, noticing the subtle shifts in your physical sensations and emotions.

After practicing with sustenance for a period of time, pick other needs and follow the cycle in a process of ongoing self-connection and mindfulness.[177]

---

[177] Manske, J. & Manske, J. reprinted with permission. All rights reserved. http://radicalcompassion.com

390

Empowering Questions

This list may give you some ideas, but the most empowering questions use the speakers language.

Design Co-facilitator Relationship

What guidelines would support us in working together?

What support do we need from each other?

What excites you about working together?

What intentions are you setting?

What are you hoping to learn?

What needs are you hoping to meet?

What would be a stretch for you?

Foster Heart Connection

How do we open our hearts fully?

What's alive in you now?

What are you hoping for?

What are you curious about?

What sensations and feelings are you experiencing right now?

If you were really honest right now, what would you share?

How can we express ourselves vulnerably?

Engage participants

How do we set the tone?

How can we create a space where everyone belongs?

How can we engage them fully from the start?

How do we create opportunities for inclusion?

What can we do to honor diversity?

How can we engage every voice in the first five minutes?

How do we create sacred space for transformation?

How can we create a conscious relationship that supports us and the group?

Set Intentions

What is your vision?

What specifically do you want to achieve?

What's the big picture?

What excites you about the future?

Imagine your time together produces desirable results – what do you see?

What change would you like to see happen, personally and collectively?

What collective outcomes do you want?

What are the short and long term goals?

Enhance Possibilities

What do you want to co-create together? What's important about that?

How do we stretch into the unknown?

What do you envision in the ideal future?

How do we weave our dreams together?

What are you yearning for?

How can you open to the great mystery?

What makes your hearts soar?

Clarify Needs and Values

What do you care about in this situation?

What value does this experience have for you?

What does your heart say?

What do you want? If you have that, then what do you want?

What is underneath that strategy?

What's behind your desire?

What's going on internally?

What do you feel?

What physical sensations can you identify?

What happens if you sit with those sensations?

Foster Understanding

Can you reflect the feelings and needs of the person who just spoke?

How do you feel about what was just said?

What do you imagine others feel or need?

What understanding do you want from others?

Can you acknowledge the underlying motivation?

What hopes and dreams are you hearing?

What needs to happen to collectively honor the needs of the group?

What do you want back from the group so that you are fully heard?

Point to Transformation

What is emerging?

Out of the chaos, what is possible?

What are we avoiding?

What really matters?

What is the group giving birth to?

How do we make room for the unheard voices?

In the spaciousness, what is wanting to be born?

Address Resistance

What are the obstacles?

What would you like to ignore?

What is wonderful about this problem?

What if you were able to get past this?

What's stopping you?

What are you stepping over?

Expand Options

What are your choices?

What are you overlooking?

What impact would you like to have?

What actions are possible now?

What inspires you?

What is the gift in this challenge?

Set Stretch Goals

What is impossible?

If you had a magic wand, what would you do?

If you knew you'd succeed, what would you do?

If you were to raise the bar what would it look like?

How can you play a bigger game?

Looking at the whole, what makes the most sense?

How can you expand what's already working well?

What if you had unlimited resources?

What if you had unlimited support?

Elicit Wisdom

What stands out?

What might you do differently next time?

What are you missing?

How is your time going to change over the next month?

How else can you think about this?

What can you do to create more balance?

What does your heart tell you about this?

When you're at your best, what's different?

How do you invite the flow of effortless manifestation?

Break through Barriers

What will be different when you have the solution?

What will get you going?

In an ideal world, how would you face this problem?

What would motivate you to change?

What does it cost if things remain the way they are?

What if you pretend you know the answer?

If you had to find a way right now, what would it be?

Honor Needs

What request do you have of yourself that will meet your needs and others?

What request do you have of others that honors everyone's needs?

What can you ask that would build connection?

To build connection, would you like a reflection from someone in the group?

To ensure collective understanding, would you like someone to synthesize what you said?

What can you request that would get you started?

What do you want?

Take Action

What strategies would honor the collective values?

What will move you forward?

What action would you like to take?

What do you want to take responsibility for?

What do you choose to do about this situation?

How do you plan to achieve that?

What will you say yes to?

What's next?

Get Support

What do you need help with?

Who can help you with that?

What can you delegate?

What resources do you need?

To get the support you want, what request can you make?

How can you turn this into a win-win?

Who has the answer?

If you knew they'd say yes, who would you ask for help?

Who has done this before?

What if you completely trusted yourself and others?

Reduce Sense of Overwhelm

What can you say "no" to?

What can you stop doing so that you can make room for what's important?

What can you stop tolerating?

If you only focused on one thing, what would it be?

What is out of harmony, and how do you restore it?

What will happen if you don't move forward?

Commit

How can you break that down into smaller steps?

What are you going to do? By when? Who will you tell?

What's compelling or inspiring about moving forward?

What else do you need to do?

On a scale of 1-10, how committed are you to this plan?

If you take this step, what would you do next?

How will you hold yourself accountable for making the change you've described?

Evaluate

How does this plan honor your values?

What are you committed to?

How can we create structures that empower everyone involved?

How will we track progress on the plan?

What value did you get out of our session?

Feelings

Affectionate – amorous, compassionate, friendly, loving, nurturing, open- hearted, sympathetic, tender, warm

Engaged – absorbed, adventurous, alert, curious, eager, fascinated, interested, intrigued, involved, playful, stimulated, touched

Excited – amazed, astonished, eager, energetic, enthusiastic, invigorated, motivated, passionate, surprised, stimulated

Hopeful – amazed, awed, confident, empowered, encouraged, expectant, inspired, open, optimistic, safe, secure, uplifted

Joyful – amused, delighted, glad, happy, pleased, tickled, thrilled, stimulated

Peaceful – blissful, calm, comfortable, centered, composed, content, fulfilled, grounded, relaxed, relieved, satisfied, serene, trusting

Refreshed – energized, enlivened, rejuvenated, renewed, rested, restored, revived

Grateful – appreciative, moved, thankful

Confused – anxious, confused, embarrassed, hesitant, insecure, jittery, nervous, perplexed, puzzled, reluctant, skeptical, torn, uncomfortable, uneasy, worried,

Scared – afraid, alarmed, distressed, fearful, horrified, nervous, shocked, tearful, terrified, regretful, worried

Angry – annoyed, aggravated, agitated, bitter, disappointed, enraged, exasperated, frustrated, furious, hostile, infuriated, mad, upset

Disinterested – alienated, aloof, ambivalent, apathetic, bored, disconnected, distant, distracted, indifferent, lethargic, withdrawn

Tired – drained, dull, exhausted, fatigued, sleepy, weary

Embarrassed – ashamed, chagrined, flustered, guilty, mortified, self-conscious

Grieving –agonizing, anguished, bereaved, devastated, grief-stricken, heartbroken, hurt, lonely, miserable, mourning, regretful, remorseful

Sad – depressed, dejected, despairing, despondent, disappointed, discouraged, disheartened, forlorn,

Yearning – envious, jealous, longing, nostalgic, pining, wistful

Tense – anxious, cranky, distressed, distraught, edgy, fidgety, frazzled, irritable, jittery, nervous, overwhelmed, restless, stressed out

Vulnerable – fragile, guarded, helpless, insecure, leery, reserved, sensitive, shaky, protective

Agitated – alarmed, rattled, restless, disconcerted, disturbed, shocked, startled, surprised, troubled, uncomfortable, uneasy, unnerved, unsettled, upset

Pseudo Feelings

Abandoned
Abused
Attacked
Belittled
Betrayed
Bullied
Cheated
Coerced
Cornered
Degraded
Despised
Detested
Diminished

Discounted
Disrespected
Distrusted
Hated
Interrupted
Intimidated
Intruded Upon
Let Down
Manipulated
Marginalized
Misunderstood
Patronized
Picked on

Provoked
Put-Down
Rejected
Ripped off
Shamed
Taken for Granted
Unappreciated
Unpopular
Unwanted
Used
Worthless

Leadership Competencies

Too often leadership performance is evaluated or feedback is given based on vague attributes, such as "is motivated to succeed" or "demonstrates integrity." In contrast, when we describe leadership competencies in terms of observable behaviors, the feedback is more tangible, so it's much easier for the recipient to develop a leadership plan from the results. To follow are some competencies that describe observable behaviors. Notice they each competency starts with an action verb, so that we can actually determine if people have demonstrated the behaviors.

Change Management
- Proposes new initiatives to improve operations.
- Creates a work environment that is receptive to change.

Coaching and Developing Others
- Stimulates resourcefulness in others, evoking clarity, action and insight.
- Inspires enthusiasm, ownership, commitment and a desire to reach full potential.

Communication
- Simplifies complex issues and expresses ideas clearly and concisely.
- Gets messages across with the intended impact and ensures quality information is received.

Customer Orientation
- Understands and meets expectations of internal and external customers.
- Changes and adapts work processes to meet changing customer demands.

Decision Making
- Solicits input and facts from those involved before making a decision.
- Chooses from a range of decision-making techniques to ensure alignment and implementation.

Delegation
- Clarifies roles and responsibilities.
- Ensures people have the resources and authority to carry out responsibilities.

Diversity
- Leads an inclusive workplace that values differences and maximizes the talents of each team member.
- Recruits, develops and retains a high-quality, diverse workforce.

Emotional Intelligence
- Demonstrates awareness of feelings, needs and interests of employees at all levels.
- Listens and expresses with compassion.

Expertise
- Accesses a wide base of knowledge and keeps up to date with industry trends, policies, best practices, and information.
- Understands organizational culture, shows awareness of relevant issues, and demonstrates cross-functional knowledge.

Feedback
- Encourages two-way communication about expectations, responsibilities and performance.
- Approaches problems as positive learning opportunities for growth and development

Innovation
- Encourages creativity and experiments with innovative ways of doing things.
- Challenges people to create solutions to problems and take advantage of new opportunities

Learning
- Challenge old ways of doing things, seeks innovation, takes risks, and shares new insights.
- Learns from experience and modifies behaviour based on feedback.

Facilitation
- Establishes meeting purpose, clear goals, action plans, and accountability structures.
- Encourages open expression of ideas and opinions on controversial issues.

Motivation
- Commits to high performance and achieves goals despite obstacles and opposition.
- Fosters a work environment that welcomes humor, joy and celebration of important goals

Relationships

- Cultivates a network of supportive relationships
- Explores ways encourage the heart and expresses appreciation for other's contributions.

Team Work

- Builds trust, enthusiasm and commitment to goals among team members
- Empowers people to build and sustain collaborative working relationships.

Transparency and Authenticity

- Self-expresses transparently, openly and authentically.
- Demonstrates congruency between emotions, language, body, thoughts, and actions.

Vision

- Inspires people to think long term and fosters development of a shared vision.
- Anticipates future trends and communicates a compelling vision.

Liberate Your Dream

By Roberta Wall, inspired by Barbara Larson, included with permission.

Your Dream

1. What are you longing to say or do (your dream)? Write it down (one concise sentence) across the top of the paper.

NO Way Thoughts

2. What "no way" thoughts are you telling yourself—why this won't work, won't happen? In column two, spend 20 minutes or more writing these down, reflecting, adding, really connecting with all those lurking "no way" thoughts you are telling yourself. They have a lot of intelligence in them and are connected to some precious needs.
3. Rank thoughts in order of intensity of charge.
4. For each thought: Write in the column next to it the feeling associated with the thought.
5. For each thought: Write in the column next to it what the precious need is behind that thought.
6. Breathe in the need…..connect with its beauty. Spend as much time savoring the need until you really feel the energy of what beauty your thoughts are longing for.
7. If new or previously-unframed thoughts have appeared, add them to the list and do the same process.

Back to the Dream

8. Now go back to your dream: What are the precious needs behind the dream?
9. In the first column, list the precious needs you are dreaming of meeting with this dream.
10. Connect with their beauty, one by one.
11. Sit for some moments, savoring, connecting with all the needs.

Integration/Action Phase

12. Go back to the needs behind the thoughts: how can you meet those needs? (Doable strategies or requests to yourself in relation to the dream)
13. Go back to the dream. Do you have any new requests of yourself about that?
14. How can you meet both sets of needs that are still alive?

Experiential/Sharing Phase

15. In dyads, each person takes 15 minutes or so to talk through their process while their partner listens or coaches if asked.[178]

---

[178] Roberta Wall created this process, inspired by Barbara Larson. 2007. www.steps2peace.com

Meeting Facility Check List

- ❏ Accessible location
- ❏ Ease of transportation
- ❏ Available parking
- ❏ Square footage
- ❏ Comfortable seating
- ❏ Round tables
- ❏ Seating options – circle, rounds, classroom
- ❏ Lighting, windows, ambience
- ❏ Visibility (posts or other barriers that prevent people from seeing each other)
- ❏ Quality of interaction with support staff
- ❏ Wall space for flip charts
- ❏ LCD projector with tech support
- ❏ Flip charts, markers, supplies
- ❏ Food and beverage
- ❏ Temperature control
- ❏ Advance access to set-up the event
- ❏ Bathroom and kitchen facilities
- ❏ Cost

Needs and Values

Belonging – identity, community, participation, receptiveness, interdependence, trust, bonding, inclusion, cooperation, unity, synergy, integration, loyalty, participation, partnership, social acceptance, empathy, acknowledgment, community, group identity, connection, respect, consideration, support, emotional freedom, emotional safety

Freedom – autonomy, authenticity, self-expression, celebration, vitality, humor, passion, creativity, imagine, dream, romance, inspiration, direction, independence, choice, individuality, space, spontaneity, will, self-empowerment, options

Meaning – purpose, conviction, awareness, clarity, consciousness, creativity, hope, learning, purpose, effectiveness, growth, discovery, spirituality, aesthetics, bliss, order, serenity, grace, faith, inspiration, hope, passion, transcendence, communion, celebration, presence, accomplishment, mourning, celebrating grief, learning, mastery, competence, self-awareness, God

Understanding – clarity, comprehension, open-mindedness, awareness, belief, reflection, discrimination, critical capacity, curiosity, intuition, honesty, integrity, openness, trust, respect, equality, centeredness, identity, respect, composure, mental stimulation, communication, focus, discernment, memory

Connection – love, esteem, affection, warmth, closeness, respect, sensuality, intimacy, companionship, mutuality, nurturance, touch, physical affection, sensitivity, tenderness, caring, bonding, comfort, appreciation, empathy, support, consideration

Authenticity – expression, celebration, vitality, humor, passion, creativity, imagination, dream, romance, inspiration, integrity, presence, openness, trust, respect, equality

Contribution – generosity, creation, imagination, boldness, inventiveness, curiosity, vision, dreams, passion, mastery, growth, service, enrichment, empowerment, support, acknowledgement, assistance, building, change, encouragement, energy, help, facilitation, nurturance, appreciation

Leisure – play, recreation, imagination, tranquility, spontaneity, adventure, challenge, daring, risk-taking, thrill, fun, humor, amusement, laughter, pleasure, sensuality, harmony, peace, security, order, mischief, consistency, calm, stability, relaxation, comfort, ease, solitude, ecstasy, delight, stimulation, excitement, beauty, dance, music, art, humor

Subsistence – air, food, health, movement, nutrition, physical survival, rest, safety, sex, sleep, shelter, water

Supporting Body Awareness
- Notice your body.
- Pay attention to your breath.
- Exaggerate that gesture.
- Scan your body and notice any sensations.
- Express that in movement.
- Breathe louder.
- Loosen any restrictions, relax your throat.
- Stand up and dance – whatever comes to you.
- Notice what your flexed left foot wants to say to you.
- You are holding something in your hand. Open your hand.
- You just removed lint from your shirt.
- Try a pensive posture to see what thoughts you generate.
- Your body is collapsed in on itself.
- Your body has a message for you.
- Assume everything you communicate verbally or non-verbally has meaning.
- Try saying that again while looking skyward with a smile on your face.
- Repeat that, "I have so much weight on my shoulders," while I press on your shoulders.
- Breathe out what you wish to give; breathe in what you wish to receive.
- Describe your posture right now.
- Make a sound to go along with the movement in your arms.
- When you speak to her, you look at me.

Supporting Voice Awareness
- Make the sound that expresses your internal feelings.
- You swallowed hard. Say the words you've been trying to swallow.
- Relax the back of your throat and say that again.
- You have something to say.
- Give voice to your pelvis.
- Amplify one word.
- Make the sound that expresses your deepest desires.
- Repeat that phrase louder.
- Sing a phrase from a song – whatever comes to you.
- Say that again, pausing after every noun.

Supporting Language Awareness
- Try saying the first thing that comes to you.
- If you weren't being polite, you would say.
- Change "I should" to "I choose to".

404

- Say that again without qualifiers.
- Contradict what you just said.
- Say it directly to her. "Cheri, you …"
- That sounds like an aside, but it has meaning.
- Change that question into a statement.
- Say the headline only.
- Change that to an "I" statement.
- Change "I can't'" to "I won't."
- Shift from the hypothetical to what is real for you.
- Refer to him as "you" instead of "him."

Expanding with Imagery
- You have a gift.
- Notice the first image that comes to you.
- Breathe deeply into the part of you that needs more oxygen.
- Let yourself fantasize.
- Imagine you are killing something.
- Ask your future self for advice.
- Chew on your experience. Describe the texture and flavor of the food.
- Give yourself full permission to.
- You are giving birth to.
- I see you in a boat.

Clarifying Observations
- Notice what captures your attention.
- Try saying the exact words that trigger you.
- Pay attention to what stands out for you.
- Become aware of what grabs you.
- Remember the moment when you were first irritated.
- Put your attention on what matters most.
- Notice what's coming up.
- Name the observation that stimulates your judgment.
- Something is ringing in your ears.

Clarifying Feelings
- Change "You make me feel," to "I feel."
- Something is happening to you.
- Your feelings are a gift.
- Stay with your feelings.
- Act out your feelings.
- Your fear wants to protect you.
- Unleash the pain.
- Affirm the hurt.
- Vent.

- Get the rage out.
- Speak to your feelings.
- Connect to the internal experience of your emotions.
- Experience the fullness of your relief.
- Notice where the joy lives in your body.

Clarifying Needs
- Notice what energizes you.
- Connect with your heart's longing.
- You're choosing that strategy because you want something.
- Slow down. Check in with yourself.
- Open your heart first to yourself. Now to the other person.
- Take a moment to cherish your needs.
- Make a list of all the things you appreciate about yourself.
- Hold onto your needs and rock them like a baby.
- Unfreeze the need and imagine that need completely fulfilled.
- Underneath that need is an even more important need.
- Take a minute to sit with the beauty of your needs.
- Connect with what enlivens you.

Clarifying Requests
- Imagine asking for what you really want.
- Make that into a request.
- You want to connect, so ask for what you want.
- Propose a doable request.
- Start your request with, "Will you…"
- Now that you're in touch with your needs, generate three possible requests that are likely to meet your needs.
- Try reconnecting with the need before asking for what you want.
- Make "I want you to respect me," into a doable request.
- Imagine what would meet your needs for respect. Ask for that.
- Make a request of yourself.

REAL Model for Organization Development

In the Sensing and Discovery phase of Organization Development, we have the opportunity to support everyone in the organization in becoming more REAL with themselves and each other.

Relate

To discover how people relate to each other and determine the level of trust, we ask ourselves:

- What are they longing for?
- How do they express their passion?
- How do they share their emotions and vulnerability?
- How do they confront or challenge each other?
- What brings out the life giving forces of the organization?
- How do they appreciate and acknowledge each other?
- How do they facilitate and manage differences and diversity?
- How do they foster creativity and innovation?
- What stands out about their relationship with customers or clients?
- How do they celebrate, express humor, have fun?
- How do they share feedback?
- How do relationships enhance self-esteem and sense of power?
- What attracts people to this team or organization?
- How are relationships and networks built?
- What metaphors do people use to describe their relationships?
- How do conversations get initiated?
- What triggers inter-personal and team interactions?
- What are the signs of conversations 'wanting to happen' or 'aborted'? What triggers such expectant/ resigned behavior?
- What formal and informal spaces exist within the organization for people to express their feelings and values?
- Who are the go-to people in times of crisis e.g. non-achievement of business results, personal crisis, team crisis, customer escalation etc?
- What are the visible behaviors that promote collaboration?
- What process do people use to resolve conflicts?
- How are customer relationships and employee relationships the same or different?
- How does the organization listen to the voice of its stakeholders – customers, shareholders, employees, and business partners?

Explore

Engaging in dialogues with work teams at multiple levels, including the senior leadership team, we can choose from a wide range of questions to explore beneath the surface. Naturally we don't bombard people with hundreds of questions, but we choose empowering discovery questions that help people get clarity about what is worth exploring.

- How would you describe the power structure?
- What challenges does the team face?
- What is the external environment calling out for, compelling us to be?
- How do structural factors facilitate or impede communication?
- How do leaders promote co-creation, delegation, and empowerment?
- How do people address power dynamics or authority issues?
- What holy cows or undiscussable issues are held sacred?
- What have been the defining moments for the organization in its evolution?
- What conflicts or disagreements need to be addressed?
- What's lurking underneath polite conversations?
- What mechanisms exist to deepen inquiry into issues raised by any individual?
- What are the paradoxes in the group?
- What are the polarities that create a push and pull in the team?
- What kind of fragmentation exists and what values are at stake?
- What is unique about the organization in its industry?
- How does customer dissatisfaction get converted to customer delight?
- How do people deal with "impossible tasks?"
- What triggers curiosity, creativity, anticipation, and wonder?
- What triggers judgment, disconnection, resignation, and disengagement?
- When have people felt intense trust?
- How do failures and mistakes get handled in the organization?

Adapting

To develop an understanding of the transformational process of the individual, group, and organization, we periodically develop a map of the state of affairs of the team that includes what is changing.

- What changes or milestones from the past can be leveraged in the future?
- How are the dreams of the founders or the top management team evolving?
- When they state their aspirations what feelings are evoked?
- What learning has been most empowering for the organization?
- What are the biggest perceived future risks?
- How is the leadership team planning to mitigate risk?

- How have dreams, sense of uniqueness and perceived risks changed across the organization?
- What changes and shifts will help develop this team/organization?
- What evidence do you see that the organization is ready for more change?
- How ready is this organization to try out new ideas and perspectives?
- What does it take to get others to listen to your ideas and suggestions?
- How flexible are the plans and processes within the organization?
- How has coaching the leaders impacted the team and the organization?
- How is the team changing as a result of the coaching process?
- What is new and exciting about this place?

Learning

How people support each other's learning is key to any organization's success. Our questions generate new awareness about how the organization integrates learning.

- How does the organization foster creativity and innovation?
- What new insights and learning are emerging?
- How is leadership capacity developed?
- How will we expand team learning and organizational learning?
- What metaphors describe this organization?
- What is the team longing for?
- What motivates or drives people?
- What blocks or releases the energy of the team?
- What are the life-giving forces of the leader and the team?
- How are failures and mistakes addressed in the organization?
- How does the organization identify high potential leaders?
- What formal structures exist to engage the development of individuals?
- What knowledge is critical for the organization? How is crucial knowledge disseminated?
- How is new knowledge created (R&D, experience, experimentation, co-creation with customers/ business partners, etc.)?
- What learning and development areas are encouraged?

Books

Coaching

Appreciative Coaching: A Positive Process for Change by Sara L. Orem, Jacqueline Binkert, and Ann L. Clancy. 2007

The CCL Handbook of Coaching: A Guide for the Leader Coach by Sharon Ting and Peter Sisco. 2006

Coaching: Evoking Excellence in Others by James Flaherty. 2005

Coaching for Performance: Growing People, Performance and Purpose by John Whitmore. 2002

The Coaching Organization: A Strategy for Developing Leaders by James M. Hunt and Joseph R. Weintraub. 2006

Coaching Skills for Nonprofit Managers and Leaders by Judith Wilson and Michelle Gislason. 2009

Coaching that Counts: Harnessing the Power of Leadership Coaching to Deliver Strategic Value by Dianna Anderson and Merrill Anderson. 2004

Co-Active Coaching by Laura Whitworth, Henry Kimsey-House & Phil Sandahl. 2006

The Heart of Coaching: Using Transformational Coaching to Create a High-Performance Coaching Culture (3rd Edition) by Thomas G. Crane and Lerissa Nancy. 2007

Communication

Connecting Across Differences: A Guide to Compassionate, Nonviolent Communication by Jane Marantz Connor and Dian Killian

Fierce Conversations: Achieving Success at Work and in Life, One Conversation at a Time by Susan Scott. 2004

Getting Real: 10 Truth Skills You Need to Live an Authentic Life by Susan Campbell

Nonviolent Communication: A Language of Compassion by Marshall Rosenberg. 2004.

Facilitation

The Complete Facilitator's Handbook by John Heron. 1999

Extreme Facilitation: Guiding Groups Through Controversy and Complexity by Suzanne Ghais. 2005

The IAF Handbook of Group Facilitation by Sandy Schuman. 2005

Nine Disciplines of a Facilitator by Jon and Maureen Jenkins. 2006

The Secrets of Facilitation by Michael Wilkinson. 2004

The Skilled Facilitator by Roger Schwarz. 2002

MultiCulturalism

Coaching across Cultures: New Tools for Leveraging National, Corporate, and Professional Differences by Philippe Rosinski. 2010

Diversity Consciousness: Opening our Minds to People, Cultures and Opportunities by Richard Bucher and Patricia Bucher. 2009

Diversity in Coaching; Working with Gender, Culture, Race and Age by Jonathan Passmore. 2009

Generations at Work by Ron Zemke, Claire Ranes and Bob Filipczak.1999

Privilege, Power and Difference by Allan Johnson. 2005

Understanding Whiteness: Unraveling Racism by Judy Helfland and Laurie Lippin. 2001

Organization Development

The Change Handbook: The Definitive Resource on Today's Best Methods for Engaging Whole Systems by Peggy Holman, Tom Devane, and Steven Cady. 2007

Courageous Visions: How to Unleash Passionate Energy in your Life and your Organization by Martha Lasley. 2004

Diagnosing Organizations: Methods, Models, and Processes by Michael Harrison. 2004

An Experiential Approach to Organization Development by Donald R. Brown and Donald Harvey. 2005

The NTL Handbook of Organization Development and Change: Principles, Practices, and Perspectives by Brenda B. Jones and Michael Brazzel. 2006

Organization Development and Transformation: Managing Effective Change by Wendell L. French, Cecil Bell, and Robert A. Zawacki. 2005

Organization Development: A Jossey-Bass Reader by Edgar H. Schein and Joan V. Gallos. 2006

Organization Development: Principles, Processes, Performance by Gary N McLean. 2005

Organizational Culture and Leadership by Edgar H. Schein. 2004.

Practicing Organization Development: A Guide for Consultants by William J. Rothwell and Roland Sullivan. 2005

Process Consultation Revisited: Building the Helping Relationship by Edgar H. Schein. 1998

Personal Transformation

Carl Rogers on Personal Power: Inner Strength and Its Revolutionary Impact by Carl Rogers. 1978

Create Change Now: Reflections for Personal Transformation by Cari LaGrange Murphy. 2009

Fire in the Soul: A new Psychology of Spiritual Optimism by Joan Borensenko 1994.

Practice

The Business and Practice of Coaching: Finding Your Niche, Making Money, and Attracting Ideal Clients by Lynn Grodzki and Wendy Allen. 2005

Get Clients Now!: A 28-day Marketing Program for Professionals, Consultants, And Coaches by C.J. Hayden. 2006

Getting Started in Personal and Executive Coaching: How to Create a Thriving Coaching Practice by Stephen G. Fairley and Chris E. Stout. 2003

Social Change

The Chalice and the Blade by Riane Eisler. 1994

Creating a World Without Poverty: Social Business and the Future of Capitalism by Muhammad Yunus 2009

How to Change the World: Social Entrepreneurs and Power of New Ideas by David Bornstein. 2007.

Pedagogy of the Opressed by Paulo Freire. 2001

Power-Under: Trauma and Nonviolent Social Change, by Steven Wineman 2001

Social Entrepreneurship: New Models of Sustainable Social Change by Alex Nicholls. 2008

The Soul of Money by Lynn Twist. 2003.

Three Cups of Tea Three Cups of Tea: One Man's Mission to Promote Peace . . . One School at a Time by Greg Mortenson and David Oliver Relin. 2007.

The Powers That Be: Theology for a New Millennium by Walter Wink. 1999

Articles

Appreciative Inquiry: a Strategy for Change in Systemic Leadership That Builds on Organizational Strengths, Not Deficits by Dawna Markova & Bea Mah Holland, Bea Mah. 2005.

Beyond Good And Evil: Marshall Rosenberg On Creating A Nonviolent World, by Dian Killian. 2002
  ⸱ Paper by Veronica Conway

Coaching from Multiple Perspectives by Philippe Rosinski

Coaching the Global Nomad by William Bergquist and Agnes Mura

Diversity in Coaching by Pete Sayers

Executive Coaching Project: Evaluation of Findings CompassPoint. 2003.

From domination to partnership: reclaiming our future - sex roles and society by Riane Eisler

Magnify Diversity and Coaching by James Gehrke

Through the Lens of Culture: Building Capacity for Social Change and Sustainable Communities by Patricia St. Onge, Breonna Cole, & Sheryl Petty 2003.

Unpacking the Invisible Knapsack by Peggy McIntosh

A White Male Network: You're Kidding, Right? by Bill Proudman

Web Sites

Association for Global New Thought's Principles for Spiritual Activism http://www.agnt.org/snvSpiritActive.htm

Caroline Casey's Center for Visionary Activism http://www.visionaryactivism.com/

Center for Nonviolent Communication http://cnvc.org/bookchap.htm

Coaching that Works http://CoachingthatWorks.com

CompassPoint http://compasspoint.org

Conscious Evolutionary Agentry http://www.co-intelligence.org/EvolutionaryAgentry.html

Eugene Gendlin's On-line Library. http://focusing.org/gendlin/gol_a_better_world.asp

Mahatma Gandhi http://mkgandhi.org/

Max-Neef on Human Needs and Human-scale Development Http://www.rainforestinfo.org.au/background/maxneef.htm

NVC Academy http://nvctraining.com

Riane Eisler and The Partnership Way http://www.partnershipway.org/

Robert Rabbin's Circles of Light http://www.circlesoflight.com/spiritual-activism

Satyana's Principles of Spiritual Activism http://www.satyana.org/principles.html

The Center for Visionary Leadership http://www.visionarylead.org/articles/sp_approaches.htm

The Co-Intelligence Institute's pages on Co-Intelligent Activism http://www.co-intelligence.org/CIPol_CIactivism.html

The Network of Spiritual Progressives http://www.spiritualprogressives.org

TIKKUN magazine http://www.tikkun.org/

Selling Questions that Build Relationships

Upfront Agreements

1. We have about an hour to talk, right?
2. I value authenticity, so can we start with an agreement that we tell each other the truth, even if it may be disappointing?
3. If for any reason you decide not to work with us, or we decide not to work with you, we'll be honest about it, rather than waste each other's time. Okay with you?
4. Besides you, who else will be involved in making the decisions?
5. Can we get all the decision-makers in the room or on the phone?
6. What role do other key players have in this situation?

Objectives

7. What do you hope to accomplish in this meeting?
8. If you could have things any way you wanted, what would you change?
9. In an ideal world, how will things be different?
10. What results do you want a year from now?
11. What is your main objective?
12. What are your goals?
13. What do you want to accomplish?
14. What changes in behavior would you like to see?
15. If you had a magic wand, how would you use it?
16. If you had unlimited resources, what would you do differently?
17. Is there anything else you'd like to see?

Connect with Needs

18. What do you need most?
19. What prompted you to look into this now?
20. What keeps you awake at night?
21. What is the biggest problem you face right now?
22. What other problems do you experience?
23. What recent examples come to mind?
24. So your personal distress about this is about a need for…
25. Is there anything else about your current situation right now that you don't like?

26. What does your organization need right now?

27. If you could change only one thing, what would it be?

28. What motivates you to change?

29. Are there any other headaches you'd like to eliminate?

30. What's your most important priority?

31. What does the team do really well already?

32. What challenges do you face?

33. What opportunities are on the horizon?

34. What are you currently doing to address your situation?

35. What stakeholders are affected?

36. What have you done so far that's worked or hasn't worked?

Budget

37. How much would it be worth to make the changes we've talked about?

38. How much will it cost you if nothing changes?

39. In round numbers, what is your budget?

40. Off the record, what do you really want to pay for this program?

41. What would make your investment worthwhile?

42. Before we start looking at solutions, it helps if we have a ballpark budget. Sounds to me like this program could cost roughly $100 – 150 K. We don't want to design the $150 K program if your budget is $100K, so can you give us some guidelines?

43. How do you plan to finance this program?

44. What other resources do you have available?

45. Who else might sponsor this with you?

Options

46. What do you have in mind for addressing these issues?

47. How do you plan to achieve your goals?

48. What is your strategy for creating the ideal future?

49. What other ideas do you have?

50. What effect would these solutions have on your situation?

51. What alternatives have you considered?

52. What benefit would you personally realize as a result?

53. How would others benefit from this program?

54. Who else are you considering using? What do you like about them? What's missing?

55. What programs you using now? What's the best part of the program? What do you like least?

56. If you don't go with us, who would you work with, or what would you do instead?
57. What criteria will you use to choose the provider?

Solutions and Action

58. How do you see us helping you?
59. What would you like from us?
60. What else?
61. Based on what you've told us, would you like to hear our recommendations?
62. If I understand what you want, would you also consider…?
63. How will you measure the success of this program?
64. Is there anything we've overlooked?
65. What question should I be asking you?
66. Are there any questions you would like to ask?
67. On a scale of one to ten, how confident do you feel about working with us? What would it take to get that up to 10?
68. What do you need to move forward?
69. It sounds like you're not really interested in working with is. May I ask why?
70. What would make you wildly excited about moving forward?
71. What keeps you from working with us?
72. When would you like to start getting results?
73. Are you working with a deadline?
74. What does your time line look like?
75. What is the next step?
76. How soon would you like to start?
77. To save time, we don't write proposals until we know exactly what you want. What are the key components you'd like to see in the proposal? (only if they ask for a proposal)
78. Are you sure you want to move forward?
79. How would you like us to invoice you?

Follow-up

80. When shall we get together again?
81. We'll call you next week, say on Thursday at 10, or is there a better time?
82. Anything else you'd like from us?

416

Tell Your Vision

1. **History: Milestones and Possibilities**

   Share a story about a peak experience. Choose a time when you felt empowered.

   What life milestones are important to you?

   What about your past will help you embrace the future?

2. **Values: Prioritizing Your Values**

   Examine your peak experiences and milestones for your personal values.

   Prioritize your top seven personal values.

   Which value is most important to you right now?

3. **Action: Future Behavior and Capabilities**

   What personal capabilities do you already have that you will use even more in the future?

   What new competencies do you need to master to meet future challenges?

4. **Environment: What do you want?**

   In a perfect future, describe your ideal environment.

   What surrounds you, who is there, and what is your inner experience?

   If you had a magic wand, how would you change your physical environment and the ambience?

5. **Identity: Choosing your Image**

   Brainstorm the identity or nicknames you would like to earn from people who meet you in the future.

   Imagine that you overhear people talking about you. What do you want them to say?

   Ten years from now, when people are still talking about you, what do they say?

6. **Contribution: How do you Serve**

   Identify all the potential ways that people benefit from your success.

   What do you contribute that's unique? In the short term? In the long term?

   What do you consider the most important contribution that you can make?

7. **Vision: Picturing Your Future**

   Imagine a front-page article written about you; what headline introduces the cover story?
   You are quoted in the article. What do you have to say about your success? What is the visionary story of your life?[179]

---

[179] Adapted from Lasley, M. (2004). *Courageous visions: How to unleash passionate energy in your life and your organization.* Discover Press.

Round 1: Judgment

1. In silence, notice the first judgments or thoughts that come up for you. Without speaking, move to the part of the circle that best describes any judgments you may have.
2. Which judgments would you *most* like to avoid? Move to that section of the circle.
3. Which judgment would you like to understand better?

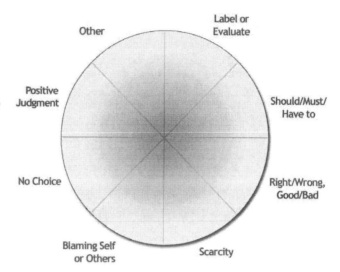

Round 2: Attention

1. Where are you putting your attention? What stands out for you? What's ringing in your ears? Move to the part of the circle that best describes where you are putting your attention.
2. Where do you *not* want to put your attention?
3. Where *else* would you like to explore or put your attention?

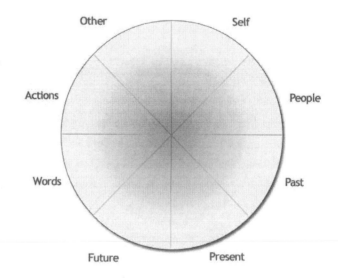

Round 3: Reaction

1. What is your first reaction? Move to the part of the circle that describes your inner experience.
2. What emotion would you like to avoid? Move to that part of the circle. Notice your internal experience as you imagine feeling this way.
3. What feeling would you like to understand better, either in yourself or others?

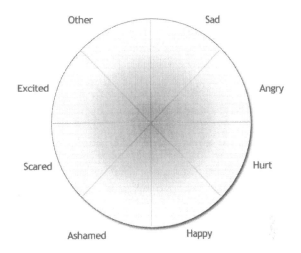

Round 4: Needs

1. In which area are you most satisfied or fulfilled? Move around the circle trying on areas until you land in the one where you feel most satisfied. Savor that for a moment.
2. What needs of yours are unmet? Move to that area of the circle and connect to your deepest desire. Notice how much you'd like to have this need fulfilled. Imagine how it would feel to have this need fully met.
3. What needs of others are you curious about or would like to better understand?

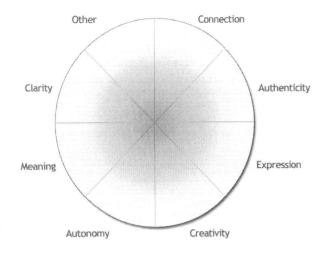

Round 5: Actions

1. Stay with the energy and desires of the group as you explore actions. What are you saying "no" to?
2. What are you saying "yes" to?
3. What will you do now? Would you like to make a request of someone?

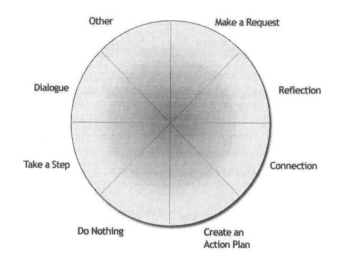

Transforming Anger in Three Breaths by Gail Taylor

Begin by rating rate yourself on a scale of 0 to 10 on your level of stress right now. Score:		
Thoughts (Inner Critic)	**Release Work (Feelings and Needs)**	**Requests (Action)**
		After you've done release work, rate yourself on a scale of 0 to 10 on your level of stress right now. Score:

Preparation

Here's how the practice works for beginners. Use the form in the resource section on page 421 to rate yourself on a scale of 0 to 10 on your level of stress right now using the upper left box (before). If you feel triggered, disconnected, or scattered, you may rate yourself somewhere below five. If you're feeling clear-headed, connected to your core, self-aware, and present, then you might rate yourself six or higher.

These three columns represent the 3 breaths:

Column 1: Thoughts (inner critic, monkey mind, or venting)

Write all the comments that express your upset. Keep each line in a single phrase. For example, you might write:

- I can't believe he lied to me.
- I let myself be betrayed once again.
- Now I don't know what to believe.

Column 2: Feelings and Needs (release work)

A) Translate each line from Column 1 into a single word for what you feel and a single word for what you need. You may want a list of feelings and needs in front of you. If you're feeling frantic, overwhelmed, and exhausted, pick one that feels the most accurate right now. Then choose the need that is connected to the feeling. For example, maybe you are feeling exhausted because you really need some rest.

B) Look for the underlying need or a core value that might be trying to express itself in this line. Avoid the temptation to do analysis or find solutions in this column. "I need to take a vacation" is a solution; instead of fixing the problem, first connect with the underlying yearning for rest.

C) Release-fully sit with the feeling and the need you just wrote. One way to *sit with* it is to say them over and over, for example, "I'm frustrated because I really need more rest." Exhale as you fully experience the feeling as if releasing the emotion with your breath. As you connect to your desire for the need, inhale as if breathing in the value and the beauty of that need. Continue your release work on this line until you experience a "shift" – if you feel calmer, happier, or more restful after a few seconds of this release work, "shift" is happening. Continue this step until the emotional charge reduces to almost nothing. Un-resisted, and undistracted, most emotions shift in 90 seconds or less.

Inhale what you want, exhale what you're releasing, and check into your body for shifts. Getting in touch with your underlying need, you'll go from the crisis expression deeper into your soul. Connecting deeply with yourself in this way, you'll find your motivation. You'll move away from what you don't want and move toward what you do want as you repeat the words. Find out what's really driving that crisis voice. Breath work stimulates the parasympathetic nervous system (the relaxation response) and also helps to release the emotion.

Another option for doing release work is to invoke your imagination. When you exhale, what does the emotion you're exhaling look like? Maybe you imagine that you're exhaling the emotion as black tar or frantic smoke. When you inhale the underlying value that you identified, maybe you imagine that you're inhaling cleansing white light.

Release work helps you reorient your conscious and unconscious processes, which affects your biochemistry, your posture, and your ability to create optimal solutions. When you focus on what you don't like, your chest collapses, contributing to a sense of depression and hopelessness. In as little as 15 seconds, focusing on what you do want, you can create a more open feeling in the chest, a sense of possibility, creativity, and curiosity.

After sitting release-fully for 90 seconds with the line you just created in Column 2, you will likely notice a tremendous shift and more relaxation in your body. If you still feel an emotional charge, take another 90 seconds with this line until you feel some release. When you have completed your list, you're ready to move on to Column 3.

Column 3 – Requests (Action)

Now is your chance to decide, "What do I do from here? Do I go back to do more Release Work? Do I take action based on what I uncovered? Or am I totally done and able to get on with life without taking action?" Ask yourself for each line in Column 2, "Is there a request I could make of myself or someone else that would start to attend to this need?" In some cases, you won't have any desire to make a request at all; the Column 2 self-empathy and release work may be enough, and you may feel "done" with the issue entirely. In some cases, you'll have something you want to request of yourself or of someone else. In formulating your request, ask for actions that can be completed within the next ten minutes. For example, if my Column 2 need is "rest," I might make a request of myself to take a half hour nap this afternoon, but I agree to it now. Or I may decide to take two days off next week, but I ask for the time off now.

If you notice that you still have more thoughts or venting showing up, go back to Column 1 and add the comments to your list. Repeat Column 2 for everything that you write down. Then approach Column 3 again.

Wrapping It Up

Once you complete all three columns, check in with yourself again. Rank your level of stress now on a scale of zero to 10. Overall, do you feel the same as before, or do you feel lighter? Do you feel more upset, stressed, or anxious, or do you feel softer, more relief, more relaxed? Choose a number that represents your level of stress now and write this in the lower right-hand after box. Has a shift occurred? Report what is true for you.

With practice, you'll be able to do this three-column process in three breaths, and you won't need to write it down anymore. The three breath practice is generative, positive, proactive, and resolution-oriented, which allows you to release and complete. This restorative process is very different from placing blame and seeking revenge (e.g. "She lied to me. She's a jerk who needs to be punished, and therefore I won't see her again," or "I blame myself for trusting some idiot who lied to me.") Still pay attention to those thoughts, but only as a first step in a healing, releasing, restoration-oriented process. Instead of a downward spiral of blame and retribution, this three-breath practice gives you an alternative that's more effective, less costly to your well being, and more connected to what you *do* want and how you might tangibly go about getting what we want.[180]

---

[180] Gail Taylor personal interview 5/27/2008. http://www.integratedcoaches.com

Violent Metaphors and Alternatives

Worth a shot: might take root, could bear fruit

Aimed at: looking toward

To have ammo: to have information to share, to have tools for the task

Stick to your guns: dog for your needs

Have enough clout: have the energy to inspire

Make an impact: shine light on the issue

Sure fire method: will bear fruit

Take a stab at it: start the journey, take a step, plant the seeds

Hold the line: clarify the issues, take a stand

Magic bullet: a panacea, sure cure

Keep your powder dry: keep your options open

On target: focused, clear about hopes and needs

Bite the bullet: face the music

Spearheading: to inspire and lead, gathering the energy for this project

The only weapon left: the clearest, most effective option, shining star

Bang for the buck: a great harvest

Hold the line: stay in the game

Kill two birds with one stone: feed two birds with one scone

Rule of thumb: law of nature

Give it a shot: take a chance

Not by a long shot: no way

Shoot for it: go for it

Going great guns: full speed

Killing time: waiting until

Plan of attack: action plan

Shoot holes in an argument: unravel a ball of yarn

Double edged sword: two sides of a coin

Dress to kill: dress to thrill

Made in the USA
Charleston, SC
05 May 2011